ACCOUNTING FOR SLAVERY

Accounting for Slavery

MASTERS AND MANAGEMENT

Caitlin Rosenthal

Harvard University Press

Cambridge, Massachusetts
London, England

First Harvard University Press paperback edition, 2019
Second printing

Library of Congress Cataloging-in-Publication Data
Names: Rosenthal, Caitlin, author.
Title: Accounting for slavery : masters and management / Caitlin Rosenthal.
Description: Cambridge, Massachusetts : Harvard University Press, 2018. |
Includes bibliographical references and index.
Identifiers: LCCN 2017058060 | ISBN 9780674972094 (hardcover : alk. paper) |
ISBN 9780674241657 (pbk.)
Subjects: LCSH: Slavery—Economic aspects—United States—History—
18th century. | Slavery—Economic aspects—United States—History—
19th century. | Slavery—Economic aspects—West Indies, British—History—
18th century. | Slavery—Economic aspects—West Indies, British—History—
19th century. | Human capital—United States—History. | Human capital—
West Indies, British—History. | Plantations—United States—Accounting—
History. | Plantations—West Indies, British—Accounting—History. |
Plantation owners—United States—History. | Plantation owners—
West Indies, British—History.
Classification: LCC HT905 .R67 2018 | DDC 331.11/734097309033—dc23
LC record available at https://lccn.loc.gov/2017058060

For my parents, Jim and Cindy

CONTENTS

FIGURES AND TABLES

Figures

Figures

Tables

PREFACE

When I began this project, I did not intend to write a book about slavery. I had just finished two years working as a management consultant with McKinsey & Company. It was a job I enjoyed. Every few months I found myself working at a different corporation on a different problem. There were always new industries, new ideas, and, of course, new data. I was just out of college, and as the most junior person on a team—the "business analyst"—I often manipulated the spreadsheets of numbers that we relied on to help us make our recommendations.

Sometimes it felt a bit like alchemy: by simply combining a firm's resources in new ways, we could help the company earn higher profits. And, as far as I could tell, it often worked. It did not seem to matter that I had not met most of the people represented in the data or that I barely grasped the technical details of the products. In fact, this distance gave me an advantage. Viewing a large division or even a whole company as an abstraction made it easier to lay out a strategy for profit. From basement conference rooms, twenty-two-year-olds calculated paths to increased efficiency, slicing and dicing data that might shape the lives of thousands of workers and many more customers.

I had the good luck to be there during a boom economy, so we were hiring, not firing; growing businesses, not cutting costs. And yet it sometimes made me uneasy. What did the models and numbers cover up? What stories was I missing by encountering production through a spreadsheet? When I started graduate school, I wanted to understand the history of this outlook and the scale that accompanied it. When did we begin to think about workers as cells in spreadsheets? What happens when businesses grow so big that they can only be comprehended quantitatively? How do labor relationships change when managers and owners encounter workers primarily as numbers—when CEOs are separated from thousands of workers by layers and layers of hierarchy?

During my first year of graduate school, I studied historical account books. I began my research where I assumed the story began, at least in America: in the New England textile factories and iron forges usually at the heart of the Industrial Revolution. The records I found advanced in fits and starts. Manufacturers sometimes kept time books and occasionally calculated output per worker, but their efforts were often thwarted when workers quit. Neat grids optimistically laid out to record data ended up partially blank or abandoned when workers left for new opportunities or to try their luck on a farm.

Around my second year of graduate school, the renowned economic historian Stan Engerman handed me a copy of Thomas Affleck's *Plantation Record and Account Book*. The volume blew me away. This was the most complex and comprehensive record book I had seen up till that point, and it included a detailed balance sheet as well as per-worker picking records. Further research would reveal that planters actually used these books very unevenly, with some of the same fits and starts of northern books. However, the most calculating slaveholders kept records as comprehensive as contemporary manufacturers. And Affleck's book was not the first or only example of sophisticated plantation accounting. As I followed leads from other scholars, I uncovered other remarkable sets of accounts, including detailed records for West Indian plantations, which were among the largest businesses of their time.

In the end, the direct ties between these plantations and today's data practices remain murky. This is not an origins story. I did not find a simple path where slaveholders' paper spreadsheets evolved into Microsoft Excel.

FIGURE P.I. The View from the Planter's Desk. Book plates like this were sometimes pasted inside the opening cover of plantation account books. It offers a romantic view of southern business that elides the circumstances of production. "John W. Madden: Stationer, Printer and Lithographer, New Orleans, Jan. 8, 1815." Bookseller label, Bookseller Collection, Box 2, Range 4, Station B. Courtesy of the American Antiquarian Society, Worcester, Massachusetts.

The narrative that emerged was far more complicated: many businesspeople in different geographies were developing new data practices independently. What I saw was a series of interconnected business histories that show how data practices often thought of as quintessentially modern coexisted with and even complemented slavery. Planters' control over enslaved people made it easier for them to fit their slaves into neat numerical rows and columns. To borrow a twenty-first-century business buzzword, slavery and quantitative management were synergistic.

Studying the ways profit and innovation can accompany violence and inequality is particularly important in the world of modern capitalism. The mythology of capitalism suggests that many individuals pursuing their own interests can make whole societies wealthier. In our current moment, it is a commonplace to hear people argue that the "freer" the market, the greater the profit and the faster the growth. Generally, those offering such explanations assume that a free market does not include slavery, but as I have conducted my research, I have come to see things differently. From the perspective of slaveholders and other free whites, the freedom to enslave was an economic freedom. They feared abolition because of the ways it would restrict their rights to control labor and property. Viewed in this light, the abolition of slavery was a triumph of market regulation that restricted their economic freedoms even as it offered freedom to so many others.

It was remarkably easy for slaveholders to overlook the human costs of their profits, and it can be similarly convenient for modern managers (and consumers) to forget the conditions under which goods are made. For me, the image in Figure P.1 captures this forgetting. Elaborate engraved book-plates were sometimes pasted inside the front cover of account books. This one advertises the services of a New Orleans stationer selling blank books. A slaveholder might have flipped past it as he reviewed an inventory of lives or a record of cotton picking. The peaceful illustration offers a desktop land-scape of pens, pencils, account books, and scrolls. The "S" in "stationer" is a dollar sign, connecting the paper technology of accounting with profit. The calendar celebrates Andrew Jackson's victory at the battle of New Orleans. A stag—perhaps a paperweight—completes the pastoral view from the planter's desk. This view does not include slavery. For me, the image conveys some-thing of the distance between the calculations of the planter and the violence of slavery. It shows how easily the connections between capitalism and slavery can be overlooked. From the comfort of the countinghouse—or a basement conference room—it is perilously easy to render human figures as figures on paper, and to imagine men, women, and children as no more than hands.[1]

ACCOUNTING FOR SLAVERY

Introduction

THOMAS WALTER PEYRE's plantation journal looks like a lab notebook. Peyre opened the book in December 1834, and what began as a simple daily diary was soon punctuated with tables and experiments. In 1842, he calculated and recorded average picking rates for cotton and peas for each of the enslaved men and women laboring on his plantation. Peyre recalculated average picking rates again in 1847 and compared them to outputs in 1849—though this time he shifted from averages to maximums, perhaps optimistic he could accelerate the pace of labor. All along the way he monitored the state of his workforce, tracking time lost to sickness and noting details on enslaved women's pregnancies and the all too frequent deaths of their children. Peyre also ran frequent "experiments in cotton": he tracked output across a dozen types of manure. He compared seed varieties, measured the ratio of picked to ginned cotton, and tested the effects of topping plants. He even experimented with the spacing of potatoes, comparing results when planting 8, 10, 12, and 14 inches apart. Peyre's potatoes were not for sale, but by his estimate, they fed his workers from "August 29 to December 17th," almost all of the picking season. In this way, potatoes could be metabolized into cotton and thus into profit.[1]

Peyre practiced scientific agriculture, or what critics sometimes disparaged as "book farming." He and other book farmers appealed to data as well as experience, believing that careful record keeping and numerical analysis led to increased output and higher profits.[2] Today, this outlook is familiar: businesspeople quantify almost everything. Ratios and totals enable them to set targets, establish benchmarks, and make comparisons. Even intangibles, like human capital, are regularly expressed in numerical terms. Though modern practices are rarely compared to slaveholders' calculations, many planters in the American South and the West Indies shared our obsession with data. They sought to determine how much labor their slaves could perform in a given amount of time, and they pushed them to achieve that maximum. Many kept extensive records—account books and reports that reflect their experimental and often brutal management practices.

Slaveholders left behind thousands of volumes of account books. These extensive archives have been widely studied, but rarely as business records.[3] This book uses them to reconstruct the management practices of American and West Indian slaveholders from the late eighteenth century through the American Civil War. The portrait that emerges from plantation records is that of a society where precise management and violence went hand in hand. Spared many of the challenges faced by manufacturers relying on wage labor—those of recruiting and retaining workers—slaveholders built large and complex organizations, conducted productivity analysis akin to scientific management, and developed an array of ways to value and compare human capital. The limited rights and opportunities of the men, women, and children laboring beneath them facilitated these efforts. Put differently, slavery encouraged the development of sophisticated management practices. Like other entrepreneurs, slaveholders strove to mobilize capital and motivate labor, regularly turning to numbers as an aid to profits. But on plantations, the soft power of quantification supplemented the driving force of the whip.

Slavery and Capitalism

The history of plantation business practices is part of a broader effort to answer a larger question: How does the history of American slavery fit into the history of American capitalism? This question is not new. Generations of historians and scholars have asked it in different ways since emancipation and even before. The precise reply still depends on how you define "capitalism," but to a great extent we know the answer: slavery was central to the emergence of the economic system that now goes by that name.[4]

Scores of historians and economists have contributed to this debate. A tradition of radical scholarship dating from at least Eric Williams's 1944 *Capitalism and Slavery* proposed deep connections between slavery and industrialization.[5] More recently, American and Atlantic historians from James Oakes to Joseph Inikori to Sven Beckert have traced the relationship between slavery and global economic change.[6] Scholars of the "second slavery" have argued that during the late eighteenth and the nineteenth centuries, slavery was not declining but systematically expanding—growing alongside the emerging wage-labor economies typically identified with capitalism.[7] A very different literature in economics has examined the extent to which plantation slavery could be highly profitable and even innovative.[8] While aspects of these literatures conflict, and rates of profit and moments of change have been rigorously debated, the overall picture is undeniable. At a minimum, slaveholders (and those who bought their products) built an innovative, global, profit-hungry labor regime that contributed to the emergence of the modern economy.[9]

Given what historians know about slavery, the fact that many slaveholders were accomplished managers should not be surprising. We know that large planters were among the wealthiest businesspeople of their time. We know that slave-grown sugar was the most valuable commodity of the eighteenth-century Atlantic world and that slave-grown cotton was antebellum America's most important export. We know that the textile industry—by most accounts the leading industry of the Industrial Revolution—wove cloth from this cotton. We know that the amount of capital invested in slaves was massive, by some measurements as large or larger than the amount of capital invested in factories.[10] And finance stretched deep into the American South through slave mortgages and insurance policies.[11] Slaveholding businesspeople—and those who bought their products—benefited from control over enslaved people. Control enabled them to manage with great precision, transporting people to distant plots of land and manipulating labor processes in minute ways.

Control has always been at the heart of modern accounting practice. The word "control" itself comes from an accounting document: the *contreroulle,* or counter-roll, a duplicate of a roll or other document, which was kept for purposes of cross-checking. At its origins, the word first meant "verification," but by the late sixteenth century it had come to encompass the direction, management, and surveillance that verification required.[12] These origins are often overlooked today, though the top accounting officer in a corporation is still called the controller or the comptroller. Slavery became a laboratory for the development of accounting because the control drawn on paper matched the reality of the plantation more closely than that of almost any other early American business enterprise.[13] In nineteenth-century America, manufacturers employing wageworkers developed a range of strategies to increase their control over laborers' lives, from building company towns to hiring private investigators to conduct surveillance. In some ways, all the great labor battles of the late nineteenth century can be seen as struggles for control: control over work conditions and processes, over earnings, and over leisure. These were battles planters rarely had to fight because the law gave them extensive power. Even the most remarkable intrusions into free workers' private lives bear no comparison to the minute manipulations of lives perpetrated by slaveholders.[14]

Of course, control should never be mistaken for consent. Account books show both the extent of planters' control and its limits. Slaves resisted, sometimes employing the same strategies that wage workers used in factories. They slowed the pace of work, took supplies, and shared resources. They defied planters' efforts to reduce them to columns of capital and units of output, sharing information and building families and communities. They ran away, they rebelled, and they conspired to commit arson and murder. They even took their own lives, both to escape from bondage and to destroy masters' property. But they could not quit, and planters blended information systems with violence—and the threat of sale—to refine labor processes, building machines made out of men, women, and children.

Slavery and Management

As much as these plantation records can tell us about the history of capitalism, they can tell us at least as much about the history of business practices. How should we write the history of management as a profession? Very few histories of business practices ever touch on slavery. Most range across a familiar

array of industries, inventors, and executives usually associated with innovation and the coming of capitalism—eighteenth-century merchants;
nineteenth-century textile manufacturers, canal diggers, railroad tycoons,
and financiers; and twentieth-century automobile manufacturers, high-tech
founders, and consultants. Some of these stories have taken on near mythical
status for modern businesspeople. Take Frederick Winslow Taylor, founder
of the famed system of "scientific management," discussed in Chapter 3. No
history of American management practices fails to linger over Taylor. Slide
rule and stopwatch in hand, the Philadelphia engineer is best known for his
time and motion studies. By observing and reorganizing the motions of
workers, Taylor claimed to be able to achieve massive gains in productivity.
At its core, Taylor's system consisted of the belief that a skilled manager could
reconfigure labor processes to make workers more productive: to make
more goods with less labor in less time.[15]

In many ways, the emphasis on Taylorism in the history of management
is arbitrary: both its scientific credentials and the extent of its direct influence are open to debate. In 1974, two management scholars called Taylor's
most famous experiment, which redesigned the simple task of lifting pig iron
into trucks, a "pig tale," concluding that it was "more fiction than fact."[16] A
search of management literature turns up no estimates of how widely the
system was actually implemented. Indeed, in 1912, when Taylor was asked
by a congressional committee, "How many concerns, to your knowledge, use
your system in its entirety?" he replied, "In its entirety—none; not one."[17]

And yet, scientific management's symbolic power is undeniable. Buoyed
by a Progressive Era fervor for improvement, scientific management's rise
coincided with the founding of America's most prestigious business schools—
Wharton in 1881, Tuck in 1900, and Harvard Business School in 1908. In a
sense, Taylor not only offered advice for managers but also justified their
existence. In the world of scientific management, even the work of the most-
skilled laborers could be improved by "the close observation of a young college man."[18] And though few implemented Taylor's principles, he reached
a large readership. By 1915, his 1911 book *The Principles of Scientific Management* had been translated into eight languages, and it helped inspire the first
consulting firms.[19] Taylorism even offered a founding theory for management as an academic discipline: it would be scientific management that
scholars pushed back against when they advocated for "human relations."[20]

Though Taylor marketed his system as new, even revolutionary, slaveholders using scientific agriculture had already experimented with many of the same techniques. At its peak, scientific agriculture influenced the practices of thousands of planters and overseers. The most calculating practitioners conducted experiments akin to time and motion studies, recording more data than Taylor or his disciples.[21] Culling from the surviving records of 114 plantations, economists Alan Olmstead and Paul Rhode recently compiled a data set of 602,219 individual observations of daily cotton picking—far more than the meager and distorted data used to construct Taylor's "pig tale."[22]

Despite this, slavery plays almost no role in histories of management. Even business histories that consider plantation slavery tend to be constrained by the assumption that innovation occurred despite slavery, not because of it. Take Alfred Chandler's now classic study of American business history, *The Visible Hand*. Chandler recognized that the plantation overseer may have been the "first salaried manager" in the country, and he was aware that many overseers kept detailed account books, but he nonetheless declared the plantation an "Ancient Form of Large-Scale Production." In his footnotes, he remarks on the South's limited investment in capital—but he excludes human capital from his totals. Changing the calculation radically changes the picture, depicting a society where slave capital actually exceeded capital invested in machinery.[23]

Pointing to the general neglect of slavery in most business histories, management scholar Bill Cooke has described what he calls the "denial of slavery" in management studies. He points out that in 1860, "when the historical orthodoxy has modern management emerging on the railroads" in the United States and Europe, 38,000 plantation overseers "were managing 4 million slaves." Moreover, they were doing so "according to classical management and Taylorian principles." Cooke charges management scholars not with ignorance but with "denial" because evidence of slaveholders' management practices was readily available in published historical literature. He did not have to seek out rare or hard-to-access archival sources to find persuasive evidence.[24]

Southern and West Indian slaveholders were not the only eighteenth- and nineteenth-century businesspeople to foreshadow Taylor's practices. Their burgeoning numeracy was part of a broader expansion of quantitative information practices into new sectors. As one scholar has written, an "avalanche

of numbers" was permeating public and private life.[25] A related "infrastructure of pens and paper" was transforming business practices.[26] But
slaveholders' practices offer a particularly powerful alternative narrative.
Including them in histories of management raises fundamental questions
about the implications of "sophisticated" business practices and their compatibility with vastly unequal power and wealth. Taylor claimed—though
workers often argued differently—that his system, properly implemented,
resulted in better conditions for all: higher profits for business, higher earnings for laborers, and lower prices for consumers.[27] His worldview fit into an
emerging capitalist narrative where markets rewarded management innovators and helped workers along the way. No such illusions can be sustained when studying slaveholders' practices. There, masters' extensive
power and access to violence increased their ability to implement all kinds
of management experiments.

Plan of the Book

This book unfolds both chronologically and thematically. The structure
helps illuminate both the long history of slaveholders' management practices
and the remarkable similarities between these practices and famous advance-
ments in the history of business. I begin in the eighteenth-century West Indies, advance to the antebellum United States, and conclude with the labor
systems that emerged in the South after the American Civil War. Each chapter
also focuses on slaveholders' use of a particular set of business practices
or strategies: the rise of plantation hierarchies akin to the multidivisional
form (Chapter 1), the standardization of accounts that enabled a form of the
separation of ownership and management (Chapter 2), the spread of productivity analysis similar to scientific management (Chapter 3), and finally the
refinement of valuation practices, particularly the calculation of appreciation and depreciation (Chapter 4). Chapter 5 changes direction, exploring
the transformation of management after emancipation. This final chapter
compares planters' efforts before and after the U.S. Civil War, showing how
they lost control over the minute details of freedpeople's lives but reestablished economic power and profitability through law and violence. This
comparison, like those in earlier chapters, brings the managerial advantages
of slavery into sharper relief.

In some ways my comparative choices are arbitrary—as previously suggested, systems like scientific management often had more symbolic than real influence on managers' ideas and identities. Henry Ford or Josiah Wedgewood might have been substituted for Frederick Winslow Taylor. This is not an origins story, but in each of the cases I address, slaveholders dealt with complex challenges in sophisticated ways, often concurrent with and sometimes prior to managers in other settings. Their business innovations were as central to the emerging capitalist system as those in free factories.

As a business history of plantation slavery, the goal of this book is not to describe typical or average plantation practices. Business histories rarely seek out the typical; more often, they describe the businesses that were the biggest and the most profitable. They focus on Carnegies, Rockefellers, and Vanderbilts, and when they look to smaller enterprises, they tend to choose innovators. Though I sample records from a range of regions and periods, my cases follow this pattern. I have sought out the best records and the largest enterprises, following leads to uncover particularly adept managers. Some of the records analyzed here were kept by planters who earned large fortunes and owned hundreds, occasionally thousands, of men, women, and children. Others come from planters who enslaved only twenty or thirty people but kept particularly excellent records. In short, these are the histories of exceptional businesspeople who, but for the nature of their business, would already be included in canonical business histories.[28]

Frederick Winslow Taylor is still regularly mentioned in management textbooks and on the pages of journals like *Harvard Business Review* (*HBR*). When *HBR* marked its ninetieth anniversary in 2012, Taylor made it into all three featured essays, offering an inspirational touchstone for the ability of managers to transform the economy.[29] The symbolic power of slavery's scientific management is less inspirational but perhaps even more important. We live in a global economy where the labor of production is often invisible. Distance and quantitative management facilitate this erasure, and assumptions about capitalism and freedom help conceal it. Neither "free" trade nor "free" markets have any necessary relationship with other kinds of human freedoms. Indeed, the history of plantation slavery shows that the opposite can be true.

I

Hierarchies of Life and Death

ACCOUNTING AND ORGANIZATIONAL STRUCTURE

IN THE BRITISH WEST INDIES

O N DECEMBER 31, 1767, the attorney or overseer on one of Joseph Foster Barham's Jamaican plantations sat down to balance the books. In neat handwriting, he recorded the progress of the year, tallying up pounds and pence earned and expended on Island Estate. He prepared a variety of reports, including an "Account of Negroes," which took the form of a balance sheet. But this was no ordinary balance sheet: it was denominated in the units of human life (see Figure 1.1).[1]

From an accounting perspective, this balance sheet of life and death was relatively simple. At the beginning of the year, the bookkeeper took an inventory of the enslaved people toiling on the plantation. He then credited the results "to inventory" on the left-hand side of the account: 176 men, women, and children lived on the estate. As the year continued, he charged the account for each baby born on the estate. In 1767, there were two: in October, Martha delivered Ephrahim; in December, Clara gave birth to Shely. On the right side of the balance sheet, the bookkeeper "credited" the account for lives lost over the course of the year: June died of yaws, Nero of fever, Sue of dropsy, and Dolly of eating dirt—possibly a suicide.[2] And the list continued. One slave succumbed to old age, but most died of the many diseases that plagued the Caribbean plantation complex. On December 31, the bookkeeper

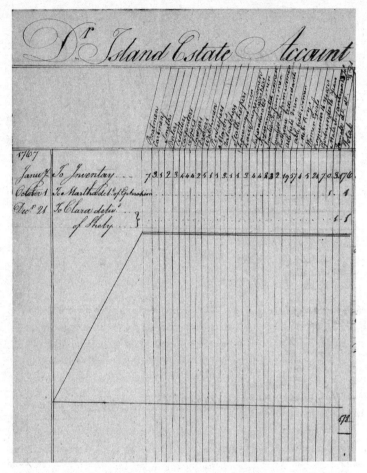

FIGURE 1.1. Island Estate "Account of Negroes," 1767. Some planters kept balance sheets denominated in the units of life and death. The left side sums the inventory from January and births over the course of the year. This total equaled deaths plus an inventory taken at the end of the year. Though these operations yielded a formal balance, deaths vastly outnumbered births. West Indies Inventories of Slaves etc., 1754–1819, The Barham Papers (MS. Clar. dep. b. 37 / 1–2), Clarendon Deposit, Department of Special Collections, Bodleian Library, University of Oxford. Courtesy of the Earl of Clarendon.

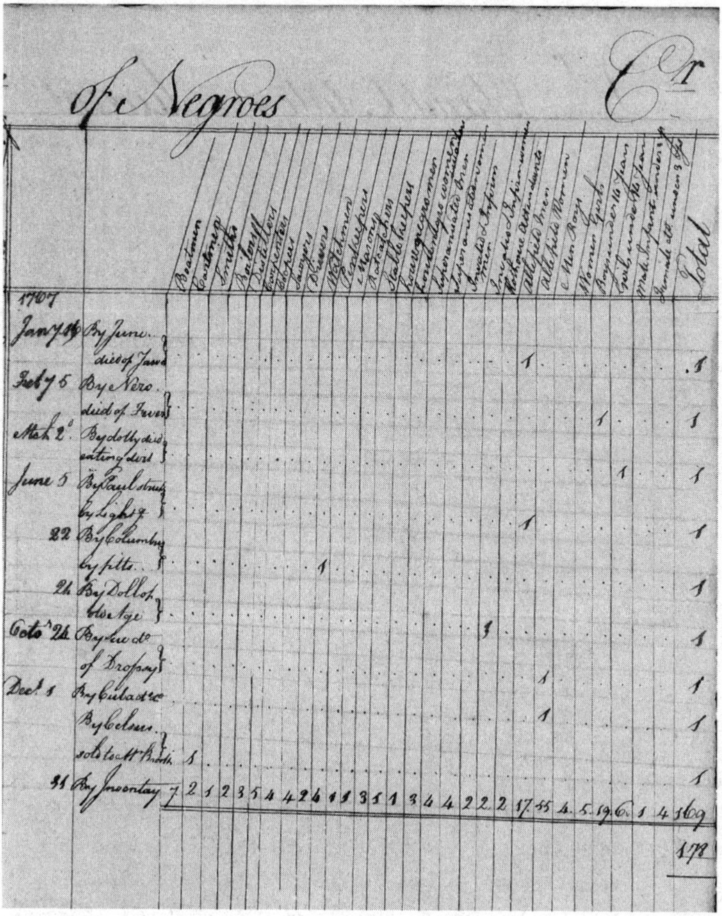
of Negroes
Cr
Boatmen
Smiths
Distillers
Carpenters
Coopers
Sawyers
Watchmen
Stablekeepers
Total
1767
June 5
22
Decr 1
31
By Nero
died of Fever
of Dropsy
By Inventory
169
178

took another inventory and entered it on the bottom right. The two sides then struck a formal balance: the initial inventory (176) plus the births (2) equaled the final inventory (169) plus the deaths (9). Every enslaved person was accounted for. And yet this balance sheet was fundamentally unbalanced: across the Caribbean, death rates dwarfed reproduction.[3]

Accounts of life and death are among the oldest genres of records, dating to the first censuses and birth registries. But plantation account books also considered the enslaved as property, noting their deaths as diminished inventory—as capital and labor lost. The losses were large: enslaved people died at catastrophic rates, not just on plantations like Island Estate but in every stage of the Atlantic labor supply chain. In Africa, as many as 10 percent died in the process of capture, and another 25 percent in the harrowing march to the coast. Still more perished in port towns, and those who survived found themselves tightly packed into the holds of ships bound across the Atlantic.[4] An estimated 12.5 million embarked on this harrowing "middle passage," where sickness, violence, and malnutrition claimed the lives of almost 2 million.[5] Once the enslaved set foot on land, heavy labor and New World diseases killed many more. Mortality rates were staggering upon first arrival—the deadly period planters referred to as "seasoning." In the British Caribbean, some estimates suggest that as many as half of "New Negroes" died within three years of arrival.[6] Though rates eventually stabilized, malnutrition, disease, suicide, and the punishing labor of sugar production continued to claim many lives, just as they did on Island Estate.[7]

When he prepared the "Account of Negroes," Joseph Foster Barham's manager created both an inventory of capital assets and a kind of organizational chart. Beyond illuminating the human costs of chattel slavery, the balance sheet reflected the complexity of plantation operations. Each side was carefully subdivided into twenty-nine columns, each representing a category of slaves (see Figure 1.1). The taxonomy included various plantation occupations, from boatmen, cartmen, watchmen, and smiths, to drivers, sugar boilers, distillers, carpenters, coopers, and even a dedicated rat catcher. Alongside these occupational categories, planters classified children and the elderly by sex and by age. The document thus offered a view of the plantation workforce, both as it was and as it would evolve over the coming years. The lost skills of the dead could be read quickly from the chart, as could the availability of growing children who could be trained to take their places.[8]

As the many occupations listed on the Island Estate account suggest, sugar production was a complex process that combined punishing labor on the ground with careful administration from above. Writing about a very different period and industry in his business history classic *Strategy and Structure*, Alfred Chandler argued for the importance of administration to the emergence of the modern economy. In his telling, middle and senior managers who organized activities like procurement, production, and distribution were the underappreciated revolutionaries of industrial capitalism, playing a role as important as inventors and entrepreneurs. Chandler based his account on careful reconstructions of late nineteenth-century organizational charts, piecing together hierarchies that extended from a central office down through numerous operating divisions. He argued that these structures—and the administrators who made them work—were fundamental to business strategy. In his view, some of the most mundane activities of modern business were among the most important.[9]

Chandler's method of organizational reconstruction can be applied to a radically different setting: the slave plantations of the British West Indies. At first, plantations may seem far removed from the railroads and factories that would dominate the economy a century later. Chandler certainly saw it this way, calling plantations a fundamentally "ancient" mode of production and commenting that before 1850, "very few American businesses needed the services of a full-time administrator or required a clearly defined administrative structure. . . . In the agrarian and commercial economy of antebellum America, business administration as a distinctive activity did not yet exist."[10] But looking just beyond national borders to the Caribbean shows businesses of similar scale and structure a century earlier. Like the railroads and manufacturers Chandler would examine, West Indian sugar plantations required complex hierarchies of managers to coordinate their activities. On these plantations, violence and control complemented organizational innovation.[11]

Sugar and Scale

In 1767, when the manager of Island Estate counted and classified 169 slaves, Island was one of two plantations owned by absentee proprietor Joseph Foster Barham. The other, about twice as large, was Mesopotamia, located in

Westmoreland Parish some fifty miles away. Though Island and Mesopotamia plantations were large, they were not among the largest properties in
Jamaica. The biggest slaveholdings included thousands of slaves spread
across many plantations. For example, two of the richest of all Jamaicans,
Simon Taylor and John Tharp, owned 2,990 and 2,228 slaves by the early
nineteenth century.[12] The vast majority of slaveholdings were much smaller;
by one estimate, only about 5 percent included more than 150 slaves between
1725 and 1784. However, despite their small numbers, very large slaveholdings dominated the economy. From the perspective of both labor and production, they were the norm: a majority of slaves in Jamaica worked on
plantations of this scale, and they produced vast amounts of sugar.[13]

This scale was massive for the period. Measuring by the size of the workforce, what might be described as "multidivisional plantations" ranked
among the largest business enterprises of their time. Only in the mid-
nineteenth century would the largest factories begin to approach the scale
of late eighteenth-century plantations. Josiah Wedgwood's famed pottery
works, which some historians have described as the largest industrial factory
of its time, employed only 450 people at his death in 1795.[14] In Britain, most
textile mills in Lancashire employed fewer than 500 hands, and as of 1841,
only twenty-five cotton concerns employed more than 1,000 people.[15] In
North America, textile mills followed a similar pattern. By the late 1830s, the
textile mills in Lowell, Massachusetts, would employ about 8,000 workers,
but these men and women were spread across some twenty-eight mills of
200–400 workers apiece.[16] Some groups of investors owned multiple properties, but even these conglomerations did not generally include as many properties as the largest amalgamations of plantations. The New York and Erie
Railroad is usually credited with producing the first organizational chart,
described at the close of this chapter. The railroad was only about double
the size of the largest eighteenth-century plantations when it produced the
chart, and it did not reach this scale until the 1850s.[17]

Understanding the importance of scale first requires a basic understanding
of how sugar was produced. Sugar production was highly complex, requiring
an array of skills and benefiting from an extensive division of labor. The process began with preparing the soil and planting cane. Figure 1.2 shows the
grueling process of preparing the soil on Weatherill's Estate in Antigua during

FIGURE 1.2. Digging or Rather Hoeing the Cane Holes, Antigua, 1823. A high degree of division of labor helped planters coordinate operations and extract maximum output from enslaved people of different ages and abilities. Here children space the cane while adults hoe. Etching by William Clark, 1823. *Ten Views in the Island of Antigua*, from drawings made by William Clark (London: Thomas Clay, 1823). The British Library / Granger. All Rights Reserved.

the early nineteenth century. At the center, children measure and mark out the spacing for the plants with sticks. Behind them, men and women hoe the fields to match the gridded pattern. From here, one gang of slaves might prepare the holes while another followed to bury segments of seed cane. At the left of the image, a herd of penned cattle offers both manure for fertilizer and meat for food. In the distance, outlined against the sky and sea, the sugar mill stands ready to grind and boil cane.[18]

After burying the seed cane, enslaved laborers tended the plants as they matured over a period of twelve to eighteen months—a long growing season, allowed by the region's warm weather. After this period, they cut the cane, bundled it, and carried it to the mill. Grinding mills, powered first by animals and later by steam and wind, crushed the cane to extract sap, which was then boiled in a series of vats to increase its concentration. After heating and cooling the liquid sugar to a wet, granulated state, enslaved laborers packed it into barrels and drained off the molasses. The sugar was then shipped to refiners abroad, who processed it further. The molasses was sold or distilled into rum, both in the islands and overseas. Alongside this central production line, enslaved sawyers and coopers made barrels, smiths maintained the boiling machinery, and cattlemen and stable keepers cared for livestock.[19]

Sugar production was time sensitive, particularly between the cutting of the cane and the boiling of the juice. Coordinating these activities for maximum output required the mill to be near the cane fields, a co-location that led anthropologist Sidney Mintz to describe plantations as the synthesis of "field and factory."[20] Proximity, however, was not enough. Planters also needed dependable labor at every stage of the production process: drivers to coordinate the growing of the cane; sufficient field hands to plant it, harvest it, and transport it to the mill; experienced boilers to stoke the furnaces and judge the sap; distillers to manage the production of rum; coopers to make the barrels; and so on. Sugar planters also needed slaves to care for the livestock, which was needed for food, to move the crop, to power the grinding apparatus, and to provide manure to fertilize the soil. In other words, sugar production required the careful administration of the labor of a large number of skilled and unskilled workers.

Thus, the usefulness of a balance sheet of lives becomes clear: planters needed not only to monitor the increase and decrease of their human stock but also to monitor changes in skill and labor allocation. Without this information, they risked losing their crop. A breakdown in one stage of the production process could cause the whole works to grind to a halt.

As it would in factories and railroads almost a century later, scale required structure. This is clear from the multitude of skilled professions on the Island Estate plantation, and it was even more pronounced for the very largest slaveholdings. These slaveholdings most closely approximate the hierarchies typically associated with nineteenth-century capitalism, which combined central offices with multiple geographic and product-based divisions. Nobel Prize–winning economist Oliver Williamson called this the "M-form," or multidivisional form, because it combined the strategic functions of a central office with the operating efficiency of smaller divisions.[21] Large slaveholders did not refer to "divisions," but they divided their organizational structures by both geography and task, delegating management across plantations dedicated to growing sugar, and stables and pens that concentrated on raising livestock. They compared and contrasted these units, strategically allocating resources between them. Consulting their account books provides a full sense of the administrative complexity of slave-based sugar production.

The organization of the many holdings of absentee proprietor Henry Dawkins reflects a structure similar to the M-form. Dawkins owned fourteen properties in Jamaica, including plantations, pens, and pastures spread across multiple parishes. Attorney John Shickle managed these properties in Jamaica, dividing them into two sets: those in Clarendon and Vere, and those in Saint Catherine's Parish. Each property had its own hierarchy of staff, both free and enslaved.[22] Like divisions of a large corporation, each pursued management goals of its own, but the results were also reported back to Shickle, who compared output and allocated resources. Figure 1.3 shows the fourteen properties and 2,248 slaves, divided first by parish and then by property. At the left are the ten properties in Clarendon and Vere, from the massive Parnassus, with 449 enslaved and 10 free staff, down to Henko Crawle, with 14 enslaved and 1 free staff person, and the smallest holding, Bog Hole, which appears to have had no resident managers or laborers, only stock. On the right are the four properties in Saint Catherine's Parish, ranging from Tredways Estate, with 205 enslaved laborers, to a place simply referred to as "At the Bog," which, like Bog Hole, lacked permanent staff.[23]

Shickle used a multifaceted system of accounts to manage Dawkins's properties. Some of his records followed the same system of double-entry bookkeeping used by sophisticated merchants and businesspeople on both sides of the Atlantic. A set of double-entry books typically included a waste book or daybook, a journal, and a ledger. The waste book was an informal registry of all transactions, noted down in the order in which they occurred. Anyone who could read and count could use this simple book. The journal organized entries from the waste book, rewriting them in the more precise format of debit and credit. Shickle or an assistant periodically transferred the journal entries to the ledger, the central book in the system. Here, debits and credits were classified by account—for example, a trading partner or a category of business—so that the bookkeeper could quickly discern whether that account was ahead or behind.[24] Double-entry books were essential for tracking a business's exchanges with suppliers and customers—that is, for

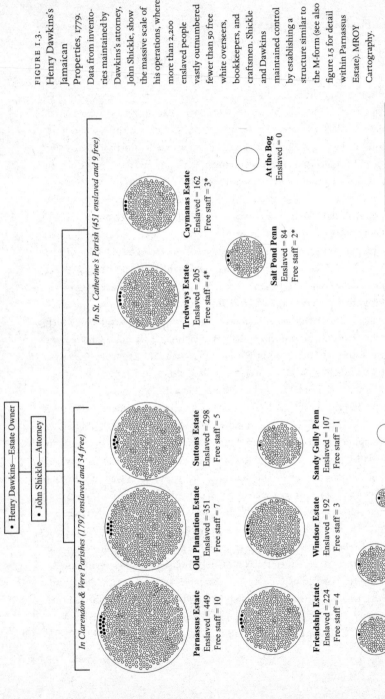

FIGURE 1.3. Henry Dawkins's Jamaican Properties, 1779. Data from inventories maintained by Dawkins's attorney, John Shickle, show the massive scale of his operations, where more than 2,200 enslaved people vastly outnumbered fewer than 50 free white overseers, bookkeepers, and craftsmen. Shickle and Dawkins maintained control by establishing a structure similar to the M-form (see also figure 1.5 for detail within Parnassus Estate). MROY Cartography.

• Henry Dawkins—Estate Owner

• John Shickle—Attorney

In Clarendon & Vere Parishes (1797 enslaved and 34 free)

In St. Catherine's Parish (451 enslaved and 9 free)

Parnassus Estate
Enslaved = 449
Free staff = 10

Old Plantation Estate
Enslaved = 351
Free staff = 7

Suttons Estate
Enslaved = 298
Free staff = 5

Tredways Estate
Enslaved = 205
Free staff = 4*

Caymanas Estate
Enslaved = 162
Free staff = 3*

Friendship Estate
Enslaved = 224
Free staff = 4

Windsor Estate
Enslaved = 192
Free staff = 3

Sandy Gully Penn
Enslaved = 107
Free staff = 1

Salt Pond Penn
Enslaved = 84
Free staff = 2*

At the Bog
Enslaved = 0

Vere Estate
Enslaved = 81
Free staff = 2

Moco Penn
Enslaved = 81
Free staff = 1

Henko Crawle
Enslaved = 14
Free staff = 1

Bog Hole
Enslaved = 0

KEY

• = One free person

○ = One enslaved person

managing its place in the market. Such records have typically been the focus of most histories of accounting practice during this period. Judged by the fragmentary account books that are available for the holdings in Shickle's care, he seems to have maintained his ledger diligently and skillfully. However, though it offers a portrait of the plantations' trading partners, it tells us relatively little about the organization of the thousands of enslaved people laboring on the plantation.[25]

More revealing are the inventories that Shickle prepared—a series of lists and tables that make it possible to decode hierarchies and reporting structures within the plantations. For each parcel of land, Shickle or his clerks compiled a detailed annual inventory of all slaves and stock. These inventories began with lists of white staff and then listed the occupations of the enslaved. The inventories closed with balance sheets of increase and decrease, much like the one prepared for Island Estate. As on Island, decrease often exceeded increase. For example, on Parnassus Estate, the largest individual property, deaths greatly outnumbered births. At the time of the previous six-month inventory in mid-1779, there had been 457 slaves living on Parnassus—this 457 combined with 3 births for a total of 460 lives. But between June 30 and the end of December, 11 slaves died, leaving just 449 men, women, and children living on Parnassus at the close of the year.[26]

After completing similar records for each of the fourteen properties, Shickle began the process of tallying up. Though the inventories occupied many pages per property, the data was neatly summarized in two sets of abstracts covering all of Dawkins's properties. These careful grids of occupations made a workforce of thousands visible in a few simple tables. Figure 1.4 shows Shickle's abstract for the nine properties in Clarendon and Vere in December 1779. Each unit is listed along the left-hand side of the table, beginning with the large plantations: Parnassus Estate, Old Plantation Estate, Suttons Estate, Friendship Estate, and Windsor Estate, worked by between 192 and 449 enslaved people; next a major animal pen, Sandy Gully Penn, worked by just over a hundred slaves; then two smaller properties with 81 people apiece; and finally tiny Henko Crawle, with just 14 slaves. Summed up, Henry Dawkins owned some 1,797 people in Clarendon and Vere parishes. Combined with his holdings elsewhere in Jamaica (added in pencil below the total), he owned 2,248 people.[27]

An Abstract of the foregoing List of Negroes from June 30 to 31st Dec 1787

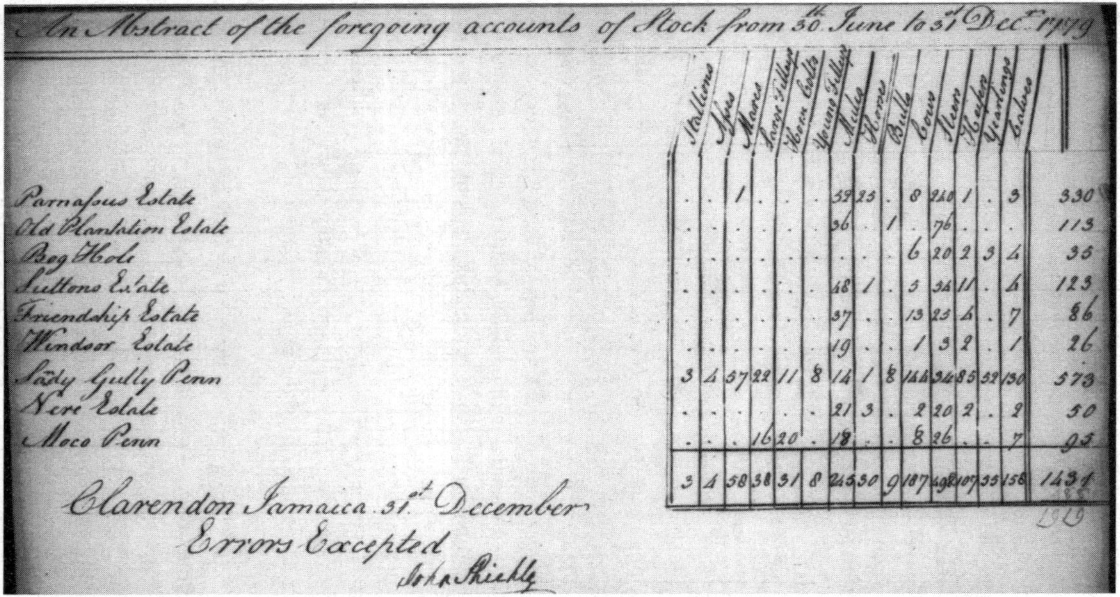

An Abstract of the foregoing accounts of Stock from the 30 June to 31 Dec.r 1779

	Stallions	Spay	Mares	Horse Kind	Horse Gelding	Young Gelding	Mules	Bulls	Cows	Oxen	Steers	Young	Grown	Calves	Totals
Parnassus Estate						5325			0	220	1	1	3	5	330
Old Plantation Estate					36			1	76					1	113
Bog Hole									6	20	2	3	4		35
Suttons Estate				48	1			5	34	11	2		6		123
Friendship Estate				37				13	23	6			7		86
Windsor Estate				19				1	3	9			1		26
Raby Gully Penn		1		8	14	1	8	4	145	29	59	30	9		578
Vere Estate				21	3			2	20	2		2			50
Moco Penn		1620		18					8	26			2		95
	3	4	1	722	11	8	50	8	2450	9	107	90	35	58	1434

Clarendon Jamaica 31.st December
Errors Excepted

John Kelly

FIGURE 1.4. Enslaved People and Livestock in Clarendon and Vere Parishes, 1779. An abstract neatly summarized the skills, ages, and health of the many enslaved people on the Dawkins plantations. Below these, the account keeper used the exact same format to keep track of animals. Jamaica Account (Box 13, Item 2.1 / 5), 1779, Wilberforce House Museum. Reproduction courtesy of the Adam Matthew Digital, *Slavery, Abolition, and Social Justice* collection, Marlborough, UK.

The record, which Shickle labeled "An Abstract of the foregoing list of Negroes," offered a detailed view of a massive workforce at a single glance. Someone consulting the abstract could tell not only how many slaves lived on each property but also their skills and occupations. On the largest of the plantations, Parnassus, Shickle classified 449 lives at the end of 1779: drivers, field men, field women, pen keepers, carpenters, coopers, smiths, brick-layers, sawyers, boatmen, cattle keepers, gardeners, and those working in the horse stable, hot-house (a hospital or infirmary), great house, new house, and overseer's house, among others. Shickle counted the boys and girls who could go to the fields and the young children who could not. He noted the number of slaves who were traveling with leave— "On the Roads"— as well as the identities of runaways and any "New Negroes" recently pur-chased. At the bottom, these categories were summed up across the parish. For example, across all the properties in Clarendon and Vere, there were 34 drivers, 336 field men, and 405 field women. There were 100 watchmen, 52 slaves working in the overseers' houses, 15 runaways, and 222 young children.[28]

Below the "abstract of negroes" was a twin record, in the same format as the first. Here, Shickle recorded the number and type of livestock living on the plantation. The 1,797 slaves labored alongside and cared for some 1,434 animals, not including smaller stock. Across all of Dawkins's properties (noted in pencil below these totals), there were 2,248 slaves and 1,919 large stock. But for the categories—stallions, asses, mares, mules, bulls, and so on—the form used is identical to the one used to classify men, women, and children. From an accounting perspective, Shickle saw these simply as two kinds of stock. At the bottom, he signed off on the report, "Clarendon Jamaica, 31st De-cember, Errors Excepted, John Shickle."[29]

All of the many occupations on the plantations fit together in complex management hierarchies. Perched atop these pyramids was a staff of free white managers. Shickle did not include them in his abstracts, for the obvious reason that they were not property, but he did include them in the lists of workers on each plantation. These lists match the description offered by eighteenth- and early nineteenth-century observers: under "an attorney (or land-agent) . . . is an overseer (or bailiff) for each estate—under the overseer are bookkeepers—and under these as many drivers as there are gangs of negroes. The drivers are blacks, the others whites."[30] The size of the white staff was usually proportional to the number of slaves, with an additional bookkeeper for each forty slaves.[31] Precise titles and ratios varied by island and even by plantation. As another author explained, on some of the smaller islands, bookkeepers were called overseers, and in Jamaica, the overseer might be called the manager.[32]

The basic structure of management seems to date to the mid-seventeenth century, and perhaps even earlier.[33] Richard Ligon, the most famous early chronicler of Barbadian sugar production, traveled to the island in 1647 specifically "to keep the accounts of a plantation of 500 acres, 99 slaves, and 28 white servants."[34] In his 1657 book about the experience, he offered a detailed set of accounts for a large plantation. Ligon's description suggests an early approximation of the hierarchies that would solidify by the eighteenth century: two hundred slaves managed by a prime overseer and five subordinate overseers, presumably playing the role "bookkeepers" would eventually fill. Ligon laid out the plantation's production and expenses in great detail, promising readers that diligent planters would earn huge profits.[35]

By the time John Shickle prepared his abstracts more than a century later, Ligon's simple pyramid had evolved into a complex hierarchy, mapped out in the organizational chart shown in Figure 1.5. At the top, the fourteen properties fan out under Shickle, the main attorney. Below these is the structure on Parnassus, the largest of the estates. Here, the white staff comprised an assistant attorney and two clerks, an overseer, bookkeepers, and several free craftspeople. Below them were enslaved drivers and head people, and finally the men, women, and children laboring in the fields, stables, houses, and workshops. Future laborers—young children—are listed to the side, as are the doctor and those in his care. Many layers of organization and management coordinated and controlled Dawkins's present and future human capital.

Free Managers

How did hierarchy function on Parnassus plantation? Walking down the organizational pyramid drawn in Figure 1.5 offers a sense of the layers of administration and middle management that enabled successful sugar

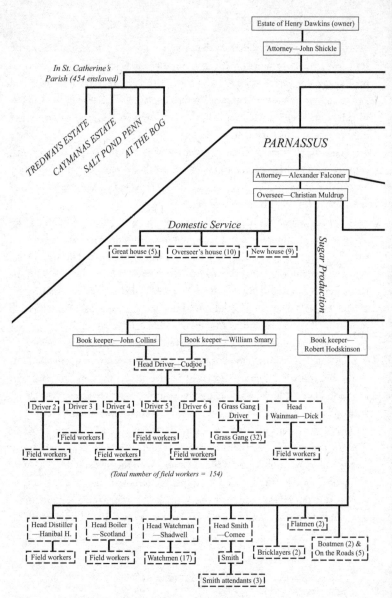

FIGURE 1.5. Organizational Chart for Parnassus Estate, 1779. Inventories from Parnassus Estate can be used to reconstruct the plantation's complex organizational structure, which included multiple layers of both free and enslaved managers. MROY Cartography.

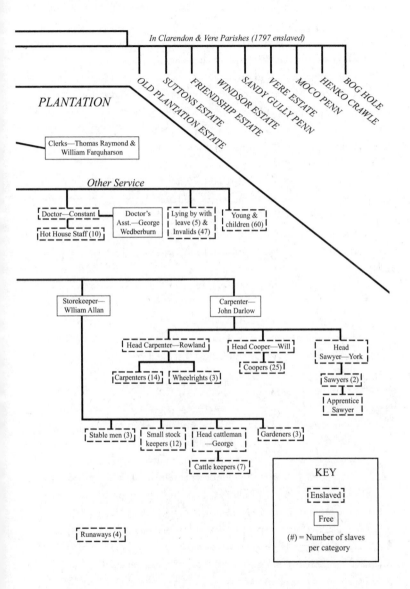

In Clarendon & Vere Parishes (1797 enslaved)

OLD PLANTATION ESTATE
SUTTONS ESTATE
FRIENDSHIP ESTATE
WINDSOR ESTATE
SANDY GULLY PENN
VERE ESTATE
MOCO PENN
HENKO CRAWLE
BOG HOLE

PLANTATION

Clerks—Thomas Raymond &
William Farquharson

Other Service

Doctor—Constant

Doctor's
Asst.—George
Wedberburn

Lying by with
leave (5) &
Invalids (47)

Young &
children (60)

Hot House Staff (10)

Storekeeper—
Wlliam Allan

Carpenter—
John Darlow

Head Carpenter—Rowland

Head Cooper—Will

Head
Sawyer—York

Carpenters (14)

Wheelrights (3)

Coopers (25)

Sawyers (2)

Apprentice
Sawyer

Stable men (3)

Small stock
keepers (12)

Head cattleman
—George

Gardeners (3)

Cattle keepers (7)

Runaways (4)

KEY

Enslaved

Free

(#) = Number of slaves
per category

production. At the top of the hierarchy was the attorney. Despite his title, a planting attorney's duties involved administration and reporting rather than law. Attorneys conducted a wide variety of plantation business on behalf of the owner, and they typically enjoyed the authority to act on behalf of absentee proprietors who had departed the islands to return to England or Scotland. Attorneys reported their progress back to these absentee landowners, but they also made important decisions in real time without prior consent. While other white staff earned flat salaries, attorneys typically worked on commission, their compensation directly connected to the success or failure of the plantation.[36]

Attorneys managed only a small proportion of the total number of properties, but these were among the largest and most important plantations in Jamaica. Historian B. W. Higman has estimated that by 1832, on the eve of emancipation, attorneys managed just 9 percent, or 1,125, of all properties with slaves in Jamaica. However, this small minority of holdings included 140,586 enslaved men and women—more than 45 percent of all Jamaican bondpeople. Limiting the sample to properties classified as estates, plantations, and stock pens shows an even greater concentration of control. A mere 745 properties managed by two hundred attorneys were worked by 42 percent of all Jamaican slaves. And among those attorneys, fifty-two men managed 5 or more properties, putting a total of 489 of the island's largest plantations under their control.[37]

The most powerful attorneys enjoyed great influence. These prominent men managed many properties for multiple owners and achieved substantial status and income. For example, in 1832, William Miller managed thirty-six properties, including twenty-six estates, eight pens, and two plantations. In total, 7,700 slaves labored under his management.[38] John Shickle, who appears to have managed properties for other absentees and also owned at least two properties of his own, would have been in this elite group.[39]

Attorneys not only maintained double-entry ledgers and detailed inventories but also performed special calculations that sought to mine this data for strategic insight. High death rates meant that to keep making sugar, Joseph Foster Barham—whose balance sheet of lives opened this chapter—had to keep buying slaves. However, he had a choice of where to buy them. To improve his purchases, he or his attorney drew up a document labeled the "List of New Negroes Bought . . . 1751 to 1774." "New Negroes" included those who had just arrived from Africa, and the compiler of this list seems to have hoped that he might discern what geographic origins yielded the longest-lived laborers. The document drew data from almost twenty-five years of plantation operations, probably from the detailed annual inventories Barham maintained. The analysis appears inconclusive—there were high death rates across the board, and almost every slave from the earliest shipments had died by 1774. Nonetheless, the data may have contributed to the eventual decision by Barham's son, Joseph Foster Barham II, to purchase only seasoned slaves from the local area.[40]

The records attorneys maintained facilitated flows of information and with them consistent management. They also made operations less reliant on any one individual—essential, given the risks of life in the Caribbean. Indeed, Henry Dawkins appears to have employed a second, or assistant, attorney. Alexander Falconer served under Shickle, assisted by two clerks. He appears to have lived on Parnassus Estate, where he oversaw the largest plantation but perhaps also prepared and reviewed accounts for other properties. His presence offered continuity in case of illness or death.[41] Such arrangements were not unknown on the largest estates; absentee owner John Pennant appointed both Falconer and another attorney to oversee his Clarendon properties in the case of Shickle's death, which occurred, of fever, in 1782. Detailed accounts and a plan of succession were essential for continuous and efficient operations.[42]

Below the attorney was the overseer. Though attorneys sometimes lived on large plantations, the overseer was typically the most senior manager permanently in residence on an individual property. On Parnassus Estate, Christian Muldrup occupied this post, part of a free staff of 10 who managed the workforce of 449 enslaved men, women, and children (see Figure 1.5).[43] Where attorneys prepared reports for owners and offered oversight, overseers concentrated on day-to-day operations. Though it is often difficult to tell exactly which records each individual kept, overseers most likely maintained mid-level accounts that monitored production and labor from week to week and month to month. Overseers likely took charge of planning production, including preparing plans for planting. For example, an overseer might have prepared the plan for the "Disposition of the several Fields" on Newton plantation in Barbados. In 1798, three fields were planted as "first crop canes," and four as "second crop," for a total of 80 acres. Guinea corn and other provisions were grown in fifteen fields, for a total of 115 acres.[44] Though overseers might have consulted with attorneys or owners about their plans for laying out the fields, they maintained authority over operations.

Overseers and attorneys offered a check on each other. In one sense, the overseer was "below" the attorney in the plantation hierarchy, but in another sense, there was simply a division of labor between the two. The attorney took charge of the commercial side of the business, including marketing and selling the crop. The overseer planned and managed production. The attorney might monitor this production through periodic visits, but operational responsibility fell to the overseer. And each could police the other, solving some of the principal–agent problems that plagued absentee owners who could not monitor their property in person.[45]

Below the overseer on the managerial ladder were the bookkeepers, whose jobs involved a wide array of tasks, many of which had very little to do with keeping books. As a critic of the system wrote after its demise, "the appellation was probably first imposed with a view to delude young men at home as to the nature of the situation." They arrived expecting to keep accounts but found that they also had to "keep swine."[46] On Parnassus, there were three bookkeepers. These men likely coordinated day-to-day labor, supervising the gangs of slaves who labored in the fields and produced sugar. Several other white staff probably managed specific aspects of plantation operations. Carpenter John Darlow likely supervised the seventeen enslaved carpenters, twenty-six coopers, and four sawyers who maintained buildings and prepared barrels for shipping crops. Storekeeper William Allan would have managed plantation goods and may have also supervised the various enslaved stockkeepers. Some plantations had even larger staffs.[47] By the 1780s, Joseph Foster Barham employed as many as seven bookkeepers to work on each of his Jamaican plantations.[48]

Despite a job description that sometimes involved more hogs than handwriting, the title of "bookkeeper" reflects the centrality of accounting to plantation operations. Indeed, if the position of bookkeeper was not the countinghouse role that young men imagined when they set out from England or Scotland, most positions involved at least some record keeping. The layers of management between owner, attorney, overseer, driver, and hand made frequent reports important for transparency and effective communications. Though most bookkeepers rarely wrote in formal ledgers, they likely contributed the many other preliminary records that connected the messy day-to-day realities of the plantation with the neat columns of reports and abstracts sent to attorneys and owners.

Bookkeepers likely maintained or at least contributed to the daily work records for John Newton's Barbados plantations. The most extensive of the surviving records are labor logs. These logs, written on thicker paper than more formal reports, begin in May 1796, picking up as if from a prior book now lost. The rough, dirty pages of the logs contrast sharply with the immaculate copies of the journals and ledgers. Their well-worn condition suggests they were completed and consulted daily, weekly, and monthly. Such records are much rarer than formal journals and ledgers. They may have been less common, but more likely they have survived less frequently than the formal records and reports that were carefully audited and often sent back to England.[49]

The labor records for Newton plantation tally up the daily activities of every enslaved man or woman who performed work there. Each slave who worked in the fields was assigned to one of three gangs and then, within each gang, to a particular activity. The records add up the total number of workers to determine the total days of labor expended. Jobs and tasks varied considerably from day to day and season to season, reflecting complex production processes. In January, the bookkeeper concentrated on maintenance and preparing food crops. Tasks included "mending the path," "moulding the still pond," "holeing for corn," "crowning pens & breaking corn." In the summer months, labor included carting, carrying letters, "minding a cow," "weeding young Canes," working "at the distilling house," and a multitude of other jobs. Though the work varied, the math was always the same. Each slave always had a job to do, and every unit of labor was accounted for. The slaves did not labor on Sundays or the annual Christmas holiday, but for every other day of the year, the allocation of labor across the tasks matched the number of slaves in each gang.[50]

The labor account books are large and soft covered, suggesting that they were completed in an office or at least at a desk. Bookkeepers may have completed them after coming in from the fields. Alternatively, they may have been secondary records, compiled each day from a smaller book or slate that was used in the field to record the activities of each gang. Almost identical documents recorded labor on Seawells, one of Newton's other plantations, and similar documents may have been kept for his third, Alleyne, though none survive. By comparing across different plantations, Newton or his overseer or attorney could see how labor was allocated on each. He could analyze how much time went into improving the land, tending the canes, growing corn, raising stock, and a wide array of other tasks. Disruptions in labor or an uptick in sickness would have been immediately apparent.[51]

Many more daily record books detailed other production processes. The small size of some of these records suggests that they may have been taken into the workplace. On the Newton plantations, a set of pocket-sized accounts monitored output of boiling the cane juice and distilling the rum. "A Boiling House Book for the Year 1798," for example, includes a daily record of the number of "Loads of Canes ground," the number of "coppers" of liquid gotten from the cane, the number of coppers of liquid boiled, the gallons of liquid boiled, the number of "Potts Sugar" made, and the total barrels of sugar filled. A tall, thin "Distilling House Book" contained a similar amount of detail, but for the production of rum instead of sugar.[52] All these accounts reflected the intersection between the demands of day-to-day accountability and longer-term planning. In the immediate term, detailed records prevented dishonesty and theft, but their uniform format would have facilitated comparisons to prior years and planning for future production.[53]

Plantation manuals offered advice or keeping these records. William Weston's *Complete Merchant's Clerk* describes a "Boiling-House-Book" containing "an Account of every Hogshead of Sugar that is potted" by date. This book, which matched the style of the Newton records, was to be "subscribed by the White-Man on Duty," presumably the bookkeeper, "and weekly delivered to the Overseer." Similarly, a "Still-House-Book," similar to the "Distilling House Book" from the Newton records, was to be delivered weekly. Occasionally these books traveled all the way up the plantation hierarchy and were "produced to the Proprietor's Attorney," where they served as a "Check, or Counter-part of the Plantation Accounts."[54] Weston expounded at length on the importance of selecting skilled clerks and bookkeepers for successful plantation management. He emphasized that it "would not be amis[s]" for an "Overseer to study the Nature of Double-Entry as well as planting; thereby making himself acquainted with what would give his Employer as much Satisfaction, as his Care of the Crop."[55]

An 1823 plantation guide mentions an even wider array of records. These included a book of accounts for the traveling agent, a book of accounts for the planter, a hot-house book recording medicines administered, a plantation book enumerating and analyzing the slave population, a breeding book, a cultivation book describing the state of the crops, and even a book recording rewards paid out for rats caught in the boiling house. Among these, the attorney probably kept the plantation book, but the overseer would have maintained many of the others, with the junior staff completing minor books such as the book of rats, designed to prevent slaves from tricking planters into paying rewards for the same dead rat more than once.[56]

Though bookkeepers occupied the bottom of the managerial hierarchy, they could rise through the ranks, achieving money and status. In order to advance, they had to learn the full system of record keeping. In his 1796 "Essay upon Pen-Keeping and Plantership," Jamaican planter Patrick Kein urged overseers to "impress the good example in the minds of his book-keepers," in order to guide them to be industrious "when they become overseers."[57] Those attaining the rank had become "the highest officer necessarily resident on the property; his salary was considerable, and in other respects his situation was comfortable."[58] The Barham records show this advancement. When the main overseer on one of Joseph Foster Barham's plantations departed in 1788, a man described as the "distiller / bookkeeper" stepped up to fill his position, while a more junior bookkeeper took over the man's former role.[59]

Enslaved Managers

The managerial hierarchy on West Indian plantations extended beyond the paid white staff to the enslaved themselves. Ten free men monitored the work of 449 enslaved men, women, and children. They thus depended on the assistance of a further hierarchy of men and women held in bondage. Parnassus had eight drivers, and the annual inventory listed them in ranking order (see Figure 1.6). Atop the hierarchy was Cudjoe, the head driver. Below him were the second through sixth drivers: John, Prince, Kitt, Mingo, and Abbo. Below them was a woman named Flora, who oversaw the grass gang—a group of field laborers that often included children. The last driver was Dick, designated the head "wainman"—the driver of a wagon team who probably coordinated the transportation of supplies and cane to and from the fields.[60]

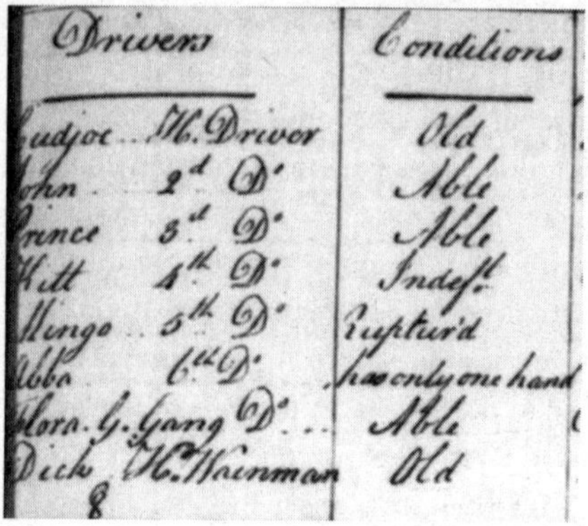

Drivers	Conditions
udjoe .. Hd. Driver	Old
ohn . 2d Do	Able
rince 3d Do	Able
Will 4th Do	Indeft
Mingo .. 5th Do	Ruptur'd
Abba 6th Do	has only one hand
lora. G. Gang Do ...	Able
Dick Hd. Wainman	Old
8	

FIGURE 1.6. Drivers on Parnassus Plantation, 1779. The eight enslaved drivers on Parnassuss managed production processes. Flora, the one female driver, oversaw the grass gang, which would have been made up of children. Jamaica Account (Box 13, Item 2.1 / 6), 1779. Wilberforce House Museum. Reproduction courtesy of Adam Matthew Digital, *Slavery, Abolition, and Social Justice* collection, Marlborough, UK.

Beyond the drivers, most categories of skilled labor also included a designated "head." Scotland was listed as both a field hand and head boiler. He probably operated the sugar house during the appropriate season. Rowland served as head carpenter; Will, head cooper; George, head cattleman; Shadwell, head watchman; Comee, head smith; York, head sawyer; and Hanibal H., head distiller. In some cases, slaves may even have directed the activities of the free white staff. The plantation report for Parnassus lists George Wedberburn, a "doctor's assistant," among the white staff. On the inventory of slaves we find two enslaved doctors: Constant, very sickly, and Harry, described as able. Two midwives, Dora and Myrtilla, as well as several nurses are all described as "Old and Weakly." Wedberburn, the white assistant, may well have aided the enslaved healers, but he probably also surveilled their work and the population in the hot-house.[61]

The presence of enslaved healers can be understood in contrasting ways. On the one hand, these men and women helped maintain the health of the plantation, probably at a lower cost than would free doctors. By offering employment for elderly slaves, these roles also helped planters exploit those who could not labor in the fields. On the other hand, they reflect the enduring influence and authority of skilled Africans—an influence that planters sometimes wished they could eliminate. In his plantation manual, Thomas Roughley described midwives as "egregiously ignorant" and "most obstinately addicted to their own way." In his view, these women often manipulated white plantation staff: one would "cunningly run to the overseer, tell him of the dangerous case, and that he should send for the doctor," but then when mother or child "expires shortly after his arrival, they dexterously assert that if he had followed their advice, all would have been well." In Roughley's estimation, these skilled women—Dora and Myrtilla on Parnassus—could not be challenged because of the position they held in the enslaved community. Though he dismissed them as "harpies," they clearly commanded the respect of other enslaved people. As Roughley wrote, they "impress, by the nature of their office and by such assertions, such an awe and reverence for them on the minds of all classes of slaves, that few practising doctors wish to encounter them." Confronted with this authority, an overseer could "do little or nothing."[62]

Head slaves rose up the ranks of plantation hierarchy, sometimes introduced to their roles from a young age. In testimony to the British Privy Council in 1827, West Indian planter Hugh Hyndman described the process of developing enslaved managers. As he explained, "When a man is first introduced to be a boiler, he begins in a subordinate capacity, and he comes on by degrees. . . . He may become, in the course of years[,] the head boiler: much depends on his skill, and his assiduity and his talent."[63] This pipeline for skilled positions is reflected in the Parnassus inventory. For example, there were four sawyers—York, the head; two additional men; and a fourth, described as an apprentice. There was also a head smith, Comee; another smith; and then three attendants, who may have eventually advanced to become smiths.[64]

Head slaves were absolutely critical to successful plantations. Colin Macrae, an experienced planter from Berbice and Demerara, explained the importance of enslaved managers. During his "five-and-twenty years" residence in the islands, Macrae had managed properties both as owner and as agent, and at one time had "as many as three thousand Negroes under my charge." In his view, the loss of "an engineer, a head boiler, or leading man" would have "very injurious effects" and "might cripple the whole concern."[65] Thomas Roughley also commented extensively on the importance of the head driver. He lamented that "a bad or indifferent head driver sets almost every thing at variance; injures the negroes, and the culture of the land. He is like a cruel blast that pervades every thing, and spares nothing." By contrast, a skilled head who was "well-disposed, intelligent, clever and active" would be "the life and soul of an estate." Beyond the head driver, he singled out the head cattleman, head mule man, head wainman, and head boiler as managers of particular importance. Below these skilled managers were "head men such as carpenters, coopers, masons, coppersmiths, and watchmen," who Roughley described as "next in succession as principal slaves on an estate." Roughley also offered advice on selecting the best candidates to fill these key roles.[66]

The few women who advanced to head roles generally supervised children, directing their activities as they learned to labor. Flora, the only woman driver on Parnassus plantation, oversaw the grass gang, which was made up of children deemed old enough to work.[67] Just as planters made use of elderly and infirm slaves as supervisors, they also made use of children on this special gang devoted to lighter tasks. On Mesopotamia plantation, also in Jamaica, children generally started to labor in the grass gang around age eight, but sometimes as young as age six. Division of labor helped planters to extract labor from the youngest workers. On Mesopotamia, the grass gang was further subdivided into a "third gang" for young teenagers and the "hog meat or fourth gang," which included older children.[68]

Children's labor fit strategically into the overall choreography of plantation production. Planters considered their tiny hands superior for the performance of certain tasks. Thomas Roughley claimed that the "supple hand of the negro child is best calculated to extract the weeds and grass." Working among young canes, children left "few breakages" because they were "more light and cautious."[69] Not only did enslaved youth perform a wide array of jobs, but by working at lighter tasks, they freed up field hands to work at heavy ones. Perhaps most important, sending children into the fields introduced them to the strenuous patterns of labor that would govern their lives, accustoming them to constant work. Planters even acquired special tools sized for children. A "list of supplies wanted for 1795 on Prospect Estate" in Jamaica requests "2 Doz'n small Children's weeding hoes."[70] Hoes were offered in different weights and sizes so that planters could make full use of enslaved labor over the life cycle. Planters sought out tiny implements for the youngest children. One Barbadian planter was disappointed to be informed by a supplier that "we have no Children hoes made smaller than No 0."[71]

The rhythm of labor that planters sought to impose on children relied on the cultivation of fear. Thomas Roughley waxed eloquently about the pleasure of seeing children go to the fields from 5 or 6 years of age—"How pleasing, how gratifying, how replete with humanity, it is to see a swarm of healthy, active, cheerful, pliant, straight, handsome creole negro boys and girls." But he also sought to instill dread among this cheer. The ideal "driveress" to "superintend, instruct, and govern this gang of pupils" should be "stern without command, fractious and severe." She would be "armed with a pliant, serviceable twig, more to create dread, than inflict chastisement."[72]

Enslaved managers generally did not contribute directly to written plantation records. However, they were part of the larger information systems that enabled their preparation. Jamaican author Patrick Kein's advice manual recommended the use of wooden tools called tally sticks to maintain accounts with enslaved pen-keepers. As he explained, "In order to obviate disputes with the pen-keepers, as well as to keep them honest and strict, I would recommend all overseers on pens, to have three distinct wooden tallies made." On one side of the first stick they would make a notch for the increase of bull calves, on the other, heifer calves. On the other sticks the same practice would be repeated for foals and cubs. The tallies were to be "made at the commencement of every year in succession, taking from the pen-keepers the half of each tally which they possess, on the last day of December in every year." In this way, the enslaved became the keepers of balance sheets of lives for livestock. By notches in wood, they tracked animals in the same ways that their masters tracked them.[73]

Wooden records did more than ensure the honesty and diligence of the individual pen-keepers. They also fed into the larger accounting systems of the plantation. As Kein remarked, the "tallies and book entries" could be "a check on each other . . . so that it will be impossible for any mistakes to happen." Notches marked by slaves could feed into or be cross-referenced with book records. Cross-referencing would help planters detect "thefts committed by the negroes . . . as the pen-keepers can have no excuse that wrong entries may be made, when they have the half of each tally in their possession until the expiration of the year."[74] Thus, like bookkeepers maintaining double-entry ledgers, enslaved men and women keeping tally sticks served not only to manage livestock but also to manage themselves. And, of course, tally sticks are just one physical aspect of information systems that were also verbal. Even when slaves maintained no paper or wooden records, their reporting would have formed many of the inputs into the more formal written records that kept the plantation operating smoothly.

Incorporating slaves into managerial hierarchies was an essential strategy both for organizing production and also for maintaining control. In addition to directing many aspects of plantation production, slaves kept security on plantations. Shadwell, the head watchman on Parnassus plantation, presided over a staff of seventeen, whose days were dedicated to "watching." His staff included men and women who were "very old," "rupture'd," and "old & sickly," and those who had lost the use of their hands or legs. Despite their ailments, they continued to contribute to plantation productivity through surveillance. Each was assigned to monitor a specific location. Peter kept watch "at the swamp," Caesar "at the works," and John and Billy "at new pasture." Six more men looked over the "negro grounds." Assigning them to distinct plantation spaces over the course of the year ensured that they could be questioned and held accountable for disturbances or theft.[75]

Of course, the leadership of drivers, the training of children to labor diligently, and the cooperation of watchers should not be mistaken for the acceptance of the structures that confined them. As Michael Craton has written, "The forces of control had to be constantly on the alert."[76] Planters could never completely extinguish resistance, so instead they strove to manage it. For example, the Parnassus records describe most of the drivers and head workers as able bodied, but the inventory also suggests that planters made use of the injured to supervise other slaves. Abbo, one of the drivers, had lost his hand, as had Shadwell, the head watchman.[77] Perhaps in using the aged and infirm as managers and watchers, planters were simply making efficient use of their capital. But surely they also realized that these slaves could be "trusted" in part because they had more limited physical capacity to escape or resist.

The peril of relying on enslaved people to conduct surveillance is clear from plantation manuals. Head watchmen—and they appear to have been mostly men—always had to be carefully watched themselves. That they frequently protected their fellow workers and misled their masters is evident from warnings in plantation manuals: unless constantly monitored, the watchman "spends the greater part of his time in gadding" or, worse, "harbouring runaway slaves whom he cheaply hires to perform some work for him." Losing control over the head watchman was "a bad example to the slave population who are ever prone to catch infection of this kind." To prevent this "noxious influence," Thomas Roughley prescribed constant contact with the overseer, who should demand regular reports "of the state of the business." Inducing enslaved people to keep surveillance over each other was necessary but perilous for masters and overseers attempting to maintain control over labor processes. Roughley recommended that the head watchman and some of the other ranking slaves be offered incentives, including rum, sugar, and "now and then a dinner from the overseers' table," but none of these measures could guarantee obedience.[78]

One of the most vexing historical questions about the West Indian plantation complex is how a small number of free whites maintained power over so many enslaved Africans. Though the ratio of 10 to 449 on Parnassus was more dramatically unbalanced than the overall proportion in the British Caribbean, by the late eighteenth century enslaved people vastly outnumbered free whites. In 1700, the population was approximately 78 percent of African descent, and by 1780, the proportion exceeded 90 percent.[79] In Saint-Domingue, similar imbalances prevailed. Planters recognized the dangers of being part of such a small minority. The imbalances that made slavery so profitable also made it perilous. Laws recognized the threat and mandated minimum proportions of free workers on plantations, usually approximately one free manager for every forty enslaved. This bare minimum was maintained in case planters needed to summon a militia.[80] But enslaved people still dramatically outnumbered free residents.

Planters' fears were sometimes realized. Scholars have painstakingly reconstructed the many ways enslaved peoples resisted bondage—from slowing the pace of work to engaging in subtle noncooperation; carving out private and communal spaces; and conspiring to commit more explicit crimes, such as arson, murder, and outright revolt. These most dramatic forms of rebellion were particularly common in Jamaica. Maroons—communities of escaped slaves—resisted in ways that sometimes rose to the level of outright war. In the First Maroon War, an escaped slave named Cudjoe led approximately five thousand escaped slaves and their descendants in a series of methodical guerrilla attacks on planters and the British colonial government. The war is often dated to the particularly violent decade leading up to 1739, but in some ways the period from 1655 (when the British captured Jamaica from the Spanish) to 1739 (when a treaty was signed) was "one long series of "revolts."[81] Some rebellions reached system-threatening proportions. On Easter day of 1760, Tacky's Rebellion began when 150 enslaved people attacked a fort in

St. Mary's Parish, which had the lowest concentration of whites in Jamaica. Though the leaders were captured within days, the revolution had already spread across the island, and it was not fully suppressed until October 1761.[82]

And yet planters maintained control, and the system survived. Account books hint at the persistence of small acts of defiance. Perhaps the name of the head driver on Parnassus—Cudjoe, the same as the Maroon revolutionary— was one such example.[83] More certain are the many individual escapes, some of them seasonal and others permanent. By running away, men and women deprived their masters of labor and property, claiming time and space of their own. At the end of 1779, when John Shickle recorded the activities and locations of the 1,797 enslaved persons on the Dawkins plantations in Clarendon and Vere, he included a column for fifteen "Runaways" (see Figure 1.4). Some of these slaves had been gone for years. On Parnassus, Quacaw had escaped in 1773, Titus in 1774, and Plato in 1775. On the nearby Suttons Estate, three of the six runaways—Sawney, Scipio, and Hanibal—had fled the plantation a carefully recorded thirteen years and five months earlier, surely plotting their escape together. Beyond these long-term disappearances, signs of short-term escape are scattered throughout the inventories. The Parnassus list labels at least four men and women "able but a runaway" or something similar. All across the Caribbean, enslaved peoples deprived their masters of labor and property.[84] But with the important exception of the Haitian Revolution, their efforts did not undermine the system itself.[85]

How could such a small minority of free whites dominate the much larger enslaved majority? Planters' strategies were—and indeed had to be—multiple. The most basic included maintaining control over weapons and horses. Most of the account books described here relate to plantation production, but some also reflected the need to maintain security. For example, accounting for tools reinforced the power structure on the plantation by helping the small white minority maintain a near monopoly on potential weapons. One lost ax might be a sign of wastefulness or carelessness, but several missing in a short period of time could be a harbinger of violence or rebellion. Tool accounts were therefore tallied up frequently. Clement Caines, author of an advice book on sugar planting, recommended balancing tool accounts weekly and summarizing overall plantation accounts in a monthly report to be sent to absentee landowners.[86] Maintaining social control was at least as important as monitoring access to weapons. By controlling information and regulating connections beyond the plantation, planters could extend their reach. For example, planters could curtail access to religion: in Barbados, following a plot by enslaved Africans to overthrow their masters, planters sought to restrict access to literacy and Christianity.[87]

Fear underwrote all of these strategies. West Indian planters used horrific and outlandish punishments to terrorize the men and women they owned: branding, slitting the nose, removing ears, gelding, and whipping and pickling—literally rubbing salt in wounds.[88] Vincent Brown has described the ways planters brutalized black bodies even after death, in an attempt to prevent suicide among the enslaved. Suicide, besides a loss of life, was a loss of property for the owner, so masters strove to give their authority "a sacred, even supernatural dimension." Spectacular displays of violence were used to "terrorize the spiritual imaginations of the enslaved," extending control into the afterlife.[89] The managers described above—especially the bookkeepers and overseers resident on plantations—had to be ready and willing to inflict terrifying violence. They had to learn to inflict the brutal punishments that supported the plantation pyramid. As Trevor Burnard has written, this violence was not some "incidental by-product" of the plantation regime; punishment and the tyrants who executed it were "the glue that held the plantation system together."[90]

Accounting complemented violence and terror, binding multiple strategies into a rationalized web of control both on individual plantations and across the islands. Just as inventories and daily work records reflect enslaved resistance, they also reveal planters' efforts to manage it. Inventories note who often ran away, and work logs recorded absences from the plantation—both with leave and without. Such records show that many escapes were temporary and that the enslaved were expected to return, adding their value once again to capital stock and labor power. Even when they eluded capture, the careful numbering and detailed accounts of the escaped might eventually help planters secure their return. And, as with records of tools, labor logs might also offer clues to conspiracy when new or different categories of enslaved peoples attempted to grasp their freedom. Such records ensured that even on massive plantations, where proprietors and overseers did not know every enslaved person, they could still know about them.

Brutal legal structures—including slave codes passed in the late seventeenth century in Barbados, Jamaica, and South Carolina—underpinned and

institutionalized masters' cruelty. These codes set out procedures for punishing the enslaved and increasingly aligned race and legal status, using racial
division as a tool for policing.[91] They also gave planters additional reasons to
keep detailed records. For example, the Barbados Slave Code of 1661 included
a "ticketing clause to curtail runaways." Masters and overseers had to write
passes for any slave who left the plantation. A failure to provide a ticket resulted in a large fine, to be divided between the public treasuries. Similarly,
a master who failed to recapture and punish an escaped African paid a fine.
Compliance with these laws required monitoring slaves absent from the
plantation. At the same time that John Shickle recorded runaways in his accounts, he listed five slaves who were "On the Roads." By clearly noting
those who had been authorized to travel, planters, by exclusion, designated
those who had not (see Figure 1.4).[92]

Planters managed resistance much as they managed production, and their
efforts to control their own property were part of the broader project of maintaining social order across the slaveholding West Indies. Records of negotiations with Maroons—escaped Africans and native peoples living off the
plantation—reveal the scale of this project. From one perspective, the very
existence of Maroon communities reflects the remarkable success of former
slaves in carving out spaces of freedom. However, in order to secure their
own safety, Jamaican Maroons signed a treaty with the British government
in 1739. The treaty required that they refuse to accept future runaways. This
offered a kind of amnesty, but it also hardened the boundaries of freedom,
enabling a more precise numbering of enslaved lives on the islands. By for-
bidding runaways from joining Maroon communities, planters made both
escaped slaves and free Maroons more manageable. Without new additions,
communities would not swell to amorphous, system-threatening proportions.
The 1739 treaty also required the Maroons to serve alongside the British militia in case of rebellion. In 1760, when slaves rose up in Tacky's Rebellion, they
navigated between the dual threat of British militias who controlled the
plantation plains and Maroon militias who controlled the mountains. Ultimately, both forces joined together to put down the insurrection.[93]

Accounting knit production, violence, religious authority, and spiritual
terror into rational and complex information systems. Reporting structures
enabled accountability and control within massive plantations and across
West Indian society. Information flowed smoothly up and down hierarchies,

from head to bookkeeper to overseer to attorney to proprietor and back again. Plantation records helped slaveholders count and control bodies, organize them for labor, and protect them as property. They did this at a massive scale—the largest collections of plantations included thousands of bondpeople and only small numbers of managers. Accounting certainly was not the main source of control in these operations. In many ways, account books were reflections of power as much as they were instruments of it. But they also augmented planters' power by weaving multiple sources of authority together into a complex and comprehensive system.

Studies of slavery alternately emphasize the overwhelming power of masters and the resistance of the enslaved. These competing genres of account ricochet between what one scholar has described as "hopeful stories of heroic subalterns versus anatomies of doom."[94] Getting inside the day-to-day administration of the plantation can help scholars escape this dichotomy because it reveals the extent to which these narratives coexisted. Account books show both the complexity and sophistication of the system faced by enslaved people *and* the moments when that system gave way. Enslaved men and women, forced to maintain the system that bound them, were transformed into instruments of their own control. Even as they resisted, they also surveilled one another, extending the eyes and ears of their masters. They became part of information systems that extended the reach of the small number of white people who resided on the plantation. These information systems combined with other technologies to enable both production of sugar and control over the enslaved as a class. They also countered informal networks of exchange and communication among the enslaved. Sometimes these informal networks enabled the enslaved to escape or even to assert the strength of their numbers, but more often planters' systems of surveillance seem to have entrapped them. Bound by both the threat of violence and the power of information, enslaved men and women were forced not only to labor together but also to manage one another.

Owners

Returning to the top of the organizational chart, we find one final layer of hierarchy: plantation owners, who increasingly managed their holdings from afar. As the eighteenth century advanced, planters returned to England and

Scotland, leaving their holdings under the supervision of local attorneys. The structure of plantation life led to private enrichment, but it did not encourage regional investment. Though the region produced vast wealth, there were few schools and little investment in infrastructure. As historian David Brion Davis has written, "as early as the mid-eighteenth century, slave societies were acquiring the images of social and cultural wastelands blighted by an obsessive pursuit of private profit."[95]

The rise in absentee plantership occurred over a long period, but it dramatically increased in the late eighteenth and early nineteenth centuries. In the seventeenth century, exit rates from Barbados were relatively similar to those in New England. But outmigration soon diverged, eventually reaching double or triple the rate found in even the New England towns with the highest turnover rates. Of course, not all of those departing the islands were leaving property in the hands of attorneys and overseers, but the owner-attorney-overseer arrangement seems to have been in use by the 1680s and 1690s, and it became more common in the eighteenth century.[96] By 1775, about a quarter of the approximately 775 sugar estates on the island of Jamaica were managed by someone other than their proprietor, and this number was rapidly increasing. By around 1825, more than three-quarters of Jamaican planters were absentees.[97]

A previous generation of historians described the rise of absenteeism as a catalyst for West Indian decline. Historian Lowell Ragatz called it the "curse of absenteeism," arguing that the gradual exodus of rich whites for England contributed to the deterioration of local governance.[98] The lack of infrastructure and amenities surely contributed to the departure of plantation owners, but their return to England can also be interpreted differently. As owners departed the sugar islands, many continued to take an interest in plantation management. Far from neglecting their operations, men worked to develop management systems that enabled them to maintain control over great distances. This distance both constrained and stimulated the development of plantation management.

Examining the rise of absenteeism through the lens of business history offers an alternative to the decline thesis: absentee proprietorship can be seen as an early case of the separation of ownership and management. Business historians have long seen the separation of ownership and management as a characteristic of modern corporate governance, albeit one with potentially high costs.[99] Reconsidering absenteeism through this lens reframes it as a sign of sophistication and managerial complexity.[100]

Several of the most widely cited plantation manuals were first written as instructions to facilitate the transition to long-distance management. When Henry Drax, a seventeenth-century Barbados planter, left Barbados to return to England in 1679, he left twenty-four pages of handwritten instructions for his manager, Richard Harwood. These detailed instructions covered all aspects of plantation management, including accounting. They circulated in manuscript form for nearly a century, and in 1755 William Belgrove of Boston revised and published them in a guide for planters.[101] Clement Caines wrote his 1801 epistolary manual on sugar growing as a guide for his own manager, Charles, who would manage his estate after he departed the island in 1802. Beginning with manuring the soil, he detailed the essential processes of growing sugar in a series of thirty letters, remarking periodically on accounting requirements. He completed the work with the text of a speech about the African slave trade and a series of appendices, two of which dealt specifically with bookkeeping.[102] Caines's first recommendation for plantation accounting was the preparation of a systematic monthly journal. He credited his methods to another Saint Christopher planter, William Somersall, whose methods he believed could provide "at one view every application and misapplication of labour."[103]

Specialized annual abstracts were designed to summarize the activities of the prior year. These could be sent back to proprietors alongside copies of the most important supplementary accounts. For example, each year the attorney of the Barham plantations in Jamaica sent softbound copies of the journal and the ledger (kept in complete double entry) back to England for review. At the close of these books, an abstract assessed the overall financial condition of each of the several plantations under management. These abstracts listed the staff on the plantations, which in addition to numerous bookkeepers included a specialized book poster named James Neilson. According to the ledger, Neilson received "15 pounds per annum" to "keep a set of Books for the Estate in Mr. Barham's form." This wage was lower than that received by the other bookkeepers, perhaps because Neilson was an expert accountant brought in only periodically to compile special reports for Barham's review.[104]

In an annual abstract, an attorney, an agent, or a specialized bookkeeper like Neilson would synthesize information for the proprietor of the estate.

In his 1823 *Jamaica Planter's Guide,* Thomas Roughley described the various subjects that should be reported to the proprietor. Though he urged the attorney to keep accounts "in as simple a manner as the nature of things will admit," he included more than a dozen separate items in his instructions:

> There should be laid before the proprietor, in plain legible terms, the accounts of the estate to the end of every year; a list of the slaves and stock, with their increase and decrease; the cultivation of the estate, with the returns from plant and ratoon, in curing house hogsheads of sugar; the number of acres in cultivation of canes; returns of rum; the condition of cane, grass pieces, and provision grounds; the quantity of acres laid down in a table, whether plant or ratoon; their condition and when fit to be cut; the names and number of the white people resident on the estate, with their occupations and salaries; the different island accounts, whether paid or unpaid, as they are presented; the shipments and appropriation of the crop; what balance of the crop there still remains on the estate, or at the wharf, not yet appropriated or shipped, and the list of clothing and salt provisions served to the slaves; jobbing and tradesmen's accounts, &c. &c.[105]

Beyond preparing a detailed report to be sent to the proprietor, Roughley urged attorneys and managers to prepare copies for their own use. As he explained, these "simple accounts are easily . . . transcribed," and they provide "such a memento . . . as should refresh his memory and satisfy his mind."[106]

Bookkeepers also made exact duplicates of other documents to accompany abstracts when they were sent back to plantation owners in Europe. The surviving records of John Newton's three Barbados plantations, Seawells, Alleyne, and Newton, include several exact copies. These multiples, all sent back to England, may have been distributed to the stockholders of the Newton plantations. As in the Barham books, the surviving copies of the Newton journals and ledgers contain a year-end abstract summarizing the finances of each plantation.[107] Like James Neilson on the Barham plantations, Patrick Paine, the book poster during the 1770s, was paid each year for "making a fair copy" and "for three abstracts, particularly explaining the Plantation

Accts." Paine's fees were divided out across the three plantations to enable separate calculations of profitability.[108]

Some absentee proprietors required only annual accounts, but others requested more frequent reports. For example, when Richard Pennant took over from his father, John, in 1781, he instructed his attorney to supply "twice yearly accounts" of his Clarendon estates.[109] Henry Drax requested that his manager send him quarterly accounts. As he wrote, all of the "accompts Concerning my plantation I would have keeptt as formerly they have bene" and "Coppies of the Same to be Sentt me Every three months." He specified a precise calendar for reporting, requesting copies of the journal, rum account, and sugar account on the "firstt shipp that Sayles" after the first of April, the first of July, the first of October, and the first of January.[110]

Written records tied the whole system together. From the attorney's desk—or the proprietor's across the Atlantic—a hierarchy of reports made many layers of managers and laborers easily visible. Proprietors and attorneys who never encountered individual slaves nonetheless knew about them. They could reflect on each day's labor from the comfort of an office, or query a chain of managers about the success or failure of day-to-day operations. At the same time, the reports of many plantations could be laid out side by side and used to take on more strategic questions about how to invest, what to plant, and how to acquire or reallocate land and slaves. An attorney like John Shickle could survey and compare many properties. And proprietors like the Barhams could reflect on their holdings, asking pointed questions about gaps in the records or strategizing about how to reallocate their investments.

The word "absentee" is almost always a term of critique, and it is one that has been employed in the critique of modern businesses. In 1923, long after emancipation in both the West Indies and the American South, Thorstein Veblen leveled the charge of "absentee ownership" at the twentieth-century business corporation. Veblen argued that with the rise of large corporations and faceless bureaucracy, owners became increasingly disconnected from the workers they employed and the customers they served. Though there were no oceans separating them from the labor they controlled, Veblen argued that a virtual distance created anonymity and disconnection.[111] This critique parallels the one historians would level at West Indian planters: as they returned to England they neglected their holdings, leading to less oversight, poor management, and declining productivity. Yet fortunes continued to be made. Whether the departure of proprietors actually improved or undermined the profitability of the Caribbean plantation complex remains an open question. Distance created obstacles to control in a society where control was paramount, but accounting helped overcome these obstacles. And distance also offered advantages for owners, including connecting them to distant capital markets, as well as professionalization and standardization of management practices on the islands.

Indeed, as the challenges to slavery became increasingly political, being located in England could even be a strategic advantage. Planters promoted their interests in and around the British Parliament, seeking advantageous trade arrangements, including protectionism, which safeguarded their existing sugar markets, and more open trade to the now independent and growing North American markets. Eventually their focus shifted from trade policies to defending against abolitionism. When abolition began to appear likely, it shifted further to securing compensation. As objections to slavery increased, protecting property required both control in the West Indies and political action back in England.[112]

Like big business today, absenteeism presented both costs and benefits. Contemporaries sometimes described scale and distance as sources of inefficiency. One nineteenth-century critic lamented that the planter's "dependence is upon the manager; who again looks to the overseer or bookkeeper to execute his orders. Thus the moving power is transmitted through a long line of inferior agents, and is nearly or quite exhausted before it reaches the point of application."[113] But account books went a long way to solving this problem. Flows of information offered the potential for sophisticated coordination of operations on a remarkable scale. P. J. Laborie's guide to coffee planting gave a long description of the information he saw as important. A journal should compile "the ordinary as well as extraordinary": everything from the daily "works and employment of the negroes" to the "deliveries of coffee" to the "tools utensils and cloathes delivered to the negroes." Carefully prepared, these records enabled an honest manager "to lay his administration open."[114]

The rise of absentee ownership and the accounting practices that accompanied it should be seen as an early case of the separation of ownership and management. This separation did not reflect a lack of interest by proprietors but rather a shift in its form. The distances of the Atlantic constrained their control, but distance also stimulated the advancement of accounting. Communications that had happened in person had to happen on paper, and managers and attorneys drew up regular abstracts and annual reports. Proprietors reviewed these documents, requesting further details and making suggestions for management. Through complex hierarchies of laborers and managers knit together by a wide array of records, proprietors could monitor and manage complex organizations from great distances.

The managerial hierarchies made visible in plantation accounts look remarkably similar to those of multidivisional corporations more than a century later. There were of course other large eighteenth-century hierarchies, including churches, branches of government like the Royal Navy, and even large landed estates back in England. What distinguished plantations—and made them look so much like large industrial corporations—was the way they combined attention to operations with strategic oversight, blending the two in pursuit of profit.[115] Careful record keeping tied together complex pyramids of owners, attorneys, overseers, bookkeepers, and enslaved managers. Owners and attorneys at the top of these hierarchies could consider strategy and capital allocation, while the lower rungs of the hierarchies focused on operations.

Of course, planters do not appear to have actually drawn organizational charts like the one depicted in Figure 1.5. But neither did the large railroads and manufacturers usually identified as pioneers of the M-form corporate structure. Historians generally date the first organizational chart to 1855, when Daniel McCallum, the superintendent of the New York and Erie Railroad, commissioned a lithographer to draw up an elaborate diagram of the railroad. The resulting picture was part map, part chart, with the appearance of a tree. The president and board of directors were the roots, the superintendent was the trunk, and the various lines and functional units were the branches, with each employee appearing as a small leaf or berry. Information flowed up and down these branches, enabling the smooth operation of the line.[116] McCallum's beautiful document was an outlier. Organizational charts are exceptionally rare before the early twentieth century. Indeed, when business historian Alfred Chandler wrote his histories of the multidivisional corporation, he does not appear to have seen *any* actual charts created by mid-nineteenth-century businesses. Though he knew of McCallum's diagram from a description of it published in a railroad journal, he never actually located the chart itself. Instead, he based his revolutionary analysis of organizational structure on account books and internal records, painstakingly reconstructing reporting structures from a paper trail of reports and memos.[117]

In other words, Alfred Chandler did for late nineteenth-century corporations what I have done for late eighteenth-century sugar production. Closely analyzing plantation records in order to uncover reporting structures yields similar conclusions to those Chandler drew about nineteenth-century factories: management and administration were essential tools for building ever-larger enterprises. Control over massive organizations—slave or free—depended on complex hierarchies and careful records. In the case of slave plantations, however, managers blended these information technologies with terrifying violence. They mixed harsh punishment with careful organization to maintain control over enslaved communities that dramatically outnumbered them. Account books are studded with evidence of enslaved people's heroic efforts to resist and escape, but they also show how planters successfully managed these disruptions, even forcing enslaved people to manage one another.

West Indian plantations thus present a brutal preview of the modern multidivisional organization. Detailed account books offered visibility from the attorney's office—or the proprietor's desk back in England—while delegating operating responsibility and day-to-day management to those on the ground. Regular reports enabled owners and attorneys not only to monitor their operations but also to think strategically about capital optimization and allocation. In this case, however, the laborers on the ground were enslaved people and much of the capital being allocated was human capital. Slavery did not undermine management and accounting. To the contrary, by the end of the eighteenth century, practices on many plantations were becoming highly standardized, and by the early nineteenth century, planters could choose between an array of systems to record their data. This process of standardization is the subject of Chapter 2.

2

Forms of Labor

O N SATURDAY, AUGUST 27, 1785, a hurricane struck the island of Jamaica. On Stephen Attlay's Prospect Estate, the storm "came on with
heavy floods, broke down the trash House, & five Negro houses flat with the
ground." Winds and rain badly damaged the water wheel, the overseer's
house, the boiling house, and part of the cattle mill. The corn house was
"blown down with the Chimney," and across the property, "all the wooden
gutters . . . broke all to pieces." The storm devastated the plantation, but work
stopped only briefly. The manager or overseer recorded the incident in script
at the bottom of the week's work log, which shows that labor resumed as
usual on Monday. The hurricane does appear to have sickened plantation
workers. Only one enslaved person died in the first half of the year, but six
died in the second half: "a Man called Dublin"; "a child called Judea"; "an old
woman called Casandra"; "Juba's child"; "a new Negro man called Portland"
and another "called Rogir." Yet even a string of deaths did not disrupt work:
in late November, when Juba's child died, she and the gang of thirteen
enslaved people under her—likely children—labored uninterrupted in the
cook room. As the seasons shifted, labor continued relentlessly: the categories of work changed but not the laboring bodies.[1]

A steady supply of labor adapted well to the steady production of accounts. Patterns of plantation labor were remarkably consistent, and these patterns fit neatly into preformatted journals and reports. Stephen Attlay's overseer relied on hand-lined forms, but soon that would be unnecessary. Attlay died in 1786, and when his son took over management he purchased specially formatted journals tailored to the job.[2] By the early nineteenth century, planters could purchase an array of standardized journals and preprinted reports designed to facilitate plantation management. Like blueprints for a machine, preprinted forms guided planters who sought to turn human labor into salable commodities.

Preprinted forms were an important and overlooked technology for organizing plantation labor. This chapter explores the emergence of this paper technology and compares plantation reports to those produced in free labor settings. Though preprinted forms were occasionally available in other industries, most businesses used custom lined books. Account books for the largest American factories—textile mills in New England—were almost always ruled by hand.[3] These records also hint at one reason for the difference: proprietors of free factories struggled to recruit and retain workers. By contrast the supply of labor on plantations like Prospect Estate remained nearly constant, and work logs show how the plantation consumed its daily allowance like a great machine.

Though a hurricane might pause work, little less than a natural disaster could. No one quit. Even runaways were sometimes included in labor totals. After all, planters expected that they would eventually return to work. On Prospect Estate, births and purchases replaced the dead, and by the end of 1785, the enslaved people on the plantation numbered 161, an increase of three from January's count of 158. All told, annual labor turnover was less than 5 percent. During a period when labor turnover in free enterprises regularly reached 100 percent or more over the course of a year, Caribbean sugar planters experienced almost none.[4] Factory owners had to negotiate, but planters simply purchased men and women and compelled them to work. The steady supply of labor they extracted from enslaved people fit neatly into formatted volumes and standardized reports. These reports traveled well, enabling careful management from great distances.

Forms of Labor

Stephen Oakeley Attlay Sr. took over management of Prospect Estate from his father in 1786, shortly after the devastating hurricane. Oakeley Attlay Sr. managed Prospect Estate from abroad—it is unclear whether he ever traveled to Jamaica from England to visit the plantation. But distance did not prevent him from taking an interest in his property, and when he assumed control, he purchased preprinted journals to help monitor operations. The journals he selected came from John Leapidge and John Bailey, who ran a stationer's business from an office under London's Royal Exchange. They sold an array of mercantile documents, such as tables to aid in the purchase of shipping insurance. Among these supplies were the preformatted, fill-in-the-blanks journals purchased by Oakeley Attlay Sr. The journals were designed to organize a full year of sugar planting. Along with pens, desks, and trained clerks (who could be interviewed at Leapidge & Bailey's offices), they were part of an information system that adapted well to the circumstances of slavery.[5]

Leapidge & Bailey's journals contained nine different forms, each printed in sufficient quantities for a year of planting. The first page recorded the use of land, detailing the various fields planted in different types of cane. The second and third forms comprised a kind of daily diary. Further forms documented goods received on the estate, produce sold, and lists of slaves, mules, working steers, and breeding cattle. The "List of Negroes" included space to record every slave, as well as his or her employment, age, and condition. Prospect Estate supplemented this book with other records, including a daybook, a ledger, and a book of increase and decrease similar to those described in Chapter 1.[6]

The diary, titled "Daily Occurrences," occupied the majority of space in the journal (see Figure 2.1). The right side of the form offered a neat grid for entering quantitative data while the left side of the form provided space for qualitative comments. On January 1, 1787, the "Account of Working Negroes" on the right side summed to 121. Of these, 40 men and women were laboring in the fields or at the works; 7 were tradespeople; 5 were keeping stock; 7 were watchers and rat catchers; 39 made up a small gang, likely composed of older children; 6 were working at different jobs; and 17 were ill—"In the Hothouse." The column for runaways was blank, yielding a total of 121 hands.

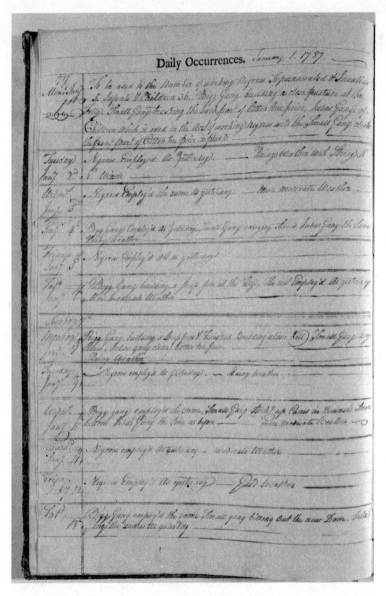

FIGURE 2.1. Work Log for Prospect Estate, 1787. Printed by Leapidge & Bailey in London, these formatted journals contained a variety of different forms that planters could use to manage labor and organize their operations. Here the manager carefully completed the labor record but left spaces for sugar production blank. Prospect Estate Plantation Journals, 1787–1793 (0627-0019). Courtesy of Barclays Group Archives, Manchester, UK.

Date	NAMES	Gallons of Liquor	Hogsheads	Tierces	Potts	Puncheons	Gallons	Gallons fold	Delivered to the Distiller	Field and Works	Tradesmen	Stock-keepers	Watchmen and Rat-catchers	Small Gang	Different Jobb	In the Hothouse	Run-aways	TOTAL
		Cane Pieces	Sugar made			Rum made		Melasses		Account of Working Negroes								
Monday										40	7	5	7	39	6	17	—	121
Tuesday										40	7	5	7	39	6	17		121
Wednesday										40	7	5	7	39	6	17		121
Thursday										40	7	5	7	39	6	17		121
Friday										41	7	5	7	39	6	16		121
Saturday										41	7	5	7	39	6	12		121
Sunday																		
Monday										40	7	5	7	38	6	16		121
Tuesday										39	7	5	7	39	6	16		121
Wednesday										39	7	5	7	39	6	16		121
Thursday										39	7	5	7	39	6	16		121
Friday										39	7	5	7	39	6	16		121
Saturday										39	7	5	7	39	6	16		121
Sunday																		

- 53 -

On the left-hand side, opposite the numbers, the bookkeeper recorded more detail in narrative form. He noted that there were 5 "superannuated & invalids" as well as 36 "Infants & children" to be "added to the number of working Negroes." Thus, the activities of 162 men, women, and children—every slave on the plantation—were accounted for.[7]

Data from a journal like the one used on Prospect Estate could be copied into other standardized forms, including monthly reports that summarized information into neat abstracts occupying a single folded sheet of paper. Reports from plantations Hope and Experiment in British Guiana offer an early example of the genre. Very few records from Hope and Experiment survive— only two monthly reports for April and June 1812, each at a different archive. But the precision and detail of these reports suggest that they drew on extensive records similar to those from Prospect Estate. The various sections of the reports also parallel the detailed sections of the Prospect journals, suggesting that they may have been designed to summarize the most important information from a larger set of plantation records.[8]

Monthly abstracts served a different purpose from day-to-day records. They were prepared not for internal coordination on the plantation but for analysis from afar. They synthesized the contents of larger journals, distilling the most important information so that plantation owners could review it quickly and easily. The first and most prominent item on the reports for Hope and Experiment was a daily record of plantation activities (see Figure 2.2). This record included three subsections, the first focused on the activities of the enslaved workers (labeled "Negroes"); the second on their output ("Cotton"); and the third an open space for comments ("Plantation Work, Occurrences, and Remarks"). Looking below this record, a reader would find the amount of acreage that had been planted in cotton and in plantains, and by flipping the sheet over would see records of "Articles Received" and "Articles Delivered." Next to these, a "Negro Account" and a "Livestock Account" summarized the state of human and animal capital. Taken together, the records condensed the activities and output of some 270 enslaved people and their white managers into the space of a single sheet.[9]

The simple format facilitated review and accountability. A planter scanning the report could detect shifting labor patterns as the seasons changed. The daily record of labor that occupied the front of each report allocated one line to each day, with columns for many different categories of enslaved men,

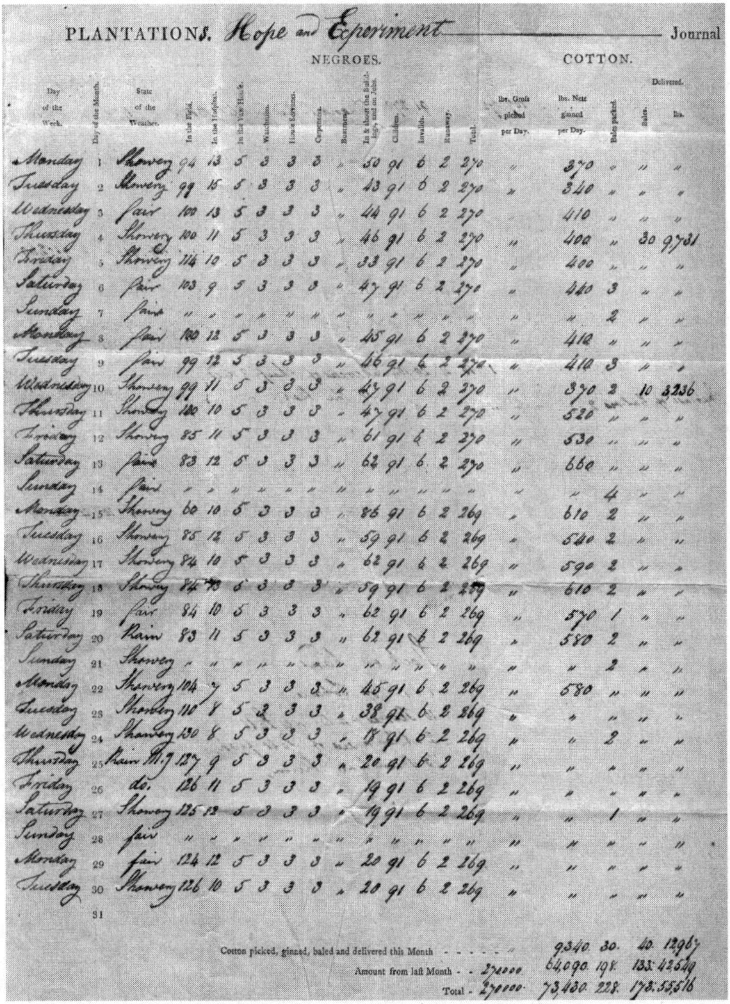

PLANTATIONS. Hope and Experiment Journal

Day of the Week.	Day of the Month.	State of the Weather.	NEGROES. In the Field.	In the Hospital.	In the Yaw House.	Watchmen.	House Servants.	Coopers.	Boatmen.	In & about the Buildings, and on Jobs.	Children.	Invalids.	Runaway.	Total.	COTTON. lbs. Gross picked per Day.	lbs. Nett ginned per Day.	Bales packed.	Delivered. Bales.	lbs.
Monday	1	Showery	94	13	5	3	3	3	„	50	91	6	2	270	„	370	„	„	„
Tuesday	2	Showery	99	15	5	3	3	3	„	43	91	6	2	270	„	340	„	„	„
Wednesday	3	fair	100	13	5	3	3	3	„	44	91	6	2	270		410	„	„	„
Thursday	4	Showery	100	11	5	3	3	3	„	46	91	6	2	270	„	400	„	30	9731
Friday	5	Showery	114	10	5	3	3	3	„	33	91	6	2	270	„	400	„	„	„
Saturday	6	fair	103	9	5	3	3	3	„	47	91	6	2	270	„	440	3	„	„
Sunday	7	fair	„	„	„	„	„	„	„	„	„	„	„	„	„	„	2	„	„
Monday	8	fair	100	12	5	3	3	3	„	45	91	6	2	270	„	410	„	„	„
Tuesday	9	fair	99	12	5	3	3	3	„	46	91	6	2	270	„	410	3	„	„
Wednesday	10	Showery	99	11	5	3	3	3	„	47	91	6	2	270	„	370	2	10	3236
Thursday	11	Showery	100	10	5	3	3	3	„	47	91	6	2	270	„	520	„	„	„
Friday	12	Showery	85	11	5	3	3	3	„	61	91	6	2	270	„	530	„	„	„
Saturday	13	fair	83	12	5	3	3	3	„	62	91	6	2	270	„	660	„	„	„
Sunday	14	fair	„	„	„	„	„	„	„	„	„	„	„	„	„	„	4	„	„
Monday	15	Showery	60	10	5	3	3	3	„	86	91	6	2	269	„	610	2	„	„
Tuesday	16	Showery	85	12	5	3	3	3	„	59	91	6	2	269	„	540	2	„	„
Wednesday	17	Showery	84	10	5	3	3	3	„	62	91	6	2	269	„	590	2	„	„
Thursday	18	Showery	84	13	5	3	3	3	„	59	91	6	2	269	„	610	2	„	„
Friday	19	fair	84	10	5	3	3	3	„	62	91	6	2	269	„	570	1	„	„
Saturday	20	Rain	83	11	5	3	3	3	„	62	91	6	2	269	„	580	2	„	„
Sunday	21	Showery	„	„	„	„	„	„	„	„	„	„	„	„	„	„	2	„	„
Monday	22	Showery	104	7	5	3	3	3	„	45	91	6	2	269	„	580	„	„	„
Tuesday	23	Showery	110	8	5	2	3	3	„	38	91	6	2	269	„	„	„	„	„
Wednesday	24	Showery	130	8	5	3	3	3	„	18	91	6	2	269	„	„	2	„	„
Thursday	25	Rain M.9	127	9	5	3	3	3	„	20	91	6	2	269	„	„	„	„	„
Friday	26	do.	126	11	5	3	3	3	„	19	91	6	2	269	„	„	„	„	„
Saturday	27	Showery	125	12	5	3	3	3	„	19	91	6	2	269	„	„	1	„	„
Sunday	28	fair	„	„	„	„	„	„	„	„	„	„	„	„	„	„	„	„	„
Monday	29	fair	124	12	5	3	3	3	„	20	91	6	2	269	„	„	„	„	„
Tuesday	30	Showery	126	10	5	3	3	3	„	20	91	6	2	269	„	„	„	„	„
	31																		
Cotton picked, ginned, baled and delivered this Month															„	9340	30	40	12967
Amount from last Month															270000	64,090	198	133	42549
Total															270000	73430	228	173	55516

FIGURE 2.2. Monthly Report for Plantations Hope and Experiment, June 1812. This excerpt includes the first two sections of a preprinted monthly report for Plantations Hope and Experiment in British Guiana. Such forms compiled information from larger accounts to be sent back to absentee owners living abroad. Plantations Hope & Experiment Journal, June 1812. Wilberforce House, Hull City Museums and Art Galleries, UK / Bridgeman Images.

women, and children: "In the Field," "In the Yaw House," "Watchmen," "House Servants," "Carpenters," and "Boatmen." Then it listed those "In & about the Buildings, and on Jobs" and finally "Children," "Invalids," and "Runaways." Each day, every slave on the plantation was allocated to one of these categories. At the beginning of April 1812, there were 267 slaves and in June there were 270 (see Figure 2.2). If labor was fully accounted for, this total would remain steady from day to day, changing only with births, deaths, purchases, and sales. And if labor was being used well, more slaves would be allocated to productive categories and fewer would be ill or idle.[10]

An attentive planter might track the proportion of enslaved people going to the field. At the beginning of April, there were 64 people in the field and some 81 "In & about the Buildings, and on Jobs." Their varied activities probably included ginning, packing, and moving cotton. Those in the field were likely tending to the seedlings, weeding, and caring for other crops (in Guiana, plantains offered an important source of food). By June, the proportion had shifted dramatically toward field labor (see Figure 2.2). On the first of the month, 94 enslaved people went to the fields, and soon more than a hundred were laboring there. While the balance varied from day to day, it continued to shift as the month advanced. By Wednesday the 24th, a peak of 130 people went to the fields, and only 18 attended to other jobs. The commentary on the right side of the report tells us that they were tending to young cotton. By the end of the month, picking had begun. On Saturday the 27th, the men were weeding cotton and the women were picking. By Monday the 29th, the journal reads "All hands picking cotton."[11]

Proprietors could also use this information in many ways. They could see how their labor (and thus their capital) was allocated. They could check the sums, taking note of illnesses and runaways. They could track their expanding acreage, taking account of new land brought into production. By comparing with other years, they could check the progress of the crop. They could monitor running totals of cotton "picked, ginned, baled, and delivered," perhaps tracing aberrations or deficiencies to changes in the health of the workers or to poor weather. Neither of the surviving Hope and Experiment reports includes daily totals for cotton picking, though there was space on the form. Perhaps these blanks reflect the fact that picking had only just begun at the end of June. In future months, maybe the overseer included these weights, which would have enabled the owner to calculate how many pounds of cotton were picked per field hand.[12]

Over the long term, planters could use the reports to monitor the increase and decrease of their human property. For each day, all the columns were tallied up and recorded in a final total at the end of the row. This sum equaled the total number of slaves laboring on the plantation, and a glance at these daily totals would show any changes in the workforce. Both April and June offered a mixed picture. A planter scanning the "total" column for April could see that on Monday the 6th, the human population dropped from 267 to 266 before rising to 268 on the last day of the month. The "Negro Account" on the back explained these changes: on the sixth, "The Negro Man named Cato died in consequence of old ulcers." And at the end of the month, "Diana & Charlott delivered one Child each, the former a Male and the Latter Female." The report for June repeats the calculation. As of June 1, 1812, the total number of enslaved people living on the plantation had risen to 270 (see Figure 2.2). The total remained constant until June 15, when the number fell to 269. In this case, the balance sheet on the back of the form tells us that "Diana 1st" "died in child bed." Either this is the same Diana who gave birth more than a month earlier, or it is another enslaved woman by the same name—perhaps indicated by "1st." If the latter is true, then her child apparently did not survive long enough to be recorded on either side of the form.[13]

Below the "Negro Account" was a nearly identical "Live Stock Account," recording the fate of horses, mules, oxen, cows, calves, sheep, pigs, and goats. The subcategories were, of course, different, but the method of taking an inventory, recording increase and decrease, and taking another inventory to carry to the next month was the same as that used for humans. During June 1812, when Hope and Experiment lost "Diana 1st," the plantation also lost eight sheep and gained twelve calves.[14] Similarities like this were not lost on slavery's critics, who lamented the fact that human and animal "stock" were tracked using the same system. Writing against the slave trade, Andrew Thomson criticized the influence of such practices. An apprentice employed in "the writing of invoices and instructions" would become "accustomed to note in the ledger, under the head of profit and loss, a number of men, women, and children, purchased in Africa, of whom so many were thrown overboard, and so many were found unsaleable." Through these daily calculations, he would become "inured to all the horrors of the system." Thinking about human beings as interchangeable commodities for sale, or abstract units of labor power, would lead merchants and planters to see human capital in much the same way that they saw animals. And, by the time a young apprentice became a partner, he would feel "no more remorse in fitting out a ship for the purpose of trading in human flesh, than he would have done in sending her to catch whales or seals."[15]

Standardized reports and the outlook they represent appear to have become more common in the early nineteenth century. Although only scattered examples survive, their variety suggests that planters could choose between several options. A disproportionate number come from British Guiana, previously Dutch Guiana—possibly a legacy of excellent record-keeping practices in the Dutch empire. In any case, by the 1820s there were many variations of reports available to planters. Examples from plantations Good Success (in Dutch Guiana) and Castle Wemyss (in Jamaica) use a very similar layout to that of Hope and Experiment, but with different columns to accommodate the production of rum and sugar. Both sets of forms appear to date to the early 1820s. Some of the records for Good Success were completed in the 1830s, but the preprinted year at the top of the form reads "182_," suggesting it was printed in the 1820s and may have been in circulation for some time.[16]

Planters experimented with rearranging data to make new information visible. One striking example comes from Friendship plantation—likely also in British Guiana, though properties of the same name dot the Caribbean. The form used on Friendship plantation, signed by "Mr. Greaves, Manager," offers an alternative method for tracking plantation demographics (see Figure 2.3). Where previous forms just listed a single set of categories that blended occupation, sex, and age, this form juxtaposed sex and age against occupation. Across the top, six columns classified the enslaved as "Men," "Women," "Boys," "Girls," or "Children." Down the left-hand side, a series of categories listed tasks and skills, as well as reasons the enslaved could not work. These categories included "In the Field," "About the Works," "On Different Jobs," "House Servants," "Coopers," and "Carpenters," as well as "Pregnant Women," "In the Hospital," and "In the Yaw-House." The final rows offered space for those too old or too young to work as well as anyone absent from the plantation. Within this grid, each slave was classified in two ways, first by age and sex and then by the various categories of labor.[17]

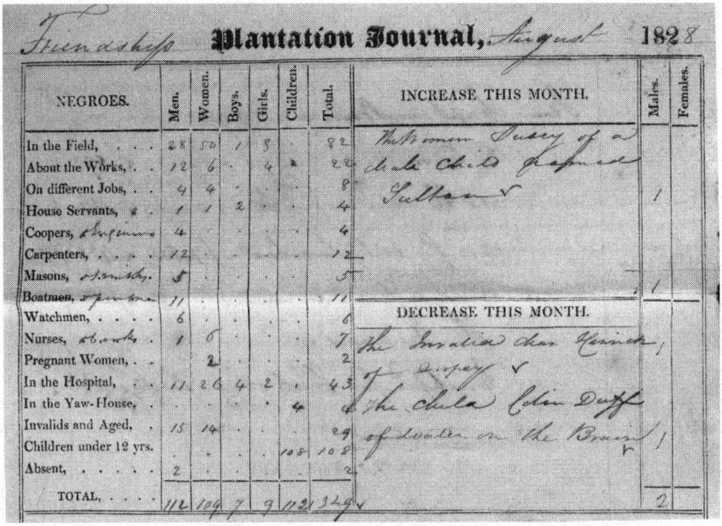

Friendship **Plantation Journal,** August 1828

NEGROES.	Men.	Women.	Boys.	Girls.	Children.	Total.
In the Field,	28	50	1	3	.	82
About the Works,	12	6	.	4	.	22
On different Jobs,	4	4	.	.	.	8
House Servants,	1	1	2	.	.	4
Coopers,	4		.	.	.	4
Carpenters,	12	.	.	.	.	12
Masons,	5	.	.	.	.	5
Boatmen,	11	.	.	.	.	11
Watchmen,	6	.	.	.	.	6
Nurses,	1	6	.	.	.	7
Pregnant Women,		2	.	.	.	2
In the Hospital,	11	26	4	2	.	43
In the Yaw-House,	.	.	.	.	4	4
Invalids and Aged,	15	14	.	.	.	29
Children under 12 yrs.	.	.	.	.	108	108
Absent,	2	.	.	.	.	2
TOTAL,	112	109	7	9	112	329

INCREASE THIS MONTH.	Males.	Females.
[illegible]	1	
	1	

DECREASE THIS MONTH.	Males.	Females.
[illegible]	1	
[illegible]	1	
	2	

FIGURE 2.3. Monthly Report of Increase and Decrease on Friendship Plantation, August 1828. This section of a preprinted monthly report for Friendship Plantation shows a method for tracking births and deaths by age and skill, a practice that would have facilitated workforce planning. *Friendship Plantation Journal*, August 1828. Wilberforce House, Hull City Museums and Art Galleries, UK / Bridgeman Images.

The Friendship account offered a view of the plantation workforce not just as it was but also as it would be. In the form for August 1828 (Figure 2.3), among the nine girls old enough to work, three labored in the field while four were "About the Works"; one older boy joined the girls in the field while two others worked as "House Servants." Almost a third of the population was "Chidren under 12 yrs" who may have been working at light tasks as they prepared to join the workforce. The forms also reflected training efforts. A few years later, on the report for October 1831, Greaves noted that there were three men working as coopers and smiths as well as two boys training in these skills. The form thus united a demographic record of human capital with a record of human capital as businesspeople think of it today—as skill. At a quick glance, the proprietor of Friendship plantation could see the distribution of labor across the different parts of the plantation as well as the supply of children available to join the future workforce. The category for pregnant women even offered a view of potential increase. In August 1828, two women were expecting babies.[18]

The neat report for Friendship paints an alarming picture of the state of human health and labor on the plantation. In August 1828, 43 of the 237 adults and older children on the estate were "In the Hospital." None of the 112 young children were in the hospital, but some were likely ill. That month, there were two deaths—an invalid "of Dropsy" and a child of "water on the brain." Three years later, on the form for October 1831, circumstances were no better. Of the 241 adults and older children on the estate, 43 were again "In the Hospital." That month saw one death—"The Boy Francis Baily Died of Dysentery." Elsewhere, the manager's report for October 1831 indicated illness and unrest. Under "General Observations," he wrote "Negroes unhealthy." He reported that Jessamine was absent, but offered no explanation. The livestock account noted that one of the estate's two calves had been slaughtered— "Killed for the sick negroes." Twenty acres of plantains should have served as the plantation's main food source, but they were "very much diseased." The account of articles received shows that the manager had to purchase more plantains to supplement the plantation's own crop. Perhaps discontent and the threat of illness also contributed to turnover among the overseers and white tradesmen. The form shows that two had just been hired to replace two others that had "quitted the estate."[19]

All of this and more could be gleaned from a single sheet, neatly folded into a packet the size of an envelope. This packet was labeled with the most important details of the contents—an abstract of an abstract. For October 1831, this terse summary read:

Pl Friendship
Monthly Return
October
1831

===

1 Death a Boy
1 Absent Jessamin
Sugar Casks.
Tare 151 lbs Dutch[20]

After being labeled and folded, the report may have been bundled with reports from other months or other plantations. A methodical system organized loose documents so that they could be consulted in the future.

The system of bundling papers and storing them with similar documents constituted a practical filing system, and the wrapped packets that this system relied on can be found throughout eighteenth- and nineteenth-century archives. The practice has preserved loose accounts for modern historians, no doubt because it was carefully designed to preserve and organize information for account keepers themselves. Each report or other document was first folded to a uniform size (a bit narrower than a standard #10 envelope). These packets were labeled with abstracts and then sorted with similar papers into the small cabinets of a pigeonhole desk.[21] Some were classified by type while others were simply inserted into the cabinet in the order they were received. When a cabinet was full—or at the end of a period of accounting—these papers were bound together, wrapped in paper, and labeled again. For example, a year of monthly plantation reports might be bundled and wrapped together. A proprietor hoping to recall or confirm a detail of their management needed only to find the correct bundle, unwrap it, and locate the desired report. Surviving bundles are sometimes pristine, sometimes dirty and perforated with wormholes. But their survival at all is testament to the system's success.[22] Bundling even helped information to travel: Pigeonholes were primarily a feature of desks, but the term also referred to storage space on ships. There, a locker, or "pigeon-hole," was "a kind of Box or Chest made along the side of a Ship to put or stow anything in."[23] Wrappers protected paper bundles as they crossed the ocean, affording abstract accounts of human capital more care than the individuals they represented.

The market for paper evolved to meet the needs of planters managing their holdings from afar. In 1830, sugar broker George Richardson Porter published a manual on sugar growing that included an appendix on bookkeeping. Porter described the need to keep a detailed set of records on the plantation and to send summaries and copies to absentee owners living off the plantation. Special paper could be purchased for each task. As he wrote, "It is usual to print these forms upon paper of different descriptions, one set remains bound together for reference on the estate, and the other, on thinner paper, is transmitted by the post to Europe."[24]

West Indian stationers imported and sold a large selection of specialized paper goods, eventually producing some forms locally. In 1770, Harman Child of Bridgetown, Barbados, offered a wide range of plantation goods, including "Negroes Cloathing, Childrens shoes," and "an Assortment of blank Books, ditto of Writing Paper and Quills, brown, whited-brown, and blotting paper."[25] In the same year, John Thomas, an ironmonger in Bridgetown, advertised "for Cash or short Credit" a diverse assortment of goods, including "Indian Ink, and Ink Powder, Red Ink, Blank Books sorted, spare Alphabets, A Variety of Pocket-books, . . . American Negotiators, Navigators Books."[26] Soon specialized stationers began to produce account books in the Caribbean. In 1781, Alexander Aikman of Saint Jago Printing-Office in Jamaica advertised that he had an assortment of the best stationery "by the last FLEET from *LONDON*." He included a detailed list of "BLANK books of various sizes, bound in rough calf."[27] Aikman was still in business in 1816, by which time he had begun ruling and binding account books in Jamaica. He still advertised books from London but also specified that "Merchants' Account-Books" could be "ruled and bound to any pattern with neatness and dispatch."[28] From the 1780s onward, the more developed islands were all supplied by specialized stationers and printers who offered an assortment of blank books, at least some of which were prepared in the islands.

A set of forms used on the Hamer Estates in the 1820s reflects the availability of specialized job printers. Where the other forms described here could be adapted to any plantation, the forms for Hamer were customized, with "Journal for Estates of Hamer for the Month of ___" preprinted across the top of each form. These documents replicated the general form of the Hope and Experiment plantations, but with even more detailed categories for classifying the enslaved. Perhaps responding to the challenges of sickness, the form included subdivisions for slaves in the hospital, those suffering from yaws, and invalids. Each category was divided into males and females, though under "Hospital" the form's keeper scratched out these categories, instead dividing the slaves into those who were "Sick" and those with "Sores." The forms were likely used on Mon Repos and Endraght plantations in British Guiana, owned by William Attwick Hamer, who resided in Gloucestershire in southwest England. Why Hamer chose to have custom forms printed is not clear. Perhaps he favored a specific format, or maybe he had trouble getting a dependable supply of generic forms. Whatever the issue, he continued to have custom forms prepared. Surviving reports from 1821 and 1825 are nearly identical, but with slight variations in title and printing format.[29]

Indeed, paper technologies of accounting were just that—technologies. These were not isolated records but small pieces of large information systems. Standardization made comparisons easier—reports could be compared across multiple plantations and over time. Preprinted forms also made management less dependent on any individual, a key advantage given the turnover in overseers and bookkeepers employed by plantation owners. By offering set categories and classifications, the forms allowed planters and attorneys to extract consistent information, which enabled and encouraged continuity and control. Armed with such information, they could both hold overseers and bookkeepers accountable and delegate tasks more efficiently.[30]

Accounting for Control in Northern Factories

The significance of standardized monthly reports, with their columns of precisely allocated labor, becomes clearer when compared to books for contemporary factories employing wage workers. Where plantations exercised extensive control over the enslaved, industrial factories struggled to attract and maintain staff. Their success depended more on keeping enterprises running than on reducing costs and increasing output. On monthly reports, plantation managers filled in neat columns of numbers that summed to even totals. By contrast, time books kept by factory owners hiring wage laborers are full of blanks. Names changed from month to month because workers often quit. Where slaveholders could allocate and reallocate labor at will, those employing free laborers had to negotiate. And when negotiation failed, as it so often did, they had to learn to live with high turnover. Taking a detour to explore these challenges of coordination and control brings the managerial upside of slavery—and of violence—into sharper relief.

In 1821, the same year William Attwick Hamer was reviewing the activities of the five hundred slaves laboring on his sugar plantations in British Guiana, Pierson & Company was in the midst of an expansion of its manufacturing facilities. Located about thirty-five miles outside New York City, the firm had been founded by three brothers in the late 1790s. Jeremiah, Josiah, and Isaiah Pierson began by constructing a foundry and a rolling mill to prepare iron for manufacturing nails. Over the coming decade, they gradually expanded their nail factory into a diversified manufacturing center that included "a cotton mill, furnaces for making blister steel, a screw factory, a stove foundry, and a hoe factory." The cotton mill began operations around 1816, and within a few years the firm sold a wide variety of products, including "Heavy Sheetings, Shirtings, Checks, Stripes, and Cotton Yarn." Production of blister steel began around the same time, and a screw factory opened in 1829.[31]

The brothers located their factory on Ramapo Creek, then an almost "unbroken wilderness." The selection was strategic: nearby forests offered ample lumber for producing charcoal, and the "water-power was unrivaled."[32] But it also meant that a supply of wage labor was not locally available. And, unlike slaveholding planters moving to remote locations in search of fresh soil, the Piersons could not just transport workers at will. They had to recruit men and women and persuade them to stay.

In the first years of operation, when the Piersons' need for labor was smallest, a single ledger was the centerpiece of their bookkeeping system. This book contained accounts related to every aspect of the business, including individual accounts for every laborer in the factory. Like some of the planters described in Chapter 1, the Piersons maintained the ledger according to the centuries-old method of double-entry bookkeeping. Most systems of double-entry bookkeeping included three books, where transactions were recorded and rerecorded. The most important of these was the ledger—the book at the center of the Piersons' first labor management system.[33]

Though some slaveholders used double-entry bookkeeping, they did not use it to manage labor, for the obvious reason that slaves were not paid.[34] By contrast, during the early years of operations at Pierson & Company, every individual who worked for the firm had his or her own account in the ledger. Accounts of common laborers appeared next to accounts of suppliers of raw materials, customers purchasing output, and miscellaneous other business-people. Aside from dealing in smaller sums, the accounts of these workers resembled the accounts of major trading partners. These accounts included a wide range of entries, reflecting highly individual relationships. Wage levels and structure varied, reflecting the process of negotiation with each worker. A slip of "memorandums and agreements" tucked into the earliest daybook describes some of these negotiations. For example, John Sidman both labored at a daily rate and sold meat to the Piersons, while Sam Peterson was paid for "1900, 580, and 700 shingles," as well as for 4½ days of work. Although amounts were always translated into currency, exchanges had the flavor of barter, and some workers never actually took cash payments. Instead, they exchanged their time and effort for food, rum, felt hats, bitters, cloth, and an array of other goods.[35]

From a management perspective, the Piersons' ledger provided a great deal of personal information about each individual worker but relatively little information about the workforce as a whole. While the company was small, the system seems to have worked well and may have had advantages. The Piersons could procure small amounts of extra labor without large outlays of capital or long-term contracts. However, as the workforce grew, the ledger became thick and unwieldy. Although it is difficult to pinpoint the precise size of the workforce, records suggest more than four hundred employees worked at the factory by 1816–1817, a scale that would have put it in the ranks of the largest American businesses.[36]

A second surviving ledger, covering the years 1816–1817, shows how the Piersons adapted to their emerging scale. An index—absent from the first volume—listed the entire workforce, making individuals easier to find. The variety of laboring arrangements also diminished: with few exceptions, most workers received a set daily wage. The Piersons also recorded labor more methodically, crediting workers on a regular weekly schedule. A more dramatic shift in accounting practices occurred in 1817, when the firm began using a dedicated time book. Instead of being credited for the "amount of labour up to date" or the "amount of son's labour up to date," workers received payment for "labour as per time book." In the time book, the left side of each page listed each worker's name, and days of the month stretched across the top. In the resulting grid, the Piersons recorded labor in quarter-day increments. On the far right, they calculated each worker's monthly wages; and in the margin, the bookkeeper noted conflicts with workers.[37]

The time books reflected both a new way of organizing information and a shift in the way the Piersons related to their workers. Instead of transacting with and accounting for each man individually, the structure of the books focused on the status of the workforce and the worker's place within it. Structuring payments in orderly columns also made all kinds of calculations easier. Information on costs that had been scattered throughout the ledger was now visible in the space of a few pages, and by the late 1820s, the Pier-sons had begun to tally up labor costs at the bottom of each page. Informa-tion that had been dispersed in individual accounts could now be assessed from a single monthly metric. The company began to treat "the hands" as a collective unit instead of an array of trading partners. In the 1820s and 1830s, the quarter day was the basic unit of recorded time in the time books, but occasional notes in the ledgers suggest that time was measured much more precisely. In 1829, marginal notes indicated the measurement of hours and even minutes. For example, a sheet of calculations noted that the "mill owes the hands 55 minutes last week" and the "hands owe the mill 20 minutes this week." Slightly later, a clerk noted that the "mill stopped evenings this week, deduct 1 day of time."[38]

In theory, this transition might have produced records that looked more or less like plantation work logs and the monthly abstracts that summarized their results. Both sets of managers were adapting new ways of synthesizing information about laborers for easy interpretation. In both cases, previously obscure information could be clearly read from new abstracts and running totals. But looking closely reveals radical differences. Where plantation man-agers were busy allocating labor to the many tasks of sugar production, fac-tory owners faced a messier reality on the ground. Early nineteenth-century factories were plagued with turnover. Various scholars have calculated that voluntary turnover often exceeded 100 percent per year, and that total turn-over sometimes reached 200 percent or more.[39] Writing of Samuel Slater's innovative Rhode Island mills, one historian noted that Slater could "con-struct buildings and machines but not staff them."[40] Instability constantly disrupted day-to-day operations. In contrast with planters who could simply reallocate (and even relocate) enslaved people, northern factory owners had to recruit workers and entice them to stay.

Turnover posed a continuing challenge for Pierson & Company. In just one typical period of instability, March and April 1819, twenty-two people quit, and others disappeared, some for weeks at a time. All told, the firm lost almost 30 percent of its workforce in two months.[41] Marginal notes describe the variety of reasons for these departures. For example, in another period of instability, Eliza Dehol was "discharged for intemperance and improper conduct," Sally Jennings died, John Still ominously "quit and stays at home for reasons not here mentioned," and Amy Corwine "went to school."[42] Although there were periods of greater stability, the Piersons started anew every time they expanded their work or launched a new operation. When the brothers expanded the screw factory in 1833, the first month's ledger was filled with notes like "Discharg'd–lazy," "Sick," and "Ran Away."[43] Time books measured labor in similar ways to plantation work logs. Each entry allocated a day of labor to a particular task. In practice, however, records were often partial—a reflection of the partial control on the ground. Though these records offered a view of the workforce as a whole, they also reflected the ongoing need to negotiate with individuals.

Similar challenges plagued other early nineteenth-century firms, including textile factories at Lowell, Massachusetts. Hamilton Manufacturing Company, which ran three mills in Lowell, experienced the high turnover typical in the industry. In a payroll ledger from 1826–1827, the bookkeeper noted the various reasons why operatives departed. Clarissa Needham, Marinda Dodge, and many others "Left without leave or notice," and Mehitabel Woodruff ran away. Others gave notice and were "regularly discharged." Many women left for family reasons—because a child was sick or to get married. But not all the operatives left willingly. Otis Wildneth was "Discharg'd" because "the overseer did not like him," and he had too much "nightwork on hand to work in the day time." Lucy Haskell was "discharged for disobedience of orders, and died suddenly." Sophia Ingalls was so "Hysterical" that the "overseer was fearful she would get caught in gearing." And Martha Coburn, Rebecca Hunt, and several others were ominously "discharged for mutiny"—perhaps the manager's word for some kind of labor organization. In the first twenty-five pages of the ledger, there are accounts for thirty-eight workers, 60 percent of whom departed over the course of that year.[44]

Labor turnover had high costs. The largest factories of the day, most of which produced iron or textiles, required large investments in energy and machines, and without adequate labor, these valuable investments would go to waste. Forges were particularly sensitive to turnover. The multistage process of producing iron meant that the loss of a small number of workers could shut down operations. Among all the tasks necessary for production, chopping lumber and preparing charcoal demanded the most labor. Everything hinged on these workers because without a steady supply of charcoal, smelting would "grind to a halt."[45] And though firms like Pierson & Company might dominate local industry, workers could go elsewhere. In 1825, John Williams, an agent of Dover Manufacturing Company in New Hampshire, complained about the need to "make frequent changes in our Girls who have very frequently been induced to go to the neighboring establishments." This created "a great deficiency in [not only] quantity but quality also, for new hands must learnt & we cannot expect good Goods from them until they have had some experience."[46]

The first step toward managing turnover—and succeeding despite it—was to document and communicate changes in the labor force. Time books and payrolls vividly revealed periods of instability that remained obscure in a ledger. For example, at Hamilton mills, details and anecdotes about workers' behavior were sprinkled throughout the payroll ledgers. However, changes in their frequency or character could not be detected without consulting and comparing many pages. A string of "mutinies" noted in the margins might foreshadow a strike, but patterns were difficult to see in ledgers. By contrast, in the time books used by Pierson & Company and in abstracts eventually prepared at Hamilton Mills, changes in employment patterns could be read from a few pages or even a series of numbers.[47] As on plantations, new types of reporting offered owners access to the details of management without ever visiting the site of production. But such changes came haltingly, and the degree of standardization was more limited than it was on contemporary plantations.

New England textile mills and iron forges represent just one highly contingent setting employing wage labor. This setting was particularly susceptible to workers' departure because of the relative abundance of land and scarcity of labor in North America. Workers could choose between alternatives, both on farms and sometimes in competing factories. They could quit even when alternatives were not available. Economists have seen competition for labor as a key impetus to the invention of labor-saving devices and investment in machines. These replaced some workers but also magnified their power—without labor, manufacturers could not keep machines running.[48] Labor turnover was a long-term challenge, which would continue to face American manufacturers into the twentieth century.[49] Succeeding despite turnover required a whole range of managerial adaptations and innovations, from time cards and payrolls to fringe benefits and welfare capitalism.[50]

If accounting for wage labor shows the ways manufacturers strove to keep machines running, then the contrasting picture that emerges from slaveholders' journals is that of the plantation itself as a great machine.[51] Instead of cogs, the parts of this machine were humans. And instead of raw materials, the commodity input was slaves. Alongside charcoal converted into steam and cane converted into juice were lives converted into sugar and cotton. Put differently, it was not the grinding apparatus that made Caribbean plantations factorylike; it was the choreography of labor. As historian Manuel Moreno Fraginals has written about sugar production in Cuba, planters expanded their production and thus their fortunes not through superior technology but through labor:

> Production could only be expanded by reorganizing the work. If hands and not machines were to be decisive, the big innovations had to be introduced into the work itself. A phrase of the period sums up the new attitude: "Sugar is made from blood." The cruel significance of the failure of the machine now becomes clear: the *hacendado* introduced into his mill the rigid disciplines of big industry. Along with the European bourgeoisie, he realized that seconds are bits of capital, and he began a special Creole speed-up system, or "Taylorism," which consumed Negroes as the trapiches consumed cane.[52]

Slaves were, quite literally, the denominator against which sugar output was measured. In Cuba, sugar was packed into boxes, and output was measured in "arrobas per Negro."[53]

Parallel logic operated in the British West Indies, where productivity was measured per acre and per slave. Muscovado sugar was packed into barrels called hogsheads, which were set against these denominators. In 1807, the author of *The West-India Common-Place Book* estimated of sugar productivity by island, expressing the totals in both hogsheads "per acre" and "per negro." As he explained, more of both were required where lands were poorer in quality. He estimated "two-thirds" hogshead "per negro" and "one-half per acre" in Jamaica, the same in Dominica, "three-fourths hogsh. per negro and acre" in Grenada, "one-half hogsh. per acre, and one-half per negro" in Antigua, and the list continued. The small island of Saint Vincent received his highest estimates, with "one hogsh. and one-fourth per acre and per negro."[54]

Enslaved people became, quite literally, a unit of analysis. Plantations operated as factories that consumed one commodity and produced another. But rather than pounds of cotton converted into yards of cloth in a textile mill, lives were converted into hogsheads of sugar and bales of cotton. Writing about the kinds of work logs described here (Figures 2.1 and 2.2), another historian of the British Atlantic has written that planters "conceptualized time as currency."[55] The numbers that filled work logs were days of enslaved time. Planters owned all of this time. The more effectively they could spend it, the more sugar or cotton they could make. Over a week, the supply of days would be seven times the number of working hands on the plantation. (Or, if a day off was allowed on Sunday, six times the number of laboring men, women, and children.) Labor was a fixed cost and a form of capital that planters sought to calculate and allocate efficiently.

Of course, the process of production was far more complex and violent than the practice of calculation. To produce goods, planters, overseers, and bookkeepers had to care for and maintain control over massive hierarchies of labor, and just as plantation records reflect coercion and control, they also show its limits. Runaways, sickness, death, and a multitude of smaller and larger obstructions delayed and diminished production. Looking back at the Prospect Plantation records that opened this chapter reveals regular disruptions in the orderly allocation of labor. Some of these are explained in the prose that accompanied quantitative work logs, but at other times the numbers simply do not add up. And after periods of diligently completing records, the bookkeeper sometimes seems to have simply abandoned them. Still, compared with time books kept by contemporary free factories, their completeness and consistency is remarkable. The labor logs from Hope and Experiment, for example, show months of largely uninterrupted labor, punctuated only by illness, childbirth, and very occasionally escape.

Distance facilitated abstraction, enabling men, women, and children to be seen as little more than inputs of production. In an era when factory owners had grasped the theory of interchangeable parts but were struggling to put it into action, slaveholders had implemented a version of the system.[56]

But in their great labor machine, the interchangeable parts were human beings. This outlook, which saw human bodies as standardized inputs of production, is strikingly visible in late eighteenth-century price currents, which sometimes listed enslaved people alongside the commodities they grew. For example, in 1785, the *Columbian Herald* of Charleston, South Carolina, advertised the sale of "New Negroes, 45l to 50l cash—75l at 6 or 9 months credit" (Figure 2.4).[57] Viewed from a distance—say, from the comfort of an absentee planter's desk across the Atlantic—sorting through reports, comparing production totals, and consulting price currents could make earning profits appear as no more than a problem of multiplication.

Account books from both plantations and factories enabled management as scale increased. These records made new information visible by condensing data about large numbers of workers and long periods of time into small spaces. But the problems these records dealt with were very different. On plantations, work logs and monthly reports highlighted allocation of labor. In factories, records focused on the problem of turnover and ways to manage it. Plantation records suggest that planters saw their operations as machines geared with human beings. Factory records show how manufacturers tended machines despite unstable workforces and high turnover.

Networks of Expertise

And yet something is lost in the process of comparison—as if we can pretend that these are two isolated case studies to be tested against each other. Instead, they were deeply connected, two faces of an expanding culture of accounting. As the circulation of paper technologies—from standardized reports to price currents—attests, the remarkable numeracy of West Indian planters did not develop in isolation. Many New England textile mills had extensive ties to both southern and West Indian plantations—ties that extended beyond the cotton they purchased.[58]

Numbers traveled well, and as they moved, they carried not only the details of production but also the methods of accounting. Distance both constrained and stimulated the development of bookkeeping practices. Though distance could inhibit communication, it also required that decisions about management be written down on paper. Reports that might have been given verbally were sent across the ocean in standardized quarterly and annual

PRICE CURRENT.

Anchors	per lb.	6d	Rice, 100lb.	12/6
Bees-Wax	1/2	1/3	Rum, Jamaica gal. 2/4 2/8
Butter	6½d 8d		Windw. Island 1/10 2s
Boards per M	100s		New-England	1/8
Bar iron ton 17l 10s 13l.		Taffia	1/2
Beef, Irish mess ba. 46/8 50	Staves, white oak pipe
common	42s 44/4	per M.	7 guineas
Bricks, per M	40s	hogshead	5 do.
Brandy, gal.	2/6 3/4	Shingles, M. 21/5 23/4
Candles, tallow lb.	7d	Scantling, M.	140s
spermaceti	2/4	Salt, bush.	2s 2/4
Cheese,	6d 7d	Sugar, d. refi.loaf, lb. 10d
Cyder, bar.	16/4	single	7d 8d
Coffee, lb.	8½d 9d	brown, 100lb. 28s 32s
Cordage 100lb 28s 40s	Snake-Root, lb.	2/4
Corn, Indian bushel 3/6	Ship Bread 100lb. 18s 18/6
Coals, ton	20	Sole leather 6½d 7d
Deer-skins in hair lb. 1/3	Tar, bar.	7s 8s
Indian dressed 1/5	Turpentine,	14s
Flour, super. bar. 35s 37/4	Tea, Bohea, lb.	2/4
common	28s	Souchong 3s 3/6
Ginsang lb.	2s 3s	Hyson 6s 6/6
German Steel lb. 4½d	Tobacco, 100lb. 24/6 25/8
Geneva, cask 20s 21/9	Wine, Madei. pipe 25l 50l
Gunpowder, lb. 1s 1/8	Port 25l 39l
Indigo, lb. 2s 4/8	Sherry 15l 20l
Mackarel, bar. 23/4	Lisbon 18l 40l
Mahogany, foot 6d 7d	European dry goods, 25
Molasses, gal. 1s 1/2	to 33⅓ per cent. if well
Pitch, bar. 9s 10s	laid in.
Pork, Irish mess 56s 60s	New Negroes, 45l to 50l
American 45s 50s	cash——75l at 6 or 9
Pink-Root, lb. 9d	months credit.

FIGURE 2.4.
Price Current, 1785. Enslaved people were advertised alongside the commodities they grew. This list offers "New Negroes at 45l to 50l cash" or "75l at 6 or 9 months credit." *The Columbian Herald*, Charleston, South Carolina, 1785.

reports. Bookkeeping practices developed as part of a trans-Atlantic print culture that included forms, manuals, and instruction books. They circulated in essays and planting manuals, eventually disseminating across a range of industries and geographies. These traveled back and forth across the ocean, stimulating an exchange of ideas that may have been as important as the trade in goods.

The circulation of forms, books, and magazines all contributed to the spread of plantation accounting practices. Manuals like William Weston's *Complete Merchant's Clerk* drew on Atlantic experiences and aspired to reach global audiences.[59] Although Weston published his manual in London, he drew on his experience as a merchant in Jamaica.[60] His 1754 edition included two parts, the first devoted to double-entry bookkeeping and the second to plantation accounting "as at present used in the Islands of Barbadoes, Nevis,

St. Christophers, and other of his Majesty's principal Settlements in the West-Indies." Weston paid particular attention to Jamaica, which he called the "Grand Mart of the British America." But his intended audience extended even beyond the Caribbean. He believed that the knowledge of West Indian systems would "render any Man capable of managing a Set of Books"—not just in the Caribbean but "in any Factory in Europe, or Asia"—for these methods had been found "by long Experience" to be "the best, and most expeditious," techniques for the "dispatch of business generally."[61]

Clerks and bookkeepers carried manuals as they traveled through the Atlantic world. In the dedication of his bookkeeping manual, William Weston recommended his methods to the "young Clerks, who are daily sent" to "Factories abroad." Indeed, before his departure from Lancashire for Jamaica in 1764, a young man named John Birly received a copy of William Weston's book as a gift.[62] In Jamaica, he worked for the firm of John Inman, Lancaster merchant. Conditions for clerks in the islands were poor—probably similar to those experienced by bookkeepers on plantations. Birly experienced a near-deadly fever, worked long hours, and ate poorly. But unlike the human chattel exposed to the same diseases and worse rations, Birly eventually escaped back to England, where he became a partner in the firm of Thomas Langton.[63] Middling businessmen in England sometimes sent their sons to pursue apprenticeships and opportunities in the West Indies. Men like John Meabry, "son of a tradesman in London," were "sent out" to the West Indies to complete their training as plantation bookkeepers.[64] These men carried knowledge of bookkeeping with them to the Caribbean and returned to England with ideas about the application of this knowledge.

Planters' children also migrated in search of education. In 1750, British pamphleteer and author Malachy Postlethwayt published a prospectus for a business school targeting an array of "gentlemen," including the sons of American planters. Postlethwayt planned to establish a "Merchant's Public Counting House," where young men would be "bred to Trade" with "great advantage." Over a period of two years, students would develop "expertness in mercantile computations" and study an array of topics, ranging from arbitrage to rates of exchange, the stock market, foreign languages, and written and spoken business communication. Postlethwayt went into great detail about the exact kind of students he hoped to attract, including "the sons of American planters." For most of his target audiences, Postlethwayt gave a detailed explanation of why his curriculum would be useful, but for the sons of American planters, he did not elaborate, assuming that the benefits of a business education for planters and their sons would be self-evident.[65] Though Postlethwayt seems not to have realized his plan, both American and West Indian planters sent their sons abroad for additional education. This practice was so common that historian Selwyn Carrington has described it as a "severe drain" on planters' resources.[66] But the expense also contributed to the circulation of practices. Planters' children took the experience of plantation life with them and returned with new knowledge of bookkeeping and accounting.

Classified advertisements reflect the mobility of young clerks and bookkeepers. Young men seeking positions mentioned their willingness to relocate to distant geographies. In 1764, a "young Man, aged 25 Years," described his services to the readers of the *Boston Gazette*. Not only did he write "a tolerable good Hand" and "understand Accompts," but he was "willing to go to any Part of America, or the West Indies, and would be willing to do any Thing in his Power to render himself useful to his Employer."[67] Another job seeker advertising in a London paper in 1787 touted "a good plain hand" and knowledge of "common accounts." He had "no objection to go to the East or West Indies, or any part of America."[68] Employers sought those who were willing to relocate. An 1820 notice in the *New-York Daily Advertiser* requested an "Experienced Book-keeper and accountant" "to go to the W. Indies." The ideal candidate would be a "perfectly competent" accountant, "capable, if required, to attend to the correspondence of a commission house."[69] Sometimes advertisements were truly trans-Atlantic in scope. A 1788 advertiser in a Charleston, South Carolina, paper sought "a discreet, sober young man" to go to Jamaica. The precise position is not mentioned, but the candidate had to be able to "read or write well." He could be "from any country," but applicants were sought *particularly from Edinburgh in Scotland.*[70]

Bookkeepers who had returned from the West Indies could trade on their experience abroad when they returned to the United States or to England and applied to positions at home. In 1802, a man seeking a situation in a merchant's countinghouse in New York touted his "eighteen years experience . . . in Europe, this country, and the West Indies."[71] Many young men migrated from Europe to the islands and from the islands to North America, bringing the

experience of West Indian slavery with them.[72] Among these, a disproportionate number became clerks and bookkeepers, a reflection of the importance
of written records to the Atlantic economy.[73] Highly mobile planters, overseers, and bookkeepers became vectors for the transmission of plantation
technologies, moving methods across the Atlantic and between the colonies.
Through this circulation, knowledge of accounting moved both north to
south and south to north, and in both directions across the Atlantic. Information practices crossed boundaries between slave and free and between different regions of slaveholding.[74]

Standardized plantation account books would soon make their way to
the American South. American planters drew on West Indian expertise in
their record keeping. Take the case of Scotsman Farquhar Macrae. Macrae
departed Jamaica in 1833, driven out by what he called "the mad abolition
act of the infatuated English government."[75] The British Parliament had
just ended slavery throughout its colonies, including Jamaica. Though Macrae
lamented his "sacrifice of property and prospects," he did not leave the
West Indies empty handed.[76] The abolition act included a provision for
compensating slave owners for the loss of their human capital. In effect,
Parliament bought them out, paying more than £20 million in total compensation to former slavers.[77] In Jamaica's Clarendon Parish, where Macrae filed
for compensation, the largest individual claims reached nearly £10,000 for
more than five hundred enslaved Africans.[78] Macrae's share was smaller:
£237 10s. 6d. for eleven men and women.[79] Though he later styled himself
a "sugar planter," accustomed to planting on a "very large scale," the
modest size of his claim suggests a more middling stature. Macrae was
probably a manager or planting attorney with charge of a large estate.[80]

Macrae chose Florida as his new home, settling on the Wacissa River
near Tallahassee, where he planned to begin planting sugar. By March 1834,
he had a plot of land and had purchased a gang of slaves to till it, perhaps with
the help of his share of the British payout. But like other emigrating farmers,
clerks, and overseers, Macrae brought more than capital to America. He arrived with knowledge of sugar planting, opinions about management, and
expertise in accounting. Trading on his West Indian origins, he became corresponding secretary for the local agricultural society and wrote a series of
articles for wealthy Virginia planter Edmund Ruffin's popular magazine, the
Farmers' Register.[81]

Macrae covered the subject of bookkeeping in his first article for the *Farmers' Register*. In one of only a handful of two-page illustrations from the magazine's ten-year run, Macrae drew a precise diagram after which planters could format their books (Figure 2.5). His forms were adapted for one month, and he recommended binding twelve sets together to create "an authentic record" of all operations on an estate over the course of a year. Macrae claimed that the system was so brief and simple that almost anyone could keep them correctly, having "nothing to do save to fill up the heads and the columns." He described the forms as "made and printed after my own experience," but they were not original. Although it is impossible to confirm where Macrae became familiar with the genre of the monthly report, the system he recommended closely replicated the structure of the pre-printed monthly reports that had been circulating in the Atlantic world for decades, particularly the forms used on Hope and Experiment.[82]

Macrae's document begins with a record of labor. At the left is a daily quantitative record of activities; at the right is a narrative of production and a record of cotton picked. As Macrae explains in the accompanying article, the editor recommends that these "blank forms" be "printed on a large sheet." The first portion was to "occupy two entire pages facing each other," thus replicating the layout from the West Indian forms used on Hope and Experiment, Good Success, and the Estates of Hamer. Beyond this record of labor, Macrae listed an array of other records, also similar to those on the West Indian monthly reports, including a "Negro Account," recording increase and decrease, and a nearly identical "Cattle Account" (though the headers include all large livestock, not just cattle as on the West Indian forms). Other than minor differences in phrasing and organization, the structure and contents of Macrae's forms replicate those circulating in the Caribbean in the early nineteenth century.[83]

Macrae brought accounting practices with him to Florida and disseminated them through his essays. Articles like his reached large audiences. In 1834, the first year Farquhar Macrae subscribed to the magazine (and the year before his first contribution), the *Farmers' Register* listed just over thirteen hundred subscribers across sixteen states and the District of Columbia. The vast majority of these subscribers were from the South—especially Virginia, where Ruffin published the magazine. But the magazine also reached subscribers as far away as New York, Ohio, Philadelphia, and Illinois.[84] Macrae

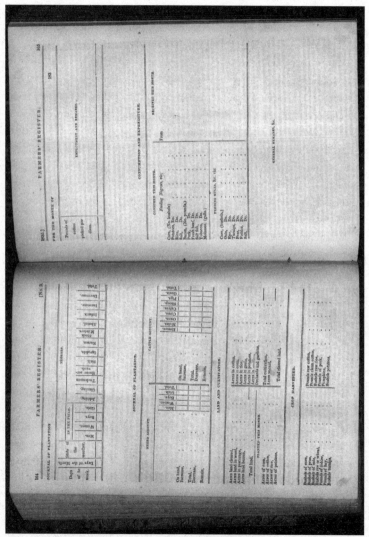

FIGURE 2.5. West Indian Practices Suited for a Southern Plantation, 1835. *The Farmers' Register* recommended that American planters adopt the kind of monthly reports that were used on West Indian plantations. They reprinted a form from Farquhar Macrae that very closely resembled the forms used on Hope and Experiment and other plantations (see Figure 2.2). *The Farmer's Register*, vol. 3, no. 3 (Petersburg, Va.: Edmund Ruffin, 1836). Courtesy of The Library Company of Philadelphia.

touted the particular usefulness of such forms for absentee planters. Absenteeism was much lower in the United States than it was in the Caribbean, but some owners left their plantations seasonally. Others owned multiple properties, sometimes at considerable distances from each other. In these cases, clear forms for reporting were particularly useful. As Macrae explained, "When proprietors travel for the summer, or reside off their plantations, this sheet neatly folded, will as a letter, inform them of all the operations of the farm, and even its daily proceedings." [85]

Accounting excelled as a technology of distance. Highly mobile proprietors, agents, and overseers carried more than money and goods. They claimed expertise in an array of management practices and farming techniques, and as they moved, they took this knowledge with them. They codified their opinions in books and periodicals, cultivating an exchange of ideas as important as the trade in commodities. Accounting played a central role in this project: planters shared advice on how to keep their books, and they used data from their ledgers and journals to advocate for new seed varieties, forms of fertilizer, and methods of management. Accounting was both an object of exchange and the language through which it took place.

In Macrae's case, the tumult of emancipation seems to have actually encouraged the spread of practices. The decline of slavery in one location strengthened its hold in others. Dale Tomich and others have written of a "second slavery," suggesting that the spread of free labor and the expansion of slavery could be mutually constitutive: abolition in one location could spur the extension of slavery in another. Abolition provoked a flurry of resettlement among men like Macrae, some of whom brought bookkeeping practices with them. And their movement was only the latest in a series of migrations within the British colonies and the larger Atlantic world. Scholars of slavery in Cuba have described similar patterns in the Spanish Caribbean, arguing for the importance of geographically mobile sugar masters in the eighteenth century and chemists and "plantation technocrats" in the nineteenth century. These men were the white-collar staff of the Caribbean sugar complex, and they moved from plantation to plantation, taking technical knowledge with them. The disruptions and upheavals of Atlantic slavery—most dramatically the Haitian Revolution—accelerated the movement of experts. French sugar masters fled Haiti for Cuba, where they raised the level of technological know-how on Cuban plantations. Just as Macrae departed Jamaica in search of a new place to use his knowledge of plantation management, sugar experts moved through the Caribbean seeking opportunities to deploy their expertise. Conversations about management crossed geographic and industrial boundaries, and planters' efforts became part of an Atlantic repertoire of ideas about management. Merchants and manufacturers drew on old methods in new ventures, blending and combining ideas as they saw fit.[86]

By the early nineteenth century, slaveholders faced first amelioration and later rising tides of abolition. For the British Empire, these would lead to the closing of the slave trade in 1806–1807 and eventually the abolition of slavery in 1833. These measures and others can be thought of as waves of market regulation, a lens that casts planters and overseers as entrepreneurs playing at a game of regulatory arbitrage. They moved to new imperial jurisdictions that allowed them to continue to exploit their human property or, when they could not take their slaves, at least the skills and expertise they had honed in exploiting them. Seeing abolition as a form of market regulation recognizes the ways it restricted slaveholders' property rights: abolition prevented the sale of men and women and thus restricted the right to contract. Faced with limitations on their economic choices, planters scanned the hemisphere for new opportunities to use their knowledge—and to redeploy the capital paid out as compensation by the British government.[87]

The circumstances of slavery had prepared slaveholders to play this geographic game. By contrast to land and buildings, humans were a highly mobile form of capital that could be moved to new locations in pursuit of profit. And the paper technologies that planters, attorneys, and overseers had developed allowed for management at great distances. Standardized plantation account books became like blueprints for factory production—designs for machines made out of humans. Even when planters could not move enslaved people to new geographies, they could transport their techniques and their ideas, seeking out new regimes where their skills could be put to use.

Moral Reckoning

The mobility of plantation records did not always work in the ways planters anticipated. Just as accounting made sugar plantations visible to absentee planters, reports and journals also put evidence of slavery's brutality into the hands of abolitionists. The same accounts that helped absentee planters to control overseers and overseers to control slaves could also make enslaved people visible to new audiences. Because these records bound together information and violence, they could also make violence and destruction visible to slavery's critics.

Abolitionists could consult plantation records for evidence against slavery. At least one critic of the system even turned an account book prepared in the pursuit of profit into a powerful illustration of the human costs of slavery. This striking example comes from British lawyer James Stephen. Stephen analyzed and published evidence from a plantation journal, using it to reveal "the treatment of the slaves and its fatal consequences." His short pamphlet reconstructed death rates for two plantations on the island of Saint Christopher. The absentee proprietor, a Mr. Wells of Piercefield, had leased his holdings—two plantations and 140 enslaved—in 1812. By April 1815, the resident population had plummeted to a mere 108. The deaths continued: "In April 1816, they were reduced to 102; in April 1817, to 98; in April 1818, to 91; in 1819, to 86." This tragic decline continued despite the purchase of additional slaves and the birth of children. Making allowances for losses in these groups, Stephen estimated that over the course of a decade, "80 out of 140 human beings" had perished.[88]

Stephen followed his calculations with descriptions of punishment excerpted from the daily entries in the plantation journal. On May 29, 1817, "Statia Jack, who had feigned sickness on Thursday, Friday, and Saturday last," tried to escape from the deadly grounds of the plantation. He was brought back and brutally punished. As Stephen remarked, "That sickness or debility was not feigned by him is highly probable . . . for we find a few months afterwards that he was bloated with dropsy, and died." On Wednesday, June 7, the manager "cart-whipped" a long list of other slaves. He lashed Priscilla thirty-nine times, also punishing Domingo, Lena, Betsy Peters, Joe, Mary Danie, and Betsy. Santy, who had run away, was harshly beaten and had salt rubbed in his wounds: "Gave him at two o'clock thirty-nine SEVERELY, AND THEN PICKLED HIM." The manager whipped Santy and Priscilla again the following day, and following the whipping steeped hot peppers from the garden and used the water to bathe Priscilla and Domingo. Santy again ran for freedom on July 13. He was brought in almost immediately and brutally lashed. Again on July 31, the manager whipped him thirty-nine times and put an iron collar around his neck.[89]

And so the journal continued. Stephen included numerous other excerpts, and also encouraged readers to consult the journal themselves. As he explained, "I will deposit it with my booksellers for the inspection and perusal of any gentleman, giving his name, who may wish to satisfy himself that it is genuine, and that my extracts are correct." In different hands, the same document could be either an instrument of labor control or a tool in discourses of emancipation.[90]

As planters and their brutal production methods came under fire, accounting also became a tool for controlling planters and overseers. Ameliorationist measures—meant not only to reduce the brutality of slavery but also to strengthen the larger system—included limitations on how enslaved people were to be punished. These laws regulated the number of lashes that could be inflicted, by whom, and under what conditions. They took advantage of standardized, preprinted forms to help enforce these restrictions, sometimes requiring the keeping of a "punishment record book."

Records of punishment recorded the regular and shocking brutality of what was supposedly a more humane, more regulated version of the slave system. "William King's Punishment Record Book of Plantation Friendship" is one such example. On this preprinted record, the master or overseer was to record the date, the name of the slave, the offense, and the time and place of the punishment. The form included space to note by whose authority, by whom inflicted, and those who witnessed the punishment. Regulations varied by sex, so separate space was allotted for the extent and nature of punishment for men and women. For example, in early March 1829, a slave named Kathleen was punished for insolence. Her punishment, three days of solitary confinement, occurred in the hospital. In January, Frank received twenty-five stripes in the yard. The manager authorized each punishment, also noting who inflicted the lashes and who witnessed each measure.[91]

Records such as this one and the corroboration of the witnesses who signed them were meant to ensure that regulations were followed. Local officials required their submission regularly. The record of punishments inflicted on Plantation Friendship actually appears to be a duplicate made for reporting purposes. The bottom reads "a True Copy," and it is signed off by the copyist—perhaps an attorney or a colonial official. By means of records such as this one, the authority of accounting became an aid to amelioration.

Chains of witnesses confirmed that slaveholders and their employees followed regulations. Of course, such records also protected planters and white workers. They could present the "punishment record book" in court, and call witnesses when planters were accused of violating the regulations. When a slave was maimed or even killed, a record such as this one might protect the manager or the man who administered the lashes.[92]

Viewed through a modern lens, the calculations of ameliorationists can seem as darkly abstract as those of planters. Joshua Steel of Barbados wrote a series of letters on the "mitigation" of slavery that contained detailed accounts on the advantages of raising slaves rather than purchasing them from Africa. Steel was arguing against the slave trade, and he advocated for gentler treatment to facilitate the health and reproduction of enslaved people. He was careful to clarify, however, that his views must not be confounded with the "Emancipation of the Slaves." In his letters to William Dickson, he planned to show "from unexceptionable *data,* that the returns of sugar estates have long been inadequate to the expense of this wasteful and oppressive system." In his view, unprofitability was due not to any features of the slave system but to the choice of West Indian planters to purchase new slaves instead of raising them on their own plantations. In Steel's letters, it is "arithmetically *demonstrated,* that, for very many years, BOUGHT *slaves in general, have not refunded their purchase-money, far less yielded a profit.*" Consequently, he argued that it was "in the interest of *proprietors* to raise their laborers on their own estates, instead of buying them, as may still be done, from various West Indian sources, quite independent of Africa."[93]

Data interpreted at a distance could be turned to multiple purposes: it could be a tool for management or become evidence for amelioration. Read closely, records could even reveal the suffering and resistance of enslaved people. But the overarching portrait that emerges from these grids of numbers tends not toward individuality but toward abstraction. As Stephanie Smallwood has written about records of the slave trade, through their "graphic simplicity and economy, invoices and ledgers" efface the "personal histories that fueled the slaving economy."[94] The archives that plantations left behind can help us to write their history, but as Saidiya Hartman writes, they also dictate "the kinds of stories that can be told about the persons cataloged, embalmed, and sealed away in box files and folios."[95] So much was recorded and also so little: birth, death, output, and consumption were diligently noted, but the details of so many human lives are lost between the lines.

In the late eighteenth and early nineteenth centuries, accounting practices across the Caribbean and North America varied widely. Both planters and manufacturers experimented with new modes of record keeping, feeling their way to greater precision and profitability. But elite Caribbean planters were beginning to standardize their methods in ways that went beyond those used in contemporary New England cotton mills. Preprinted forms were distributed to attorneys and overseers, carefully completed, and sent back across the Atlantic to England. By contrast, labor records from many textile mills appear haphazard and irregular—a result of high levels of turnover. Free workers could quit—and did. Enslaved people enjoyed far fewer opportunities to negotiate, circumstances that enabled regular management and record keeping.

Planters and overseers thought about enslaved people as abstract, interchangeable inputs of production. This outlook translated well to standardized reporting, and planters increasingly relied on preprinted forms to help them record and allocate day after day of uninterrupted labor. The forms contain neat columns of numbers that show how plantations turned people into profitable commodities. In a sense they offered blueprints for machines made of men, women, and children. Neatly folded, the forms could even be shipped across the Atlantic, allowing planters to monitor these human machines from great distances. Enslaved people defied planters' expectations, and read carefully, reports also reveal their resistance. Occasionally they even revealed this resistance—and its high costs—to abolitionists. But, more often, the records helped planters to control overseers and overseers to control slaves. The overarching picture that emerges is of the sophistication of the system that enslaved people were up against as they attempted to survive. Compared to manufacturers employing free labor, planters wielded immense control, and they maintained that control both through violence and through careful accounting.

By the 1830s, preprinted forms—designed to help move information over great distances—were traveling to the American South. Even before Farquhar Macrae advertised his methods to American planters, they were beginning to collect data and use it to analyze productivity. Eventually, standardized forms would have an even greater influence in the South than they had in the Caribbean. Planters would come to rely heavily on preprinted forms to monitor plantation business, particularly the growing of cotton. In cotton picking, they would take productivity analysis to new heights, monitoring enslaved productivity on an individual basis. Where West Indian planters had focused on labor allocation and on maintaining accountability over distance, American cotton planters would turn their attention to pushing up output per slave. By the 1840s and 1850s, some would be measuring labor output with an intensity approaching that usually attributed to scientific management. These efforts are the subject of Chapter 3.

3

Slavery's Scientific Management

PRODUCTIVITY ANALYSIS IN THE ANTEBELLUM SOUTH

O N MONDAY, OCTOBER 10, 1842—"A beautiful day" on Pleasant Hill
Plantation in Amite County, Mississippi—Eli J. Capell noted the precise amount of cotton picked by each of his fifteen slaves. Every hand, including the enslaved overseer, picked at least 100 pounds, and Capell's top
pickers—Terry, Isaac, and Peter—exceeded 200 pounds apiece. All told, they
brought in 2,545 pounds, "the best ever done here in one day."[1] Capell knew
that the day was remarkable because he was in the habit of keeping diligent
records. He kept a yearly plantation journal that tracked his output, and his
records show that over the coming decades, his workforce would repeat the
achievement of that October day many times. As he increased the size of his
workforce and improved the methods of his management, he pushed daily
picking totals ever higher.

Capell and other "book farmers" in the American South paid close attention to how efficiently enslaved men and women picked cotton, frequently
experimenting with new methods for maximizing output. These plantations
were not the giant hierarchies of the West Indies. Though some were worked
by hundreds of slaves, many were worked by only ten or twenty. Their free
staff was typically limited to an overseer, and sometimes planters managed
for themselves. These plantations were distinguished not by their sheer scale

but by their data practices. Planters recorded and analyzed information diligently and precisely, keeping accounts and comparing them year after year. Their efforts—as well as those of planters growing sugar, rice, wheat, and other staples—were remarkably sophisticated for their time. Planters paid more attention to labor productivity than did many northern manufacturers, foreshadowing the rise of scientific management in the 1880s and beyond. They excelled in determining the most labor their slaves could perform and in pushing them to attain that maximum.

Understanding the relationship between slavery and management practices in the American South is the subject of this chapter and the next. In the simplifying language of twentieth-century economics, there are three inputs of production: land, labor, and capital. Slaves confounded the last of these categories, at once labor and capital, and planters analyzed them in both ways, using accounting both to understand labor productivity and to estimate capital increase. This chapter explores the ways calculation structured slaves' days and weeks, focusing particularly on estimates of productivity and output. Chapter 4 turns to longer time scales, asking how plantation accounting structured slaves' practices from year to year and life to life, as planters sought to maximize the value of human capital.

The precise records planters left behind make clear that sophisticated accounting techniques were not incidental to plantation slavery: power enabled precise management. Instead of attracting and retaining labor, slaveholders acquired it and accelerated it, aided by the threat of violence. In essence, they subjected men and women to experiments, directing labor at will, planning meals and lodging, and measuring and monitoring production with great precision. To be sure, slaves resisted planters' efforts, but a combination of calculation and control constrained their attempts. Slavery became a laboratory for the use of accounting, because neat columns of numbers translated more easily to life on plantations than they did in many other early American enterprises.[2]

The clearest examples of these practices can be found on cotton plantations, most notably those using a set of popular journals published by Thomas Affleck. This chapter begins with these account books, which reveal planters' efforts to accelerate the pace of daily labor through calculation and comparison, bonuses and incentives, and, of course, punishment. From here I turn to record keeping more generally, including that on sugar plantations. Though sugar production was less suited to productivity analysis than was cotton, in some ways its complexity made coordination even more important. Planters could not track output per slave as meticulously as they could for cotton production, but they pursued increased efficiency through systematic labor allocation. Taken together, these efforts paint a picture of elite cotton and sugar planters as relentlessly calculating, aspiring to exploit every aspect of the lives of the people they enslaved.

Plantation Journals

Eli Capell took over the management of Pleasant Hill Plantation after the death of his father, Littleton Capell, in the mid-1830s. Under his direction, the plantation thrived, expanding from a farm of less than 1,000 acres into a plantation of 2,500 acres, worked by a force of eighty slaves.[3] Capell recorded his progress in a series of detailed journals stretching from 1842 to 1867. In the earliest of these records, he experimented with a variety of differently formatted diaries and blank books, but none suited his needs. On days when he attempted to record every slave's individual picking, his calculations spilled into the margins.[4] In 1850, he remedied the problem by adopting Thomas Affleck's preprinted *Plantation Record and Account Book*. Affleck's journal was an all-in-one account book designed to facilitate plantation management.[5]

Thomas Affleck was a planter and gardener in the small town of Washington, Mississippi, about fifty miles west of Capell's plantation in Amite County. Born and educated in Scotland, he migrated to the United States in 1832, moving from the East Coast to Ohio before relocating to Mississippi, where he began to plant cotton. His background combined experience in finance, scientific agriculture, and publishing. In Edinburgh, he had worked as a bookkeeper for the Bank of Scotland, and he boasted in his correspondence that the experience had accustomed him "to the strictest business habits."[6]

When he arrived in Mississippi, Affleck found that although some of his neighbors "had kept regular plantation books for many years," their records varied dramatically, lacking the uniformity and regularity that would enable comparisons across plantations. In response, Affleck "prepared 2 books with the pen," giving one to each of his overseers. After testing the journal and revising it, he published his first edition.[7] The *Plantation Record and Account Book* contained a preprinted, all-in-one system for planters wishing to improve their accounting practices. As advertisements boasted, his journal combined "Day Book, Journal, Stock Book, Ledger and Daily Record" all in "one large folio volume."[8]

Affleck published his journal in six versions, specialized by crop and plantation size (see Figure 3.1).[9] Eli Capell originally used Affleck's smallest book, designed for cotton plantations with 40 or fewer slaves, but by the late 1850s, his operations had outgrown this volume, and he purchased the *Cotton Plantation Record and Account Book, No. 2,* for plantations with up to 80 hands.[10] Affleck offered an even larger edition with space to record the work of as many as 120 working hands, and by 1860, he had published a fourth edition for up to 160 working hands. He also offered two volumes for sugar plantations with 80 and 120 working hands. Because many enslaved men and women were too young, old, or infirm to labor in the fields, the largest volumes targeted elite planters whose holdings could reach as high as 200 or even 300 total slaves. The smallest journal sold for $2.00, and the prices of the larger editions increased in increments of $.50. These prices were higher than those of other blank books but a small expense relative to the total investment involved in operating a large plantation.[11]

The cotton journals contained fifteen different forms, labeled A through O (see Table 3.1). Each form addressed a different aspect of plantation production, and together they comprised an interlocking system that enabled planters to make sophisticated comparisons and calculations. Planters filled in some of the forms every day, including the record of activities and the record of cotton picked. Other pages in the journal—including the inventories of tools, supplies, and the slaves themselves—were to be completed only quarterly or annually. As Affleck explained, the inventories would be particularly useful for non-resident planters who could not supervise everything directly. These forms would save the planter "much vexation and loss" and the overseer "undeserved blame." Several forms offered opportunities to cross check, providing space for both the overseer and the planter to enter information. For example, on Form H, the overseer recorded the weight of every bale of cotton, the total of which should match the total from Form M, on which the owner recorded the weight of the bales as they were sold. Comparing the weight of cotton bales after ginning to the weight at time of

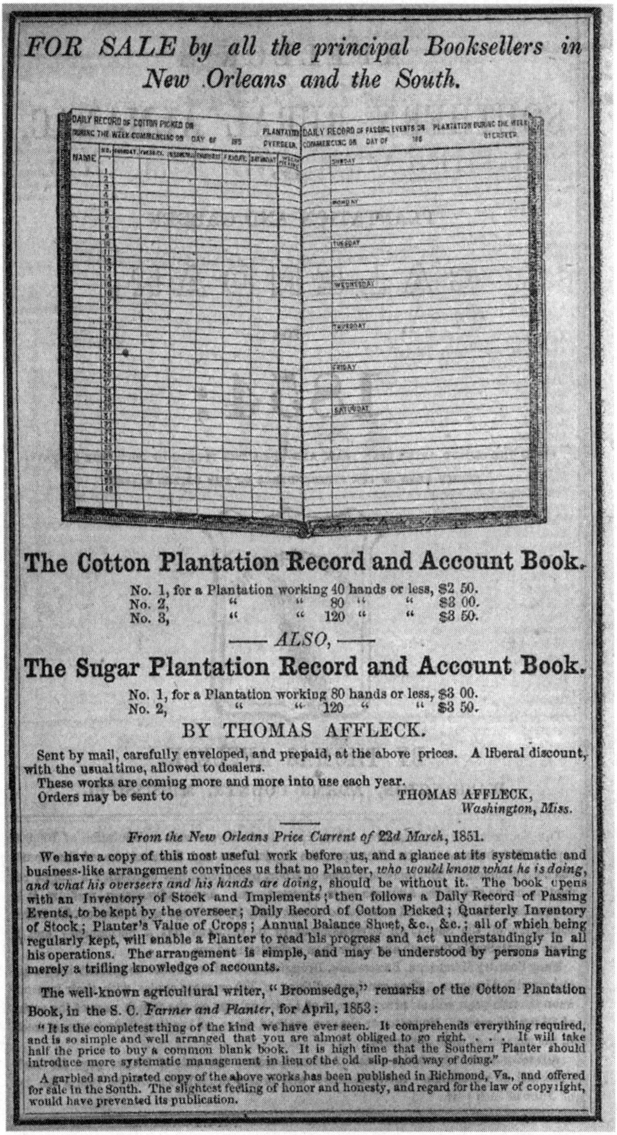

FIGURE 3.1. Advertisement for Thomas Affleck's *Plantation Record and Account Books,* 1854. Affleck's preprinted ledgers came in specialized versions tailored to plantation crop and size. Affleck's Southern Rural Almanac, and Plantation and Garden Calendar for 1854 (Washington, Miss.: Thomas Affleck, 1854). Courtesy of Louisiana and Lower Mississippi Valley Collections, Louisiana State University Libraries, Baton Rouge.

TABLE 3.1. Forms included in Thomas Affleck's *Cotton Plantation Record and Account Book*

Form	Title	Frequency completed?
A	Daily Record of Passing Events	Daily
B	Inventory of Stock and Implements	Quarterly (Monthly in 1st ed.)
C	Daily Record of Cotton Picked	Daily from late July, weekly totals
D	List of Articles Given Out to the Negroes	As distributed
E	Overseer's Record of Supplies Delivered to Him	As received
F	List of Births and Deaths	As needed
G	Check on the Physician's Account	As needed
H	Weights of Cotton by Bale	At weighing and sale
I	Planter's Annual Record of his Negroes	Beginning and end of the year
J	Planter's Annual Record of Stock	Beginning and end of the year
K	Planter's Annual Record of Tools	Beginning and end of the year
L	Statement of the Several Products of the Plantation	Yearly
M	Statement of the Sale of Cotton	As sold
N	Condensed Account of the Expenses of the Plantation	Yearly
O	The Planter's Annual Balance Sheet	Yearly

sale could help planters to monitor their overseers, while comparing the ratio of cotton picked to ginned could help overseers to monitor the enslaved.[12]

Affleck's journal culminated in Form O, an end-of-year balance sheet on which planters could calculate their yearly profits. This balance sheet ensured that every cost and revenue was tallied, drawing inputs from five different forms elsewhere in the book. Capital costs—including land, slaves, tools, and stock—were charged to the balance sheet at 6 percent of their value, in keeping with what Affleck judged to be the prevailing interest rate. By consulting the balance sheet and comparing it with prior years, planters could assess their overall profitability and identify the cause of their success or failure: improvement to their property, sale of cotton, or change in the value of slaves.[13]

Despite their complexity, Affleck's journals required very little specialized knowledge of bookkeeping. As he explained in an 1860 advertisement, "The plan of the book is so simple, and yet complete, that any man who can write at all legibly, whether or not he has any knowledge of the principles and practice of book-keeping, is capable of making his entries correctly." The detailed instructions and fill-in-the-blanks balance sheet meant that only basic addition and subtraction were required to strike a "true balance" and to determine "whether the year's labors have resulted in profit or loss."[14] This relative simplicity made Affleck's journals ideal for monitoring overseers, who rarely had any skill in bookkeeping. When James Henry Hammond complained to Affleck that he had "no hope of ever getting an overseer who will or can keep such a book" in South Carolina, Affleck replied that in Mississippi, there were many such men. He recommended making the completion of the books a stipulation of their contracts, giving newly hired overseers little choice in the matter.[15]

Affleck applied the same entrepreneurial calculations to his publishing business that he instructed planters to use with their crops. In a letter to a potential partner, he described his business plan in detail:

> The Acct. books can be got out at 60c to 70c p copy—say an average of 75c. Weld writes me he has got over $650 of advertisements for this coming edition. I feel confident that 5,000 copies of all the editions, Sugar & Cotton can be sold per annum, at an average retail price of $3.00, Netting $2.00, counting freight &c. &c. & losses. $500 can be had for adverts., reducing the cost of the books 10c. p copy. I am keeping a long way within bounds. Say 5,000 copies net $1.35 each = $6, 750.[16]

In practice, Affleck appears to have had difficulty realizing his projections. He claimed that this was due not to a lack of demand but because of difficulty finding and maintaining a dependable printer. Over the run of the journal, Affleck employed several printers, at least one of whom "absquatulated," leaving Affleck with neither the funds nor the volumes for several months.[17]

Affleck's journals appear to have sold well, remaining in print until the Civil War and running to eight editions. Although it is difficult to verify their circulation, Affleck claimed annual sales of two thousand and believed that he could reach five thousand if production were managed efficiently. By 1860, he touted a print run of three thousand. These rates would have reached only a small fraction of all slave-owning cotton farmers. Assuming Affleck's—probably generous—estimate of three thousand was correct for 1860, he was still reaching less than 3 percent of all slaveholding cotton planters. However, most of these farmers had very small operations, with about half owning ten or fewer slaves and a large majority owning thirty or fewer.[18] A circulation of three thousand would have reached a much larger proportion of mid- to large-scale planters—nearly 15 percent of plantations worked by more than thirty enslaved people. Figure 3.2 shows the distribution of plantations and of cotton production grouped by number of slaves. While there were many small farms and plantations (see the light columns to the left), these produced relatively little cotton (dark columns). Larger plantations worked by many slaves (counted in the light columns to the right) were fewer in number but produced much more cotton (dark columns). These large plantations were the target of Affleck's books. In combination with competing volumes, preprinted journals like his probably reached a substantial fraction of these planters.[19]

Though Thomas Affleck's series of books were the most popular plantation blanks, they were not the first to reach the American South. Farquhar Macrae advertised his methods in the *Farmers' Register* in 1835, though he appears not to have manufactured them for sale.[20] By 1840, Andrew Flynn of Mississippi was using a simple preprinted book, with space to keep an inventory and pages to record the daily allocation of labor. Unlike Affleck's volumes, which comprised a complex system of interlocking accounts, this book simply offered space to track labor.[21] Like Macrae's recommendation, this volume more closely resembled the West Indian work logs highlighted in Chapter 2 than Affleck's system of record keeping. Still, the preprinted journal seems to have been on its way to becoming a well-developed genre of printing in the South well before Affleck published his volumes.

In 1852, J. W. Randolph of Richmond, Virginia, published the most comprehensive alternative to Affleck's book. Randolph did not disclose the author, referring to him only as "a Southern Planter."[22] A review describes him as one of the "best and most systematic farmers in Virginia," claiming the journal could save its users "hundreds of dollars."[23] Where earlier volumes were simpler, Randolph's book was in some ways more extensive than Affleck's. The text included, among other things, a draft contract with a manager, recommendations on books to consult, and space to list the volumes in

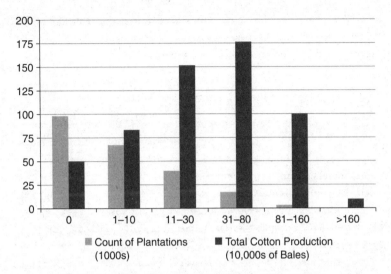

FIGURE 3.2. Output and Number of Plantations by Size of Slaveholding, 1860. Although there were many small farms (see the light columns to the left), these produced relatively little cotton (dark columns). Large plantations worked by many slaves (counted in the light columns to the right) were fewer in number but produced vast amounts of cotton (dark columns). Data comes from the Parker-Gallman Sample, which includes 1860 data on 5,228 farms, or 1.67 percent of all farms in 405 major cotton-producing counties in the South in 1860. Numbers presented here are for all farms producing cotton, scaled up assuming a random draw. William N. Parker and Robert E. Gallman, "Southern Farms Study, 1860," ICPSR07419-VI, Ann Arbor, MI: Inter-university Consortium for Political and Social Research [distributor], 1991.

the planter's library. A large section of "Miscellaneous Information, Tables, and Data" covered everything from weights and measures to planting distances and guidance for a system of crop rotation.[24]

Affleck railed against competing texts, considering them inferior substitutes for his own. In 1854, he requested a copy of one "bastard acct. book" from bookseller B. M. Norman.[25] A year later, when someone alerted him of a copycat book being sold by a "Mr. Bland," he exclaimed in reply that "such plagiarism" was "quite common," complaining of "an almost literal reprint of my books—but with the part of Hamlet omitted! Most shabbily gotten up & some of the most important records left out."[26] Still, despite Affleck's lamentations, his books were simply the most well known of a broader genre. By the 1850s, planters could choose from several different systems to monitor plantation business. However, this is less remarkable than what it allowed planters to do: to analyze data and put it to use.

Putting Numbers to Work

Planters not only recorded information systematically, they also put their data to work, analyzing it in order to increase the productivity of their operations. Determining how much cotton an enslaved man or woman could pick was a near obsession among southern planters, and they used careful records to help determine this maximum. Planters used Thomas Affleck's books unevenly, often leaving many forms incomplete. But almost without exception, they completed Form C, the "Daily Record of Cotton Picked." This form tracked the pounds of cotton each slave picked every day (see Figure 3.3).[27] The first column noted the name of each enslaved person, and to the right of this list were columns for each day of the week (Monday through Saturday). These columns could be tallied to determine each workers's weekly output, and these numbers could be summed for a weekly total across the force. In combination with an array of other management strategies, planters relied on this routine of weighing and recording to accelerate the pace of labor.

Some planters had been recording data on cotton picking for many years before blank books were widely available. For example, Francis Terry Leak of Tippah County, Mississippi, kept a daily record of cotton picking in a single book covering the period from 1841 to 1865. On the volume's hand-lined pages, he listed every slave laboring in the fields. To the right of this roll of names were six columns, representing space for every day of the week except Sunday, when he tallied up the week's results. He kept this cotton record separate from his general journal, but he returned to it each year when the picking season began, usually in late September or October, and it continued as long as the picking continued—usually until December but sometimes into January or February if weather permitted. Records of cotton picking like Leak's often included hundreds of data points each week and thousands over the course of each season.[28]

The regularity of picking records reflects regimented procedures for measurement on the plantation. After emancipation, minister and former slave Charles Thompson recollected the basic process of picking, weighing,

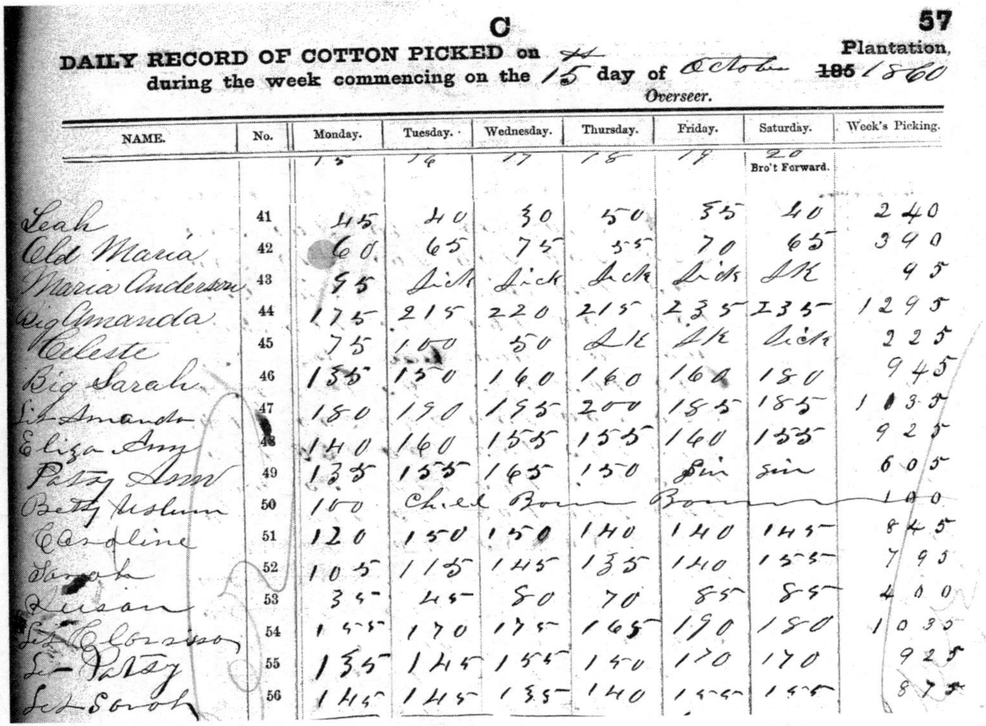

FIGURE 3.3. "Form C," Daily Record of Cotton Picked on Eustatia Plantation, 1860. Planters used Form C to record the number of pounds of cotton picked by each slave every day. Betsy Uslum (no. 50) picked until her child was born and resumed labor within the month. G. R. Clark, Eustatia Plantation, Mississippi. Account Book, 1861, Ohio Historical Center Archives Library. Courtesy of Ohio Historical Society, Ohio History Connection (Img 59, Vol 649), Columbus.

57

C

DAILY RECORD OF COTTON PICKED on ___ Plantation.
during the week commencing on the 15 day of Octor. 185 /860

Overseer.

NAME	No.	Monday.	Tuesday.	Wednesday.	Thursday.	Friday.	Saturday.	Week's Picking.
							Bro't Forward.	2.0
Leah	41	45	40	30	50	35	40	240
Old Maria	42	60	65	75	55	70	65	390
Maria Anderson	43	45	Sick	Sick	Sick	Sick	Sick	95
Armanda	44	175	215	220	215	235	235	1295
Violett	45	75	100	50				225
Big Sarah	46	135	150	160	160	164	150	945
Lit Amanda	47	150	160	175	200	155	185	1035
Eliza Ann	48	140	160	155	155	155	155	925
Patty Ann	49	135	135	65	130			605
Hebron	50	170	Sick	Born			Sick	140
Caroline	51	120	150	150	140	140	145	845
	52	105	115	145	135	140	155	795
	53	35	45	50	70	55	55	400
	54	155	170	175	165	190	150	1035
	55	135	146	154	140	170	170	925
	56	145	145	135	140	155	155	875

and accounting for cotton. As he wrote, "Each picker had a 'stint' or daily task to perform; that is, each of them was required to pick so many pounds of cotton." Thompson was "placed over the hands as 'boss' and cotton-weigher." He described measuring each slave's progress as often as "three times each day." Such frequent weighing enabled the enslaved to track their progress and to strive toward their full task. Thompson could add and write, but he had to conceal these skills due to laws against educating slaves. Nonetheless, his owner benefited from his ability. Being numerate allowed him to report "the weights of each hand separate and correctly" to the overseer each night.[29]

Some planters used incentives to accelerate picking, relying on the use of precise calculation. After his escape from slavery, Henry Bibb described the use of contests to speed up the pace of labor. As he explained, instead of extorting picking from their slaves "by the lash," some planters would "deceive them by giving small prizes." An overseer began by "dividing the hands off in three classes" by skill, and "offering a prize to the one who will pick out the most cotton in each of the classes." By this means, they encouraged slaves of every ability to increase their pace. After repeating such challenges several times and "weighing what cotton they pick every night," the overseer could tell "just how much every hand can pick." Later he would use these achievements as benchmarks and punish those who did not reach them. Reward and punishment worked together, with one generating data and the other relying on it.[30]

The most complex incentive systems stretched over the course of the year. In 1851, a Mississippi planter who owned forty-nine slaves explained his scheme. As he wrote, "I pay them money at the end of the year. . . . The amount given to all depends on the crop and the price; the amount to each one upon his good behavior, his activity, obedience and efficiency during the year." He allocated the payment by class: "The negro who has discharged all his duties through the year most faithfully is put in the first class. As many as deserve it are put there and all get the largest and same amount of Money. The amount paid them is lessened as they fall into lower classes." Slaves could draw on their accounts throughout the year, and the planter furnished "any extra clothing that any of them may want," charging their accounts, and "at pay day, as they call it, it is brought up against them."[31]

Incentives could be used to reward and punish entire communities of enslaved people. In 1842, a planter and minister from Virginia described the payment system that he used to enforce slaves' honesty. Every year, he gave "each laboring hand a barrel of corn, or its equivalent in money," to be settled at Christmas. If any theft or "depredation is committed, *no matter by whom,* my negroes are responsible for it, and double its value is deducted from the Christmas present." However, if "the thief is given up . . . the whole responsibility rests on him." Thus, he explained, "a few barrels of corn are made the means of saving my property to perhaps ten times the amount the whole year." Accounting practices allowed sophisticated systems of incentives and punishments to work together.[32]

Record keeping could make punishment just as calculating as payment. Some book farmers advocated more humane treatment, but others relied primarily on the threat of violence. They meted out lashes in precise relation to picking, whipping slaves as many strokes as the number of pounds they fell short of during their daily or weekly tasks. In the 1840s, Henry Watson described a state of almost constant terror on the plantation where he labored. As Watson wrote, "Each individual having a stated number of pounds of cotton to pick, the deficit of which was made up by as many lashes being applied to the poor slave's back."[33] John Brown described the same cruel system: "For every pound that is found short of the task, the punishment is one stroke of the bull-whip." Though Brown himself "never got flogged for short weight," many others did, "and dreadful was the punishment they received."[34]

Even for those who avoided punishment, the weighing of cotton could be harrowing. Solomon Northup's 1855 slave narrative described the fear that motivated him to accelerate his work. As Northup wrote, "A slave never approaches the gin-house with his basket of cotton but with fear. If it falls short in weight—if he has not performed the full task appointed him, he knows that he must suffer." But the cost of success was high. As Northup reflected, if "he has exceeded it by ten or twenty pounds, in all probability his master will measure the next day's task accordingly. So, whether he has too little or too much, his approach to the gin-house is always with fear and trembling."[35] On the plantation where John Brown labored, management expected a hundred pounds for a new picker, but on the first day, he "picked five pounds over this quantity." Much to his "sorrow," Brown found that because he had "picked so well at first, more was exacted of me, and if I flagged a minute, the whip was liberally applied to keep me up to the mark." By constant driving, the overseer gradually pushed Brown's task higher until he "at last got to pick a hundred and sixty pounds a day."[36]

Enslaved men and women recognized the high stakes of tactics designed to reveal their maximum picking rates. Many saw prizes and payments for what they were—a ruse that masters could discontinue once they knew what work could be performed. And they responded with subtle modes of resistance. Frederick Law Olmsted described enslaved men's and women's attempts to slow down plantation speedups in *The Cotton Kingdom*. As he explained, slaves "very frequently cannot be made to do their master's will." They do not "directly refuse" to obey orders but rather rebel more subtly, undertaking their tasks "in such a way that the desired result is sure not to be accomplished." Olmsted labeled the passage in which he described this behavior as "sogering," a term that he defined approximately a decade earlier when describing the slow pace of work on a packet ship in England. Sogering, he wrote, is "pretending to work, and accomplishing as little as possible." Management scholar Bill Cooke has traced sogering to the same root as Frederick Winslow Taylor's "soldiering," also meaning to shirk, or to pretend to work in order to obscure true ability.[37]

Instances of enslaved defiance are particularly remarkable considering the legal power slaveholders wielded over their human property. Though specific legal circumstances—based on both statutes and case law—varied from state to state and over time, the collective picture is one of legally sanctioned domination. Short of killing enslaved people, planters enjoyed tremendous autonomy to extract obedience from the men, women, and children they owned. In the 1834 North Carolina case *State v. Will,* the judge summed it up as follows: "Unconditional submission is the general duty of the slave; unlimited power is, in general, the legal right of the master." This power had few exceptions, usually only restricting "the unlawful attempt of [a] master to deprive [a slave] of life."[38] In 1842, a Tennessee judge concurred that "the right of obedience and submission . . . is perfect in the master; and the power to inflict any punishment, not affecting life or limb, which he may consider necessary for the purpose of keeping him in such submission, and enforcing such obedience to his commands, is secured to him by law."[39] In a North Carolina case, Justice Thomas Ruffin reflected that though "a principle of moral right" repudiated such treatment, by the nature of the institution of slavery, masters nonetheless enjoyed "uncontrolled authority over the body" of a slave.[40]

The threat of violence offered a powerful tool to extract labor, and the law offered little protection. Even fatal beatings were frequently excused in practice, though theoretically prohibited by law. In an 1860 Mississippi case, a master was initially found guilty of killing a slave named John, but an appeals court reversed the conviction on the grounds that the slave had been resisting his master's lawful authority. As the judge explained, in such cases "the master may use just such force as may be requisite to reduce his slave to obedience, even to the death of the slave." The conflict that gave rise to John's supposed disobedience appears to have been a version of the "sogering" described by Olmsted. As the overseer testified, "He did not seem to work fast enough, and Oliver [the slaveholder] told him to work faster and the negro didn't do it, and Oliver took the shelling-stick from him and killed him with it."[41] Enslaved people could neither defend themselves physically nor defend themselves in court. They typically could not give evidence, and in some states a master could clear himself simply by giving an oath, though this practice was eventually called into question.[42] Still, it is important not to overstate the extent to which enslaved people were outside the law. Despite substantial barriers, some found ways to use the courts. For example, though they were themselves property, enslaved people often owned some property, and in some cases they defended this property in court—even against claims from free whites. That enslaved people sometimes managed to protect their property using a system that offered so little protection for their lives reflects the extent to which the law privileged property rights over enslaved lives.[43]

Case law adjudicating what masters could and could not do to manage the enslaved is remarkably scarce. Plantation spaces were, in a sense, "privatized"—held outside the law but within the master's control. Those few cases that made it to court tended to be extreme, suggesting that masters enjoyed extensive power and that courts only reluctantly policed space within plantations. As Jonathan Bush has written, even in settings where slave law was relatively underdeveloped, it was "offset by private 'rule-making,' described in plantation manuals and rule-books, and enforced with whipping and other punishments, including death."[44]

Plantation accounting was part of this system of private rule-making, and masters used measurement and calculation to uncover enslaved resistance. Israel Campbell, a slave who struggled repeatedly to meet his task, described hiding "a good sized melon" in his basket before it was weighed. The possibility of discovery terrified him, but he knew that otherwise, "a whipping was sure." At first Campbell thought himself "pretty smart to play such a trick . . . but a day of reckoning was to come." Before the cotton was sold, "it had to be ginned. . . . As they always put down the amount picked, allowing so much for waste, they could calculate very nearly the amount it ought to make." Comparing these weights revealed a shortfall, and though the overseer never implicated Campbell, he could not repeat the trick.[45]

The many surviving account books from southern plantations suggest that by the early to mid-nineteenth century, sophisticated accounting practices were relatively widespread. Amid the destruction of the Civil War, it is remarkable how many volumes were preserved. And these records—typically the most formal elements of plantation accounting—only scratch the surface of the ways numbers were used on plantations. Outside of bound books, there would have been loose paper notations and still more impermanent slates that were filled and erased daily. Only traces of these more informal technologies are visible in account books. For example, on Eli Capell's plantation, the column for Monday, September 13, 1852, has no data. Instead, a scrawled notation reads, "To days picking was Rubbed off the Slate."[46] In several narratives, enslaved authors also recall overseers setting down the weights of cotton on slates.[47]

Scattered clues, like references to slates and scales, suggest that numbers permeated plantation life to an even greater extent than daily picking records reveal. The three-times-daily measures Charles Thompson described did not make it into the account books, but they may have been recorded on slates. Perhaps a low midday total spurred slaves to pick faster to meet their targets. But a high one surely provided no relief, as the manager might raise their targets. Relentless measuring offered both details for surveillance and an incitement to effort. Like progress reports tacked to the walls of modern corporations, these constant notations made the data of plantation operations daily visible.

King Cotton

Though many of the account books produced and sold by men like Thomas Affleck were only partially completed, planters almost always filled in the detailed records of cotton picking. By the late 1850s, planters could even purchase books dedicated to the harvest of cotton. A printer named W. H. Fox offered one such volume for sale. This reformatted journal contained only one form, the "STATEMENT OF COTTON Picked," which nearly exactly replicated Affleck's Form C. Each page contained space to list the names of the enslaved, and across the top were columns for Monday–Saturday, space for a total, and a final column for remarks. The record could be used on any size plantation, with planters simply using as many pages as needed to list the members of the enslaved workforce.[48]

In 1859, Robert Stewart of Natchez, Mississippi, used a dedicated cotton book to record the picking of the enslaved men and women laboring under him. Page after page is filled with daily tallies of individual and plantation picking. The results are extraordinary: by the time picking season was in full swing, the most skilled pickers were regularly bringing in more than 400 pounds per day, sometimes more than 500 pounds. The weaker pickers harvested at least 100 and often 200 pounds per day. In the last week of October, an enslaved man named Oskar brought in more than 500 pounds every day, for a total of 3,160 pounds over the course of the week. The following Monday, perhaps fresh from his Sunday rest, he brought in 615 pounds, reaching 3,295 pounds over that week. The following year, during the boom cotton season of 1860–1861, Oskar would top this daily record again. On January 4, coming back to what must have been full fields after a few days of ditching, Oskar picked an astonishing 735 pounds. That same day in January, Stewart's other top pickers, Little Ellick and Margarette, picked 670 pounds apiece.[49]

These remarkable totals were far above the average for the late 1850s— probably between 150 and 200 pounds per day. However, they would have been unheard of half a century earlier, when average picking rates may have been as low as 50 pounds per day.[50] Analysis drawing on records like the ones described in this chapter has demonstrated a tremendous increase in productivity during the sixty years preceding the American Civil War. Between 1801 and 1862, the average amount of cotton picked per slave per day increased about fourfold, or 2.3 percent per year.[51]

Economists and historians have disagreed about the source of these gains in cotton productivity, with economists pointing to biological innovation—especially the adoption of new strains of cotton—and historians putting greater emphasis on violence toward enslaved people.[52] Plantation account books show that planters pursued both strategies in combination, weaving agricultural innovation and coercion together in strategies to grow more cotton. New strains of cotton, most notably the Mexican hybrid Petit Gulf, undoubtedly accounted for a large part of efficiency gains. Planters sought varieties with higher and earlier yields, extending the picking season. They also sought strains that were more "pickable" and thus could be harvested faster. Pickable strains had boles that opened more widely, enabling the cotton to be plucked from the pod more easily than in other varieties. Ideally, many boles also opened simultaneously, allowing slaves to harvest more on each pass by a plant. In their pursuit of new strains, planters tested varieties from different sources—imports from all over the world, as well as the most productive plants in their own fields. By the late antebellum period, they could choose from many varieties based on climate, yield, cost, and available labor.[53]

"Pickability" did not automatically yield more cotton: enslaved people had to be induced to pick more. Without biological improvement, it would have been impossible to increase the pace of labor beyond some theoretical maximum—force could speed the work of enslaved laborers but not change what was possible. The converse was also true: though new seeds changed what was possible, they did not automatically increase the amount of cotton that enslaved people actually plucked from the fields. By keeping careful records, planters could compare different seeds, select the best varieties, and recalibrate expectations for how much they could require workers to pick. They could then blend rewards with punishment to push enslaved people to achieve these maximums. Focusing too narrowly on either biological innovation or on coercion overlooks the complex ways planters wove these tools together to expand production. New strains of cotton resulted in higher yields only because planters could calculate and enforce a faster rate of picking. And punishment, no matter how brutal, could accelerate productivity only because new strains changed what was possible.[54]

Data and management practices thus underpinned increased productivity. When planters adopted easier-to-pick strains of cotton, daily picking records enabled them to set new targets, thereby extracting higher output from their slaves. Careful record keeping also facilitated the dissemination of innovations and the recalibration of expectations across the South. When Thomas Affleck first published his account book, he touted both its benefits for individual planters and the salutary influences he expected them to have on agriculture in the region. As he exclaimed to James Henry Hammond in a letter recommending the books, "Think of the advantage to both planters & overseers, of even 1,000 books written from day-to-day experience, scattered over the country!" Such books, kept in a standardized format, would enable precise comparisons, turning the full community of southern farmers into a vast laboratory for agricultural improvement.[55]

If planters seem to have cared about the last pound of cotton, they cared more about the last bale. From one perspective, pound-by-pound records of daily cotton picking are the most distinctive and impressive aspect of late antebellum plantation account books. They show a relentless drive to quantification. Slave-by-slave accounts seem designed to extract every possible pound from enslaved pickers. But on another level, these relatively simple records are less impressive than the larger systems of coordination and control that were developing alongside them. Looking beyond picking shows the many other ways planters attempted to increase their output. Account books not only helped monitor labor but also enabled planters to decide when to try new seeds or purchase equipment. Calculation and record keeping became flexible tools that helped planters reap productivity gains from all kinds of sources.

Growing cotton was complex, and it was sometimes difficult to uncover the source of large yearly fluctuations in output. Was a surplus or shortfall the result of the weather? Of the seed? Manure? The diligence of the slaves? Francis Terry Leak's journals of cotton picking and his accompanying diary show how he attempted to disentangle multiple influences. In his records of cotton picking, leak often included a variety of other calculations. He kept a running total for the year as well as subtotals for individual fields, some of which were planted with different seeds or enriched with different manures. He used these running totals to make projections, attempting to anticipate the success of the cotton crop and making what adjustments he could when the year's harvest began poorly. For example, midway through the 1843 picking season, he drew up a table of production and wrote, "If the deficiency for the whole season is proportionate to that occurring up to 7 Feby, it will amount to 605000 bales." But if the "balance of the season should be at the rate of that occurring from 17 January to 7 Feby, it will amount to 696000 bales."[56]

Southern planters were obsessed with cotton, but they were not mono-culturists, as historians have sometimes represented them. True, cotton was "king" in both the eyes of southerners and their northern critics, but this drove them away from monocropping, not toward it. Though historians once believed that cotton plantations grew little food, plowing all their resources into cash crops, we now know that this misconception resulted from trade statistics that did not reflect the fact that a large proportion of the midwestern foodstuffs that arrived in New Orleans were exported to consumers beyond the South.[57] Planters grew many crops. Most grew large amounts of food, including corn, potatoes, and an array of garden crops. They also raised hogs and sometimes other livestock. All these practices could complement the production of cotton: crops could be rotated, and pigs yielded not only meat but also manure, to enrich the land for growing more cotton. Perhaps most importantly, corn and cotton were countercyclical, enabling the steady use of enslaved labor over the course of a year.[58] Planters could use the off-season from cotton to grow corn to feed their slaves (and to feed their hogs). By carefully choreographing their crop mix, planters smoothed labor requirements over the course of the year.[59]

What plantation account books reveal is not just that cotton and corn were complementary but that they were complementary *by design*. Among the most important of Francis Terry Leak's calculations was his estimation of how he should divide his land between cotton and corn, a subject he commented on regularly. Leak's account books show that the smoothing of labor was not simply a characteristic of the crops but a result of careful calculations of when to plant and tend each. In April 1845, he noted a variety of "hints to be attended to another year." Among these, he included instructions on how to stage the planting of cotton and corn. Early in the season, he aimed to "plant Corn early enough to plough, hoe, & thin it, before Cotton comes up." Following this, "the scraping of the Cotton should Commence as soon as the cotton begins to come up." In order to have enough time to plant corn, the planting of the cotton crop had to happen quickly. So that "the scraping may commence in time, the whole planting of the Cotton Crop should not exceed 8 or 10 days. This Year we were too long planting." Speed during potential bottlenecks could be enabled by preparation during the off-season. For example, "It would be desirable to break up the Corn land before planting, or to break out the stalks immediately after planting as in either Case the ploughs might not be kept in the Corn, after it comes up longer than to run round it."[60]

Seasonal planning hinged on how quickly planters could expect enslaved people to work. Efforts to understand the pace of labor are most evident from picking records, but planters also made estimates of more difficult-to-measure tasks. Below his notes on the relation between cotton and corn, Leak commented on the pace of labor he expected in chopping: "In chopping through Cotton the men should have 13500 yards & the women 10600 yards for a task." Leak's journal commented repeatedly on when he started and finished various tasks. Optimally planned, labor requirements could be smoothed over the course of the year. Staged properly, there would be no off-season. Even those tasks that were less time sensitive could be choreographed to allow perfect timing for those that were. Ginning, for example, could be completed during poor weather or pushed to the end of the picking season. But it could only be pushed back so far, or it would interfere with the planting of the next season's cotton. When Leak noted, for example, that he "finished ginning Wednesday 22nd March at 12 O'clock," he was completing the task just in time to tend to the next year's crop.[61]

Because planters controlled the activities of slaves year round, they sought to smooth labor requirements from season to season. These efforts had been underway for decades. George Washington proposed growing wheat of different varieties to stagger the harvest. This would have obviated the need to hire additional labor to assist his slaves. As he wrote in his diary, "If Wheat of different kinds are sowed so as to prevent the Harvest coming on at once, it is my opinion that hirelings of any kinds may be dispensed with."[62] By timing their planting, masters could grow more of everything without hiring additional labor. Indeed, across a variety of regions, success in growing staple crops tended to be associated with success in growing food crops. The two activities were complementary because they kept enslaved laborers working at a constant rate while also reducing expenditures on food.[63]

Control over labor over the course of the year also mitigated risks associated with harvest variation. Not only could planters plan the year to make use of labor from season to season, but they could deviate from this plan when opportunities for large profits arose. During an outstanding season, a planter could earn outsized profits—much larger than in a typical year. But he could only earn these profits if he could actually bring in the harvest. A planter pursuing maximum profits thus might sow extra acres in cotton. If the harvest was small, he could reallocate enslaved labor to other tasks and food crops. If it was large, he could purchase food and focus on picking cotton. Taking the risk of planting a very large crop without a captive, controlled labor force made little sense. But under slavery, planters could reallocate from other tasks when opportunities arose.[64]

Slavery made it possible to turn years with exceptional crops into exceptional profits. In a free labor economy, a cotton planter might not be able to recruit labor to bring in a rare bumper crop, which would likely coincide with high labor demand across a region. By contrast, under slavery, planters could plant more cotton with the assurance that they could command labor during the harvest. One such year was 1860, and some planters were able to translate the large crop into massive profits. Take Robert Stewart's plantation. In 1859, the picking season began in mid-August and extended to early December. When the picking concluded, he allocated labor to other tasks. But during the famously productive season of 1860, picking began in late August and stretched into February. Stewart had planted enough cotton for his slaves to continue picking for almost two more months when the opportunity arose.[65] Economist Gavin Wright has argued that the key to understanding southern productivity lies in crop mix. Those farms that concentrated more land and labor in cash crops like cotton tended to be more productive. Of course, concentrating resources in cash crops, rather than in subsistence crops like corn, brought the risk that planters would have to purchase foodstuffs in case of a shortfall. But slavery allowed planters with adequate resources to take on this risk, allocating relatively more resources to cotton.[66]

Planters also tried a wide array of other strategies to increase their cotton yields. Francis Terry Leak conducted an array of such experiments. Some of these constituted little more than dabbling with new methods, but others were designed to isolate the influence of particular techniques. For example, in the 1850s, Leak described a well-planned "experiment" in the "Southwest Corner of the 58 acre Gin field." He fertilized even rows with various manures: "the 2nd, 4th, 6th & 8th rows are plastered for about 10 hills; the 10th, 12th, & 14th have hydraulic Cement 8 hills the 16th Ripley marl; & the eighteenth & twentieth Ashes only." Leak left the odd numbered rows unfertilized as controls, a strategy that would have made it easy both to isolate the effects of the various additives and to compare one fertilizer to another. More basic experiments included sowing different varietals, including "India cotton," "Nanking Cotton," Petit Gulf strains procured from different sources, and seed that he harvested from his own plants when he observed their boles opening particularly early. Leak also measured stalks as they came up and planted a garden where he attempted to determine how a red rot afflicting his cotton spread.[67]

Historians who have described planters as cotton-crazed get something important right: cotton was certainly king. However, planters grew it not single-mindedly but thoughtfully, with attention to their bottom lines. In their efforts to grow more cotton, planters both diversified crop mix and planted as much cotton as they could harvest. Understanding planters' goals also explains why their books look different from the accounts of merchants and manufacturers. Many did not frequently balance their books. Historians of accounting have focused disproportionate attention on striking a balance and on double-entry bookkeeping more broadly, sometimes describing it as "high capitalist accounting."[68] One of the reasons for this focus is the way double-entry bookkeeping enables businesspeople to both calculate their rates of profit and determine where those profits came from. For a merchant with many trading partners or a manufacturer with multiple product lines, the use of double-entry bookkeeping helped estimate and increase profits. By contrast, cotton planters knew where their profits were coming from: *cotton*.[69] To earn greater profits, the key was to grow (and pick) more cotton. Thus, what is most remarkable among planters' records is not their calculation of rates of profit—only occasionally attempted—but their analysis of labor output and the way it enabled them to grow more cotton and thus to earn higher profits.

Sugar and System

Record keeping also played a role in the success of sugar planters, though their account books were at once more complex and less regular than those of cotton planters. Sugar production was more complicated than growing cotton. As on the West Indian plantations described in Chapters 1 and 2, success involved more machinery, more processes, more tasks, and more potential bottlenecks. Sugar cane had to be planted, cut, and milled promptly to capture as much juice as possible before the cane dried out, then the resulting juice had to be boiled quickly to avoid spoilage. Because of this compressed schedule, the growing of raw ingredients and the early stages of processing were closely integrated and typically co-located. In a sense, it was as if textile mills had been located amid the cotton fields.

Sugar production in the American South, predominantly Louisiana, was even more time-sensitive than in the West Indies because of the shorter growing season. The risk of frost meant that the cane did not have as much time to reach maturity, and near the end of the growing season, planters faced the choice of whether to begin milling earlier at a lower rate of yield or to wait longer but chance an early frost. Harvesting typically began in the second half of October or early November, and then within a span of six to eight weeks, everything had to be harvested and processed into sugar.[70] The complexity of production and the exigencies of the crop made the potential rewards from aggressive labor management particularly large. The faster the harvest, the longer the planter could wait, and the more sugar he would produce. But a planter who pushed too hard might encounter resistance or a spike in runaways during this critical period.

Cotton had the convenient characteristic of being easy to weigh and easy to attribute to individuals, producing a number that could be used to reward or punish enslaved workers. And though fluctuations in price would of course mean changes in profit, this easy-to-collect metric related closely to a plantation's final productivity. By contrast, sugar planters lacked any single such measurement. The cutting and boiling of cane could not be easily quantified and attributed to individual slaves. Sugar making was an industrial, high-risk operation that benefited from regular record keeping. But sorting out the most valuable measurements and optimizing them was a far harder task. As a result, practices were often complex but also highly uneven.

Thomas Affleck's sugar plantation account books reflect these circumstances. They included many more forms than the cotton journals. Where the cotton books included fifteen forms, lettered A–O, the sugar books included twenty-one, lettered A–U (see Table 3.2). The sugar books changed more over the course of Affleck's publishing career, and planters used them even more unevenly than they used his cotton books. For example, on A. Ledoux & Company's plantation in Louisiana, overseer Samuel Leigh appears to have used the books as little more than a daily diary. He noted the weather and plantation activities daily, but he completed the other inventories only sporadically.[71]

On James Pirrie Bowman's Frogmoor Plantation, overseer George W. Woodruff used Affleck's books more extensively. He recorded clothing and supplies given out to slaves, births and deaths, and physician's visits. However, even he did not use all the recommended forms. His script filled the daily diary spaces from margin to margin, and when grinding season began, he simply wrote across the columns Affleck included for quantitative measurements. These five calculations ("Strength of Juice," "Lime Used," "Number of Strikes," "Number of Hogsheads," and "Cords of Wood") might have yielded valuable insights over the long run, but the payoff to recording them was far more distant than for the weighing of cotton. Woodruff ignored the instructions and simply offered more detail in narrative form. In similar fashion, he completed the inventory of slaves but left the valuations blank. He kept a detailed record of sales, but he did not bother to tally everything up in the final balance sheet.[72]

Woodruff did take advantage of occasional opportunities when output could be attributed to individuals. For example, he kept a detailed slave-by-slave record of cutting wood. First he recorded the daily task in the appropriate column (most often 1½ cords, but it ranged considerably by slave), next he filled in the amount cut each day, and finally he summed that total over the course of the week. Maintaining a sufficient supply of lumber was critical to the success of the mill; without enough to burn, the entire operation would grind to a halt. And unlike most of the other processes on the plantation, woodcutting could be easily monitored on a slave-by-slave basis.[73]

The comparative lack of standardization in sugar accounting should not be mistaken for a lack of sophistication. Rather, it reflects the exigencies of the crop: instead of minute productivity monitoring, planters focused on

TABLE 3.2. Forms included in Thomas Affleck's *Sugar Plantation Record and Account Book*

Form	Title	Frequency completed?
A	Daily Record of Passing Events	Daily
B	Inventory of Stock and Implements	Quarterly (Monthly in 1st ed.)
C	Daily Record of Passing Events (with grinding data)	Daily from start of grinding season
D	Record of Wood Cut	Daily
E	Record of Cooper's Work	As needed
F	Record of Clothing, Tools, &c., Given Out to the Negroes	As distributed
G	The Overseer's Entry of, and Receipt for, Supplies	Beginning of the year and as received
H	Record of the Weight of each Hhd. of Sugar made	
I	Record of each Barrel of Molasses made	
J	Record of the Shipments of Sugar and Molasses	As shipped
K	Overseer's Record of Births and Deaths of Negroes	As needed
L	Record of the Physician's Visits	As needed
M	Planter's Annual Record of his Negroes . . .	Beginning and end of the year
N	Planter's Annual Record of Stock	Beginning and end of the year
O	Planter's Inventory of Implements and Tools	Beginning and end of the year
P	Planter's Annual Inventory of Sugar-house . . .	Beginning and end of the year
Q	Planter's Record of the Amount and Value of Crops . . .	Beginning and end of the year
R	Planter's Record of the Sales of Sugar	
S	Planter's Record of the Sales of Molasses	As sold
T	Condensed Account of the Expenses of the Plantation	Yearly
U	Planter's Annual Balance Sheet	Yearly

Samuel Leigh, Observations of weather and crops, 1856–1857, A. Ledoux & Co. Plantation Journal, Pointe Coupee [Iberville?] Parish, Louisiana, January 5, 1856–January 18, 1857. Kenneth M. Stampp; Randolph Boehm; Martin Paul Schipper; Library of Congress, Manuscript Division, *Records of Antebellum Southern Plantations from the Revolution through the Civil War*, Series I: Selections from Louisiana State University, Part 1: Louisiana Sugar Plantations (Frederick, Md.: University Publications of America, 1985).

overall coordination and supervision. Richard Follett's excellent study of the business of sugar making describes the wide range of techniques planters adopted to make their operations more efficient. He describes how they instituted "assembly-line production," subdivided tasks, and introduced "systematized shift work," imposing a "regimented order that proved both exacting and relentless." In Follett's analysis, it was "a punishing agro-industrial system that, at the very least, anticipated several aspects of modern industrialization."[74]

Planters' efforts to increase production focused on coordination and supervision. As planter William Hamilton wrote, "I am a lover of order and system." He strove "to have a certain way of doing everything and a regular time for doing everything."[75] As in the Caribbean, planters developed extensive labor hierarchies and corresponding reporting structures. Compared to cotton, sugar required more slaves per acre, which made direct surveillance easier. Men supervised what the scale could not. Planters also sought a perfect balance between planting the cane, preparing it, cutting wood, grinding, and boiling. Timing was the key to maximizing the final output of sugar and molasses.

The journal for Robert Ruffin Barrow's Residence Plantation, in Terrebonne Parish, Louisiana, reflects the importance of "system." Residence was part of Barrow's extensive holdings. By some accounts, on the eve of the Civil War he owned sixteen plantations and more than seven hundred slaves. Barrow's journal shows his efforts to optimize production. Coordinating and categorizing labor was a year-round challenge. Every day, multiple gangs of slaves labored at a variety of tasks, from planting to plowing to hoeing to milling. Barrow's top manager was Ephraim A. Knowlton. Knowlton and the overseers below him kept running totals to track their cumulative progress at each of these tasks, hoping to ensure that everything was prepared for the harvest. As the year advanced and winter bore down on the plantation, the challenges of coordination intensified. The enslaved worked frantically to bring in the crop and turn it into sugar, often in multiple shifts over the course of the day. But there were many potential bottlenecks that could bring everything to a halt. Without enough wood, the boilers could not boil. Without the right boards and hoops, they could not make barrels. Without enough barrels, they could not store the sugar. On top of all this, cane had to be brought from the field at a steady pace and continuously fed into the grinder. Any mechanical malfunction could disrupt this continuous flow of production.[76]

To keep the works running, either Knowlton or Barrow (perhaps together) laid out a roster of the many tasks on the plantation. They titled this form the "classification of Han[d]s at Residence of 1857." The first classification was drawn up in mid-November, at the beginning of the grinding season. The chart divided the various categories of labor into two groups, presumably each feeding a boiling apparatus. Each group included a broad distribution of categories: "engine," "cane cutters," "shucking cane," "kettles," "furnace," "wood hauler," "cane shed," "loaders," "wagoners," "juice boxes," "wagon greasers," "cook till 12 o'clock," "sugar potters," and "cook for negroes." The messy document appears to have been modified repeatedly, with categories crossed out and altered. The journal also refers to it repeatedly, noting that the rest of the hands are at work as "per the classification."[77]

A few weeks later, perhaps with a better idea of how each process could be staged, the classification was redrawn (see Figure 3.4). This classification divided the various categories of labor into two groups, one for each "tower." Under the new division of labor, the whole plantation operated as if a machine of many parts—a continuous-process assembly line on a grand scale. This document is neater than the first classification, but the proto–assembly line still required constant adjusting. Knowlton explained at the bottom: "The above is how the Hands worked this day. They are however changed most every day. Those on 1st Tower are put on 2nd Tower, it is hard to keep up with the changes as it is almost requisite to make a new classification every day if a currency is required. EAK." And despite this effort, a variety of bottlenecks could and did sometimes bring the works to a halt.[78]

Coordinating and classifying labor was an ongoing challenge, but the legal conditions of slavery made it far easier to keep the works running. In a northern factory, labor could not be reclassified without consent from the workers. A new job might require new negotiations and higher wages. Negotiations often resulted in high rates of labor turnover—a challenge that manufacturers in free factories would continue to face into the twentieth century.[79] By contrast, planters could simply and quickly reallocate labor from day to day without renegotiation. On cotton plantations, this meant a secure labor force when the crop came in. On sugar plantations, this offered regimented control over the whole factorylike production process. Several ob-

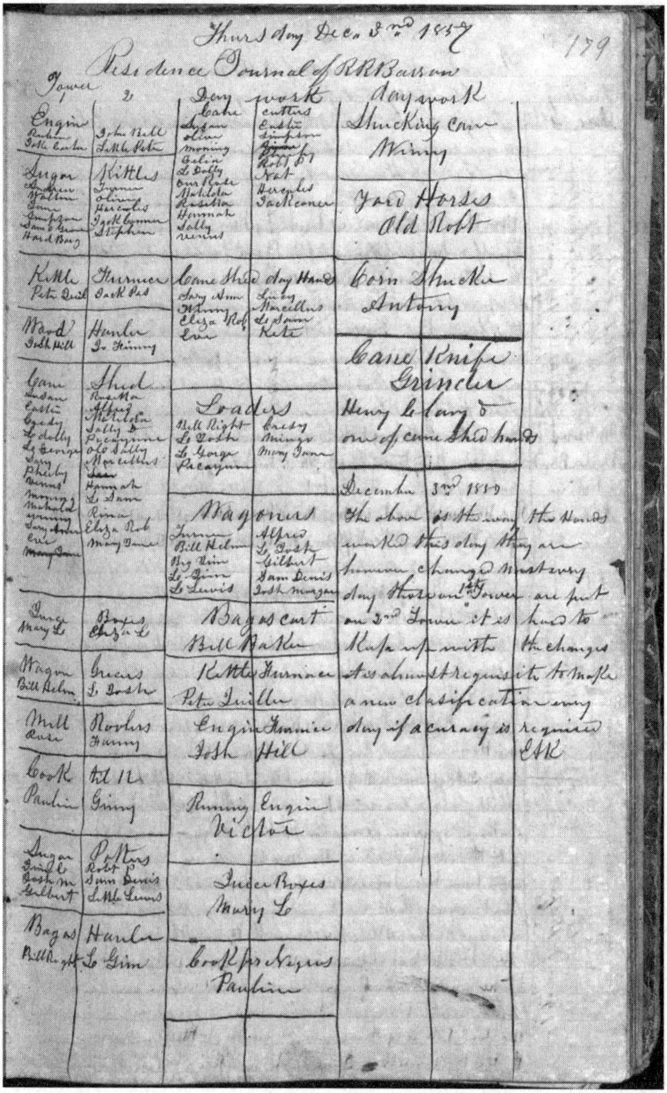

FIGURE 3.4. Classification of Labor on Residence Plantation, 1857. Labor on Residence Plantation was regularly classified and reclassified as the sugar-making season advanced. Courtesy of the Southern Historical Collection, Louis Round Wilson Special Collections Library, University of North Carolina at Chapel Hill.

servers commented on the advantages of superior organization. Timothy Flint explained that one hundred slaves "will accomplish more on one plantation, than so many hired free men, acting at their own discretion."[80] Robert Russell concluded, "Free labor cannot compete, in the manufacture of sugar, with better organized slave labor."[81]

The challenges of turnover were not entirely absent on southern plantations, which often employed free workers as well. Because he had such large holdings and was often absent from the plantation, Barrow employed a manager and a team of overseers. Just managing this small free staff frequently presented problems. Ephraim Knowlton, Barrow's top manager, had charge of production and remained on the plantation throughout the year. However, the overseers below him quit or were fired every few months. In late April, after a disagreement about the livestock, Robert Ford told Knowlton that he planned on "quitting and cease Overseeing," and Barrow told Knowlton to "let him quit." Several months (and another overseer) later, Ford would return. At first Ford seems to have been resigned to follow Barrow's orders, but he quit again after only a few weeks. A man name Gaither quit after thirty-eight days because "he thinks he does not suit Mr B." After Gaither, N. B. Holland arrived. Barrow decided to employ Holland "on trial," but conflicts over scheduling and coordination arose almost immediately.[82]

For enslaved people, the only way to quit was to run away, risking capture and deprivation not only for themselves but for loved ones they left behind. If the law neglected to reach inside the plantation except in the most egregious cases, it did police its boundaries. From the colonial period to the Civil War, slave patrols monitored movement off plantations and enforced pass systems, securing the system of slavery. In some cases, elite masters preferred not to extend too much power to patrollers, restricting their authority on plantations or refusing to write passes for their own slaves. Generally, however, masters supported patrols while also taking steps to make sure that they maintained authority within the boundaries of their plantations. Patrols safeguarded slavery by restricting enslaved mobility, while planters controlled the enslaved within the plantation.[83] On a national scale, planters used the law to protect their authority, with the Fugitive Slave Act of 1850 as the most prominent example. Even when enslaved people took the immense risk of fleeing beyond the state or region of their masters, they were not safe from their authority.[84]

Enslaved people could not quit, but their owners could sell them. Slave-holders used the threat of sale to increase their power. Occasionally statutes limited planters' rights—for example, restricting the sale of children away from their mothers. But even these statutes placed few practical restraints on planters' power. For example, an 1854 Georgia law prohibited the executors and admin-istrators of wills from selling children under the age of five without their mothers. But this restriction only applied if practicable: if a will could not be executed without selling children away from their mothers they could be sold.[85] The threat of sale could be used to extract obedience, even from beyond the grave. The 1861 will of Edward Winning of Saline County, Mis-souri, expressed his aspiration that after his death, his slaves would be allowed to "choose their new homes, and if it could be done to be kept in the family." However, any who became "unmanageable and disobedient" were to be sold or hired as the executor wished.[86]

The plantation worked as a kind of human machine. As one commen-tator wrote in the *Southern Cultivator*, "A plantation might be considered as a piece of machinery; to operate successfully, all its parts should be uniform and exact, and the impelling force regular and steady; and the master . . . should be their impelling force."[87] Reallocation of labor occurred not only in response to changing seasonal labor requirements but also as a result of sickness and injury. When a human cog in the machine became ill, manage-ment could simply rotate him or her to a lighter task. On Barrow's Residence Plantation, this occurred when the hands were struck with measles. Knowlton and Barrow established a "measles gang" to make use of those hands deemed well enough to work. Pregnant women and those with young children were similarly reclassified during confinement and after birth. Barrow's journal records the regular tasks of a "sucklers gang," which would have been com-posed of nursing women.[88] Planters sought to allocate the labor of enslaved people of all ages and capabilities, and they distributed tasks according to strength and ability. The lightest tasks could be assigned to children or to those recovering from illness. Though the nature of work might change over the course of a day, a season, or a life, the expectation was always that labor would continue.[89]

Some of the incentive systems masters employed resembled those used in free labor systems, but planters could be far more intrusive than managers of wage laborers. Not only could they threaten punishment, but they could manipulate almost every aspect of slaves' daily lives—from access to food to housing, clothing, curfew, and contact with children and family. Private and community life could be manipulated to improve production. Evidence of this minute level of control can be found in the ways planters reconfigured plantation life during periods of peak labor. Some adopted centralized kitchens to spare field hands the need to cook during the grinding season. Cooking facilities also enabled overseers and planters to monitor slaves' diets during times when maximum effort was required.[90] The recommendations were part of a larger literature on how food influenced output. Planters debated slaves' consumption in much the same way they considered the addition of marl or guano to southern soils, hypothesizing about what foods and beverages might expedite labor and increase yield. One writer to an agricultural periodical proposed serving coffee with lots of sugar during the winter months,[91] while another recommended refreshing slaves with a blend of water, ginger, and molasses as they toiled in the fields.[92]

Of course, planters' domination had limits. The exigencies of the grinding season gave slaves a modicum of power, and they did what they could to secure better conditions. Slaves might receive Christmas presents, more food, and small sums of money for diligent service.[93] Frederick Law Olmsted observed that on one plantation the slaves seemed to have fewer grievances during the season of hardest labor. The "reason of it evidently is, that they are then better paid; they have better and more varied food and stimulants than usual."[94] But incentive schemes always paid planters better than slaves. As on cotton plantations, planters used bonuses and prizes to stretch out the working day and drive slaves harder during times of peak labor. And the circumstances of slavery meant that planters did not have to pay very much. Slaveholders could buy the diligence of many slaves for a pittance compared to total costs.[95]

Accounting for Control

The language planters used to describe their efforts to improve labor productivity bears a striking resemblance to the late nineteenth-century language of scientific management. In his 1911 classic *The Principles of Scientific Management*, Frederick Winslow Taylor described the goals of his experiments in labor productivity. As he wrote, "Our endeavor was to learn what really constituted a full day's work for a first class man; the best day's work that a man could properly do, year in and year out, and still thrive under."[96] More than half a century earlier, South Carolina planter Plowden C. J. Weston described the fundamental maxim of good management in almost identical terms. As he emphasized in his instructions to his overseers, *"In nothing does a good manager so much excel a bad, as in being able to discern what a hand is capable of doing and in never attempting to make him do more."*[97] Virginia wheat planter Pleasant Suit urged his overseers to use "every means" in their power to understand "what is a day's work for a hand in every variety of plantation business."[98]

The fundamental aim of scientific management was to discern and extract the maximum amount of labor from workers. Managers and owners thought about men and women as inputs of production that could be adjusted and improved in the same manner as machines—and trained and rewarded like animals learning new tricks. When Taylor described the ideal profile of a pig-iron handler, he revealed this mind-set. Those who were "fit to handle pig iron as a regular occupation" should be "so stupid and so phlegmatic" that their mental capacity "more nearly resembles . . . the ox than any other type."[99] The circumstances of slavery lent themselves to a similar mode of thinking. Taylor's "first class men" were seen in a similar light as the "prime hands" who labored in the cotton fields. Taylor and the "college men" he hired to follow them and study their motions thought of them as "first class" only in their ability to perform physical work.[100]

In exceptional cases, the level of observation planters applied to their slaves approached the time and motion studies of scientific management. One particularly striking contribution to the southern agricultural press came from a planter writing under the proto-Taylorist pseudonym "One Who Follows His Hands." In 1848, this unnamed planter wrote two essays titled "A Day's Work." The articles enumerated exactly how much work a prime field hand could complete across an array of tasks. The prime hand could plow 20 to 24 miles (with allowances for turning the plow and team), open furrows for sowing 12 acres of cotton, drop cotton seed across 7 to 10 acres, and haul out 6 to 800 yards; in addition, three "good fellows" could "make a ditch 3 feet wide at top, 2 feet deep, and 2 feet wide at bottom, 220 yards long." In this way, the author continued specifying what constituted "a day's work" across dozens of tasks. Throughout his experiments, he claimed literally to follow his hands, requiring that every hand be closely observed, for "unless he is watched he will not do it."[101]

The essayist appears, at first, to be prone to exaggeration, and perhaps he was. Still, readers took him seriously enough to respond in detail and on his terms. One skeptical reply contributed by "A Voice from the Seaboard" chose to precisely analyze his calculations. "Really, Mr. Editor," he wrote. "Let us take his example in ditching, under the most favorable circumstances. He says—'Three good fellows, somewhat versed in spade &c. can make a ditch three feet wide at top, two feet deep, and two feet wide at bottom, 220 yards long in a day in old land.' Or 3,300 cubic feet (being 1,100 cubic feet apiece). . . . What sort of hands has he . . . ?"[102]

Similar analysis can be found in the *Plantation and Farm Instruction Record and Account Book,* published by J. W. Randolph. The appendix offered task recommendations in a short section on "data in mechanics and rural economy." For example, the author explained that "in plane earth excavations, one man ought to execute each day 10 cubic yards with spade and wheelbarrow, depositing the dirt at any distance within 120 feet." He similarly concluded that a man or boy with a horse and plow could be tasked with about 1 and 1 / 3 acres per day. For him, figuring out labor was simply a matter of multiplication: "given the width of the furrow-slice cut by any plough, the number of hours at work, and the rate at which the team travels per hour," the "surface that such plough and team can plough per day, may be calculated." Ironically, the author's example included a large arithmetical error, but he nonetheless offered it as a general rule. This same author offered further estimates that an active man, "working to the greatest possible advantage," should be able "to raise 10 lbs. 10 feet in a second, for ten hours in a day; or 100 lbs. 1 foot in a second, or 36,000 feet in a day; or 3,600,000 lbs. 1 foot in a day." A good horse could "in general, draw no more up a steep hill than three men can carry." And so he continued, treating men just as he treated horses, and both as he treated machines.[103]

The logic of multiplying human labor out over time again resembles Frederick Winslow Taylor's investigations into scientific management. In *The Principles of Scientific Management,* Taylor described repeated attempts to determine "what fraction of a horse-power a man was able to exert, that is, how many foot-pounds of work a man could do in a day." Through a series of experiments, he concluded that "to our surprise," there was no "constant or uniform relation." In some activities a man could do "not more than one-eighth of a horse-power," but in others he might achieve "a half a horse-power of work." Despite his empirical findings, however, Taylor remained "quite as firmly convinced as ever that some definite clear-cut law existed as to what constitutes a full day's work for a first-class laborer." Eventually, through collaboration with Carl Barth, Taylor would settle on a relationship, if not quite a law. And he would maintain his mechanistic view of human labor as he developed the theory and practice of scientific management.[104]

Taylor's efforts and those of southern planters even appear to share an overlapping heritage. The analysis of the "labor of an active man" included in Randolph's plantation journal appears to come from an 1814 book by Scottish civil engineer Robertson Buchanan. Buchanan's work was also a source for Julius Weisbach's *Principles of the Mechanics of Machinery and Engineering,* a chapter of which appeared in a textbook used at the Stevens Institute of Technology while Taylor was in residence.[105] Just as in the late eighteenth- and early nineteenth-century West Indies, management advice sometimes circulated widely, even crossing oceans and moving between economies based on free labor and those based on slavery. Though slavery's "scientific management" does not appear to have any direct influence on the system that would later go by that name, both were embedded in broader networks of managerial expertise. Both reflected the same mechanistic view of human labor, and both relied on the belief that careful observation would reveal the physical laws that governed maximum output.[106]

Southern blank books spread innovative, comprehensive accounting systems. Books like Thomas Affleck's were remarkably precise and specialized, and planters used them both to monitor the activities of overseers and to extract maximum effort from enslaved people. Among the many kinds of records contained in these journals, planters focused by far the most attention on the records of cotton picking. Planters used these forms to track the number of pounds picked by each individual slave every day. They recorded thousands of data points, tracking productivity with a level of precision that would not be regularly attained in northern factories until the late nineteenth century with the rise of scientific management. They wove this data together with violence to accelerate the pace of labor, enabling planters to grow more cotton and thus to earn higher profits.

Though slave-by-slave records of cotton picking are in many ways the most impressive artifacts of plantation data practices, they were only one piece of a larger system of experimentation and innovation. Carefully kept records helped planters to increase their output through a variety of agricultural innovations ranging from new seeds to fertilizers. These new technologies made it possible for enslaved people to pick more cotton, and assiduously collected data helped planters to reset their expectations and to design incentive systems (of small rewards and brutal punishments) to drive enslaved laborers to reach new frontiers of productivity. Enslaved people sometimes slowed the pace of work in an attempt to thwart this speedup, but careful records limited their success. The constant surveillance of the scale made both overages and shortfalls perilous. Slaveholders' control guaranteed them a steady supply of labor. Though they were not monoculturists, they were obsessed with growing as much cotton and sugar as possible, and their domination of enslaved people made it profitable to sow larger crops because they could be assured of labor at harvest time.

Systematic accounting practices thrived on antebellum plantations—not despite slavery but because of it. The soft power of numbers complemented the intimidation of the whip and the threat of sale. Planters blended innovation, information, and violence as they drove up the pace of labor, conducted experiments, and distributed incentives. On the pages of account books, the power of masters over slaves transformed men and women into units of labor power, labor power into bales of cotton, and cotton into profit. Chapter 4 turns to a complementary set of calculations—of enslaved people's value as capital. Here planters estimated not just how much work people could be expected to perform, but how much they were worth on the market as tradable assets. Of course, the transformation of enslaved people into units of labor and units of capital was never complete; the complexity and humanity of individual people constantly subverted full commodification. But planters advanced remarkably far in their efforts to capitalize human lives.

4

Human Capital

VALUING LIVES IN THE ANTEBELLUM SOUTH

I N 1856, TWELVE BABIES were born on Canebrake Plantation in Adams County, Mississippi: six boys and six girls. The first, Kate, arrived on January 21, born to Beck, age thirty. The last came just before the New Year—Jenny, born to Susan, age twenty-three, on December 29. One, a baby girl born to Peggy on November 12, did not survive the month. If she received a name, we do not know it. But the rest lived long enough to be entered into the inventory of lives for the following year. There, Canebrake's proprietor, James Green Carson, noted their names, ages, and values. He priced each baby at $25 except for Kate. He rounded her age up to one and set her value at $75. Thus, the births of 1856 became $325 in human capital at the beginning of 1857. Many years before he would begin to measure their labor, Carson had already entered them into his account books as capital.[1]

Chapter 3 described the ways planters attempted to accelerate the pace of labor from day to day, keeping detailed records in order to determine how much work their slaves could perform and to pushing them to achieve this maximum. But slavery also offered another kind of profit: capital appreciation. Slaves were, quite literally, human capital, whose value could appreciate through maturation, reproduction, and health or depreciate due to illness, age, and disobedience. Slaveholders' calculations show that they were keenly aware of the impact of human processes on profits and losses, and they attempted to manipulate enslaved lives to increase their earnings. Where Chapter 3 examined planters' efforts to quantify output, this chapter explores their efforts to estimate and maximize the value of men and women themselves.[2]

In their attempts to value and price human capital, planters, southern industrialists, and slave traders estimated the value of the enslaved in many different ways. They began to speak the language of "depreciation" decades before it would become a common accounting technique, evaluating lives in much the same way that the railroads were beginning to value trains and tracks. Slave traders and auctioneers printed price lists and advertisements, grading slaves into standard categories. These schemes treated the enslaved like the commodities they grew, attempting to attribute value without reference to specific individuals. Of course, where labor was also capital, accounting for the two often overlapped. Slaveholders' system of "prime hands" rated men, women, and children on a fractional scale that could be used both to assign daily labor and to estimate market value.

Though not all of these genres of calculation were widespread, they reached a large audience through politics. Data on the massive market capitalization of enslaved property appeared in speeches and pamphlets defending slavery and eventually arguing for Southern secession. As war threatened and enslaved people sought their freedom, it became clearer than ever that politics and power were as important as management practices to the preservation of enslaved property. Though slaveholders' careful calculations suggested that prices were efficient and correct, beneath their rationalizing patina was the fundamental reality that property was political—especially property in people.

Depreciating Lives

James Green Carson began every year by taking an inventory. First he listed each man, woman, and child, noting the age and sex of each (see Figure 4.1 for the first page). Though he had no immediate plans to sell any of them, he also made estimates of their prices. In 1857, there were 151 entries. The most valuable, Thomas, Carson rated at $1,200. The eldest, Hercules, Sawney, Sue D, and Sophy, he valued at $00. Between fifty-six and seventy-five years old,

they were past the point of profitable labor. The rest fell somewhere in between: Aaron, age twenty-one he rated at $800; Eliza, age five, $175; Edward,
age two, $100; Lucinda, age fifty-two, $450; James, age forty-one, $800. Sum-
ming the values, Carson found that he had a total of $59,450 invested in
human capital.[3] Inventories like Carson's were planters' most basic tool for
measuring and monitoring their human capital, and they had been relatively
common since at least the mid-eighteenth century.[4] Early inventories were
little more than lists of names, but they sometimes included details like age,
occupation, sex, health, and family relationships. By the late antebellum period (and sometimes earlier), planters regularly included estimates of value.[5]

Within this framework of monetized human life, any change in a slave's
value was a change in a master's capital. Carson recorded his annual inventories on Form I from Thomas Affleck's *Cotton Plantation Record and Account
Book*. Affleck's journals, described in detail in Chapter 3, facilitated plantation accounting by combining a wide range of blank forms in a single volume.
Using these journals, planters could keep sophisticated records simply by
filling in the blanks. Affleck titled the annual inventory "The Planter's Annual Record of his Negroes." A competing volume printed by J. W. Randolph
in Virginia titled the list more plainly: the "Inventory of Negroes."[6]

Both Affleck's and Randolph's journals instructed planters to take an inventory at the beginning and the end of the year so that they could track
changes in their capital. Comparing these inventories helped planters measure the "appreciation" or "depreciation" of their human investments. As Affleck wrote, the balance sheet "is charge-able . . . with any depreciation in
the value of the negroes, occasioned by overwork and improper management." By contrast, if "the strength and usefulness of the old [has] been sustained by kind treatment and care; the youngsters taught to be useful, and
perhaps some of the men instructed in trades, and the women in house manufactures, the increased value of the entire force will form a handsome addition to the side of *profits*."[7]

Following these instructions, James Green Carson repeated the process
of valuation at the end of the year (Figure 4.1). He accounted for the increasing
value of the young people, noted the declining value of the elderly, and wrote
down the value of lives lost. In 1857, there were three deaths: two more of
the babies born the prior year, and Richmond, a boy of eight. Nonetheless,
Carson likely reflected on the columns of numbers with satisfaction. Tallied

116

THE PLANTER'S ANNUAL RECORD of his NEGROES upon Plantation, made at the commencement and at the close of the year 185_

Children under 1 year of age $25 ... more ... $75 ... for each additional year up to 10, $325—

	MALES					FEMALES			
	NAME	Age.	Value at commencement of the Year.	Value at end of the Year.		NAME	Age.	Value at commencement of the Year.	Value at end of the Year.
1	Fish	5?	600	600	1	Sue L	54	600	600
2	Henry x	37	800	800	2	Louisa	35	600	600
3	Bob	12	450	500	3	Peggy	55	100	100
4	Rolla	5	175	200	4	Milly	20	600	600
5	Edward	2	100	125	5	Sue J	22	600	600
6	Baptly	61	400	400	6	Lydia	2	100	125
7	Charley	25	800	800	7	Florinta x	33	570	550
8	Fisher	13	500	600	8	Finah	10	300	350
9	Sam	30	800	800	9	Beck	31	600	600
10	Sure B	38	900	800	10	Kate	1	75	100
11	Sure I	10	300	350	11	Amy	32	600	600
12	Joe	8	250	275	12	Jenny	58	800	300
13	Nathaniel	2	100	125	13	Amelia	13	450	600
14	Isaac	32	800	800	14	Shina	57	100	100
15	George	8	25	75	15	Sophaline	34	600	600
16	Peter	17	800	800	16	Cynthia	15	650	600
17	Sam	14	550	650	17	Affee	10	300	350
18	Scott	8	250	275	18	Phillis	9	225	250

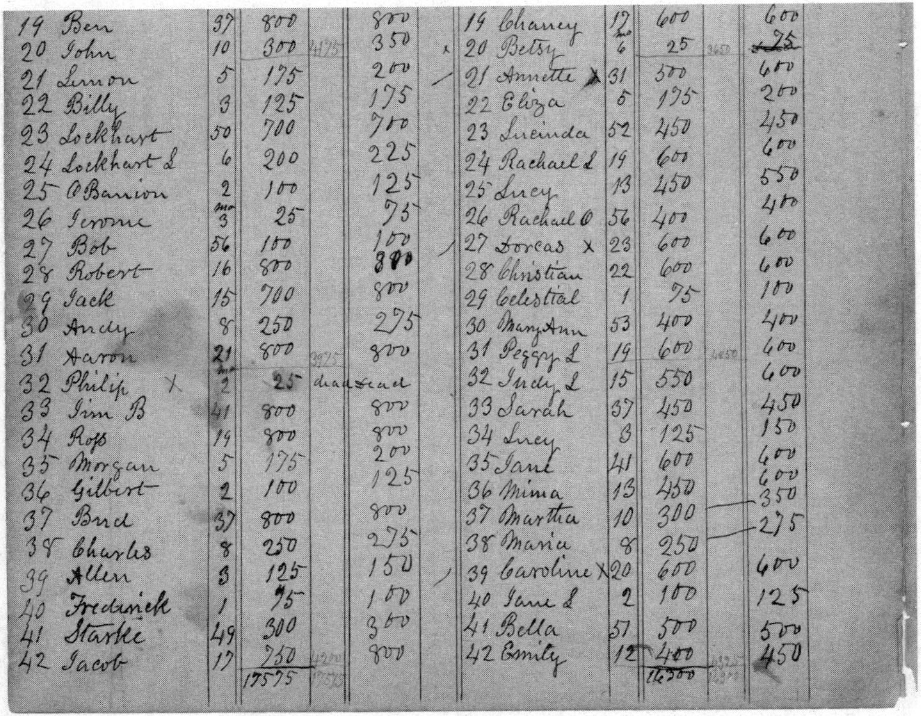

FIGURE 4.1. "Form I," Inventory of Lives on Canebrake Plantation, 1857. James Green Carson's inventory recorded the value of his human capital at the beginning and the end of the year. Above the inventory, he included specific instructions on how he valued children: "Children under 1 year old $25," "children over 1 year old $75," and "for each additional year up to 10, $25." James Green Carson, Record Book, 1857. Recorded in Thomas Affleck's Plantation Record and Account Book. Cane Brake Plantation Records, 1856–1858 (di_11072), Box 2B177. Courtesy of Dolph Briscoe Center for American History, University of Texas at Austin.

up, the end-of-year values came to $62,675, a gain of $3,225—more than 5 percent over the prior year. Records from the following years suggest that these results were high, but not unusually so.[8]

The prices attached to enslaved people changed for many reasons: age, sickness or health, the acquisition of skill, and changes in the market. Carson strove to be systematic in his valuations, and he noted his method for pricing children in the margin of his inventories. Babies "under 1 year old" were valued at $25, those over a year at $75, and "for each additional year up to 10," he added $25 to the total. Older children's prices increased more rapidly as they approached prime age, around fifteen to seventeen years old. At this peak, Carson appraised most of the men at $800 and the women at around $600, values they might retain until their mid-forties, when they began to decline in value. Plotted on a graph and viewed from a distance, Carson's data produces a neat picture. Figure 4.2 shows the prices from the beginning of 1857, divided by sex and plotted by age. The neatly advancing arcs of men and women suggest predictability—particularly below the age of ten, when Carson used his formula to estimate value. But the scatter of dots also reflects the complexity of the act of valuation and the diversity of the individual men and women being valued.[9]

Pricing lives was an alternation between the twin poles of standardization and individuality. Prices reflect standardization but also diversity and idiosyncrasy. For example, thirty-one-year-old Annette's value increased by $100 over the course of 1857.[10] The only clue to the cause is the birth of a baby in November—perhaps the added value recognized her fertility. Or, take Frank and Ephraim, both eleven years old at the beginning of 1856. Their values had advanced in lockstep from birth, and at the beginning of the year, each was priced at $350. By the end of the year, however, Frank's value had leapt to $450 compared to Ephraim's at $400. Perhaps Ephraim was injured, or his owner judged him disobedient. Maybe Frank was simply taller and stronger. Over time, the disparity grew: five years later, Ephraim was still priced at $400, whereas Frank's value had increased to $700.[11] The dual reality of slaves' commodification and their individuality is visible in Figure 4.2. The data points are a spray of values, but they cluster around a general pattern. Efforts to rationalize and commodify played out in the aggregate: even as each data point reflected individual circumstances, taken together they populated predictable curves.

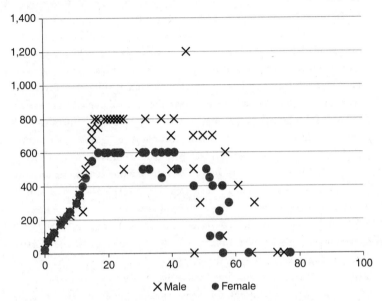

FIGURE 4.2. Valuations for Enslaved People on Canebrake Plantation by Age and Sex, 1857. Up to age ten, enslaved boys and girls were valued along a standard line. Adult valuations varied dramatically, reflecting individuals' health, strength, skills, and temperament.

From a business history perspective, the calculation of depreciation may be the single most remarkable aspect of plantation accounting. Widely regarded as a landmark in the advancement of management practices, depreciation involves allocating capital costs over the useful lifetime of an asset.[12] Affleck's methods comprise a hybrid of what we now call "mark-to-market" and "straight-line" methods of calculating depreciation. When planters assessed the value of men, women, and children, they were in a sense "marking them to market"—making an assessment of their likely prices were they to be put up for sale. They adjusted the value of their chattel with swings in the market. In practice, however, some planters combined this with something closer to a straight-line method. In modern straight-line depreciation, the value of an asset is marked down in equal annual increments over its useful life. James Green Carson's method of calculating appreciation looks like the inverse of this method. He increased the value of children by an even $25 per year, smoothing their impact on his capital stock.

Plantations were not the only southern businesses to prepare inventories of lives. At least as early as 1833, the South Carolina Canal and Rail Road Company included the value of slaves in its annual report. By the late 1840s, the South Carolina Railroad Company entered the enslaved as capital on its annual balance sheet. And by the mid-1850s, scattered mentions had given way to systematic reporting. At the end of 1857, the railroad owned eighty-seven hands, valued at $76,238.49. The manager preparing the report took this value from an inventory of slaves included in the report (see Figure 4.3). Each entry includes the name of the enslaved person, the date of purchase (from April 1836 through December 1857), from whom he or she was purchased, and the cost. The railroad's inventory of names very closely resembled—albeit in simplified form—the inventories of engines a few pages later.[13]

The logic for calculating depreciation on slave plantations parallels the reasons managers adopted the practice in factories and railroads. Historians of accounting typically connect the emergence of depreciation with increased investment in complex, long-lived assets like railroad cars and tracks. The high capital costs of these investments required managers to distribute costs over time in order to calculate profits and set prices. Planters saw the value of the enslaved in similar terms. Their value as capital evolved over the course of their lifetimes, making them as important a source of profit or loss as the commodities they grew. Ownership of slaves' productive potential—from day to day, season to season, year to year, and generation to generation—made depreciation useful. That is, understanding enslaved people as complex, long-lived capital assets made owners aware of the complexity of measuring their value.[14]

Put differently, without considering depreciation, both railroads and plantations risked bringing in enough to cover their operating costs but actually losing money over the long run. Once a track and trains were built, the variable costs of moving a load of freight down the line were very low. However, selling at rates that merely exceeded variable costs (like fuel) ignored capital costs as well as ongoing expenses like wear and tear on the road and cars. In the same way, a planter who brought in more than he spent might actually be losing money due to the falling value of lives or land. Not all southern planters understood this danger. A commentator on the Panic of 1837 criticized those who were content to be making "what is called a support"—that is, when "plantations require no outlay over and above the money they make."

No.	Name of Negroes.	Date of Purchase.	From whom purchased.	Cost.
	Brought forward..............................			$42,920 00
53	Edmund Brownlee.....	April,	1852	J. C. Sproull & Co......	912 25
54	Stephen Garmany......	"	"	"	922 50
55	Aaron Gaskins........	"	"	"	917 37
56	Ned Larkin...........	"	"	"	660 12
57	Nelson Skinner........	"	"	"	963 50
58	Ben Cothran..........	"	"	"	871 25
59	Andrew Jackson......	May	"	F. Schwartz...........	860 00
60	Ben.................	August,	1853	N. Calderbank........	1,050 00
61	Isaac.....	Dec'r,	1853	Jos. L. Inabinet.......	1,000 00
62	Robert	March,	1854	J.J. Chisolm & J. Bryan, T's of Mrs. C. L.Chisolm.	1,101 00
63	Bob........	April,	1854	Est. Geo. F. Raworth..	850 00
64	Markly.....	"	"	do.	850 00
65	Peter...............	"	"	Warren Wells.........	1,000 00
66	Philip...............	May,	1854.	do.	900 00
67	Austin..............	Dec'r,	1854	Nathan Calderbank ...	900 00
68	Bill.................	"	"	T. J. Robertson	1,000 00
69	Harry	March,	1855	Samuel George........	1,010 50
70	William.............	July,	1855	James Coward........	1,000 00
71	Abram..............	"	"	Mrs. M. E. Purse	900 00
72	Crockett............	"	"	E. M. Gilbert........	1,000 00
73	Tom...............	Sept'r,	1855	James Coward........	900 00
74	Jim.................	Nov.,	1855	Jacob H. Wells........	1,000 00
75	Levi................	"	"	do.	1,000 00
76	Daniel	"	"	C. T. Scaife.........	1,000 00
77	Andrew	"	"	do.	1,000 00
78	Adam...............	Jan.,	1856.	H. E. Walpole........	900 00
79	Pompey.............	April,	1856	Thos. P. Smith.......	700 00
80	Ben...	"	"	George P. Elliott	1,200 00
81	John...............	Jan.,	1857	Dr. M. C. King........	1,200 00
82	Jim.................	"	"	E. W. Bancroft.......	800 00
83	Peter...............	February,	1857	W. J. Magrath........	900 00
84	Alexander...........	"	"	do.	1,000 00
85	Andrew.............	"	"	S. Kingman...........	800 00
86	Davy...............	April,	1857	D. A. Ambler..........	1,050 00
87	Maurice.............	Dec.,	1857	B. S. Gibbs, Trustee...	1,200 00
				$76,238 49

FIGURE 4.3. Inventory of Enslaved Capital for the South Carolina Railroad Company, 1857. The South Carolina Railroad Company included a record of enslaved people in its annual report. This report listed values at purchase price rather than appreciating or depreciating them from year to year, although elsewhere the report makes adjustments for new purchases and loss of life. *Annual Reports of the President and Directors and the General Superintendent of the South Carolina Railroad Company, for the Year Ending 31st December, 1857* (Charleston, SC: Walker, Evans & Co., 1858).

In these cases, he argued, the planters were overlooking "the loss of interest on the capital employed, and the depreciation of value in lands and negroes by use."[15]

Failing to calculate appreciation could cause planters to underestimate their profits. If James Green Carson had failed to construct inventories, he would have overlooked the not insignificant profits he was earning from reproduction. American planters had been benefiting from these profits for generations. Half a century earlier, Thomas Jefferson calculated the supplemental income he earned from the reproduction of his slaves. In 1792, while recounting the profits of the prior year in a letter to George Washington, he relayed his estimates, explaining that—in addition to his usual business—he was earning a 4 percent profit through the birth of children. Jefferson later offered an even more generous projection of the possibilities for "silent profit," recommending that a family in financial distress lay out "every farthing . . . in land and negroes, which besides a present support bring a silent profit of from 5. to 10. per cent."[16]

Summarizing inquiries from across the South, British traveler and naturalist Robert Russell offered a range for the returns from reproduction, estimating that planters earned "from two to six percent throughout the cotton region." As he explained, there were two ways to think about this level of profit. On the one hand, the "breeding of slaves could, under no conceivable circumstances, be profitable on its own account." After all, as he explained, it was "scarcely equal to the ordinary rate of interest of money." On the other hand, combined with the production of staple crops, such an increase could substantially add to profits. Through this lens, the value was very high. A rate of return that "almost amounts to the interest of the capital invested" made slave labor effectively "free."[17]

The question of slave "breeding" or "raising" has long generated controversy among both historians and economists. An earlier generation of scholars found very limited evidence of deliberate slave breeding as a stand-alone business.[18] But this research approached the question too narrowly. Planters did not think about "increase" as a solitary business enterprise, nor did it make sense for them to do so; rather, they calculated that reproduction would earn a profit in combination with other kinds of exploitation. More recently, scholars have argued for a broader definition of "breeding" that incorporates experiences recounted by former slaves. A broader definition would account for the myriad ways that masters violated enslaved people, including rape, rules about marriage practices, and family separation. In the space between outright breeding and adequate respect for private lives, planters constantly intruded. Though they may not have frequently remarked on the profits to be earned from violating intimate relationships, they were augmenting the value of their human capital at the same time that they drove enslaved people to earn more immediate profits.[19]

Even Thomas Affleck, accountant and nurseryman, styled himself an expert on matters of reproduction, offering recommendations on how long mothers should be allowed to nurse their children. He advised that bond-women breastfeed for nine months, an interval that historian Richard Follett points out would have limited lactational amenorrhea—the period of reduced fertility that accompanies extended breastfeeding. Separated from their nursing children for extended periods, women quickly returned to fertility.[20] Though planters may not have stated this goal, their influence—intentional or not—can be seen in the extent to which reproduction varied by crop. In the harsher labor regime of sugar, where women joined in punishing labor shortly after giving birth, they also conceived again sooner. Female slaves on sugar plantations experienced a birth interval between nine and ten months shorter than that of enslaved women in cotton country.[21] Of course, there were limits to planters' control. Follett argues that slave women often disobeyed orders to cease breastfeeding and that some used other modes of preventing pregnancy. But even when women chose to continue nursing their children against planters' wishes, their regimented schedules would have reduced lactation's contraceptive effects.[22]

Though planters' frequent and often violent efforts to manipulate reproductive life surely paid well over the long run, calculating appreciation and depreciation could be misleading in the short term. Just as "earning a support" might obscure lost capital, planters' optimistic calculations of appreciation due to the increase of slaves could conceal losses in other areas. In 1850, cotton planter Eli Capell completed every form in Affleck's journal, including the balance sheet. At the end of the year, his calculations showed a profit of approximately $10,000. But this profit reflected appreciation in the value of slaves and stock, not the sale of cotton. On Form I, where he had inventoried his slaves, Capell's calculation showed an increase of more than $13,000 in human capital (see Figure 4.4). But absent any intention to sell his

94   **I**

THE PLANTER'S ANNUAL RECORD *of his Negroes upon* Pleasant Hill

Plantation, *during the year* 1850   E. J. Capell   Overseer.

MALES.				FEMALES.			
NAME.	Age.	Value at commencement of the year.	Value at end of the year.	NAME.	Age.	Value at commencement of the year.	Value at end of the year.
John	70	850 00	75 00	Hannah	60	100 00	125
Tone	49	1000 00	1200 00	Mary	34	800 00	900
Sandy	38	600 00	800 00	Fanny	23	800 00	900
Edmund	45	1000 00	1300 00	Rachel Sen	32	675 00	750
Piney	40	700 00	950 00	Martha	27	675 00	700
Solomon	38	700 00	950 00	Celia	28	675 00	750
Peter		700 00	950 00	Rachel Jun	24	675 00	750
Isaac	30	700 00	950 00	Diana	31	600 00	700
Anthony	25	800 00	950 00	Chany	32	600 00	675
Scott	25	800 00	950 00	Lucy	28	600 00	750
George	20	750 00	1000 00	Set	28	650 00	650
Lim	37	800 00	950	Azaline	13	600 00	700
Dotson	20	700 00	900	Amanda	13	400 00	600
Bill	18	700 00	900	Sarah	9	350 00	450
William	24	1000 00	1200	Harriet	8	300 00	400
Charle	10	500 00	650	Bet	7	350 00	400
Henry	9	375 00	400	Hannah	7	350 00	450
Henderson	8	300 00	350	Maryan	7	275 00	300
Johnson	6	250 00	275	Ellen	6	200 00	350
Stephen	4	250 00	225	Louisa	5	175 00	200
Tom	5	250 00	275	Susan	4	200 00	250
Monroe	4	200 00	225	Melissa	3	100 00	125
Daniel	2	150 00	175	Matilda	5	200 00	225
Sim	2	150 00	175	Ginny	3	150 00	150
Aaron	3	175 00	200	Caroline	3	150 00	150
Ferry	1	75 00	100	Frances	2	100 00	125
		9625 00	11675 00	Laura	1	100 00	125
				Amarintha	1	75 00	100
				Saraan	6m	75 00	100
				Rose	6m	75 00	100
						10975 00	12850
				Ann			100
				Delia			100
							13050

slaves or tools, the surplus was deceptive. Perhaps Capell could have used it to secure a loan, but otherwise the profits he realized on paper did not match his cash in hand. For all practical purposes, he was in the red.[23]

Confronted with this mismatch between his calculations and his experience, Capell changed his accounting practices. In 1851, he skipped the calculation of depreciation. He still recorded the value of each person he enslaved on Form I, but at the end of the year, he left the second column blank, choosing not to sum up the change in the overall value of his human chattel. He still cared about the evolving prices of his capital. At the beginning of the following year he recorded each slave's adjusted value in a new book, so he had everything he would have needed to calculate depreciation at his fingertips. But he chose to focus his attention on day-to-day productivity, something over which he exercised more control. Slaves' appraised value could rise and fall due to factors within the planter's influence: health or sickness, increased skill, or disobedience. But price could also swing wildly as the market changed, a force beyond the control of any planter, if no less important to his bottom line.[24] Scholars who are critical of slaveholders' business practices have sometimes pointed out that planters did not often calculate their annual profits. This is true, but it should not necessarily be seen as evidence of poor management. Rather, planters concentrated their efforts on tracking data that was immediately useful. Metrics like the amount of cotton picked and baled actually helped them to earn more money in the short term. Men like Capell were well aware of the potential profits to be earned from capital increase, but calculating these profits was useful only occasionally.[25]

Plantation inventories could be useful for plantation operations, but planters likely prepared them for broader audiences as well: banks, slave traders, and others who might lend them money. While records of cotton picking focused on questions of internal productivity—highlighting relationships between masters, overseers, and slaves—valuations in dollars reflected

FIGURE 4.4. Inventory of Enslaved People, Pleasant Hill Plantation, 1850. Eli Capell filled in prices for the beginning and end of the year and used them to calculate the appreciation and depreciation of individual slaves as well as his entire slave force. He would later abandon the calculations. Pleasant Hill Plantation Record and Account Book, 1850. Capell Family Papers (Mss. 56, v. 15). Courtesy of Louisiana and Lower Mississippi Valley Collections, Louisiana State University Libraries, Baton Rouge, Louisiana.

concern with and performance for the outside world. The inventories of lives prepared by southern slaveholders would have helped them to secure loans in at least two ways. One was partly performative—planters seeking loans could produce neatly kept books as evidence of careful business practices and past returns. Scholars of accounting have long argued that well-kept ledgers and journals helped slaveholders to project an image of credibility and authority. Carefully kept records could augment a reputation for thrift and care in business, and a good reputation could help secure a loan.[26]

Beyond improving planters' reputations, inventories could also be used to identify the value of specific enslaved people who could serve as collateral for loans. Mortgages secured by human collateral were common. Drawing on a large sample of southern loans, historian Bonnie Martin has recently shown that approximately 40 percent of mortgages from both the colonial period and the nineteenth century were secured by slaves. Moreover, these mortgages tended to be larger than average, securing more than 60 percent of all credit in both periods.[27] Most mortgages operated in one of two ways, both of which parallel the operation of modern housing markets. In the first, an enslaved person might serve as collateral for his or her own sale. Buyers with only a small amount of cash could use it as a down payment on a more valuable slave. As Martin explains, when purchasing a slave, "buyers made a down payment, promised to pay the rest of the price plus interest in install-ments, and used the same slaves they were buying as collateral for the loan. The seller kept legal title . . . similar to rights a bank keeps today on a home mortgage."[28] Inventories would have been even more useful in helping planters secure a second type of loan, similar to a home equity loan today. In these cases, those who wanted to buy additional slaves or land used slaves they already owned as collateral. These owners thus "made liquid and usable the savings invested in their human property without having to sell that property."[29]

Enslaved capital helped expand southern financial networks, offering pos-sibilities that other large capital investments, such as land and buildings, could not. In comparison to land, human bodies were liquid and mobile, of-fering a more flexible basis for credit. Southern planters enjoyed an array of financial opportunities unavailable to northern farmers: "Slaves represented a huge store of highly liquid wealth that ensured the financial stability and viability of planting operations even after a succession of bad harvests, years of low prices, or both."[30] Inventories offered a simple information technology for manipulating this flexible form of human capital, enabling it to compound in multiple ways simultaneously. They tracked the birth of children and the appreciation of enslaved populations. By documenting this growing capital inventories made it easier to secure loans to buy land, seed, livestock, and more lives. In some cases, issuers of mortgages based on human collateral even issued bonds based on these mortgages—securitizing assets based on enslaved wealth for sale across the United States and abroad.[31]

The language of depreciation can be found in court records, which reflect some of the many reasons why human capital fluctuated. Health and age were among the most common causes of lost value. In Franklin County, Virginia, Abram Childress asked the court for permission to sell two slaves on behalf of his wards to guard against "depreciation, natural to slaves in the decline of life."[32] In Louisiana, Thomas Couch petitioned for damages after discovering that the sixteen-year-old girl he had purchased was afflicted with "syphilis" or "Gonorrhoea." Couch argued that the seller concealed the illness and sought $500 compensation for the cost of a physician and the "depreciation" in her value.[33]

Enslaved people also depreciated when they ran for freedom. In 1854, Dr. Henry Daret sued the captain of the steamship, *Eldorado*, which had carried a family of enslaved people as they attempted to escape from him. Enos and Phillis, and their children, Rosette and Perrine, were arrested on board the ship. Though they were captured and returned to their owner, the father, Enos, was not as valuable as he had been before running away. Daret sought $400 in damages for "depreciation of the value of the said slave." Before his escape, he had been worth "fully $1000 to $1200," but after, he was not worth "more than one half of the amount . . . from the fact of having run away." Daret advertised Enos for sale at $1,000, but he only brought $600.[34] In a similar petition from 1840, Francois Barthelemy LeBeau sought compensation from the owners of the ship *Tecumseh*, which he believed had harbored his property, Harrison and Aimee, as they ran for freedom. LeBeau demanded that the ship "be seized and sold" to compensate him for the "depreciation on his slaves" as well as the property they had taken.[35]

Enslaved men and women facing sale sometimes used the terminology of "depreciation" to describe changes in their own value. Recounting his own sale for $1,000—$500 less than his previous price—Solomon Northup speculated that perhaps "the small pox had depreciated our value."[36] Henry Bibb remarked that in 1839 he was sold to a Louisville, Kentucky, slave trader "at a depreciated price because I was a runaway."[37] Historian Daina Ramey Berry has recently offered a rich account of how slaves were priced and sold over the life cycle—from before birth to beyond the grave when cadavers were sometimes sold for medical experiments. Berry uses the phrase "soul value" to denote what could not be priced—the "self worth of enslaved people." Her work reflects on what enslaved people actually made of their situation. For some, "no monetary value could allow them to comply with slavery. Others, weakened by enslavement, negotiated certain levels of commodification to survive their experience. Still others were socially dead." In all of these cases, the value of the soul could not be rated in dollars.[38]

Soul value and market value did not move in tandem—sometimes they moved in opposition. In Josephine Brown's account of her father's life in slavery, she reflected on the relationship between freedom and depreciation: "As the slave becomes enlightened, and shows that he knows he has a right to be free, his value depreciates. A slave who has once ran away is shunned by the slaveholders, just as the wild, unruly horse is shunned by those who wish an animal for trusty service."[39] Escape (or evidence of an attempt) could dramatically depreciate a slave's market value. But the costs for enslaved people were incredibly high. Whenever they could, sellers concealed slaves' efforts to escape. Jacob D. Green described his master explaining to him that he would take "that collar off your neck, not because I think that you are sufficiently punished, but because there are some gentlemen coming . . . and they want to purchase some negroes . . . and mind you don't tell them that ever you ran away, for if you do none of them will buy you."[40] Sometimes slaveholders responded to attempted escape by selling recaptured slaves away from local communities where their actions were well known. Although William Wells Brown—Josephine's father—would eventually claim his freedom, his daughter noted that most of those who were caught were "pretty sure of being sold and sent off to the cotton, sugar, or rice fields of Georgia, or other slave-consuming States."[41]

Running away was, of course, only one dramatic example of how behavior could drive market price. Enslaved people were well aware of the ways they could influence their own prices, and some sought to augment or undercut their own value in order to influence sales.[42] Sometimes, how-

ever, comportment, personality, and attire could not conceal the truth. Enslaved people wore the evidence of escape on their bodies. Isaac D. Williams
described being examined after his capture. The doctor counted "twenty-nine
shot in my right arm and forty in my right leg" and criticized my captors,
"not . . . on the grounds of humanity" but "because we had depreciated in
value, being not so marketable."[43]

Grading Lives

Slave traders approached valuation from a shorter-term perspective than
owners. Planters prepared inventories so that they could understand and
compare the evolving value of their investments over the long term. By contrast, for slave traders, inventory was meant to be turned—that is, the faster
they could buy and sell, the more quickly they could use and reuse their capital.[44] The preparation of price lists reflects this reality. These lists attached
value not to individual men, women, and children but to a set of categories,
or "grades." In price lists, the standard subsumed the individual.

The Richmond, Virginia, firm of Betts & Gregory used standardized
price lists to share up-to-date market data whenever it received an inquiry
from a potential customer (see Figure 4.5). These price lists took the form of
a pre-formatted letter, the auctioneer's equivalent of Thomas Affleck's fill-
in-the-blank account books. The letter opened "Dear Sir: We beg leave to give
you the state of our Negro Market, and quote them as follows." Below this
opening, the firm listed a range of categories. At the top of this list were the
three categories of men: "Extra" (presumably for extraordinary or extra fine),
"No. 1 do." (likely the equivalent of a prime or full hand), and "Second rate
or Ordinary do." Below these were the same categories for women and for
boys priced by height (in 3-inch increments up to 5 feet tall). Girls "of same
height of boys" were being sold for "about the same prices." To the right of
each category, the form offered space for price ranges, which the traders could
fill in by hand. For example, on January 5, 1861, "Extra Men" were being sold
for $950–$1,000, while boys 4 feet tall were priced at $275–$300. At the bottom
of the page was a space for additional notations about special categories
or the state of the market. In this sample, Betts & Gregory noted that a
"Good young woman and first child" would fetch $850–$900. This higher
price ("Extra" women were being sold for $800–$850) recognized the value

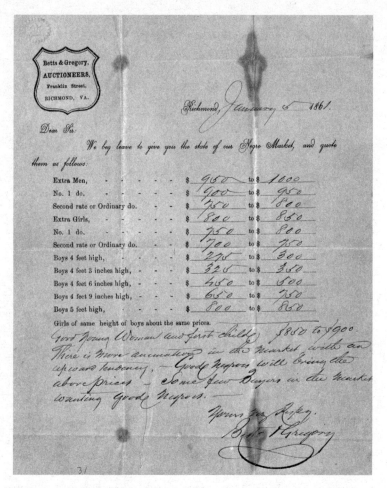

FIGURE 4.5. Pricing Lives by Height and Sex, January 5, 1861. The auction house Betts & Gregory advertised prices using standardized grades that resembled those used to rate commodities like grain and cotton. Below these grades they described pricing in special circumstances, such as the sale of a mother with her first child, here advertised at "$850–900." American Slavery Documents Collection (RL.11093), Box 2, Folder 36. Courtesy of David M. Rubenstein Rare Book & Manuscript Collection, Duke University, Durham, North Carolina.

of the infant as well as the mother's fertility. But such values were only slightly higher because of the time the mother would spend caring for her child and the long period before that child could begin to work.[45]

Betts & Gregory's price lists resembled the commodity grading schemes that were emerging elsewhere in the American economy during the mid-nineteenth century. Just as the grading of wheat turned the diverse crops of myriad farmers into a "golden stream of grain," the grading of men and women into price categories and fractional hands attempted to render them as fungible inputs of production.[46] Near identical language was used to categorize slaves and agricultural crops like grain and cotton. For example, in labeling men and women as "Extra," "No. 1," and "No. 2," the auctioneers followed conventions that were being used for other commodities. In its first annual report (for 1858), the Chicago Board of Trade described the categories used to grade wheat, corn, oats, rye, and barley. For wheat, grades included "Club," "No. 1," "No. 2," and "Rejected." Across other grains, the categories were simply "No. 1," "No. 2," and "Rejected."[47]

Walter Johnson's evocative history of slave markets, *Soul by Soul*, considers the aspirations of price lists to make human beings "fully fungible." In slave traders' tables, "any slave, anywhere, could be compared to any other, anywhere else." These neat documents collapsed the infinite complexity of individual lives into a set of rough-and-ready categories. The prices made the incommensurable commensurable, enabling "even the most counter-intuitive comparisons—between the body of an old man and a little girl . . . or between the muscular arm of a field hand and the sharp eye of a seamstress, or, as many nineteenth-century critics of slavery noted, between a human being and a mule." As Johnson writes, "That was commodification: the distant and different translated into money value and resolved into a single scale of relative prices."[48]

Traders used a variety of techniques to translate the distant and the different into a single scale. Whenever possible, grading relied on simple, measurable characteristics. Betts & Gregory's list assigned value to children by height and sex. By contrast, earlier handwritten price circulars from Dickinson, Hill & Co. divided the enslaved by sex and age, offering corresponding age and price ranges.[49] But categorizing based on height had distinct advantages. Sellers did not always know the precise ages of the children they put up for auction, but heights were relatively easy to measure and to verify at the moment of sale. Perhaps more important, the enslaved could not dispute their measurements in the way they might have contested their ages or skills to influence a transaction.

Biometric pricing strove to make values as objective as possible, facilitating agreement between buyers and sellers and minimizing the potential influence of the enslaved. Though height appears to have been more common, traders dabbled in pricing by the pound, particularly for youth. Slave trader Tyre Glen wrote to his brother Thomas, instructing him to make "some purchases at this time if they can be made at fair prices." He then offered a series of ranges for what these prices might be. He recommended "5 to six dollars per pound," for plow boys, but "if the boy is very likely and weighs 60 to 90 or 100. 7 [dollars per pound] may be given."[50] Similarly, escaped slave John Brown recollected his master striking a deal to sell him according to his weight. The purchaser, Starling Finney, weighed his own saddle to confirm the accuracy of the scale, and then Brown sat in a rope looped from the scale's hook. The two men struck a deal for $310, and the ten-year-old Brown was "marched off" without time to bid his mother good-bye.[51]

To make standardized categories work, slave traders strove to present enslaved people as uniform, compliant examples of the grades they represented. Former slave John Brown wrote of how traders required that enslaved people look "'bright and smart' when the buyers were choosing." As he explained, "The price a slave fetches depends, in a great measure, upon the general appearance he or she presents to the intending buyer. A man or a woman may be well made, and physically faultless in every respect, yet their value be impaired by a sour look, or a dull, vacant stare." Traders went to great lengths to encourage "bright and smart" appearances, a goal which theoretically might have limited violence. Instead, however, slave traders sought out modes of punishment that preserved market value.[52]

Those who did not present a bright demeanor faced the horror of a punishment designed specifically to cause a maximum amount of pain without leaving physical evidence. As John Brown explained in his narrative:

> It is a rule amongst "nigger dealers," not to flog with any instrument that will cut the skin, because this would depreciate the value of the "property"; therefore the punishment is inflicted with what is called a "flopping paddle." The "flop" is of leather,

about a foot-and-a-half long, and as broad as the palm of the hand;
perhaps a little broader: the handle is of wood, and about two feet
long. Men, women, and girls are all punished alike. They are
brought in and stripped stark naked, and laid flat on the floor . . .
whilst the whipper lays on, "flop, flop, flop," for half an hour. . . .
The punishment is dreadfully severe, for all no blood is drawn.[53]

Slave traders' carefully calibrated punishments reflected their proximity to
the market. They stood to benefit immediately from manipulating the enslaved without leaving a mark. By contrast, a planter interested more in an
enslaved person's labor than his or her sale might not be concerned with scar-
ring. The same marks that a trader avoided could prove a valuable reminder
of punishment, spurring those who wore them and those who saw them to
work more diligently. Under slavery, the whip was a technology that could
be used in many ways depending on slaveholders' needs.

What happened to enslaved peoples who fell below the lowest grade—the
human equivalent of "rejected" grain brought to the Chicago Board of Trade?
The most vulnerable slaves often cost more to maintain than they yielded in
output—they were unlikely to be protected even as property. In the case of
children, planters might hope to recoup their investments a decade or more
down the road. But the very elderly, who by law often could not be freed,
would only be a drain on resources.[54] In the language of twentieth-century
business, these slaves had a negative net present value, meaning the market
deemed them less than worthless. On annual inventories, planters and overseers typically assigned infants and the very elderly some value. At a minimum, they recorded their prices as zero. But these prices were in some way
imaginary: no one had actually agreed to pay. Even appraisals that were used
to secure credit were estimates. To fully collateralize a loan, the perceived
value of the enslaved need only exceed the amount of the debt; it did not
matter by how much. By contrast, on auction blocks, value had a sharper edge.

The existence of negative prices reveals the calculating gazes of men and
women as they shopped for slaves. The same planters who rated the elderly
and infirm at zero on their own inventories would not have "purchased"
these men and women for free. Traders offered them at negative prices by
selling them in groups, or lots—a practice that they claimed was particularly
humane. And, indeed, the sale of slaves in family groups sometimes kept

slaves with their loved ones. But it also had a pecuniary upside because it bundled the elderly and infirm with their more valuable kin. An 1859 list of enslaved people being priced for sale reflected this practice. After the death of planter Duncan Clinch, the 257 men and women who had toiled on his Georgia estate were divided into lots. The elderly were scattered among these groups, presumably based on family connections. In lot No. 27, for example, the cost of Katy (−$100) was deducted from the combined value of Cato, Hagaar, Frank, Saturn, James, Margaret, and Will. Lot No. 44 valued Old Betty and Phillip at −$50 each, their cost offset by Betsy, Bella, and an unnamed infant.[55] Slave codes had long recognized the problem of negative value. At least since the colonial period, legal restrictions in many locations prevented masters from emancipating the elderly and infirm. In some jurisdictions, masters were forbidden from freeing their slaves simply to spare themselves the cost of food and shelter. However, like other legal limitations on sale, such laws actually offered little protection in practice. Selling slaves in lots or before their value declined below zero offered a way around the prohibition. In other cases, the enslaved elderly were "pensioned off" or simply left to scrape by with little attention to their needs.[56]

Of course, even when they were weighed, measured, and terrorized with punishment, enslaved people could not be traded in the same way as bushels of grain. But many potential barriers to exchange were easily dealt with through calculation and law, where the treatment of human property sometimes differed from that of other kinds of property. Antebellum property law was increasingly caveat emptor—with buyers responsible for inspecting their purchases and liable for shortcomings in the absence of an explicit warranty. In the sale of cotton or wheat, aided by grading systems, caveat emptor legal treatment worked well. By contrast, in the sale of immensely complex and diverse human beings, potential information asymmetries were much greater. A seller almost always had dramatically more knowledge of a slave's temperament and physical capabilities than did the buyer, and he or she might hide these characteristics in the process of a sale. The law offered a solution, and regulations for the sale of slaves usually required sellers to disclose defects and to honor implied warranties about the condition of the men and women they sold.[57]

Though the law sometimes regarded human property differently from other kinds of property, this special treatment was less a reflection of enslaved people's humanity than a practical tool for helping markets function. Courts adjudicated all kinds of property, and different rules were often applied to different goods. The law offered a flexible tool that supported markets for complex and expensive property like slaves. Rather than undermining commodity markets for the enslaved, special rules made them more efficient, enabling buyers and sellers to make certain assumptions about transactions and to expect some protection in court when they were not met. For example, courts directly confronted the question of fungibility when they allowed for specific performance in suits involving slave property. Could a suit for loss of personal property request the return of a specific slave or only monetary damages? In most cases involving personal property (rather than real property, typically land), plaintiffs could request only monetary damages. However, in some cases involving slavery, judges allowed plaintiffs to sue for the return of specific people.[58] The law thus encouraged trade by recognizing that the "value" of some slaves to their owners might exceed their market value. The law proved a flexible tool for facilitating the exchange of human property. As legal historian Thomas Morris has written, "The general trend was toward assuring an early alienability in the market."[59] Economist Jenny Bourne Wahl confirms, "Slave sales law developed in a way that minimized the cost and uncertainty of trafficking in human flesh and, thus, strengthened the institution of slavery."[60]

Slaves were more likely to be protected as property than as people. Short of barring a master from killing, neither statutes nor case law generally placed many limits on owners' use of force to secure obedience from the enslaved. However, the law did offer masters protection if their property was injured or killed by others. Transportation law made carriers like railroads responsible for most injuries to slaves, just as they were responsible for injuries to livestock. By contrast, free persons received little protection. Similarly, masters who hired out their slaves could receive compensation after the injury or death of their human property. Indeed, they received compensation more often than did the families of free laborers injured or killed on the job.[61]

Prime Hands

Of course, accounting for day-to-day productivity and longer-term value were inextricably linked. After all, the allocation of labor was also the allocation of capital. In the 1850s, some of the same railroads that were beginning to consider the depreciation of their large capital investments were also developing comparable measures of productivity, such as the "cost per ton-mile."[62] This measure enabled them to compare output across different kinds of freight carried on different lengths of track. Their practices linked the assessment of output to the rating of capital. Slaveholders devised a similar unit of analysis that enabled comparisons across the diverse men and women they enslaved. This system of fractional and prime hands was used both to assign labor to specific individuals and also to render them comparable and interchangeable inputs of production.

A "prime hand" was an enslaved man or woman whose productivity was near the maximum that could be expected from a single individual in good health. All other slaves were graded against this ideal, their value denominated in fractions of a hand. As one observer explained, "Some negroes are considered as being *full* hands, others as *three-quarter* hands, others again as *half* hands, and the young and the feeble as only *quarter* hands." Ratings evolved over time: "The young people who begin as quarter hands are gradually advanced in the scale according to their increasing bodily capabilities; while those whose strength is declining from their advanced age, or any other cause, are, on the other hand, released proportionally from their toil."[63] In 1833, the *Southern Agriculturist* published a similar account of management practices on J. Hamilton Couper's Hopedon plantation. As the author explained, the "rateable or working hands" were scored according "to his or her efficiency." There were four rates of each sex: "full hands, ¾, ½ and ¼ hands." The daily work expected was in proportion to these ratings, with "4 quarter hands being required to do the same work with one full hand."[64] Fractional hands could either be given partial tasks or be combined with other fractional hands to complete full tasks. For example, two half-hand youths could be assigned to work a full plot jointly or a child rated at one quarter might help a mother rated at three quarters.[65]

The system of fractional hands was most common on Sea Island cotton plantations. In Saint Simons, Georgia, James Postell prepared detailed schedules of the hands on his plantation. As of 1853, when he opened his account book, a community of 81 men, women, and children lived on the plantation. These included 36 males and 45 females, 44 of whom were old enough and well enough to work regularly. He rated each laborer in quarter-hand increments. Among the men who went to the field, Sumer, Robin, Hannible, Robert, and Tony were regarded as full hands, Morris a three-quarter hand, October a half hand, and four other men and boys a quarter hand apiece. Summing these up, Postell concluded that he had the strength of 7¼ men working his fields. He repeated this process for women, listing 23 names and concluding that they could be counted as 17 full hands. Adding in 10 permanent jobbers who rated as 7 hands and 37 children not yet old enough to work, Postell concluded that his 81 slaves were equal to 31¼ full hands. When he closed the journal four years later, he repeated the calculations and comparisons.[66]

Postell appears to have used this information in many different ways. His detailed inventories list not only the ages and ratings of the enslaved but also their allowances of provisions. He also used hand ratings to determine whether he had an appropriate amount of acreage under cultivation. Though he does not explain his logic, we can see his calculations. Below the inventory of hands, he took the total number of field hands (24¼), rounded down to 24, multiplied by 4, added 1¼, and then rounded the answer off again to 97 acres. He then subtracted 15, concluding that he should plant 82 acres.[67]

Planters used the unit of hands beyond the Sea Island region as well. In the Kershaw district of South Carolina, planter and attorney John McPherson DeSaussure kept a similar list of hand rankings. Before 1850, he appears to have kept simple inventories, composed of lists of names. In 1850, however, DeSaussure prepared a more precise record of every man, woman, and child who went into the field, listing names, ages, ratings, and ailments. When he summed these up, he found that his 146 hands in the field should be expected to perform the tasks of 120 prime hands (see Figure 4.6).[68]

Even when labor was not given out as tasks, fractional hands could be summed up to enable comparisons between one group of slaves and any other. Based on his observations throughout the South, Frederick Law Olmsted described the process of tallying up as it was used in different regions. On a cotton plantation in the lower Mississippi valley, he found "135 slaves, big and little, of which 67 went to field regularly—equal, the overseer thought, to fully 60 prime hands." There were also a number of highly skilled hands, including a blacksmith, a carpenter, a wheelwright, and a nurse, who "would be worth more, if they were for sale, the overseer said, than the best field-hands."[69] Olmsted found two hundred slaves on a rice plantation in North Carolina, reckoned "to be equal to about one hundred prime hands." By the overseer's

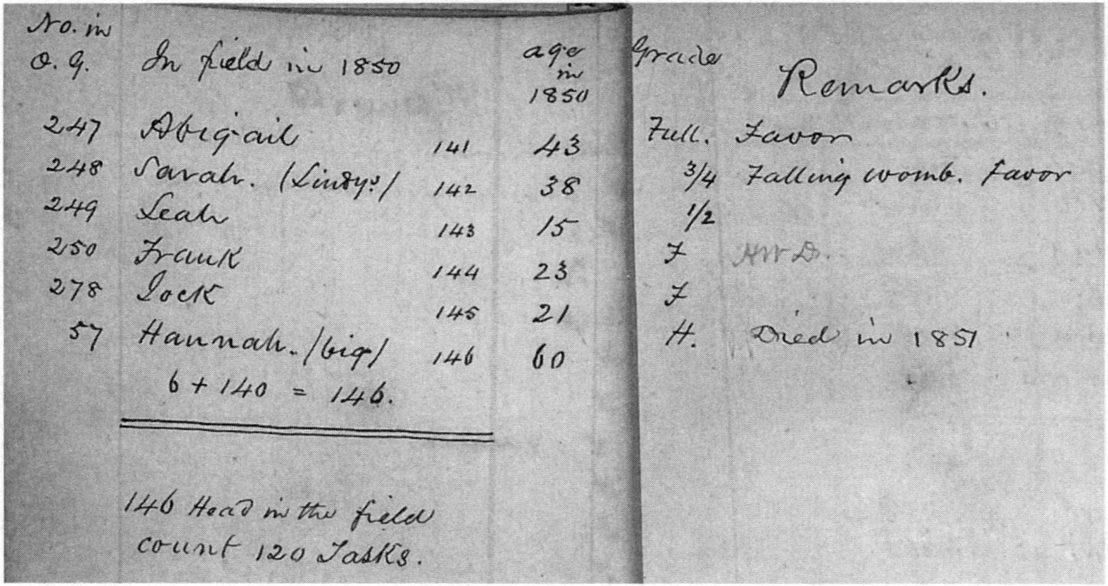

No. in O. G.	In field in 1850		age in 1850	Grade	Remarks.
247	Abigail	141	43	Full.	Favor
248	Sarah. (Lindy's)	142	38	3/4	Falling womb. Favor
249	Leah	143	15	1/2	
250	Frank	144	23	F	HWD.
278	Jock	145	21	F	
57	Hannah. (big)	146	60	H.	Died in 1851
	6 + 140 = 146.				

146 Head in the field
count 120 Tasks.

FIGURE 4.6. Hand Rankings from the Plantation of John McPherson DeSaussure, 1850. DeSaussure rated his enslaved laborers on a quarter-task scale and then summed those totals up. In 1850, he had "146 head" working in the field, the equivalent of "120 Tasks." John McPherson DeSaussure Plantation Book, 1849–1861. DeSaussure Family Papers (3304, 3371). Courtesy of the South Caroliniana Library, University of South Carolina, Columbia.

assessment, this was "an unusual strength for that number of all classes."[70] Olmsted observed that the number of hand equivalents on a large plantation rarely exceeded half the number of enslaved men and women. However, a low ratio of prime hands to total hands might not be a sign of weakness. Another planter, who described his "whole force" as having a "proportion . . . somewhat smaller than usual," explained that it was not due to infirmity or weakness among his workers. Rather, "his women were uncommonly good breeders," and thus babies brought the average productivity down. He had "never heard of babies coming so fast as they did on his plantation."[71]

In these examples, planters graded their hands both to assign labor and to compare output. By rating their workers as partial hands, planters rendered the enslaved as abstract units of labor, many of which could be summed to make a whole. And by totaling up their hands, planters owning slaves of many ages and capabilities could compare them with planters owning mostly prime hands. Planters developed a language of comparison, using hands to share production estimates in the lively southern agricultural press. For example, Alexander McDonald of Alabama sent a comparison of his profits from 1844 and 1845 to the *Soil of the South*. He owned "13 hands, mostly boys and women," but for the purpose of analysis, these could be "counted at" only "10 good hands." He calculated that the value of these hands was $5,800 and added it to his other capital, charging 8 percent interest across his profit.[72] A few years later, another contributor tabulated the results of almost two decades of growing cotton. He measured productivity in several ways, including yield of cotton per acre, average price per pound, and net proceeds per hand.[73]

When planters rated the enslaved as one-quarter, one-half, or three-quarters of a prime hand, they were in some ways attempting to benchmark their output—to figure out how much work each man or woman ought to be able to perform if he or she could be spurred to maximum efficiency. But rating people as fractional hands was also a tool for commodifying and capitalizing lives, if not in the unit of dollars. By rating the enslaved as fractions of a person, slave owners translated the infinite diversity of humanity into a parade of prime hands. Through calculation, they rendered the incommensurable abstract and equivalent—as a unit of labor that could be compared to other units of labor without reference to individuals.

Data shared in the southern press shows how planters triangulated labor with capital. In August 1857, for example, *DeBow's Review* published a

COTTON ON A LARGE SCALE.

Land—2,000 acres, bottom, at $8 50............	$17,000
50 prime field hands, at $1,000.................	50,000
50 half hands, at...... 600..................	30,000
50 quarter hands, at... 300..................	15,000
House and furniture........................	4,000
Quarters and overseers' houses.................	2,000
Mules and tools............................	2,000

Capital outlay.........................	$120,000

ANNUAL PRODUCTION.

At 4 bales per hand, of 450 lbs. 158,400 lbs., at 8 cents............		$12,672
Increase of slaves, at 5 per cent., $4,750......................		4,750
		$17,422
Deduct annual expenses..........................	$1,000	
" interest on $120,000, at 8 per cent..............	9,600	
		10,600
Clear returns..............................		$6,822

FIGURE 4.7. Cotton Production on a Large Scale. These estimates for the profits to be earned from cotton production used fractional hands, describing the capital outlay for prime, half, and quarter hands and projecting output at four bales per full hand. James D. B. De Bow, "Texas," *De Bow's Review*, vol. 23, no. 2 (New Orleans, La.: J. D. B. De Bow, August 1857), 127.

description of Texas based on Frederick Law Olmsted's account of his travels. Though the essay argued at length with elements of Olmsted's depiction, the editor nonetheless found much worth repeating, including a comparison of profits between "Cotton on a Large Scale" and "Sheep on a Large Scale." In the pro forma calculations for the cotton plantation, Olmsted listed all the investments necessary to run a plantation. Chief among them were fifty prime field hands, fifty half hands, and fifty quarter hands (see Figure 4.7).[74]

This start-up plan neatly classified slaves into fractional categories, collapsing a wide variety of temperaments, ages, and skills onto a single scale. Further, the scale yielded values that could be added up: 50 prime, 50 half, and 50 quarter totaled 87½ hand equivalents. Rounded up, these 88 hands could be expected to grow and process four bales of 450 pounds apiece, for a grand total of 158,400 pounds. Sold for 8 cents per pound and combined with a 5 percent profit from the increase of slaves, this imagined plantation would yield $17,422 in income. After deductions for expenses and interest on the capital, this left a considerable profit of $6,822. Through this process of rating, incomparable characteristics—from speed to intelligence, strength, height, literacy, recalcitrance, skill, and reproductive potential—became comparable and combinable.[75]

The hypothetical cotton plantation also shows the relationship between the commodification of lives and the commodification of land. Planters reflecting on such a plan were contemplating the pairing of abstract units of labor—hands—with abstract units of land—acres. Just as fractional grading schemes made labor available in the abstract, processes for surveying and selling land made it calculate from a distance.[76] From the hand, planters also developed a range of comparative metrics. For example, a "task acre" was a unit of land measure that might vary according to what a prime hand could accomplish.[77] In rice culture, a task acre was slightly larger than an acre, typically "a rectangle 300 feet long and 150 feet broad, divided into square halves and rectangular quarters, and further divisible into 'compasses' five feet wide and 150 feet long."[78] Profits from hypothetical plantations could be calculated without reference to individual slaves or specific places. Through accounting, human figures became figures on paper, and men and women appeared as no more than hands.

Commodification and Control

How fully commodified were enslaved people? The mark of full commodification in the sale of grain or cotton has always been the futures contract, an agreement to buy not a specific bushel or bale but any unit of a specified quality. There were no futures contracts for slaves; individual negotiations or auctions were the basis for most transactions. But the commodification of enslaved people advanced remarkably far considering the complexity and individuality of human assets. The genres of calculation described above all translated slaves into abstract units of value. Inventories rated their worth in dollars, price lists sorted them into categories, and the classification of fractional "hands" created a unit of human value that allowed a diverse array of people to be compared and combined.

For futures contracts to work, goods have to be treated as fully fungible, and for goods to be regarded as interchangeable, a number of conditions must be met. First, goods have to be *classified* into abstract categories. Both the rating of fractional hands and the price list supplied by Betts & Gregory accomplished this work on enslaved people. Next, these abstract categories had to be *standardized*. A market with fewer rating systems allows for a greater degree of commodification than where there are many competing systems. The standardization of categories for enslaved people was partial. For example, the unit of hands was widespread enough that planters could use it to make comparisons and publish those comparisons in the southern agricultural press, but closer inspection suggests that the unit meant different things to different people. It was more a rough-and-ready heuristic device than a precise and widely recognized unit of measurement.[79] Similarly, in the Betts & Gregory price lists, the categories were standard enough for the same preprinted forms to be used week after week. But the categories they supplied were ranges reflecting varying prices to accommodate diverse individuals.

To form a basis for liquid futures markets, processes for classifying commodity goods also need to be *routinized* and *generalized*. That is, rating needs to take place the same way on a regular schedule, and to be widely accepted across society. Here the processes of commodification acting on enslaved people fall short. Some planters and traders rated enslaved people regularly— for example James Green Carson inventoried his slaves annually, using the same transparent scale to price children each year. But none of the systems of abstraction described here came close to the transparent, widely accepted, and well-regulated grading practices that emerged for staple goods like wheat, cotton, and sugar.

Only rarely did practices for pricing enslaved people approach the regularity of those used for pricing other commodities. As Steven Deyle observes in his study of the domestic slave trade, readers of southern newspapers could scan tables with the current market prices for cotton, rice, hogs, and the like, but they could not find corresponding data for people.[80] This was true— generally. The vast majority of price currents did not include slaves, but in the late eighteenth century, they sometimes listed "new negroes" from Africa. Chapter 2 includes a 1785 price current from the *Columbian Herald* (Figure 2.4), which priced enslaved people alongside the crops they grew.[81] Highly standardized valuation schedules like this price current and the Betts & Gregory price list (Figure 4.5) seem to have emerged at moments when the market for slaves was particularly lively and extensive: before the end of the Atlantic slave trade and with the flourishing of the domestic slave trade in the last decade before the U. S. Civil War. During both periods, bondpeople were torn from local contexts and transported to places with labor shortages. By wrenching slaves from networks of personal ties, purchasers and sellers made enslaved people more interchangeable. If not for the closing of the Atlantic slave trade in 1807 and the coming of the Civil War in 1861, futures markets might well have emerged.[82]

Still, grading lives was a project far more difficult than grading agricultural goods like wheat and cotton, and efforts often fell short. A strict definition of commodification would require that buyers and sellers treat the enslaved as *fully* fungible and interchangeable. Even during the brief periods when the prices for enslaved people were disseminated in newspapers and price lists, the values supplied were ranges that could be adapted to the actual diversity of lives. In part, enslaved people set the boundaries of commodification. As Walter Johnson has argued, enslaved men and women understood that they were people with a price. Buyers, sellers, traders, and bondpeople all negotiated on the terrain of slaves' bodies, each maneuvering to turn the moment of sale to his or her advantage. Unlike other commodities, the sold strove to shape the course of the sale.[83]

But it would be misleading to suggest that planters pushed for standard prices and slaves struggled against them. Being a person with a price cut both ways. Even the rhetoric of "pricelessness" could be turned to an owner's advantage. This is most clear from bondpeople's efforts to purchase themselves or to secure purchase by a preferred master. A slave pursuing manumission could not buy just any prime hand. A mother working to free her child could not simply pay the price for so many pounds of flesh. Planters buying labor could choose from many slaves, but a slave seeking freedom sought something singular, and he or she had to negotiate with a monopolist.[84]

Planters asserted their slaves' value as commodities only when it was convenient and profitable to do so. Take the story of Trinidadian slave Pamela Munro. In 1824, as part of an amelioration program, the British colonial office had instituted a compulsory manumission policy. The policy established a legal procedure for pricing slaves and authorized them to purchase themselves at that price. Most cases set prices at close to the market price, but the price set for Munro was approximately double the price she would have brought if put up for auction. Munro's owner did not wish to sell her, explaining that he considered her services to be irreplaceable.[85] Here, not price but pricelessness buoyed the master's power and profit. Munro's case was unusual because it unfolded on a trans-Atlantic diplomatic stage, but it was also typical. Numerous slave narratives record the thwarted attempts of enslaved people to influence their sale to preferred masters. One slave attempting to secure his sale was told that his owner was "unwilling to part with [him] at any price."[86] Solomon Northup describes the way his fellow captive, Eliza, attempted to persuade her own buyer to purchase her beautiful daughter, Emily. But the slave trader, Theophilus Freeman, "would not sell her then on any account whatever." As Freeman expounded, there were untold "heaps and piles of money to be made of her . . . when she was a few years older." Of course, what he meant was not that she was actually priceless but that he would not sell her for any amount near the commodity price—the rate that might have been called for on a trader's list or a price current. As he explained, "There were men enough in New Orleans who would give five thousand dollars for such an extra handsome fancy piece."[87]

Planters took part in a kind of dialectic of valuation: an alternation between standardized practices and highly individual exchanges. In part, the complexity of these valuation practices reflects slaves' fundamental individuality, the reality that—as labor or as capital—men and women could not be reduced to a set of specifications. But it also reflected the power of planters to shift between different genres of valuation when it benefited them to do so. They could sort the enslaved into commodity categories, but they could also sing their praises as luxury goods. Planters' account books and traders' price lists reveal not just their skill at calculation but also their power. Control made calculation and commensuration profitable. Planters strove for rationalization, standardization, and fungibility when it served their interests. Their ownership of capital gave them the power to commodify *as they chose*.[88]

Politics and Property

Though not everyone kept the kinds of records described here, the priorities and power structures they represented reached a broad audience through politics. There, calculations of the value of enslaved capital became estimates of the value of slavery to the nation and also of the potential costs of disunion. In March 1860, while campaigning for the presidency, Abraham Lincoln spoke in Hartford, Connecticut. He reflected that even "our wisest men" underrated the conflict between North and South because they had not properly estimated its magnitude. "What is the difficulty?" he asked. "One-sixth of the population of the United States is slave. One man of every six, one woman of every six, one child of every six, is a slave. Those who own them look upon them as property, and nothing else." And the amount of this property was immense: "at a moderate estimate, not less than $2,000,000,000." As Lincoln continued, having such an amount of property has "a vast influence upon the minds of those who own it." The "slaveholders battle any policy which depreciates their slaves as property. What increases the value of this property, they favor."[89]

Lincoln's "moderate estimate" was indeed too conservative. Economists have estimated that the nearly four million slaves who lived in the United States on the eve of the Civil War had a combined market capitalization of between $3.1 and $3.6 billion.[90] The states that seceded from the Union were closer to this number when they argued for secession, triggering the beginning of the Civil War. On January 29, 1861, the state of Georgia offered a statement explaining its reasons for leaving the Union: "Why? Because by their declared principles and policy" the northern states had "outlawed $3,000,000,000 of our property in the common territories of the Union."[91] Mississippi offered an even higher estimate, writing that the property in slaves was "the greatest material interest of the world." They seceded to prevent "the loss of property worth four billions of money" and to "secure this as well as every other species of property."[92] Jefferson Davis simply put the risk at "thousands of millions of dollars."[93]

Where individual inventories and price lists estimated rates of increase at the scale of the plantation, political figures and pamphleteers calculated the trajectory of the entire South. In his secessionist tract, *The Rightful Remedy,* Edward Bryan explained that "besides the labour which is derived" from the slave, his support "yields a considerable return to the master's capital." Bryan set the "natural increase of slaves" at "3 per cent" per year, and his calculations yielded an estimate of approximately $15 million in annual capital gains across the South. To be sure, this profit in slaves was smaller than profits from cotton, but it nonetheless added considerably to planters' bottom lines.[94]

The risks of depreciation affected not just individual planters, but the whole of the South. In October 1860, commenting on the likely effect of the election of Lincoln, *The Charleston Mercury* published an essay on the terrors of secession. Among these terrors was depreciation: as the author explained, with "a submission to the rule of Abolitionists at Washington," slaveholders would seek to sell their slaves. Those in "the Frontier States" would "force their slaves on the markets of the Cotton States," and "the timid in the Cotton States," would "also sell their slaves." If masters rushed to liquidate their human capital "the consequence must be, slave property must be greatly depreciated." The authors claimed to have seen advertisements "for the sale of slaves in some of the Cotton States," with "the simple object of getting rid of them." They further warned that "standing orders for the purchase of slaves in this market have been withdrawn, on account of an anticipated decline of value from the political condition of the country."[95]

The price of slaves reached record highs on the eve of the Civil War—and with good reason: the harvest of 1860 had yielded large profits. But as political fortunes turned, prices plummeted and then ricocheted wildly. The Betts & Gregory price lists show this collapse. The list reproduced in Figure 4.5 shows that in early January 1861, "Extra Men" were bringing in $950–$1,000. Only five months earlier, in August 1860, another Betts & Gregory circular had priced the same category more than 50 percent higher, at $1,550–$1,625. Two months later, on a circular from March 1861, prices were back up. But this form was only partially completed, suggesting a breakdown in systematic pricing. Political uncertainty had turned the trade in enslaved people into a game of speculation.[96]

Property revealed its true nature: maintaining and growing capital had less to do with careful management than with politics. The risks that planters had sought to account for through their detailed calculations paled in comparison to the risk of outright expropriation. James Green Carson, the planter whose careful inventories opened this chapter, abandoned his estimates of depreciation. Green filled in prices for the beginning and the end of the year in every surviving volume except for his last—1862. Here he did not bother to complete the second record. Surely the advancing Civil War had made such calculations seem uncertain. Maybe some of Carson's property had already grasped their freedom. Whatever the reason, Carson's calculations about the value of his human capital no longer held the importance they had in prior years.[97]

Though the impending war made the politics of property particularly vivid, planters had long recognized that their property, like all property, depended on the law. In 1839, more than twenty years before Lincoln spoke in Hartford, planter and senator Henry Clay estimated the "present number" of enslaved people to be about "three millions." Setting "the average value of slaves" conservatively at "only four hundred dollars. The total value ... of

the slave property in the United States, is twelve hundred millions of dollars." "Now," he continued, "it is rashly proposed, by a single fiat of legislation to annihilate this immense amount of property! To annihilate it without indemnity and without compensation to its owners!" Foretelling the future, he predicted that this kind of expropriation would lead to "convulsion, revolution, and bloodshed."[98] Enslaved people had been uncertain property from the earliest years of the new nation: when George Washington conveyed Thomas Jefferson's calculations of "silent profit" to British agricultural expert Arthur Young, Young was critical. As he wrote, "I cannot admit of it: he reckons 60£ a year increasing value of negroes . . . to have a considerable value invested in slaves, is a hazardous capital."[99]

Slaveholders understood that the value of enslaved property—like all property—was contingent on political circumstances. It depended on social and cultural expectations and—most importantly—it depended on law. As Clay emphasized in his 1839 speech, "That is property which the law declares to be property." At the time, Clay believed that the immense size "of the slave property in the United States" rendered it immune to attack. But as this property grew, so too did the attacks on it.[100] The rising tide of abolition meant that slaveholders needed to preserve their capital not just through their management practices but also in the halls of government. Earning profits had required them to make both cotton and law. Eventually it would require them to make war.

In the preparation of inventories, the use of depreciation, and the development of standardized price schemes, southern slaveholders were at the cutting edge of nineteenth-century valuation practices. When they calculated depreciation, midsized southern planters were making use of a technique found only at a few of the largest railroads and manufacturers. By including it in his instructions for planters, Thomas Affleck advanced ahead of most accounting textbooks, which did not begin to cover the topic until the 1880s. Similarly, price lists like Betts & Gregory's used some of the same practices that were enabling innovation at the Chicago Board of Trade. And the practice of rating enslaved people as fractions of a hand helped planters to think abstractly about productivity, linking the valuation of slaves with their labor.

Planters invested vast sums of capital in complex, long-lived human assets, and their profitability depended both on extracting labor and on maintaining or increasing their capital over time. Traders sought to turn this capital: to buy low and sell high as fast as possible. They practiced a kind of human arbitrage, and their success required them to see value and the potential for it to be transformed, whether through relocation to a new market or through careful marketing and presentation. Though the commodification of enslaved people was far from complete, law and calculation combined to make enslaved people a flexible asset from which slaveholders extracted substantial wealth both as labor and as capital.

Men, women, and children were complex and unpredictable assets. Pricing and appraisal—the most inhumane of activities—were always inextricably human. Despite this, buyers, sellers, and traders imagined pricing to be a rational exercise, and their records show how they used measurable characteristics and invisible punishments in order to constrain the opportunities for enslaved people to shape the market. Though it often seems like slaveholders pushed for commodification and enslaved people struggled against it, the reality was more complex and pernicious. Masters shifted between different genres of valuation at their convenience. When they needed to think about enslaved people as interchangeable inputs of production, they relied on standardized grading schemes and the system of fractional hands. But in the throes of individual negotiations—including those with enslaved people seeking to buy themselves or loved ones—they could demand a premium price, arguing that particular slaves were uniquely valuable.

Ultimately, maintaining and increasing the value of enslaved property was as much a matter of politics and power as of calculation and management. Politicians translated calculations of human capital to a national scale. They quoted the immense market capitalization of slaves—likely between three and four billion dollars in 1860—as evidence of slavery's indispensability to the Union. Eventually they used it in their arguments for secession. When the advancing war threatened this property, enslaved people grasped their freedom. Planters lost the control that had once allowed them to dominate men, women, and children, and to analyze their labor and lives in columns of numbers. And with radically different politics and power structures came new methods of management. These new systems—and the account books that documented them—are the subject of Chapter 5. Postbellum record books show both what freedpeople gained and how their former masters succeeded in recreating new mechanisms of control.

5

Managing Freedom

REIMAGINING SOUTHERN CONTROL

I N 1859, ON THE EVE of the American Civil War, planter and nurseryman Thomas Affleck published the eighth and final edition of his
Plantation Record and Account Book. The all-in-one accounting book remained in circulation into the early 1860s, but as the war unfolded, Affleck
seems to have abandoned the business. Deep in debt, he pursued a wide
array of speculative schemes to turn his fortunes, but reprinting his account
book was not among them. Maybe he doubted that a product as prosaic as
a formatted journal could save him from financial collapse. Or perhaps he
simply recognized that the neat columns of his ledgers could not accommodate the unruly new politics of plantation life. Accustomed to almost complete control over the men and women laboring for him, he railed against
their efforts to exercise their new freedoms. Where he had once dictated
patterns of labor, provisions, and housing, Affleck found that he now had to
negotiate.[1]

In 1880, just over a decade after Affleck's death, his son saw things differently. Just as scientific management practices were beginning to emerge in
northeastern factories, Issac Dunbar Affleck published the retitled *Farm
Record and Account Book,* "enlarged on an improved plan" from the original.

The volume, published by Fairbanks, Palmer & Company in Chicago and New York, adapted Affleck's original system to the needs of the "more modern agriculturist," claiming that the "distinguishing features of the original" had been retained and rearranged "so as to apply to any system of farming and to farms of any extent." The new edition shared the original's commitment to scientific agriculture, offering space for monitoring all kinds of data.[2] But the book also shows how much had changed, erasing the forms that had made Affleck's earlier volumes so distinctive. Gone was the inventory of slaves, where Affleck recommended careful calculations of human capital. And Form C, the all-important record of cotton picked, was replaced with a series of forms, C1–C6, each of which dealt with some aspect of the now complex negotiations between a planter and his tenants or laborers.[3]

Planters found that their relationships with their workers had suddenly become market relationships. Now they would have to recruit, maintain, and pay workers. No longer could they simply purchase lives and direct labor, negotiating only at the margins. They could not manipulate diet and lodging to maximize output and minimize expense. Nor could they reallocate labor from task to task at will. To be sure, enslaved men and women had always resisted discipline, but their inability to quit radically constrained the scope of their efforts. The freedpeople could quit—and did.

Emancipation broke down the systematic processes that had enabled exacting agricultural management. Reckoning with turnover made planters' once minute focus on labor efficiency impossible. Still, planters entered negotiations with disproportionate power. They retained control over land and, after the brief electoral triumphs of Radical Reconstruction, regained control over politics. They also supplemented these structural advantages with familiar strategies of coercion, violence, and deception. Over time, planters restored cotton production, but labor productivity lagged. The results for the freedpeople were even more mixed. They grasped for new freedoms, and despite planters' efforts to bind them to the plantation, they continued to move in search of new opportunities. The labor market that emerged bears the mark of both local negotiations and national reconstruction. The harshest contracts were signed under the early black codes in 1865–1866. The freedpeople negotiated more successfully during the subsequent years of Radical Reconstruction, but they still found themselves economically subordinate.

With the decline of Reconstruction in the 1870s and its end in 1877, planters increasingly encoded social and economic control in law.[4]

Plantation account books reflect this transformation. The former slaves threw off constant surveillance, claiming time for themselves and refusing to let planters dictate the minute details of their daily labor. Records of cotton picking disappeared: planters no longer measured and monitored labor with exacting precision. A multitude of other economic arrangements emerged, including sharecropping and cash tenancy, which were established and enforced through coercive contracts and sharecroppers' ledgers. These records reveal employment terms that offered some hope of getting by but almost none of getting ahead. They also show how the former slaveholders struggled to reassert control. Many of their efforts to dominate the freedpeople succeeded, but they could not reestablish the extensive power they had once enjoyed.

Contracting for Control

After emancipation, Mississippi planter Eli Capell contracted with his former slaves to continue their work. At first, most remained on the plantation, laboring in freedom much as they had under slavery. In July 1865, Capell signed contracts with his former slaves, and work seemed to proceed as usual. That November, Mississippi would pass the first, and probably the harshest, of the southern black codes. These laws promised to help planters keep their former slaves laboring much as they had in bondage. The laws outlawed vagrancy, banned freedpeople from renting lands outside cities, and dramatically restricted the ability to quit during the terms of a contract. Those who did quit forfeited up to a year's wages, and they could even be captured and returned to their employers in the same manner once allowed by the Fugitive Slave Acts. These laws probably reassured Capell that his plantation machine would continue to operate.[5]

After Christmas, however, the freedpeople asserted their independence, refusing to resume work. Only at the end of January did Capell manage to secure contracts for 1866, and at the end of 1866, confusion erupted anew. On Christmas Day, he described the plantation as "very quiet," but less than a week later, there was "a great confusion in the country among the whites and blacks as regarding next year." This time, political support for coercive contracts was less certain. The resounding victory of Republicans in the national congress had given them the power to override President Andrew Johnson, and Radical Reconstruction began. Capell, accustomed to almost complete control over the details of labor, felt "perfectly disgusted." The freedpeople were "roving all over the country." After another week, there was still "nothing doing on my place, negroes very unsettled and won't say what they are going to do. I never saw such a state of things."[6]

For more than a decade before the Civil War, Capell had maintained meticulous records of cotton picking. Each day he had carefully measured the amount of cotton picked by every enslaved person laboring in the fields. After emancipation, he continued to keep careful records, but they show very different labor relationships. In 1867, after finally managing to get signed contracts, he used a slim, preprinted volume labeled "Account of Work Done." The form listed the names of the workers down the left-hand side and the days of the month across the top—a similar format to records of cotton picked. But in place of the detailed logs of cotton picking he had assiduously maintained for years, we find a simple daily labor record (see Figure 5.1). Where prior forms had measured productivity in the form of weights of cotton, this one simply measured days of labor.

Capell may have wanted to keep records of picking—and perhaps he even tried. We do not know why he stopped weighing cotton as he had for years. But other planters seem to have abandoned the practice as well. The change surely reflects not their preferences but those of the former slaves. The freedpeople could be made to sign contracts to plant and pick cotton, but not to do so under the minute surveillance of the scale. And though planters would eventually pay some pickers by the pound, they do not seem to have attempted it in the first years of freedom.[7] Perhaps minutely monitoring the output of each laborer generated too much resistance, too closely resembling the highly regimented labor regimens that had existed under slavery.

Enslaved people might run away, but they could not quit. The freedpeople could and did, even when planters sought to limit their mobility. Thus, Capell and other planters were plagued by turnover.[8] As historian Tera Hunter has written about a different setting—women's domestic labor—quitting was a central strategy for shaping work environments: "Quitting could not guar-

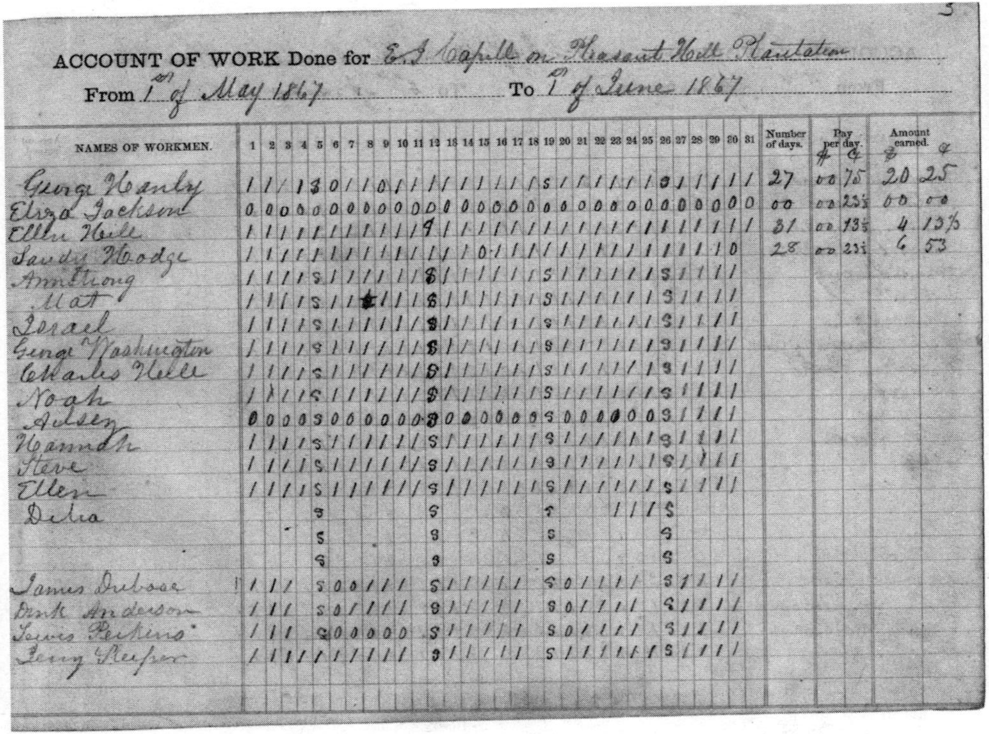

FIGURE 5.1. Work Log on Pleasant Hill Plantation after Emancipation, 1867. After emancipation, Eli Capell continued keeping records, but now he tracked days of labor rather than output. Records of cotton picking disappeared almost entirely after the Civil War. E. J. Capell, Laborer's Record Book (1867–1885), Eli J. Capell Family Papers (Mss. 674, v. 3). Courtesy of Louisiana and Lower Mississippi Valley Collections, Louisiana State University Libraries, Baton Rouge.

antee a higher standard of living or a more pleasant work environment for workers, but it was an effective strategy to deprive employers of complete power over their labor."[9] Frustrations about high levels of turnover and other kinds of labor instability echoed across the South. Planters did not wish to negotiate with the former slaves as free laborers. No matter how much they sought to re-create the circumstances of plantation slavery, labor relations were dramatically changed. Their efforts would secure the return of cotton production, which eventually exceeded the levels of 1860. However, while the new arrangements could be profitable, these farms looked little like the great machines that had dictated plantation labor under slavery. The labor market that emerged was characterized by high turnover, and profit came through skilled negotiation, debt, and exploitation, not the plantation assembly line that had turned people into cogs.

Though they stopped weighing cotton picking in the same way, planters went to great lengths to replicate other labor patterns that had existed under slavery. Contracts signed with the freedmen in the immediate aftermath of the Civil War reflect both the immense power granted by the early black codes and planters' aspiration to continue to control the lives of the former slaves. Take the records of John DeSaussure, a planter in the Kershaw district of South Carolina. On the eve of the Civil War, he held approximately three hundred slaves, whom he was in the practice of rating and tasking on a quarter-hand scale (see "Prime Hands" in Chapter 4). After emancipation, he sought to turn his system for rating the enslaved into a method for calculating compensation, a translation of practices that would leave overarching work patterns unchanged.

DeSaussure began by signing yearlong contracts with the freedpeople. At the beginning of 1866, "the Freedmen whose names are here signed" agreed to his terms. Whether all of the former slaves understood the contract remains unclear: probably few or none could read. None actually signed, instead marking an "X" by names written in DeSaussure's handwriting. The contract laid out detailed terms for labor and compensation. DeSaussure expected the former slaves to continue to work as they had under slavery; in fact, the contract stipulated that they would "labor diligently and faithfully" in any way that "JM DeSaussure or his agents may require." They would "keep no Dogs, . . . Stock, Guns or . . . spirits." They would not leave the plantation "without his permission during working hours," which were "from sunrise to sunset, daily," with only a break for the midday meal. They would perform "the usual tasks" "promptly" and "industriously," obeying "all directions given to them."[10]

Now, of course, the former slaves were supposed to be paid, and their contracts show the contours of the emerging sharecropping system. DeSaussure described his plan to compensate the freedpeople: in addition to housing and a ration of corn, "at the end of the year, they shall be paid one third part of the cotton ginned and packed in Bales—one third part of the corn, Peas + Potatoes gathered and ready for market." These thirds of the produce of the plantation were to be divided according to the same fractional hand ratings that had been assigned to slaves' labor before emancipation. Deductions for missing work due to sickness would be "twenty five cents per day"; "from any other cause" they would be "one dollar per day." The contract made no mention of a right to quit, and anyone doing so may have had to forgo his or her share entirely. By contrast, DeSaussure reserved the right to dismiss for absence or "any wrong conduct" by paying four dollars per month.[11]

Over the course of 1866, DeSaussure tallied up the results of the scheme in a kind of ledger. On the cover, he provided a key for the rating of hands between full and quarter (see Figure 5.2). Inside, he opened an account for each individual or family. As the season unfolded, he charged the accounts for food and clothing, as well as for sundry other expenses, including "taxes." Next, he charged them for lost time due to absences. Finally, he credited them for a portion of the overall one-third share of the crop. For example, the first account of the ledger is for Albert, Joel, and Pussey. Albert, presumably the head of household, is listed as a full hand, Joel as a half hand, and Pussey as a quarter hand. Over the year, they paid $54.21 for shoes, bacon, rice, beef, and taxes. At the close of the year, they were charged for $15.12 in lost time, for a total of $69.33 owed. In return, they received a one and three-quarters share of the cotton crop, amounting to $47.47. As of December, they were thus $21.86 in debt to DeSaussure.[12]

The conditions of 1866 surely satisfied few of the freedpeople. Not all of the hands ended the year in debt, but the aggregate balance swung decisively in DeSaussure's favor. When he summed up the many accounts in the ledger,

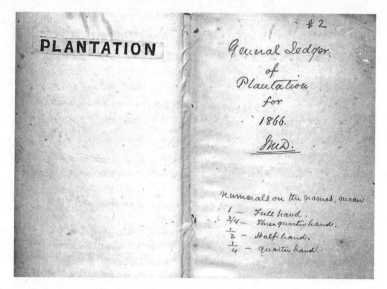

FIGURE 5.2. Hand Ratings after Emancipation, 1866. Even after emancipation, the former slaveholders continued to think of the freedpeople in fractional terms. General Ledger of Plantation for 1866, title page. DeSaussure Family Papers (3304, 3371). Courtesy of the South Caroliniana Library, University of South Carolina, Columbia.

the final totals show $303.67 "due to me" compared to a mere $194.04 paid to the laborers (see Figure 5.3). DeSaussure had managed to contract in such a way that he retained all of the crop *and* a surplus debt from the formerly enslaved. The memo book does not show whether his overall profitability actually increased, and the cost of rations and housing is not included, but in some ways he secured the labor of his former slaves for better than free.[13]

DeSaussure nonetheless seems to have been dissatisfied. Perhaps he was frustrated because dollars on paper could not be readily converted into dollars in his pocket. Though the hands owed him substantially more than he owed them, most surely could not pay—after all, he was their main source of income. Or perhaps he simply felt that they did not work enough. In the next year's contract, he created a more coercive penalty system for missed time. Now he would deduct "one-dollar for the first day, fifty cents for the second day, and if sick for more than two days, then only twenty five cents from the beginning." At these rates, even occasional absences due to illness would quickly erase earnings. Evidently the new contract did not bring the desired results or the freedpeople protested, for he returned to the original scheme in the coming years.[14]

Even as DeSaussure attempted to manage turnover and absenteeism through a penalty system, the freedpeople pursued their own aims. The sweeping victories of the Republicans in the 1866 congressional elections gave them control over Congress and the ability to launch Radical Reconstruction over the vetoes of Andrew Johnson. As on Capell's plantation, the freedpeople seem to have taken advantage of the shifting political circumstance by negotiating for better terms. On January 3, 1867, DeSaussure drew up a contract for the coming year, but not everyone signed. A week later, perhaps to secure the remaining signatures, he added further text: "After this contract was partly signed, it was further agreed on that the employees would supply themselves with corn from the first of January to 1st July 1867," in consideration of which he "agreed to pay each full hand ten dollars now—and each fractional hand with their fraction of this amount." In 1866, purchasing provisions from DeSaussure had left many in debt, and this new system offered them the opportunity to procure supplies elsewhere.[15]

Still, the contract that the former slaves signed in 1867 (and ones that they would sign in the coming years) contained harsh provisions to control their labor and restrict mobility. Reviewing other contracts from the early postbellum period shows that many planters used similar terms in their attempt to maintain the patterns of labor established under slavery. Most contracts, like DeSaussure's, were for a full year, and they gave planters extensive power.[16] For example, North Carolina planter Alonzo T. Mial signed contracts that dictated a grueling sunrise-to-sunset routine, with timed breaks for meals. Mial also required that the former slaves work beyond sunset whenever necessary. Though there was no field labor on Sundays, the freedpeople were expected to "attend to the plantation" during this time, ultimately receiving only a half day on alternate Saturdays for their own use. Should they quit before the end of the year, they would forfeit a half month's payment, which Mial held as security for their labor.[17] Other planters also continued to rate the freedpeople as fractional hands. Like DeSaussure, Peter Bascot denominated each laborer as a full, three-quarter, half, or quarter hand.[18]

63 Balances due to S.m D			64 Balances due to negros		
Albert	$ 21.86	apl 24 / may 9	Archy, Pd $10.71.38 v 11.38		
Andrew	21.20	may 9	Randal Pd Rose. mother 1.78		
Anderton	12.22	apl 24 / do / to	Alice Paid v 5.20		
Amanda	13.39		Billy drian paid 4.54		
			Cain Paid v 3 -		
Daniel	1.38	May 3	Carolina pd v 5.78		
Dick	1.41	do	Chearity Paid v 1 -		
George,					
Graci. camden		apl 24	Davy v E. Paid v - .93		
Harry	2.07 / 5.09 / 60	do	Dundy Paid v 2.90		
Jackson	2.60		Edward v Branch $1e v 2.02		
Joel	5.54	apl 24	Elizabet Paid v 2.51		
Joe	24.30	do	Elias Paid v - .71		
Joe	10.64		Hardy 31.87		
John	17.94	apl 24	Harriet of July Paid v 21.13		
John Crine	8.47	apl 24 v / may 9 / apl 24	Henry Hails Paid v 6.39		
Leah	6.84	may 3	Isaac Paid v 6.39		
			Jacob Paid v - .78		
March	7.89	apl 24	January Paid v 2.65		
Miriam	26.89		Jim v Amelia pd v 4.26		
			July paid v 23.10		

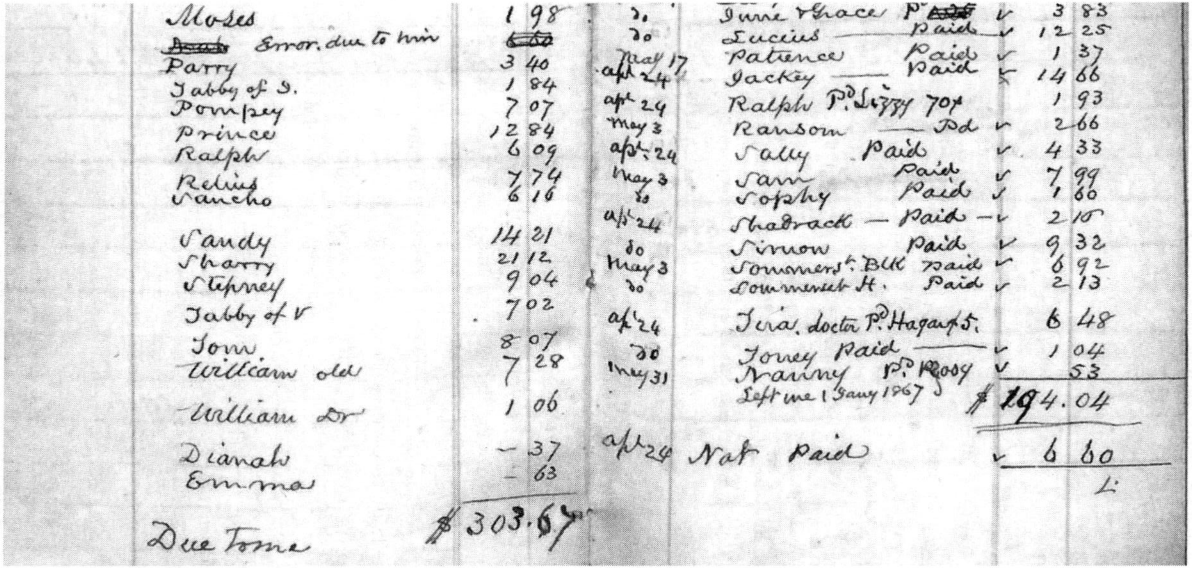

Moses	1 98	do	June & Grace Pd. [illegible]	✓	3 83
[illegible] Error, due to him	[illegible]	do	Lucius —— Paid	✓	12 25
Parry	3 40	May 17	Patience Paid	✓	1 37
Jabby of D.	1 84	apl 24	Jackey —— Paid	✓	14 66
Pompey	7 07	apl 24	Ralph Pd. Lizzy 70¢		1 93
Prince	12 84	May 3	Ransom —— Pd	✓	2 66
Ralph	6 09	apl 24	Sally Paid	✓	4 33
Relius	7 74	May 3	Sam Paid	✓	7 99
Sancho	6 16	do	Sophy Paid	✓	1 60
		apl 24	Shadrack — Paid —	✓	2 10
Sandy	14 21	do	Simon Paid	✓	9 32
Sharry	21 12	May 3	Sommers't. Blk Paid	✓	6 92
Stepney	9 04	do	Sommersett H. Paid	✓	2 13
Jabby of V	7 02	apl 24	Tira. doctor Pd. Hagar $5.		6 48
Tom	8 07	do	Toney Paid ——	✓	1 04
William old	7 28	May 31	Nanny Pd. Rosy	✓	53
			Left me 1 Jany 1867		$ 194.04
William Dr	1 06				
Dianah	– 37	apl 24	Nat Paid	✓	6 60
Emma	– 63				
Due to me	$ 303.67				

FIGURE 5.3. Year-End Balances, Plantation of John McPherson DeSaussure, 1866. DeSaussure acquired the labor of his former slaves for better than free: at the end of 1866, they owed him more than he owed them. General Ledger of Plantation for 1866, pages 63–64. DeSaussure Family Papers (3304, 3371). Courtesy of the South Caroliniana Library, University of South Carolina, Columbia.

The records of an Alabama plantation belonging to the Lewis family illustrate the shift from analyzing labor efficiency to simply trying to keep people at work. Before the war, the owner or overseer maintained a dedicated cotton book, neatly entering daily picking totals for every slave for the years 1858, 1859, 1860, and 1861. For 1858, the book's keeper even tallied up the total output for the season for each individual slave. Perhaps he intended to pay a bounty to the top pickers, or maybe he just wanted a record of productivity. In any case, as the war advanced, this detailed analysis of output stopped, and it would not resume after emancipation.[19]

However, record keeping did not stop. Instead of picking records, the book contains calculations for the payment of groups called "squads"—Sam's Squad and Arthur's Squad. A list of bales packed later in the volume includes many other names, suggesting that other freedpeople were working in squads or family units as well. Each group member was paid a "dividend" less Lewis's "acct. against" them. Unlike on DeSaussure's plantation, most of the freedpeople seem to have come out ahead in 1866—all eighteen men and women on Sam's Squad, and thirteen of the eighteen men and women on Arthur's Squad were owed a dividend at the end of the year.[20] Still, over the longer term, debts seem to have mounted. A list of "negro indebtedness" from 1873, written in the same volume, shows that by then many were indeed in debt, several by more than $100 and one by almost $400—massive sums considering the amount of their annual earnings.[21]

The most coercive contracts sought not just to regulate labor but also to control the private lives of the former slaves. Writing from Savannah, Georgia, in March 1866, northern observer Louisa Jacobs reported that "some wish to make contracts with their former slaves; but the majority are so unfair in their propositions, that the people mistrust them." Jacobs recounted the terms of one master, whom she described as being "noted for cruelty." He proposed "to make contracts on these conditions: a boat, a mule, pigs and chickens, are prohibited; produce of any kind not allowed to be raised." Further, "permission must be asked to go off of the place," and "a visit from a friend punished with a fine of $1.00." A "second offence breaks the contract."[22]

Mounting debt and harsh contract terms reflect the barriers the freedpeople faced in negotiations. In theory, Reconstruction policies offered some protection in the contracting process. The Bureau of Refugees, Freedmen, and Abandoned Lands, usually called simply the Freedmen's Bureau, was tasked with both approving and enforcing labor contracts. Though policies varied dramatically by jurisdiction, the bureau did make strides to help the former slaves negotiate. Indeed, in some districts, the existence of any contract at all was an achievement, given planters' unwillingness to negotiate with their former property. One freedman later recalled the first contracts as a triumph of Reconstruction: "White folks at first didn't want to make the contracts. . . . So the government filled the jail with them," and after that everyone "make the contract."[23]

While the existence of contracts signaled a measure of consent and agreement, successful negotiation was difficult. In the worst cases, slaves might be forced or tricked into signing. Another former slave, Jennie Kendricks of Georgia, recalled that "after the war ended and all the slaves had been set free, some did not know it, as they were not told by their masters. A number were tricked into signing contracts which bound them to their masters for several years longer."[24] Even when the freedpeople were properly informed of their rights, they entered into negotiations with the critical disadvantage that the vast majority could not read or write. Recalling the signing of contracts many years later, a freedman named Louis Thomas told an interviewer in Missouri that "in March 1868, they sent to the field for all us hands to come up to the house to sign a contract. We all went. . . . He took my hand, put it on his pen, and held it right there and signed my name himself. I got mad as a wet hen about that agreement he read to me. So he tried to make me feel good saying he was going to give me half. I knowed better."[25]

Contracts and plantation records reflect planters' disproportionate access to information. Contracts listed terms followed by a series of names, each accompanied by a slave's "mark." A freedman named Jake McLeod of Timmonsville, South Carolina, recalled, "When we signed the contract, the Yankees"—perhaps men from the Freedmen's Bureau—"give us to understand that we was free as our Massa was. [We] couldn't write, just had to touch the pen" and give the "name we wanted to go in."[26] Even when the contract was read aloud and witnessed, freedpeople's limited literacy and numeracy left them at a disadvantage. With complex terms like payment in percentages of the crop—usually after deductions for an array of expenses and rations—even a fairly signed contract could be hard to understand. Without the opportunity to check and calculate, whether you would come out ahead or behind was hard to predict, and this was compounded by the added uncertainty that the harvest might vary dramatically. Ledgers containing accounts were always written in the planters' hand. Few freedpeople could sign them, much less read them or maintain a counterrecord of their own. Planters' control over literacy, which had its origins under slavery, helped them to maintain control after emancipation.[27]

When it supervised contracting, the Freedmen's Bureau pursued multiple goals: securing payment for freedpeople and ensuring steady, regulated labor for planters. The bureau seems to have helped secure more favorable contracts for freedpeople in individual cases. Some officers forced revisions of particularly egregious contracts even after they were signed—for example, where former slaves had agreed to work for rations only. At the same time, the bureau pushed the former slaves to sign yearlong contracts, a move that limited their mobility and thus their ability to pursue other opportunities.[28] In practice, officers approved an array of harsh terms. As one scholar has observed about conditions in Florida, "Bureau agents not only approved contracts stipulating low wages, but tolerated contracts worded in such a manner that in the event of a poor harvest the Negro would get nothing."[29] Inequality in contracting extended to enforcement. Even when the enslaved managed to sign contracts with reasonable prospects, they could not count on their fulfillment. One freedman explained that his former master had sold him and others land on credit. But after he died, another man—Captain Dan Travis—simply "broke all the contracts."[30]

Lost Time, Gained Time

Among the most striking provisions from early contracts are those for "lost time," the missed days that could be charged against each freedperson's account when it came time to pay at the end of the year. The penalty system on John DeSaussure's plantation charged freedpeople for their absences, and both Alonzo Mial and Peter Bascot required freedpeople to pay for missed work. On Mial's plantation, any freedpeople who missed work without his permission were charged for unexcused time at double wages.[31] Bascot set even steeper fines for lost time: fifty cents per excused day, two dollars per unexcused day.[32]

In most free labor settings elsewhere in the United States, the penalty for lost time was simply lost wages. The freedpeople faced this penalty, of course.

If they missed work, they would sacrifice wages or (under a share contract) the potential for a larger crop due to their increased labor. But lost-time systems charged additional penalties simply for not working, and the rates at which freedpeople had to pay typically exceeded what they might be paid for the same time. Take DeSaussure's contracts. If workers were dismissed, they would be paid a rate of $4.00 per month in back wages for the time they had labored thus far. This translated to about $0.15–$0.17 per day. By contrast, they owed $0.25 to $1.00 per day for "lost time." And Bascot charged more than twice as much—$2.00—for "unexcused" missed days. On the Lewis plantation in Alabama, the planter or overseer maintained a careful record of absences (see Figure 5.4). With names down the side and months across the top, the record resembles a time sheet but tracks a debt of labor, as if the planter, not the freedperson, owned it to begin with. The record shows that increments as small as a quarter of a day were charged against the freedpeople, and that while some missed only a few days per year, others missed more than a hundred.[33]

Records of lost time, like the one in Figure 5.4, tell two stories. One reading shows the freedpeople falling behind: as days summed to weeks and even months of time, absences erased the earnings of hard labor. Another reading shows freedpeople exercising their freedom. When once their former masters might have compelled them to work, now they could choose to recover from illness or childbirth, to care for their families, or to rest. High rates of lost time reflect a new ability to choose when and where to work. This choice came at a high price, however, and planters' ability to charge their former slaves for time when they did not work shows their enduring economic power. Still, the ability to choose nonetheless reflects increased independence in work patterns and more freedom from supervision.

Freedpeople worked under an increasing variety of labor arrangements, the diversity of which can also be read both as a reflection of their preferences and as a sign of the range of economic tools available to planters. In 1866, 168 of the former slaves on John DeSaussure's plantation "signed" the same contract.[34] By 1870, however, they were working under a wide array of agreements. Sixty-seven hands agreed to contracts similar to those from 1866, and fourteen more worked under special contracts with individual terms. About fifteen additional individuals or families worked under "house rent" contracts, and around sixty-five others appear to have rented land at three dollars an

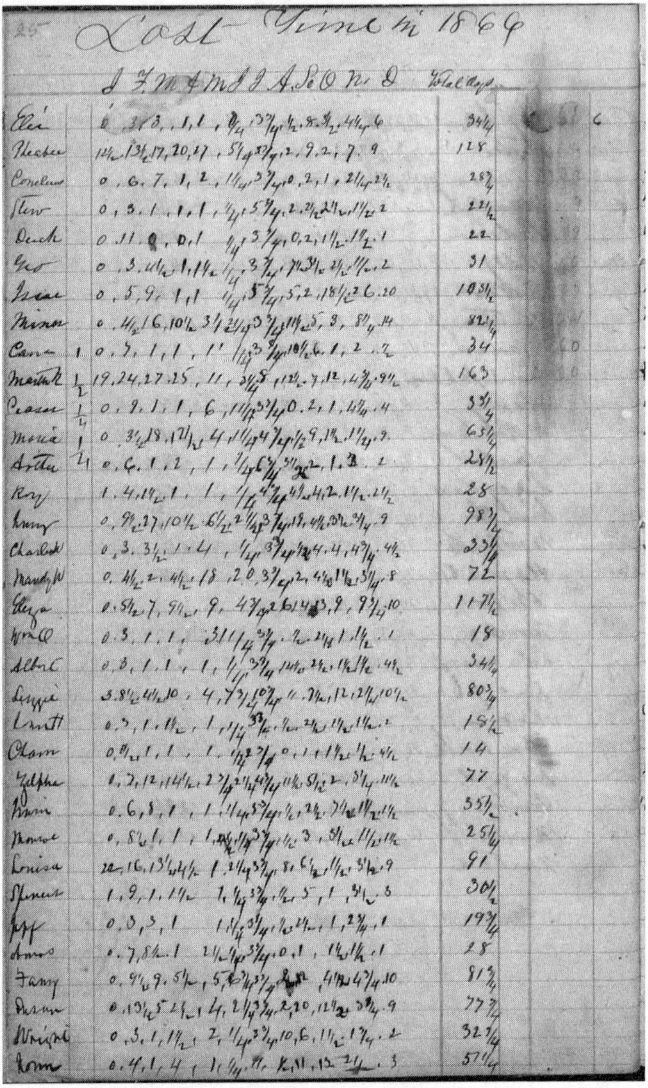
Lost Time in 1866

J F M A M J J A S O N D Total days

FIGURE 5.4. "Lost time" on the W. H. Lewis Plantation, 1866. Many planters actually charged sharecroppers when they missed work, making them pay a penalty in addition to any lost output. This practice contributed to the indebtedness of the former slaves. Lewis Plantation Papers, #2528, Folder 3, Volume 2: 1866, 1881, Scan 28. Courtesy of the Southern Historical Collection, Louis Round Wilson Special Collections Library, University of North Carolina at Chapel Hill.

acre.[35] Tenancies eliminated the control that had enabled planters to keep precise records of output and to manage the pace of labor, but they rarely benefited the former slaves economically. Planters negotiated to their advantage under all kinds of economic arrangements. They tailored contracts based on factors ranging from cotton prices to plot size to reputation of the tenant. They varied side-payment terms as well as amount of acreage. The postbellum agricultural labor market reflected in contracts reveals what economist Joseph Reid has called "economically intelligible variation": planters deployed a whole array of contracting possibilities to secure labor at a low cost.[36]

A collapse of scale accompanied the multiplication of arrangements. Before emancipation, the wealthiest planters had controlled the labor of hundreds of slaves, and many more had commanded the time of dozens. Though this scale did not approach that of Caribbean sugar plantations or the largest northern corporations, it vastly exceeded the size of most northern farms and many midsized factories. After emancipation, many landholdings remained large, but their cultivation was increasingly divided into smaller plots worked by individuals and families. As early as 1867, the editor of the *Southern Cultivator* remarked on the general dissatisfaction among planters attempting to organize labor. He explained that "the experience of the past two seasons shows that plantations on an extended scale, with free labor, cannot be made profitable."[37] Within a few years of emancipation, labor was organized in many ways. Some former slaves worked in collective units for wages or for a share of the crop, while others sought cash or share tenancies. Though the breakup of large farms into small tenancies offered a measure of daily independence, like other changes, it offered few economic benefits for the former slaves.

The breakup of large-scale production accompanied a decline in gang labor—the organization of laborers into large groups by skill and speed. Under slavery, men and women in gangs had worked side by side, moving together up and down rows of crops. Ganged labor had appealed to planters because these groups could be closely supervised and thus subjected to the same kind of speedup that would later occur on factory assembly lines. In the first years of emancipation, during the period of the early black codes, some planters appear to have been able to maintain the gang system. For example, in 1866, planter J. Alphonse Prudhomme appears to have established a gang system on his plantation in Natchitoches Parish, Louisiana. Prudhomme's father, Phanor Prudhomme, had been an assiduous record keeper before his death in 1865, using many editions of Thomas Affleck's record books. In 1866, J. Alphonse established a system of labor for monthly wages, with a separate account for each of the freedpeople. He noted the number of days worked and lost. He then included columns for recording the resulting wages as well as deductions for a hospital and for school taxes.[38] Evidence for the continued ganging of labor in the first years of emancipation is noted in the margins of Prudhomme's records: nursing women were reallocated to a separate suckler's gang. While in this gang, members' wages were reduced by half. For example, freedwoman Marie Nagot was described as a "Suckler from 4th to 15th of January" and then part of the "big gang from 15th January to 7th of August," before rejoining the suckler's gang until the end of the year. Other women also found themselves sorted between different gangs depending on how they chose to nurse their children.[39]

Thus, throwing off the gang system was an attempt by freedpeople not just to assert control over work patterns but also to escape from intervention in the most intimate choices about family life. What planters saw as lost time or lower productivity was also personal freedom, albeit obtained at a high economic cost. Though the account books contain insufficient detail to reconstruct the negotiations that unfolded between Prudhomme and the freedpeople working on his plantation, we know that they were dissatisfied and continued to push for better terms, particularly as Reconstruction offered greater political opportunities. As Prudhomme noted in his journal on January 4, 1868, "Hands not satisfied." Two days after he had read out the contract, he wrote, "Not satisfied. Told them to go and look for better elsewhere." And the following day, "Hands in a stew. Uneasy. Apparently not satisfied."[40]

The freedpeople's insistence on changes to work processes can also be seen in the labor relations between planters and women and children, who withdrew their labor from the fields, or at least from planters' supervision. DeSaussure's contracts reflect his changing relationship with the children he had once owned. In 1866, the list of names affixed to the first contract he signed included quarter hands, who were almost certainly children. But as Radical Reconstruction took hold, children disappeared from DeSaussure's lists. In 1867, fewer half hands and no quarter hands signed. The pattern continued at least until 1870, when DeSaussure's lists of ratings consisted primarily of those rated at least a three-quarter hand. Children may have still worked on tenancies and in homes, but none labored under the eye of DeSaussure and his foreman. Economists Roger Ransom and Richard Sutch estimate that before emancipation most enslaved men worked between 3,000 and 4,000 hours a year in agricultural production, while women worked slightly fewer due to pregnancy, childbirth, and recovery. Children worked fewer hours but still averaged between about 2,000 and 2,500 per year. After emancipation, all these averages dropped, but especially those for women and children.[41]

Accounting records show how emancipation shifted planters' power. Most planters abandoned what had been their most intensive data practice under slavery: recording the amount of cotton picked by every slave, every day. They no longer figured relentlessly about how to extract the maximum amount of labor from every available hand, and the breakup of plantations into small plots reduced control over the intimate details of family life. However, the former slaveholders did not stop keeping records. Rather, planting required a different set of calculations. Profit could be achieved through the right contract, and the right contract secured through negotiation. From an accounting perspective, both cash tenancy and sharecropping simplified the calculation of profitability. With cash tenancy—renting at a fixed price—a planter had full transparency into his profits. As long as his contract protected his land and investments, then his profit was equivalent to the rent—or to the rent less the cost of capital and taxes. A very sophisticated planter might think in terms of opportunity costs, but to come out ahead, such calculations were unnecessary. During slavery, planters had to account for many expenses, like food and clothing for the enslaved. With tenancy, these costs fell to the freedpeople. For their part, freedpeople exercised their ability to quit, and in doing so they gained increased control over their lives—control with implications for their ability to care for their families, build communities, and pursue politics.[42] But despite this new control, they did not make large economic gains. And with the eventual collapse of Reconstruction, their control over the shape of work would begin to erode as well.

Importing Labor

A telling, if smaller-scale, response to emancipation was planters' impulse to simply replace the former slaves. For Thomas Affleck and other southern planters, emancipation shattered fantasies of control. Watching African Americans begin to exercise their new freedoms fueled hostile racist condemnation. Affleck railed against what he saw as lackadaisical, unpredictable work habits. He resisted breaking up large plantations into small plots, unwilling to abandon the systems he had once promoted in his plantation record books. So, instead of raising wages or embracing new work patterns, he decided that the best course of action would be to replace the freedpeople altogether.

In 1865 and 1866, Affleck launched a scheme to attract immigration from Scotland, England, and Germany. Along with other planters, he worked to entice migration through the Texas Immigration & Land Agency, which offered loans for purchasing land and aid in finding work.[43] As a first step, he planned to recruit twenty-five to thirty families to come to his plantation, Glenblythe. He would settle them on his land, furnish tools and livestock, and then allow them to pick a supervisor to coordinate their labor. Once his plantation had been outfitted, he would import more white laborers, shipping livestock back to Scotland so that he could profit from the journey in both directions.[44]

Affleck went to great lengths to promote the immigration scheme, traveling to Europe to solicit candidates. Elsewhere in the South, boosters and entrepreneurs launched similar efforts, and a series of reports published in *DeBow's Review* recounted their progress. Despite many obstacles in recruiting, an agent in Stockholm promised "a large supply of hardy Swedes and Norwegians in the spring." An agent in Zurich lamented that "many influences had been brought to bear upon the minds of the Swiss, prejudicing them against the South." Nonetheless, through "publishing cards, hand-bills, and by communicating personally," he now had "thousands ready to emigrate to the State of Louisiana as soon as they have means to enable them to go." A representative of the bureau of immigration in South Carolina even reported success: "the arrival of 150 German immigrants at the port of Charleston."[45]

Efforts to attract immigration vividly displayed the way the former slaveholders continued to think about labor: as an input that could be plucked

The terms upon which I undertake to furnish the hands are as follows:

Commission, per hand............................	$5 00
Do half hands............................	3 00
Wages for men, per month............................	15 00
Do women, per month...............	$8 00 to $10 00
Do half hands............................	5 00 to 6 00

FIGURE 5.5. Imagining Free Immigrants as Fractional Hands, 1867. Planters continued to imagine their ideal laborers in fractional terms. Art X. Department of Immigration and Labor, *De Bow's Review*, vol. 4, no. 6 (New Orleans, La.: J. D. B. De Bow, December 1867), 580.

from one location and applied in another. Labor was not something to be acquired through compromise and negotiation; it was a movable, controllable resource that could be deployed at will.[46] One recruiter who established an agency in New York sought to recruit German and Irish immigrants for planters and others in the South. Drawing on the terminology of slavery, he used the language of fractional hands to set his commission: he was to be paid five dollars per hand and three dollars per half hand (see Figure 5.5). Recommended wages were also enumerated on a fractional basis.[47]

Most schemes yielded few immigrants and no profits. And even when workers came, they often did not stay. Boosters' grand claims about southern opportunity did not match the reality immigrants found upon arrival. Confronted with low wages and poor working conditions, most quickly relocated to new geographies. They did not offer the pliant, eager labor that planters imagined. The New York recruiter who charged on a fractional basis seems to have been aware of this barrier. As he explained, "I undertake to make all hands sign binding contracts with the employers before embarkation."[48]

Attempts to bring bonded Chinese labor to the South were more successful. Thousands of indentured servants arrived in the region during the postbellum period, with a large concentration working on Louisiana sugar plantations. Planters advocating for the trade highlighted characteristics like control and manageability. An article in *DeBow's Review* described this plan in much the same language once used to describe the slave trade. Employers were not attracting immigrants; they were considering the "importation of coolies." The essay extolled their reliability, describing "the free and intelligent Mongol" as "ingenious, industrious, saving and quiet but will not vote."

These workers could be controlled. They were "more industrious than negroes, far more skillful and orderly," and, most important, they would "not get
up riots or muddy the stream."[49]

Patterns of thought that favored replacement of the former slaves over
negotiation were not unique to the American South. Slavery seems to have
wrought a similar outlook elsewhere, conditioning planters to see workers
as something to be imported and purchased—a commodity not dissimilar
from the agricultural products they grew. After the abolition of the Atlantic
slave trade in 1807, planters in the West Indies also sought ways to import
more labor. Though they still enjoyed control over the enslaved, they could
no longer simply purchase more as needed. The records of the Barham plantations in Jamaica contain careful calculations estimating the profitability of
workers imported from China—an attempt to replicate familiar patterns of
labor acquisition and control.[50] The import plan contained in the Barham records is labeled "Calculation of the Profit of an estate of 3200 acres cultivated
by 500 Chinese." The plan includes projections of sugar production both for
the current works and for an expanded estate. The various calculations estimate a profit of as much as £9,500 on a £60,000 capital outlay. The cost of
labor is both included in the estimate of capital expended and deducted as a
share of final profits (one-third). Long-term contracts with the five hundred
Chinese laborers (apparently for six years) could be acquired for a capital
outlay of £10,000, or "20 per head." A draft prospectus for the scheme touted
"industry, ingenuity, frugality, and orderly conduct."[51]

Though it is unclear what became of the Barham's scheme, the British
did transport bonded Chinese laborers to the West Indies from 1806 onward.
Indentured for long periods—typically six years—these workers could not
leave in search of better working conditions. Other empires embarked on
similar paths, with large numbers of Asian bonded laborers transported to
Cuba, Peru, Surinam, and other Latin American and Caribbean plantation
economies. The trade in bonded laborers appears to have intensified at moments of abolition, adopted as a replacement for slavery, or as an alternative
to negotiating in earnest with former slaves. Programs began with the end
of the slave trade and accelerated after the British abolished slavery in 1833.
Facing labor shortages and accustomed to control, planters pursued to a trade
in long-term indentures.[52]

Planters' expectations and aspirations made them as likely to attempt to replace those they had enslaved as to pay them more. Thomas Affleck, once a chief advocate for orderly plantation labor, shifted his efforts to promoting European immigration. But his desire to turn Texas into a "white man's country" attracted few immigrants and undermined his already precarious financial situation. Mired in debt, he did what he had done before. Looking for larger payouts and new opportunities, he turned to all manner of uncertain schemes, from onion planting, to supplying grapes to distillers, to commercial fishing, to his old standby of land speculation. As failed schemes piled upon failed schemes, his mounting debt propelled him to seek new risks. In April 1868, his estate, Glenblythe, was sold at auction, and he spent his final months living above a druggist's shop in Galveston, scraping together funds to send to his family. He died on December 30, 1868, his reputation under fire.[53]

Grasping for Control

In 1869, the first Redeemer government was elected in Tennessee, with others shortly following in Georgia, North Carolina, and Virginia. Though aspects of Reconstruction continued into the 1870s, by 1872, the federal government had eliminated the Freedmen's Bureau. Campaigns of violence and the intimidation of black voters helped to bring additional Redeemer governments to power. After the inauguration of Rutherford B. Hayes in 1877, the last federal troops left South Carolina, Florida, and Louisiana, unleashing violence against the freedpeople and assuring the success of Redeemer governments there as well. The brief electoral ascendancy of the freedmen ended. Reconstruction collapsed. As southern planters regained political control, they enshrined their efforts to control the freedpeople's lives and labor in law. A growing body of legal restraints on freedpeople included measures that bolstered planters' power on the plantation: the rise of debt peonage laws, the criminalization of breach of contract, and the expansion of vagrancy laws.

New arrangements substituted one form of control for another: the power of debt for that of ownership. After a few years of labor under opaque and often coercive contracts, many of the former slaves found themselves in debt. Debt peonage laws translated the money they owed into restrictions on mobility. Laborers were bound to their creditors until they had worked off what they owed. By one estimate, in 1907, a third of large plantations in the Cotton Belt had peons working their crops.[54] For many years, historians argued that debt peonage laws effectively bound the former enslaved people to plantations.[55] However, research suggests that these laws did more than keep the freedpeople on the land. Rather, employers manipulated debt in multiple ways. Instead of simply requiring freedpeople to stay, planters could also use what they were owed for leverage in negotiations, as an incentive to keep some laborers and to push others to go. Debt peonage made debt forgiveness a powerful strategy. Planters forgave or reduced debts in order to entice the best to stay or the weakest to leave.[56]

Even those who managed to stay out of debt often found their mobility limited. White southern elites passed a whole constellation of laws to constrain freedpeople's choices, even criminalizing the breach of labor contract.[57] Writing about the early twentieth century, Pete Daniel sums up research on late nineteenth-century southern labor regimes as follows: "The structure of the postbellum southern labor system . . . was built upon a body of law" of which the "central rationale was labor control."[58] Former slaveholders solved the problems of turnover faced by northern factory owners through harsher means. Over time, some of the coercive measures that planters relied on came to be enshrined in law. When planters broke contracts, they were subject only to civil suit, but freedpeople also faced criminal suits and strict vagrancy laws.[59]

Still, even as planters rebuilt their profits and amplified their economic control, they grasped for the more extreme power they had once enjoyed. Their efforts could not resurrect slavery itself, but they succeeded in recreating pockets of extreme domination. The convict labor system that emerged in the late nineteenth century most explicitly reconstructed the circumstances of slavery.[60] Though the system had its origins in the North, it intersected with the legacy of slavery and took on new implications.[61] The convict labor system operated in several ways. Some prisoners worked directly for state and local governments, while a larger number worked for southern industrialists through the lease system. Under the convict lease system, employers bought the rights to prisoners' labor. For a fee and the cost of feeding and housing workers, they could put them to work. The result was cheap labor for industrialists and revenue for the state. Convicts enjoyed very few labor protections, and the result was a horrifying and violent system that embodied the darkest side of postbellum southern racism, replicating and even exceeding the worst of slavery.

The account books of southern industrialists who leased convicts show this vividly. Both Talitha LeFlouria and Alex Lichtenstein draw on the records of the Chattahoochee Brick Company, where managers' practices look remarkably like those under slavery, with the dangerous modification that owners no longer cared to preserve their human capital. At the brick company, James T. Casey documented his use of torture in monthly "whipping reports." With an assiduousness that went beyond that of most slaveholders, Casey "meticulously notated every 'stroke' and 'stripe' tendered by the lash."[62]

Convict lessees sometimes used task and bonus systems not unlike those under slavery. Convicts were expected to work their task and then continue laboring for compensation. However, this compensation was much lower than what they might have earned as free workers, and it was paid in company scrip. Thus, as under slavery, very small incentives could become powerful instruments of control. And tasks could of course be adjusted. As one convict testified, if a man could do his task by three or four in the afternoon, his task would be increased. But only "after about twelve beatings" for "shortage" would a task be reduced.[63] Like slaves, convicts worked sunup to sundown, and they could not quit. They could and did resist, but the costs were high. Manufacturers enjoyed near complete control, which they translated to increased output. After the state of Georgia eliminated the convict lease system in 1908, the Chattahoochee Brick Company transitioned to free labor. Managers' complaints from the time echo those of planters accustomed to dealing with slaves and newly forced to negotiate. And the business struggled: output fell and production costs soared.[64]

Historians' interpretations of the convict lease system contain some of the same deep tensions as their descriptions of slavery. The system's terrible conditions have sometimes led scholars to describe it as economically unsophisticated—as the last bastion of a dying economic system. By contrast, Alex Lichtenstein has argued that far from a laggard in the story of southern economic development, the convict lease system was at the cutting edge. As he argues, "At each stage of the region's development, convict labor was concentrated in some of the most significant and rapidly growing sectors of the economy."[65] Businesses employing convict labor drew on the disciplinary strategies of slavery. As Lichtenstein writes, "Convict labor in the

South was steeped in brutality; the rawhide whip, iron shackle, sweat box, convict cage, and bloodhound were its most potent instruments for eighty years." But, as he continues, these characteristics should not make the system seem distant—as a vestige of the backward South that had largely disappeared. Rather, the convict lease system (and its brutality) was married to the "cutting edge of southern politics and economic development, not its dark corners. Far from representing a lag in southern modernity, convict labor was a central component in the region's modernization."[66] Just as the horrors of slavery facilitated a form of scientific management, "the horrors of the southern penal system . . . played a central role in the evolution of the region's race relations, forms of labor exploitation, and burgeoning capitalist development."[67]

Still, the effect of harsh legal restrictions, debt peonage, and the convict lease system should not be overestimated. These systems limited workers' choices, creating pockets of labor with very real similarities to the slave system. On the whole, however, the labor market that emerged after the war was a high turnover market, where planters had to recruit labor and induce it to stay. The former slaves began to relocate immediately after emancipation and would continue to move even as peonage and vagrancy laws expanded. Sociologist Martin Ruef estimates that cumulative exit rates between 1865 and 1870 may have been as high as 80 percent. The reasons freedpeople gave for leaving plantations emphasized their desire for control over their living and working conditions. They sought to reunite their families and to escape the cruelty of former masters.[68] High turnover rates continued into the 1870s and beyond, as the freedpeople continued to move from place to place in large numbers. Studies of individual plantations show that during the 1870s, some experienced turnover rates of around 50 percent, and even those enjoying more stable workforces generally experienced some turnover.[69] Though these rates do not approach the high levels of turnover experienced in some northern factories, they departed radically from the captive labor of the slave system.[70]

Remarkably, despite legal changes, the former slaves continued to quit long after the end of Radical Reconstruction. In 1910, when the Bureau of the Census asked share tenants how long they had lived on their current farm, the median response was one year or less, and "more than 80 percent of black share tenants had been on their present farms less than five years."

The freedpeople were mobile not just from plantation to plantation but from county to county and from state to state, often following a path to higher wage areas.[71]

Critically, however, mobility did not extend beyond the South to the North. The southern labor market remained isolated from markets in other regions, keeping wages low for decades. Despite small amounts of outmigration, the region would remain separate from the higher wage North and West for more than half a century. Networks of immigration tend to be remarkably persistent, with those migrating in search of higher wages typically following friends or kin along similar routes. Knowledge of opportunities for agricultural workers kept migration flowing within the South. However, only very small numbers of black workers moved out of the region, and those few who did choose to leave do not seem to have paved the way for large-scale relocation until the great migrations of the twentieth century. Though the former slaves continued to negotiate, they negotiated in an environment of low wages.[72]

In the high-turnover, low-wage economy that emerged after emancipation, the former slaves gained some control over work patterns and personal mobility, but they did not gain significant economic power. And as the brief victories of Radical Reconstruction faded into Jim Crow, the state came to police private lives and mobility in some of the same ways planters had controlled them under slavery. For their part, planters continued to complain about the steadiness of labor. Though turnover was comparatively less than in most northern factories, it differed tremendously from the extreme control to which they had been accustomed. Planters also seem to have been unwilling to recognize that the two aspects of the labor market were connected—that high turnover came at the cost of low wages. As one observer reported, "We suspect the chief reason why the Negro is loth to labor is the uncertainty of his wages."[73] Raising pay or increasing shares seem to have been solutions that planters were unwilling to consider. Accustomed to near complete control over work patterns, they resisted negotiating with the freedpeople in earnest.

Historical debates about Reconstruction labor markets have alternately characterized the system that emerged after the Civil War as a variant of wage labor and as a form of peonage or even peasant labor. These two categories come freighted with a set of related interpretive connotations—was the South on a free labor, capitalist trajectory similar to that of the North? Or did it rely on a fundamentally different, premodern form of labor? Did emancipation make the South more capitalist or less so?[74]

Postbellum southern account books tell a hybrid story. On the one hand, if free labor is fundamentally defined by the right to quit, then the freedpeople fought for and exercised this freedom. After emancipation, southern planters began to experience high levels of turnover, if not as high as those in the North. On the other hand, the rise of wage labor is generally associated with a loss of control over labor processes. In most accounts of the coming of capitalism, the rise of wage labor accompanies a shift from workshop to factory that is associated with a process of deskilling—of workers' loss of control over labor patterns as they are forced to sell not their skill or output but their time. By comparison, after emancipation, the former slaves gained control over labor patterns. Though economic and political progress were severely curtailed, freedpeople's control over their work increased dramatically. They threw off the surveillance of gang labor and the scale, and the breakup of plantations into smaller farms gave them more control over daily labor patterns. In many ways, the rise of sharecropping looked more like a shift from factories to workshops than the opposite.[75] The economy that emerged included an expansion of wage-like payments as well as a rise in contracts.[76] However, these transitions accompanied a decline in the size of the average productive unit and an increase in workers' control over labor processes. Workers received pay for their labor (when the crop was good), but in some ways their labor was less commodified than it had been under slavery.[77]

The circumstances that emerged looked more like the capitalist North in some ways, and in other ways less. Familiar categories like free labor and property carried different implications for the freedpeople. Even as they sought access to property and wages, they also contested these categories. They brought the experience of slavery to their negotiations, sometimes embracing and sometimes contesting the visions of northerners and their former masters.[78] The economy that emerged reflected the overlapping but often divergent visions and interests of northerners, southerners, and freedpeople. It also ushered in a long period of comparative economic stagnation; though the economy continued to grow at a moderate pace and cotton production increased, what had been a wealthy region would not begin to approach the prosperity of other regions until after the New Deal.[79] Postbellum southern account books support what a number of scholars have suggested: that the economic system that emerged after emancipation does not fit neatly into the familiar categories offered by theories of capitalism. As Scott Marler has written, sharecropping was "a hybrid economic 'form'—not a full-blown mode of production—during a long period of unsettled social relations." It was a "compromise 'solution,'" never entirely satisfactory to either planters or freedpeople.[80]

The version of Thomas Affleck's account book that his son republished in 1880 reflects both continuity and change. In some ways, the volume replicated the commercial, calculating aspirations of the popular antebellum journals. A multitude of data could be input into a series of blank forms and the output from these could be summed up on the "Farmer's Annual Balance Sheet." The new volume, like its predecessors, also presented agriculture as deeply intertwined in a growing national economy. Purchasers flipping to the advertising section could review the routes of the Chicago, Rock Island & Pacific Railway, contemplate a luxury chair manufactured in Pittsburgh, enroll in Gaskell's Business College of New Jersey, or order "Poland-China Swine" from Waterloo, Nebraska. But the book also shows how much had changed. Gone were the inventory of human capital and the record of cotton picked. Nor was there space to measure the depreciation of human capital or to tally up output per hand.[81]

Before the end of slavery, planters had analyzed detailed information on the output (and capital value) of individuals who could not leave. They had organized their labor in large units with organizational structures that paralleled those used in big businesses elsewhere. Spared the complexity of recruiting and retaining labor to staff these enterprises, slaveholders had focused on speeding up the pace of work so that they could plant and pick more cotton. After emancipation, the freedpeople could quit and did. Though planters continued to imagine labor as little more than an input of production, the former slaves contested this outlook. They negotiated for crucial transformations in the shape of work, throwing off the surveillance of the scale, and pushing for large plantations to be broken up into smaller units. Planters attempted to limit their mobility through debt peonage and vagrancy laws, but the freedpeople continued to move in search of better opportunities for themselves and their families.

The pages of southern account books show a retreat from both large-scale production and from productivity analysis. Even as big business was on the rise in other sectors, large plantations were being divided into smaller units. And at the very moment when scientific management was beginning to emerge in other settings, the scientific agriculture it so closely resembled collapsed. The revival of Affleck's book failed with them. Though there was apparently sufficient demand to warrant a second edition in 1883, sales agents complained that they could not sell the journals.[82] The book neither transformed the business practices of American farmers nor made the publisher and salespeople much money. The emerging southern economy followed a parallel course: planters continued growing ever more cotton, many earning profits for themselves. But regional labor productivity stalled, and despite the aspirations of men like Affleck, the southern economy became increasingly isolated from other regions and the world.

For their part, the freedpeople won important concessions in the shape of work but not economic security. Daily labor patterns looked radically different from those that prevailed under slavery, and these new labor patterns accompanied increased control over individual and family life. However, despite success in winning these critical freedoms, sustained economic gains eluded the freedpeople. Wages stagnated across the region, and the former slaves labored on the edge of solvency or slipped into debt. Though many moved within the South, few ventured beyond the region. Planters complained about high turnover and workforce instability, but they did not pay higher wages. The South remained a dramatically low-wage region within a high-wage nation.

Conclusion

M ANAGEMENT EXPERTISE blended well with violence, a fact slaves understood well. In 1834, Moses Roper escaped from a plantation in West Florida. Roper traveled north and eventually to England, where he wrote an account of his life as a slave. He illustrated his narrative with a diagram of a cotton screw, a plantation appliance used for pressing cotton into bales (see Figure C.1). Roper drew on the visual style of technical diagrams to show how this common device could become an instrument of torture. The illustration labeled the parts of the machine "a" through "e," explaining the purpose of each. At the letter "a," his master, Gooch, "hung me up by the hands." A horse, "b," circled the contraption, turning the screw, "e," while Gooch followed behind, whip in hand. The turning of the screw lowered a block, "c," down into a box, "d." Eventually Gooch put Roper "into the box d, and shut me down in it." The end result was more labor. As Roper explains, after this treatment, "I . . . did my work very well."[1]

Of course, this was not the image that planters called to mind when they thought about the efficiency of their operations. Elsewhere, the cotton screw was a symbol of improvement: one adorned the masthead of the *American Cotton Planter*. There, it was the centerpiece of an orderly and productive

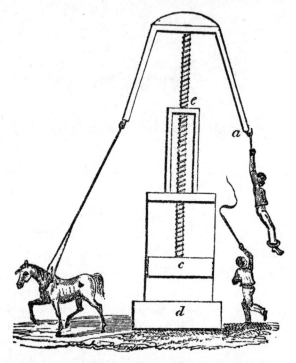

THE AUTHOR HANGING BY HIS HANDS
TIED TO A COTTON SCREW.

FIGURE C.I. The Cotton Screw as an Instrument of Torture. Technology and violence went hand in hand on the plantation, and enslaved people understood their compatibility. In his narrative, Moses Roper used the visual rhetoric of the patent diagram to illustrate his brutal punishment. Moses Roper, *A Narrative of the Adventures and Escape of Moses Roper, from American Slavery* (Philadelphia: Merrihew & Gunn, 1838), 47.

plantation landscape (see Figure C.2). In the foreground, an enslaved laborer filled a basket with cotton, while others packed the screw. A neat stack of bales documented their output, and in the distance a train and a steamship connected the plantation to the global economy, smokestacks puffing. Below this scene, a subhead declared the journal's commitment to "Plantation Economy, Manufactures, and Mechanic Arts." Roper's screw shows the synergy of violence and industry. The *American Cotton Planter*

A Monthly Journal, devoted to improved Plantation Economy, Manufactures, and Mechanic Arts.

FIGURE C.2. The Cotton Screw as an Instrument of Improvement. Planters saw the cotton screw as the centerpiece of an orderly plantation landscape, and one adorned the masthead of the *American Cotton Planter*. *The American Cotton Planter: A Monthly Journal, Devoted to Improved Plantation Economy, Manufactures, and Mechanic Arts* (Montgomery, Ala.: N. B. Cloud, Editor, 1853).

displays slavery as efficient and productive, but pushes violence comfortably offstage.

What can we learn by considering these contrasting visions of American slavery side by side? This book brings together two very different kinds of history—business history and the history of slavery. These fields rarely intersect. They are studied by different groups of scholars who attend different conferences and ask different kinds of questions. But each field has something new to offer the other. The history of slavery offers an opportunity to study the ways businesses benefit from coercion and control. And the methods of business history—using records to reconstruct management strategies and structure—can help us better understand what the slaves were up against. This conclusion takes these themes in turn, beginning with what slavery can teach us about the history of business before moving to the ways business history can help us to understand slavery.

Slavery and the History of Business

Slaveholding planters adopted innovative business practices similar to those developed by businesspeople employing free labor. They developed complex management structures (Chapter 1), standardized reporting (Chapter 2),

productivity analysis akin to what would later be called scientific management (Chapter 3), and capital valuation practices, including depreciation,
which they applied to human lives (Chapter 4). After emancipation, some
planters continued to keep detailed records, but the former slaves refused to
be measured and monitored in the same ways (Chapter 5). Many of the most
innovative southern calculations disappeared—planters carefully tracked the
debt of their former slaves, but gone were the records of cotton picking that
had accelerated their productivity.

Underlying all these business practices was the fundamental flexibility
of the slave system. From the perspective of planters, humans proved a complex and dynamic form of both labor and capital. As labor, enslaved people
could be allocated and reallocated from task to task with comparatively little
negotiation. They could be driven to labor in unpleasant jobs or moved thousands of miles to fertile soils. As capital, they multiplied—the price of slaves
rose, and women bore children. Higher prices and larger communities meant
more capital, and this capital became collateral for the purchase of more
slaves, land, and tools.[2]

Whether southern account books were more or less "sophisticated" than
their northern counterparts is hard to judge, and in some ways beside the
point. Each context produced different kinds of records, each of which excelled the other in particular ways. Slaveholders seem to have been more successful in calculating productivity, while entrepreneurs employing free
workers relied on payrolls and ledgers to manage labor. Southern books reflect remarkable standardization, whereas northern books show more nov-
elty and customization. Both settings produced both business failures and
large fortunes. And in both regions, the practices of elite businesspeople—the
focus of this book and of most business histories—advanced far ahead of average practices. Many of the agro-businesses built by southern planters were
incredibly successful. In 1860, more millionaires lived in the slave South than
in the rest of the United States. The wealthiest plantation districts boasted
concentrations of fortunes to match the wealthiest northern neighborhoods.
In his study of Feliciana Parish, Louisiana, Richard Kilbourne found that
some 10 percent of free families had been millionaires during the late antebellum period (in 1995 dollars).[3]

Planters earned these fortunes not despite slavery but because of it. Not
all of my findings about southern business practices are new. Scholars have

argued for years that slavery could be highly profitable and that some planters were adroit businesspeople. However, advanced practices have often been interpreted as scattered exceptions in an otherwise backward economic system. This account makes that interpretation untenable: the list of innovations that structures my chapters includes almost every key development in the history of management during the period. And the overarching portrait that emerges from studying these innovations is of slaveholding entrepreneurs benefiting from the circumstances of slavery. Surveying cotton fields and seeing humans as inputs of production seems to have stimulated management innovation in ways that were difficult in free factories plagued with turnover. Far from being rigid, combining only reluctantly with modern management techniques, slavery was a fluid institution that could be adapted to many settings.

In the mid-twentieth century, economist and social theorist Joseph Schumpeter characterized capitalism by its incessant change from within—a process he described as the gale of "creative destruction." For Schumpeter, the engine of capital could be found in the relentless pursuit of new consumer goods, new methods of production and transportation, new markets, and new forms of industrial organization. Economies built on slave labor certainly do not always display this creativity—slavery has existed as a comparatively static institution at many points in history. But in the late eighteenth- and nineteenth-century American South and West Indies, slavery and modern business practices strengthened each other. Slave labor and capital were deployed in the search for new markets, new crops, new production processes, and new information systems to coordinate production. Control aided planters in their pursuit of new seeds, new manures, and new lands. Slavery enabled capitalists to build machines made of men, women, and children, and also to regear this machinery on command.[4]

The "creativity" of slaveholders should not be surprising. In a sense, slaveholders operated in the ultimate unregulated market. Before abolition and amelioration measures restricted property rights, slaveholders enjoyed immense flexibility to exploit labor. Planters in both the American South and the West Indies employed wage laborers. They also purchased and sold slaves, using both positive and negative incentives to motivate their labor. Regulations placed few restrictions on the ways they could exploit their human property. In the choreography of labor and the push to accelerate its pace, planters benefited from extensive, legally permitted power over their slaves. The law allowed them to pair incentive payments with violence and the threat of sale, and thus to drive enslaved people to greater productivity and higher profits. Far from creating a barrier to efficient production, slavery offered planters tremendous flexibility in the way they managed labor.

Of course, the flexibility and dynamism of slavery was limited to a narrow class of capitalists and entrepreneurs. As a result, the varieties of innovation that accompanied slavery were different and narrower than those that emerged elsewhere. A number of studies have described slavery's negative long-term impacts on economic growth, suggesting that stagnating development results from the highly unequal institutions that usually accompany it. For example, slavery is correlated with the restriction of education to a narrow class. Even in those southern states with comparatively high levels of education for free whites, rates of education tended to be substantially lower than in the North. Similarly, in the West Indies, cultural and educational institutions flagged, which contributed to the rise of absenteeism described in Chapters 1 and 2. Patenting rates in the slaveholding South also lagged behind those in the North, though these do not capture many agricultural innovations, such as new seed varieties. Although slavery was compatible with certain kinds of economic creativity, it may have limited others—and thus, in the longer term, economic change.[5]

Still, these long-term consequences—or as economists have described them, "reversals of fortune"[6]—should not lead us to classify slaveholders' business practices as primitive or premodern. Rather, they should lead us to question our assumptions about the relationship between advanced business practices and longer-term economic development. Inequality can drive innovation, and innovation can entrench inequality, particularly in highly unregulated labor markets that put everything—even lives—up for sale.

Business and the History of Slavery

In comparison to northern farmers and manufacturers, planters exercised a remarkable level of control over enslaved people. During the nineteenth century, many northern payrolls and time books show constant disruptions: blanks and inconsistencies from when workers arrived late, stayed home, and quit—often without notice. Aggregate studies of turnover confirm this instability. By contrast, southern records are remarkably complete. Grids of cotton picking were meticulously filled, suggesting that almost every worker went to the fields every day. Gaps usually note the reasons for absences— weather, illness, or allocation to another task. Planters and overseers surveilled enslaved workers, assiduously collecting data on their output. When compared to northern (and postbellum) books, this data reflects a remarkable level of control. On plantations, the aspirations to control reflected on paper were more completely realized than in other emerging industries and geographies.

To some readers, the notion that slaveholders enjoyed extensive control over the men and women they enslaved may seem obvious. However, my emphasis on control is at odds with much recent historical scholarship. For decades, historians have focused on masters' lack of control, publishing outstanding research uncovering the various ways enslaved people eluded their owners. These studies of resistance, community, family, and culture have shown the myriad ways enslaved people carved out spaces of their own in a system of extreme domination.[7] Appreciating the importance of this scholarship requires an understanding of what came before. Studies of enslaved agency pushed back against a prior generation of research that emphasized domination, comparing plantations to concentration camps. The earlier generation of scholarship suggested that slavery did long-term damage to African American communities, families, and personalities. Among its claims was the notion that the system of slavery was infantilizing, creating certain personality types.[8] That perspective, however outdated today, was also politically radical in its own moment: it blamed persistent inequality not on racial inferiority but on slavery.[9] It also countered an even older literature that cast slavery as inefficient and even kind. This romantic distortion grew out of a vision of the slave South as more concerned with honor and social order than with profit. As one of the most prominent historians of this outlook put it, slavery served as a "school" to "civilize" the slaves.[10]

Even this cursory synthesis of a century of slavery scholarship gives a sense of the discipline's ricochet between masters' domination and slaveholders' resistance. More recently, studies focused solely on resistance have come under critique for their aspirations to recover enslaved "humanity" and "agency." As waves of scholarship before them, these histories of resistance have now been cast as inadequate and even presumptuous—as if historians were in a position to grant enslaved people humanity by telling their stories.[11]

This book recovers the insights of older literature emphasizing domination without losing the insights of scholarship focused on enslaved culture and community. My emphasis on control rather than its subversion is not meant to question the resistance of enslaved people—indeed, evidence for resistance is embedded throughout the account books I have studied. Control and resistance are not opposites. Control does not reflect a lack of resistance, nor does it in any way signal consent. To offer an adequate account of chattel slavery, historians need to acknowledge the vitality of slave culture without romanticizing it or overstating its scope. What enslaved people accomplished was remarkable but also dramatically circumscribed by systems of violence and surveillance. To understand the significance of moments of resistance, we need to comprehend the system that enslaved people sought to survive.[12]

In 1975, historian David Brion Davis began an influential study of abolition by asking "what the abolitionists were up against."[13] I ask the same question about enslaved people: What were they up against? Here, a business history approach can be particularly valuable because it illuminates the interlocking strategies planters employed to increase their profits. Rather than turning first to abstractions like hegemony and ideology to explain planters' control—though such concepts can be useful—we can begin with the material and informational technologies slaveholders used to extract labor from the people they owned.[14] Slaves seeking spaces for themselves faced complex and often quantitative information systems that knit together violence, fear, and social terror.

What were enslaved people up against? Limited access to basic necessities, including food, lodging, and rest; the threat of violence, sometimes to the point of death; the risk of sale, of both themselves and loved ones; and a legal system that was more likely to protect them as property than as people. These circumstances offered slaveholders tremendous leverage over labor processes, and planters who engaged in careful record keeping sought to bind their power into extensive systems of control. Whenever they could, they drew enslaved people into this system of surveillance. Though this book focuses on information systems and accounting, these systems were also connected to technologies of spatial and architectural surveillance, what other scholars have called the "carceral landscape"—a description taken from research on urban spaces and prisons.[15]

Modern mechanisms of management and surveillance combined with the manipulation of food and shelter to extend planters' control over enslaved people. Historian Eugene Genovese famously characterized slavery as a paternalist system where slaveholders understood themselves in part through their care for and authority over enslaved people. The notion of paternalism has come under intense criticism, not least because of the trappings of benevolence that seem to accompany the word. Genovese himself tried to specify that paternalism did not imply kindness, but the word's familial associations have left scholars appropriately uncomfortable with the category.[16] Business historians also write about paternalism—the paternalism of the company town and of welfare capitalism. Though this was a paternalism that shaped the identities of business owners, it was also a paternalism that was fundamentally in service to profit, a form of paternalism that cultivated obedience, aided by extensive surveillance that forced workers to buy basic necessities at company stores. Paternalism was a business strategy deployed in pursuit of other priorities. If slaveholders were paternalistic, it was this kind of paternalism—akin to the paternalism of the Ford Motor Company, where managers peered deep into employees' private lives, but with the crucial distinction that the whip not the five-dollar day kept workers on the job.[17]

Understanding plantation business strategies can help to connect the contrasting portraits offered by recent scholarship on the history of American and Atlantic slavery. On the one hand, scholars have unearthed vibrant histories of enslaved culture and community. On the other, they have described a system of slavery that was expanding and strengthening. For example, Ira Berlin, one of the most influential scholars of enslaved community, has argued persuasively for the ways enslaved people built distinctive cultural systems and strong social networks. Yet as Berlin also points out, during the eighteenth and nineteenth centuries, the slaveholding regions of North America transitioned from being "societies with slaves" to "slave societies." Slavery shifted from a peripheral influence on economic and social orders to a central organizing feature, and much of the American South came to be structured around enslaved production.[18]

Put differently, the business history of slavery helps to bridge the gap between stories of enslaved agency and those that show how slavery was growing stronger. It can connect a late antebellum world where slavery was expanding with the brutal war that led to its dramatic collapse. How did masters succeed in extending their control over men, women, and children who resented and resisted their dominance? In part, they did so by building sophisticated information systems. The elite slaveholders described in this book infused slavery with modern business practices that enabled them to maintain control despite opposition. To understand the significance of moments of resistance, we need to comprehend the system that enslaved people struggled to survive. Once we recognize the strength of this system, enslaved people's efforts to undermine their masters appear not as scattered interruptions but as a constant undercurrent of opposition.[19]

Understanding plantation information systems can help us to interpret small-scale resistance and to understand its stakes. Slowing down the pace of labor, stuffing rocks and melons into sacks of cotton, and covering for one another when planters suspected something all disrupted management regimes. They prevented slaveholders from extending their monopoly on information and violence. These ongoing efforts to limit masters' control also reflect a readiness to resist openly when the opportunity arose. When war began to open fissures in the system, enslaved people pried these fissures open, grasping freedom on the ground. Many of the same men, women, and children who had complied with their masters to survive suddenly made themselves unmanageable.[20]

Figure C.3 is illustrated with two images of men, women, and children picking cotton. Taken either in the final days of slavery or the first days of freedom, these two almost identical pictures are the two sides of a stereograph. Such images could be inserted into a stereoscope—a popular device not altogether different from a modern 3D headset—that merged the images, bringing three dimensions out of two. Plantation account books can be read in the same way. Seen from the perspective of a slaveholding entrepreneur, they show how units of labor could be flattened into units of profit, and how this profit could be reinvested in human capital that compounded over time. With a shift in perspective, these same account books reveal what enslaved people struggled against: a matrix of control that offered little room to negotiate. Once we

FIGURE C.3. Picking Cotton near Montgomery, Alabama. This stereograph from the 1860s shows either freedpeople or bondpeople laboring in the cotton fields. Inserting a stereograph into a stereoscope merged the images, giving users a three dimensional view of cotton picking. J. H. Lakin, photographer, *Picking cotton near Montgomery, Alabama*, [186?] Photograph. Stereograph Cards Collection (LC-DIG-stereo-1s02973), Library of Congress Prints and Photographs Division, Washington, D.C.

understand this system, enslaved people's efforts to undermine their masters—from running away, to slowing the pace of labor, to covering for each other and spreading information—become all the more amazing. And the fact that, when opportunity arose, they heroically took their freedom becomes utterly unsurprising.

Nineteenth-century Americans bought stereoscopes so that they could see distant places—so that they could travel without leaving home. Like account books and the quantitative methods they contained, these were technologies of distance. Both technologies made new information visible to new audiences, and they continue to make information visible today. Account books have helped historians to uncover the experiences of enslaved people. Read against the grain, they have helped us to see the ways men, women, and children resisted being reduced to units of labor and capital. In their own period, plantation account books sometimes even became weapons in the hands of abolitionists who took the data planters employed and turned it against them in the fight against slavery.[21] But, reading between the lines for this counternarrative is a difficult process. Account books begin with the story that slaveholders were seeking, and the stories of enslaved people reveal themselves only reluctantly—and sometimes not at all.[22] Like a stereoscope that allowed distant populations to glimpse the men, women, and children who picked the cotton they wore on their backs, account books provided planters with information at a comfortable remove.

Thinking about men, women, and children as quantitative inputs of production made it remarkably easy for slaveholders to overlook the human costs of economic exchange. Parallel patterns of thought govern many modern businesses: conditions similar to slavery are not as far away as it is convenient to think they are. They are connected to our modern economy—sometimes only a purchase or a sale away. Plantation account books remind us how easy it is to overlook the conditions of production from the comfort of a countinghouse or the safety of a computer screen. Reckoning with the ways planters accounted for slavery should encourage us to rethink the kinds of data we record and how we use it. Quantitative records can help us to see farther, but only if we remember what the numbers make visible and what they erase.[23]

Postscript

FORWARD TO SCIENTIFIC MANAGEMENT

A<small>FTER EMANCIPATION</small>, planters stopped tracking the number of pounds their laborers picked each day. But similar productivity analysis would soon reemerge in a new setting. Frederick Winslow Taylor, supposed originator of the system of scientific management, began his experiments in the 1880s at a Philadelphia factory called Midvale Steel. By the time he published *The Principles of Scientific Management* in 1911, slavery was almost half a century gone. Southerners had reestablished control by new means—by Jim Crow, by debt and the sharecropping system, and by convict labor. For their part, the former slaves had begun to make their way north and west in the first great migration. But the circumstances of slavery were far from forgotten, and as Taylor sought to popularize his methods of management, he came under fire for promoting what his critics called a new "slave driving" system.[1]

In the same year Taylor published *The Principles of Scientific Management,* a congressional special committee convened to investigate the circumstances of shop management. Workers, union leaders, and management experts—including Taylor himself—all spoke at the hearings, which extended into the following year. An experienced iron molder from the Watertown Arsenal in Massachusetts told the committee that scientific management felt to him "as if it is getting down to slavery." Managers, he said, exerted extreme control, "following you when you are at your job . . . and with a stop watch stand over you while you bend down to pick up a few rods. . . . This is too much for a man to stand."[2] The head of a machinists' union argued that the system had "reduced the men to virtual slavery, low wages," and that it had "engendered such an air of suspicion among the men that each man regards every other man as a possible traitor or spy."[3] At the close of the hearings, though the committee took little action, it agreed that elements of the system acted "the same as a slave driver's whip on the negro, as it keeps him in a constant state of agitation."[4]

Of course, the ticking of a stopwatch is wildly different from the lash of the whip—or a whip and a watch used in tandem, as was the case on some plantations.[5] But there is nonetheless something revealing about the analogy, particularly because proponents occasionally used the language of slavery as well. One example appears in the correspondence of Kempton Taylor, Taylor's nephew, who assembled material for a biography of his uncle after he died. One correspondent, Scudder Klyce, explained that scientific management was a system of "Cooperation or democracy," but he gave a very peculiar definition of democracy. As he wrote, the system "consists of the able person's taking the lead in giving 'orders' in the cases where he is of superior ability, and the others' submitting: it is the relationship of master and slave, regardless of how otherwise it may be named." From the manager's perspective, control was the essential characteristic of scientific management. What set scientific management apart from actual slavery was that the relations of control could change over time: "At any time a lathe hand may be able to show the superintendent a better way to do it; the superintendent should in that case be the slave."[6] The master had full control over the slave, with the essential caveat that these roles could change.

In the eyes of its founders, scientific management paired the efficiencies of the division of mental and bodily labor, so extreme under slavery, with the circumstances of freedom. Taylor believed that this arrangement would benefit both owners and workers. He argued that the application of scientific analysis to management would create large improvements in productivity, and that laborers could share in the fruits of these gains. But in the experience of operatives, this was rarely true. From their perspective, the system offered little freedom. A fleeting reversal of roles offered workers no enduring control. Rather, when they showed the superintendent a better way, they gave up their own power. They rendered themselves replaceable.[7]

The most striking parallel between slavery and scientific management can be found in the "task idea," which Taylor described as "the most prominent single element in modern scientific management." The task system is closely identified with Henry Laurence Gantt, who is most well known today for the Gantt chart, which still bears his name. During the heyday of scientific management, Gantt developed a "task and bonus system," which paired a flat task and a time wage with bonuses for overwork. Workers would be paid a base wage plus an additional piece rate for production above a certain minimum. By combining an achievable (rather than a maximal) task with bonuses, workers would enjoy the security of a minimum payment but also be encouraged to strive beyond it.[8]

Of course, while they introduced some details, neither Gantt nor Taylor created the task system. It has a much longer history, and was one of the principal methods of organizing labor under slavery. Many of the calculations outlined in this book, particularly in Chapter 3, demonstrate the lengths that planters went to in order to calculate appropriate tasks for the enslaved. Some even paid bonuses for achievement above these targets. Except for the base payment, the systems slaveholders used closely resembled Gantt's new system, and he and others were aware of the connection. Taylor lamented the word's "unfortunate connection with 'slave-driving.'" Gantt acknowledged that the word "task" was "disliked by many men," regarding it as a "principal disadvantage" of the method.[9]

That Gantt understood the word's historical connections with slavery is perhaps unsurprising given his southern roots. He was born on the eve of the Civil War to a slaveholder in Maryland. His father, Virgil Gantt, owned sixty-six men, women, and children. As Gantt wrote, "The term 'taskmaster' is an old one in our language; it symbolizes the time, now happily passing away, when men were compelled to work, not for their own interests, but for those of someone else." His goal was not to abolish this old system but to adapt it to modern needs. As he explained, "The general policy of the past has been to drive, but the era of force must give way to that of knowledge, and the policy of the future will be to teach and to lead, to the advantage of all concerned."[10]

Scientific managers seem to have seen their own practices not as something utterly disconnected from the history of slavery but as a strategic movement forward from it. Their rhetoric was not always of distance but of progress. Gantt apparently "liked to say that scientific management marked a great step forward from slave labour." [11] James Mapes Dodge, a Philadelphia manufacturer and early supporter of Taylor, explained in 1913 that "we cannot tell who first liberated the germ idea of Scientific Management, as it was born to the world in the first cry of anguish that escaped the lips of the lashed slave." Dodge's reference was metaphorical, to a vague and distant past where slavery prevailed, not to the slave South. But he understood that "the present generation" had inherited "from the past the relationship of master and slave" and saw it as the job of scientific management to move beyond it. [12]

This study is not the first to describe the many parallels between plantation practices and those used in scientific management. The similarities have been pointed out not just by scientific managers and their opponents but also by historians studying both systems. Writing in 1918, during the heyday of scientific management, historian Ulrich Bonnell Phillips acknowledged the parallels. As Daniel Joseph Singal writes, when Phillips described the sophistication of southern management strategies, he liked to reference a series of articles in the *Southern Planter* by H. W. Vick, whose "analysis of stance and movement" resembled some of the most advanced industrial studies of his own time. [13]

Because racial bias permeated Phillips's work—he also described slavery as a kind of "school" for the enslaved—his descriptions of southern industrial discipline are sometimes overlooked. But paternalism and industrial precision can be compatible. Indeed, Phillips's descriptions of the ways planters interacted with their slaves bear striking similarities to the ways Frederick Winslow Taylor described the interactions of managers and workers. In 1911, during the many months of congressional hearings on scientific management, Taylor attempted to distance his system from that of slavery by describing it as a school for workers who did not know how to work. In a typical passage, he railed against his critics: "This is not nigger driving; this is kindness; this is teaching; this is doing what I would like mighty well to have done to me if I were a boy trying to learn how to do something. This is not a case of cracking a whip over a man and saying, 'Damn you, get there.'" [14]

Half a century after Phillips, during a decade of heated debate over the nature of southern slavery, Keith Aufhauser again described the extent to which the theory and practice of the slaveholders conformed to Taylor's system of scientific management.[15] Aufhauser came to similar conclusions not just about the parallels between planters' tools and those advocated by scientific managers, but about the power relations they reflected. As he wrote, "This study has examined the relations of power between ruler and ruled at the point of production. As far as discipline at the workplace goes, I have argued that the master-slave relationship is quite similar to the capitalist-wage-laborer relationship in scientifically managed enterprises."[16]

Two decades after Aufhauser, historian Mark Smith would again describe aspects of plantation management that looked strikingly like scientific management. Smith focused on the role of time discipline on the plantation, pointing to the widespread use of clocks to assess how much labor the enslaved could perform.[17] Again in 2003, management professor Bill Cooke pointed out that planters had used many of the same practices we associate with the history of American business.[18] Cooke argued that our failure to appreciate these associations resulted not from a lack of research but from denial. He called it denial because his findings drew on easily accessible published research—like that of Aufhauser, Smith, and others.[19]

In some cases, the evidence for denial can be literally read between the lines. Take the example of Henry Laurence Gantt, whose task and bonus system so closely paralleled the one used by some slaveholders. Gantt is still sometimes profiled in modern management books.[20] As his biographer explains, he was born in 1861 to a family of prosperous farmers in Maryland. But "his early years were marked by some deprivation as the Civil War brought about changes to the family fortunes." Those "changes," so easily elided, were wrought by the sixty-six slaves who took their freedom in the war. The legacy of slavery is simultaneously acknowledged and overlooked.[21]

Moving beyond denial requires not only an acknowledgment that slaveholders practiced a kind of scientific management but also a broader rethinking of deep-seated assumptions about the relationship between capitalism and control. Though there are many exceptions, histories of business practices—at least those that reach a general audience—tend to be both individual and social success stories. They tell stories that are win-win, with businesspeople earning profits and customers, laborers, and communities benefiting along the way. This can, of course, be true. The shift from seeing trade as zero-sum to positive-sum was one of the most important transitions underpinning the rise of capitalism. But capitalism does not make this win-win inevitable.

Growing the pie brings no guarantee about how it will be divided. The sharing of rewards depends on how the rules are written or, differently put, on how markets are regulated. Slavery shows how one particular set of rules enabled precise management but paired its efficiencies with horrifying costs. Slavery also illustrates how certain kinds of market expansion—allowing lives to be bonded in labor and sold—can produce radical inequality. Economic growth can accompany the expansion of freedom and opportunity. But, as in the case of American slavery, the expansion of market freedoms for a few can depend on the limitation of all kinds of freedoms for others. Growth can accompany choice, but it can also build on violence and injustice.[22]

Certain kinds of management flourish when managers enjoy a high level of control over their workers. The rise of scientific management in the late nineteenth century should be seen both as a moment of innovation and as the reemergence of new circumstances of control. With the closing of the frontier, workers had fewer opportunities to leave the factory to return to the land. With immigration and rising inequality, manufacturers enjoyed access to a plentiful labor supply. The age of trust and monopoly limited outside options, and collusion meant that even when workers could legally go elsewhere, the circumstances were not necessarily better. Only in these circumstances did it make sense for managers like Taylor to attempt to calculate "what fraction of a horse power a man power is," with the expectation that this maximum rate of work could be acquired for an hourly wage, or perhaps a wage and a "bonus."[23]

Modern narratives of capitalist development often emphasize the positive-sum outcomes of many individual choices. They suggest that free, even selfish, decisions go hand in hand with growth and innovation. They also assume that vast wealth accumulated by a few accompanies improved circumstances for many. The history of slavery's capitalism warns against all these expectations. In the eighteenth and nineteenth centuries, slavery proved highly adaptable to the pursuit of profit. Free markets for slaveholders flourished, and their control over men, women, and children expedited production, both by pushing up the pace of labor and by transporting it to new, more fertile soils. Slaveholders' manipulation of human capital compounded it into massive fortunes—both through financial maneuvering and through human reproduction. The power of capital to control labor was rarely more acutely felt than where labor was capital.

NOTES

Abbreviations

AAS   American Antiquarian Society, Worcester, MA

AMD   Slavery, Abolition, and Social Justice, Adam Matthew Digital, http://www
      .amdigital.co.uk/m-collections/collection/slavery-abolition-and-social-justice/

BNA   Barbados National Archives, Bridgetown, Barbados

CLAR Clarendon Deposit, Bodleian Library, Oxford University, Oxford

DBC   Dolph Briscoe Center for American History, University of Texas at Austin,
      Austin, TX

FWP   Born in Slavery: Slave Narratives from the Federal Writers' Project, 1936 to
      1938, Library of Congress, https://www.loc.gov/collections/slave-narratives
      -from-the-federal-writers-project-1936-to-1938/

HBS   Baker Library, Harvard Business School, Cambridge, MA

JCB   John Carter Brown Library, Brown University, Providence, RI

LCP   Library Company of Philadelphia, Philadelphia, PA

PQHV Proquest History Vault; many of these records have been digitized from
      RASP. For these records, series and part have been identified to facilitate cross
      referencing.

RASP Records of Ante-bellum Southern Plantations from the Revolution through
      the Civil War [microform], ed. Kenneth M. Stampp (Frederick, MD: Univer-
      sity Publications of America, 1985–2001)

RSPE   Records of Southern Plantations from Emancipation to the Great Migration [microform], ed. Ira Berlin (Frederick, MD: University Publications of America, 2000–2003)

RUB   David M. Rubenstein Rare Book & Manuscript Library, Duke University, Durham, NC

SCL   South Caroliniana Library, University of South Carolina, Columbia, SC

SEN   Senate House Library, Special Collections, London

SHC   Southern Historical Collection, The Wilson Library, University of North Carolina at Chapel Hill

TAMU   Cushing Memorial Library and Archives, Texas A&M University, College Station, TX

UVA   Special Collections, University of Virginia Libraries, Charlottesville, VA

Preface

1. "John W. Madden: Stationer, Printer and Lithographer, New Orleans, Jan. 8, 1815." Bookseller label, Bookseller Collection, Box 2, Range 4, Station B. Courtesy of the American Antiquarian Society, Worcester, Massachusetts. The label is not dated, and may have been used after emancipation. For another label with identical imagery but a different advertiser, see "P.J. Christian & Co. Stationers Printers," Plantation Journal, 1867, folder 279, Prudhomme Family Papers 1765–1997 #00613, SHC.

Introduction

1. Thomas Walter Peyre Plantation Journal, 1834–1851, Records of Antebellum Southern Plantations, ser. B, reel 5. Original at the South Carolina Historical Society.
2. "Book Farming," *Southern Cultivator*, June 1853, 186.
3. Much of the best research about slavery in recent decades has reconstructed the histories of enslaved peoples, some of it using the same account books I analyze here. Scholars have explored the ways these archives both erase and reveal aspects of the enslaved experience. See especially Stephanie E. Smallwood, *Saltwater Slavery: A Middle Passage from Africa to American Diaspora* (Cambridge, MA: Harvard University Press, 2007); Saidiya V. Hartman, *Lose Your Mother: A Journey along the Atlantic Slave Route* (New York: Farrar, Straus and Giroux, 2007); Marisa J. Fuentes, *Dispossed Lives: Enslaved Women, Violence, and the Archive* (Philadelphia: University of Pennsylvania Press, 2016). Another related area of research comes from

literary scholars who have examined financial records, sometimes alongside narratives that describe them. See Ian Baucom, *Specters of the Atlantic: Finance Capital, Slavery, and the Philosophy of History* (Durham, NC: Duke University Press, 2005); Sally Wolff, *Ledgers of History: William Faulkner, an Almost Forgotten Friendship, and an Antebellum Plantation Diary* (Baton Rouge: Louisiana State University Press, 2010). Another exception is the rich and underutilized research of accounting historians. See note 13 below.

4. I hesitate to use the term "capitalism" because it can cause confusion. My own preferred definition of capitalism emphasizes (1) the accumulation of capital, and (2) the ways that accumulation enables the commodification of labor. Capitalism exists where capital is accumulated and deployed in such a way that labor can be highly commodified. However, the precise definition is much less important than the broader (and far less controversial) point that capitalism and slavery were intimately connected. Capitalism is an abstract category, and debating definitions can offer an interesting analytical detour. But for the purposes of this book, whether any given definition leaves slavery as "capitalism with its clothes off" or "in but not of the transatlantic capitalist world," the important thing is to recognize that the two evolved together. Scholars connected with the revival in interest in capitalism within history departments have generally preferred not to define the term, arguing instead that the history of capitalism should be a bottom-up mode of analysis concerned with the study of wealth, work, and power during the period of what is generally called capitalism. They argue that defining the term could artificially constrain this analysis—for example, excluding slavery from our understanding. For "in but not of," see, for example, Elizabeth Fox-Genovese, *Within the Plantation Household: Black and White Women of the Old South* (Chapel Hill: University of North Carolina Press, 2000), 98; for "with its clothes off," see Paul Gilroy, *The Black Atlantic: Modernity and Double Consciousness* (New York: Verso, 1993), 15; and Orlando H. Patterson, "Slavery in Human History," *New Left Review*, I, no. 117 (1979): 31–67. On resistance to defining "capitalism" in the "new history of capitalism," see Seth Rockman, "What Makes the History of Capitalism Newsworthy?," *Journal of the Early Republic* 34, no. 3 (Fall 2014): 439–466; "Interchange: The History of Capitalism," *Journal of American History* 101, no. 2 (September 2014): 517. For useful critiques of the lack of definitions, see James Oakes, "Capitalism and Slavery and the Civil War," *International Labor and Working-Class History* 89 (April 2016): 195–220; John J. Clegg, "Capitalism and Slavery," *Critical Historical Studies* 2, no. 2 (2015): 281–304.

5. Eric Eustace Williams, *Capitalism and Slavery*, rev. ed. (1944; repr., Chapel Hill: University of North Carolina Press, 1994). For an overview of this earlier tradition of scholarship, see Peter James Hudson, "The Racist Dawn of Capitalism," *Boston Review*, March 1, 2016. Hudson contends that work on the "new history

of capitalism" overlooks this tradition; my own view is that while there should be more emphasis, on balance recent scholarship seeks to bring increased attention to this literature.

6. James Oakes, *The Ruling Race: A History of American Slaveholders* (New York: Knopf, 1982); J. E. Inikori, *Slavery and the Rise of Capitalism* (Mona, Jamaica: Department of History, University of the West Indies, 1993); Sven Beckert, *Empire of Cotton: A Global History* (New York: Alfred A. Knopf, 2014).

7. For an introduction to the literature on the second slavery, see Dale Tomich and Michael Zeuske, "Introduction, the Second Slavery: Mass Slavery, World-Economy, and Comparative Microhistories," *Review (Fernand Braudel Center)* 31, no. 2 (2008): 91–100; Anthony E. Kaye, "The Second Slavery: Modernity in the Nineteenth-Century South and the Atlantic World," *Journal of Southern History* 75, no. 3 (August 2009): 627–650.

8. In economics, see, among many others, Alfred H. Conrad and John R. Meyer, "The Economics of Slavery in the Ante Bellum South," *Journal of Political Economy* 66, no. 2 (1958): 95–130; Robert William Fogel and Stanley L. Engerman, *Time on the Cross*, rev. ed. (Boston: Little, Brown, 1974; New York: W. W. Norton, 1995); Alan L. Olmstead and Paul W. Rhode, *Creating Abundance: Biological Innovation and American Agricultural Development* (Cambridge: Cambridge University Press, 2008).

9. A small selection of valuable classic texts and recent syntheses of the economic history of Atlantic and American slavery include Sidney Wilfred Mintz, *Sweetness and Power: The Place of Sugar in Modern History* (New York: Penguin Books, 1986); Robin Blackburn, *The Making of New World Slavery: From the Baroque to the Modern, 1492–1800* (New York: Verso Books, 2010); Gavin Wright, *Slavery and American Economic Development* (Baton Rouge: Louisiana State University Press, 2006); Walter Johnson, *River of Dark Dreams: Slavery and Empire in the Cotton Kingdom* (Cambridge, MA: Belknap Press, 2013); and the essays collected in Sven Beckert and Seth Rockman, eds., *Slavery's Capitalism: A New History of American Economic Development* (Philadelphia: University of Pennsylvania Press, 2016).

10. The amount of enslaved capital has been remarked upon since the antebellum period. For one set of recent comparisons, see Piketty and Zucman, "Capital Is Back: Wealth-Income Ratios in Rich Countries, 1700–2010," *Quarterly Journal of Economics* 129, no. 3 (2014): 1255–1310.

11. On finance, mortgages, and insurance, see Bonnie Martin, "Slavery's Invisible Engine: Mortgaging Human Property," *Journal of Southern History* 76, no. 4 (2010): 817–866; Richard Kilbourne, *Debt, Investment, Slaves Credit Relations in East Feliciana Parish, Louisiana, 1825–1885* (Tuscaloosa: University of Alabama Press, 1995); Calvin Schermerhorn, *The Business of Slavery and the Rise of American Capitalism, 1815–1860* (New Haven, CT: Yale University Press, 2015); Michael Ralph and

Bill Rankin, "Decoder: The Slave Insurance Market," *Foreign Policy*, February 2017, https://foreignpolicy.com/2017/01/16/decoder-slave-insurance-market-aetna-aig-new-york-life/; and work in preparation by Sharon A. Murphy currently titled "Banking on Slavery in the Antebellum South."

12. *OED Online*, s.v. "Control, n.," accessed May 27, 2016, http://www.oed.com/view/Entry/40562. For a broad theorization of accounting and control, though not of its etymology, see appendix C of Jeffrey Fear, *Organizing Control: August Thyssen and the Construction of German Corporate Management* (Cambridge, MA: Harvard University Press, 2005).

13. Scholars from critical accounting studies have long recognized the connections between accounting and control, arguing that accounting systems have helped to uphold slave regimes. The field has produced a rich literature on slavery that has been largely overlooked by historians. See, for example, Richard K. Fleischman and Thomas N. Tyson, "Accounting in Service to Racism: Monetizing Slave Property in the Antebellum South," *Critical Perspectives on Accounting* 15, no. 3 (April 2004): 376–399; Thomas N. Tyson, Richard K. Fleischman, and David Oldroyd, "Theoretical Perspectives on Accounting for Labor on Slave Plantations of the USA and British West Indies," *Accounting, Auditing & Accountability Journal* 17, no. 5 (2004): 758–778; Cheryl S. McWatters and Yannick Lemarchand, "Accounting, Representation, and the Slave Trade: The Guide Du Commerce of Gaignat De L'Aulnais," *The Accounting Historians Journal* 33, no. 2 (December 1, 2006): 1–37; Jan Richard Heier, "Accounting for the Business of Suffering: A Study of the Antebellum Richmond, Virginia, Slave Trade," *Abacus* 46, no. 1 (March 1, 2010): 60–83.

14. See, for example, David Montgomery, *Workers' Control in America: Studies in the History of Work, Technology, and Labor Struggles* (Cambridge: Cambridge University Press, 1980).

15. Branded "scientific management" at the encouragement of Louis Brandeis, the method was almost called simply "efficiency." See Jill Lepore, "Not So Fast," *New Yorker*, October 12, 2009, http://www.newyorker.com/magazine/2009/10/12/not-so-fast. On Taylor generally, see J. C. Spender and Hugo Kijne, eds., *Scientific Management: Frederick Winslow Taylor's Gift to the World?* (Boston: Springer, 1996); Robert Kanigel, *The One Best Way: Frederick Winslow Taylor and the Enigma of Efficiency*, Sloan Technology Series (New York: Viking, 1997).

16. In the pig-iron experiments, "Schmidt," a "man of the type of the ox," purportedly learns to load more than forty-seven tons of pig iron from the ground into a truck each day—a fourfold increase over the prior average productivity. On the many errors and misrepresentations in Taylor's discussion of the data, see Charles D. Wrege and Amedeo G. Perroni, "Taylor's Pig-Tale: A Historical Analysis of Frederick W. Taylor's Pig-Iron Experiments," *Academy of Management Journal* 17, no. 1 (March 1974): 6–27.

17. Taylor continued on that a "very great number" had adopted the system in part, though "as to how many in numbers, I can not say." *The Taylor and Other Systems of Shop Management: Hearings before Special Committee of the House of Representatives*, vol. 3 (Washington, DC: Government Printing Office, 1912), 1504.

18. Frederick Winslow Taylor, *The Principles of Scientific Management* (New York: Harper & Brothers, 1911), 55.

19. Rakesh Khurana, *From Higher Aims to Hired Hands* (Princeton, NJ: Princeton University Press, 2007), 96. On the development of management consulting, see Christopher D. McKenna, *The World's Newest Profession: Management Consulting in the Twentieth Century*, Cambridge Studies in the Emergence of Global Enterprise (New York: Cambridge University Press, 2006).

20. On the rise of human relations in academic context, see *The Human Relations Movement: Harvard Business School and the Hawthorne Experiments (1924–1933)*, Online Exhibition, https://www.library.hbs.edu/hc/hawthorne/; see especially Michel Anteby and Rakesh Khurana's introduction to the exhibit, "A New Vision." For an excellent account of Hawthorne, see Richard Gillespie, *Manufacturing Knowledge: A History of the Hawthorne Experiments* (New York: Cambridge University Press, 1991). For a comprehensive review of literature on human relations and human resource management, see chapter 2 of Bruce E. Kaufman, *Managing the Human Factor: The Early Years of Human Resource Management in American Industry* (Ithaca, NY: ILR Press / Cornell University Press, 2008).

21. Mark M. Smith, *Mastered by the Clock: Time, Slavery, and Freedom in the American South* (Chapel Hill: University of North Carolina Press, 1997).

22. Alan Olmstead and Paul Rhode describe their data set in these terms in a working paper, "The 'New History of Capitalism' and Slavery," December 2015, http://cliometrics.org/pdf/2016-assa/Olmstead-Rhode.pdf.

23. Alfred Chandler, *The Visible Hand: The Managerial Revolution in American Business* (Cambridge, MA: Belknap Press, 1977), ix–xiii, 64–67, 64n48. That slave capital was so large is a long known fact, whose continuing ability to surprise is evident from the way it captured a news cycle in 2014 with the publication of Thomas Piketty and Gabriel Zucman, "Capital Is Back: Wealth-Income Ratios in Rich Countries, 1700–2010," *Quarterly Journal of Economics* 129, no. 3 (August 2014): 1255–1310. Interestingly, Piketty and Zucman also choose to exclude enslaved capital from much of their analysis. There can be good reasons for this, but doing so also risks erasing a fundamental form of wealth and capital investment that may have been more like other kinds of capital than we realize.

24. Bill Cooke, "The Denial of Slavery in Management Studies," *Journal of Management Studies* 40, no. 8 (December 2003): 1895, 1898. The paradox of understanding

and denial is also evident from the coverage of Edward Baptist's recent, contested, *The Half Has Never Been Told*. Baptist pitches his book as offering a new, untold history of the blending of business acumen and hideous violence on the plantation complex. In one way, this claim is misleading: scores of historians and economists have written on the question of slavery and capitalism. But in another way, this wealth of scholarship is what makes Baptist's claim profoundly correct: despite the telling and retelling of the story of American slavery, awareness of the system's power as an engine of economic change remains limited. Edward E. Baptist, *The Half Has Never Been Told: Slavery and the Making of American Capitalism* (New York: Basic Books, 2014). For a summary of critical reception in the discipline of economics, see John E. Murray et al., review of *The Half Has Never Been Told: Slavery and the Making of American Capitalism*, by Edward E. Baptist, *Journal of Economic History* 75, no. 3 (September 2015): 919–931.

25. The phrase "avalanche of numbers" comes from Ian Hacking, *The Taming of Chance* (New York: Cambridge University Press, 1999). Hacking focuses on the mid- to late nineteenth century, but others range back further. On quantification in this general period, see Tamara Plakins Thornton, *Nathaniel Bowditch and the Power of Numbers: How a Nineteenth-Century Man of Business, Science, and the Sea Changed American Life* (Chapel Hill: University of North Carolina Press, 2016); Dan Bouk, *How Our Days Became Numbered: Risk and the Rise of the Statistical Individual* (Chicago: University of Chicago Press, 2015); Theodore M. Porter, *The Rise of Statistical Thinking, 1820–1900* (Princeton, NJ: Princeton University Press, 1986); Eli Cook, *The Pricing of Progress: Economic Indicators and the Capitalization of American Life* (Cambridge, MA: Harvard University Press, 2017); Patricia Cline Cohen, *A Calculating People: The Spread of Numeracy in Early America* (Chicago: University of Chicago Press, 1982); Gerd Gigerenzer, Zeno Swijtink, and Lorraine Daston, *The Empire of Chance: How Probability Changed Science and Everyday Life* (New York: Cambridge University Press, 1990).

26. On the "infrastructure of pens and paper," see Michael Zakim, "Paperwork," *Raritan* 33, no. 4 (Spring 2014): 34–56, 56. For other work on the growing importance of information technologies, see especially JoAnne Yates, *Control through Communication: The Rise of System in American Management* (Baltimore: Johns Hopkins University Press, 1989); and Margaret Levenstein, *Accounting for Growth: Information Systems and the Creation of the Large Corporation* (Stanford, CA: Stanford University Press, 1998).

27. For workers' critiques of Taylor, see Harry Braverman, *Labor and Monopoly Capital: The Degradation of Work in the Twentieth Century* (New York: Monthly Review Press, 1975); Hugh G. J. Aitken, *Taylorism at Watertown Arsenal: Scientific*

Management in Action, 1908–1915 (Ann Arbor, MI: University Microfilms International, 1980).

28. Another bias in my approach is the focus on plantations growing cotton or sugar. A more comprehensive business history of slavery would explore its adaptability to many more crops and industries—rice, coffee, wheat, turpentine, mining, and iron production. For a good start on wheat growing, see Daniel Rood, *The Reinvention of Atlantic Slavery: Technology, Labor, Race, and Capitalism in the Greater Caribbean* (New York: Oxford University Press, 2017); on rice production, see William Dusinberre, *Them Dark Days: Slavery in the American Rice Swamps* (New York: Oxford University Press, 1996); Peter A. Coclanis, *The Shadow of a Dream: Economic Life and Death in the South Carolina Low Country, 1670–1920* (New York: Oxford University Press, 1991); S. Max Edelson, *Plantation Enterprise in Colonial South Carolina* (Cambridge, MA: Harvard University Press, 2006); on industrial slavery, see Charles B. Dew, *Bond of Iron: Master and Slave at Buffalo Forge* (New York: W. W. Norton, 1994); T. Stephen Whitman, "Industrial Slavery at the Margin: The Maryland Chemical Works," *Journal of Southern History* 59, no. 1 (February 1993): 31–62, doi:10.2307/2210347; Robert S. Starobin, "The Economics of Industrial Slavery in the Old South," *Business History Review* 44, no. 2 (1970): 131–174; on tobacco, see Barbara Hahn, *Making Tobacco Bright: Creating an American Commodity, 1617–1937*, Johns Hopkins Studies in the History of Technology (Baltimore: Johns Hopkins University Press, 2011); and on coffee, see Michelle Craig McDonald, "The Chance of the Moment: Coffee and the New West Indies Commodities Trade," *William and Mary Quarterly* 62, no. 3 (July 2005): 441–472.

29. In 2006, a cover story described him as "arguably the most important management innovator of the twentieth century." Gary Hamel, "The Why, What, and How of Management Innovation," *Harvard Business Review* 84, no. 2 (February 2006): 72–84; Julia Kirby, "Inventing HBR," *Harvard Business Review* 90, no. 11 (November 2012): 84–88; Walter Kiechel III, "The Management Century," *Harvard Business Review* 90, no. 11 (November 2012): 62–75; Nicholas Bloom, Raffaella Sadun, and John Van Reenen, "Does Management Really Work?," *Harvard Business Review* 90, no. 11 (November 2012): 76–82. Taylor's fudged facts rarely make it into such accounts, though some contemporary scholars even excuse the many errors in Taylor's work (which they call "relatively minor discrepancies") and suggest that there is still value in Taylor's pig-iron experiment as an "object lesson" that showed that even the "most basic processes" could be improved. Jill R. Hough and Margaret A. White, "Using Stories to Create Change: The Object Lesson of Frederick Taylor's 'Pig-Tale,'" *Journal of Management* 27, no. 5 (October 2001): 585–601.

1. Hierarchies of Life and Death

1. Island Estate "Account of Negroes," 1767, West Indies inventories of Slaves etc., 1754–1819, box 37 / 2, Barham Papers, CLAR.
2. Planters thought slaves were attempting suicide by eating dirt and sometimes forced them to wear masks to prevent it. For one such example, see Jerome S. Handler and Annis Steiner, "Identifying Pictorial Images of Atlantic Slavery: Three Case Studies," *Slavery and Abolition* 27, no. 1 (April 2006): 51–71, 59. Some enslaved testimony supports this theory. For interesting examples, see Kristen Block, *Ordinary Lives in the Early Caribbean: Religion, Colonial Competition, and the Politics of Profit* (Athens, GA: University of Georgia Press, 2012), 46. For a rich discussion of another possible interpretation of the practice, see also manuscript in preparation by Kristen Block, "Dirt-Eating and Despair in Planter Rhetoric and Enslaved Experience."
3. Island Estate "Account of Negroes," 1767.
4. Joseph Calder Miller, *Way of Death: Merchant Capitalism and the Angolan Slave Trade, 1730–1830* (Madison, WI: University of Wisconsin Press, 1988), 440. Miller summarizes estimates for late in the history of the trade. Among other studies on the long-term effects on Africa, see also John K. Thornton, "The Demographic Effect of the Slave Trade on West Africa, 1500–1850," in *African Historical Demography: Proceedings of a Seminar Held in the Centre of African Studies,* vol. 2, ed. Joel W. Gregory (Edinburgh: University of Edinburgh, 1981), 691–720; Nathan Nunn and Leonard Wantchekon, "The Slave Trade and the Origins of Mistrust in Africa," *American Economic Review* 101, no. 7 (December 2011): 3221–3252.
5. Embarkation and disembarkation come from "Estimates Database," 2010. *Voyages: The Trans-Atlantic Slave Trade Database,* accessed June 23, 2014, http://www .slavevoyages.org/estimates/OzaOrAcz.
6. Michael Craton, *Empire, Enslavement, and Freedom in the Caribbean* (Kingston, Jamaica: Ian Randle Publishers, 1997), ch. 8. Death rates after arrival were somewhat lower but still terrifyingly high in Virginia and the Carolina low country, where a quarter to a third perished within the first year. Philip D. Morgan, *Slave Counterpoint: Black Culture in the Eighteenth-Century Chesapeake and Lowcountry* (Chapel Hill, NC: University of North Carolina Press, 1998), 444–445. A further source of instability and illness after "arrival" would have been the intercolonial slave trade, which appears to have been larger than previously understood. See Gregory E. O'Malley, *Final Passages: The Intercolonial Slave Trade of British America, 1619–1807* (Chapel Hill: Omohundro / University of North Carolina Press, 2014).

7. These circumstances have led historians to describe the slave trade as the "Way of Death" and the West Indies as the "Reaper's Garden." Vincent Brown, *The Reaper's Garden: Death and Power in the World of Atlantic Slavery* (Cambridge, MA: Harvard University Press, 2008); Miller, *Way of Death*. The exception to demographic conditions in which deaths exceeded births was the antebellum United States after the close of the slave trade, where populations became self-reproducing; the rates of increase and their implications for business practices are taken up in Chapter 4.

8. Island Estate "Account of Negroes," 1767.

9. Alfred D. Chandler, *Strategy and Structure: Chapters in the History of the American Industrial Enterprise* (Cambridge, MA: MIT Press, 1969).

10. "Ancient" comes from Chandler, *Visible Hand*, 64; "Very few . . ." from Chandler, *Strategy and Structure*, 19–21. Chandler acknowledged a few other enterprises he thought had "embryonic administrative structures." These included Nicholas Biddle's Second Bank of the United States, and John Jacob Astor's American Fur Company, but he argued that these did not have much effect on the development of administration in the country. A more influential early candidate (still decades after the plantations described here) was the Erie Canal (20–21). Merchants also developed systems for administrative oversight but did not often include the scale of labor management associated with large-scale production. On merchant practices see David Hancock, *Citizens of the World: London Merchants and the Integration of the British Atlantic Community, 1735–1785* (Cambridge: Cambridge University Press, 1997); Cathy D. Matson, *Merchants & Empire: Trading in Colonial New York* (Baltimore: Johns Hopkins University Press, 1998).

11. My emphasis on scale has led me to focus on sugar, but much recent work on the British West Indies has pointed to the importance of crops and other kinds of production. On coffee, see, for example, Michelle Craig McDonald, "The Chance of the Moment: Coffee and the New West Indies Commodities Trade," *William and Mary Quarterly* 62, no. 3 (July 2005): 441–472; on livestock raising, see Verene Shepherd, *Livestock, Sugar and Slavery: Contested Terrain in Colonial Jamaica*, Forgotten Histories of the Caribbean (Kingston: Ian Randle, 2009); and on diversification within plantations, see Justin Roberts, *Slavery and the Enlightenment in the British Atlantic, 1750–1807* (New York: Cambridge University Press, 2013).

12. Trevor G. Burnard, *Planters, Merchants, and Slaves: Plantation Societies in British America, 1650–1820* (Chicago: University of Chicago Press, 2015), 159.

13. Estimates come from Trevor Burnard's data on inventories. These do not comprise a random sample but do include more than 6,000 inventories and more than 190,000 enslaved people for the period 1725–1784. Burnard, *Planters, Merchants, and Slaves*, 175.

14. Arthur Bryan, "Josiah Wedgwood," *RSA Journal* 143, no. 5460 (1995): 25. On Wedgwood as a management innovator, see Neil McKendrick, "Josiah Wedgwood and Factory Discipline," *Historical Journal* 4, no. 1 (1961): 30–55.

15. François Crouzet, *The First Industrialists: The Problem of Origins* (London: Cambridge Press, 1985), 32.

16. Theodore Steinberg, *Nature Incorporated: Industrialization and the Waters of New England* (Amherst: University of Massachusetts Press, 1994), 3. This estimate matches Thomas Dublin's estimates of 20 mills and 6,800 workers in 1836, and 40 mills and 10,100 workers in 1850. Over this period, mill size seems to have increased when measured by assets, looms, and spindles, but because workers could tend more machinery, mill size actually shrank when measured by employees. Thomas Dublin, *Women at Work: The Transformation of Work and Community in Lowell, Massachusetts, 1826–1860* (New York: Columbia University Press, 1981), 133.

17. "Plan of Organization," New York and Erie Railroad, 1855, Geography and Map Division, Library of Congress.

18. William Clark, "Digging or Rather Hoeing the Cane Holes," *Ten Views in the Island of Antigua*, 1823, aquatint, London, British Library, http://www.bl.uk/onlinegallery/onlineex/carviews/d/022zzz0001786c9u00002000.html.

19. For a useful overview of the planting process, see "Kalendar," Gordon Turnbull, *Letters to a young planter . . . To which is added, The planter's kalendar* (London, 1785), 50–62. On the complexities and technologies of the planting process in the Caribbean, see Sidney Wilfred Mintz, *Sweetness and Power: The Place of Sugar in Modern History* (New York: Viking, 1985); B. W. Higman, *Plantation Jamaica, 1750–1850: Capital and Control in a Colonial Economy* (Kingston, Jamaica: University of the West Indies Press, 2008); Daniel Rood, *The Reinvention of Atlantic Slavery: Technology, Labor, Race, and Capitalism in the Greater Caribbean*, 2017. For a brief overview, see "Sugar in the Atlantic World," Clements Library, Ann Arbor, Michigan, http://clements.umich.edu/exhibits/online/sugarexhibit/sugar02.php.

20. Mintz, *Sweetness and Power*, 47.

21. Oliver Williamson would call the hierarchies that Chandler described "M-form" corporations. In more formal terms, the M-form, or multidivisional form, combined features of the unitary firm, or U-form, with aspects of the holding company, or H-form. Like the U-form, it created a central office responsible for strategy and the allocation of capital, but like the H-form, it divided operating responsibility by product or geography. The M-form combined strategy with control, offering a hybrid structure that rewarded execution and created room for longer-term thinking. As economist Oliver Williamson put it, "In contrast with the holding company . . . the M-form organization adds (1) a strategic

planning and resource allocation capability and (2) monitoring and control apparatus." Oliver E. Williamson, *The Economic Institutions of Capitalism* (New York: Simon and Schuster, 1985), 281. See also Oliver E. Williamson, *Markets and Hierarchies, Analysis and Antitrust Implications: A Study in the Economics of Internal Organization* (New York: Free Press, 1975). For a recent review and discussion of opportunities to move beyond the opposition of markets and hierarchies, see Naomi R. Lamoreaux, Daniel M. G. Raff, and Peter Temin, "Beyond Markets and Hierarchies: Toward a New Synthesis of American Business History," *The American Historical Review* 108, no. 2 (April 1, 2003): 404–433.

22. Details on the Dawkins holdings managed by Shickle and used in the following charts can be found in "Jamaica Account, 1779, providing a list of slaves, stock, cattle and horses on various plantations," 1779, box 13, item 2.1, Wilberforce House Museum, AMD. Dawkins was likely Henry Dawkins II, though the records do not specify. His father, Henry Dawkins I, had perished in 1744, leaving his estates to his sons James Dawkins and Henry Dawkins II; James died in 1757 and his Jamaican property seems to have passed to Henry Dawkins II. See "Henry Dawkins II" and linked relationships, Legacies of British Slave-ownership, https://www.ucl.ac.uk/lbs/person/view/1619404559. Shickle also managed the connected estates of the Pennant family and had some holdings of his own. See Jean Lindsay, "The Pennants and Jamaica, 1665–1808: Part 1, The Growth and Organization of the Pennant Estate," *Transactions of the Caernarfonshire Historical Society* 43 (1982): 37–82.

23. Due to slight differences in the format of the inventories, it is not possible to know the exact number of managers on the Saint Catherine's properties. Numbers indicated with an "*" are estimates based on the proportion on similar properties. Though there is no way to determine exact counts without records, the number of white staff seems very unlikely to be more than one or two higher or lower on each property.

24. Samples of the two more formal elements of a double-entry system—the journal and the ledger—survive from the Dawkins estates, though these are not from the same year. It is possible that they did not use a waste book, as skilled bookkeepers sometimes wrote their transactions directly into a journal. For the ledger, see "General Accounts, Jamaica, 1 January–30 June 1779," 1779, box 13, item 2.2, Wilberforce House Museum, AMD. For the journal, see "General Accounts, Jamaica, 1 July–31 December 1779," 1779, box 13, item 2.3, ibid. Double-entry bookkeeping has received a disproportionate amount of attention in the history of accounting, but the system was of limited use for ordering hierarchy. A double-entry system could help a merchant coordinate a large trade or track the proceeds from different products, but it was not particularly convenient for managing large numbers of laborers.

25. The literature on double-entry bookkeeping, its origins and importance, is extremely extensive and long dominated the field of accounting history. My attention to bookkeeping records goes beyond the double-entry books and looks more extensively at those related to internal coordination and control, usually referred to by accounting historians as "management accounting" and "cost accounting." On the importance of these types of records, see H. Thomas Johnson and Robert S. Kaplan, *Relevance Lost: The Rise and Fall of Management Accounting* (Boston: Harvard Business School Press, 1987). Johnson and Kaplan connect the disparity in scholarship to a decline in focus within the accounting profession from the late nineteenth and early twentieth century forward; this decline is associated with the growing focus on financial accounting (and double-entry bookkeeping) associated with the rise of professional associations and the growing importance of regulation that required reporting in double-entry form. Neglect has also applied to other kinds of accounting practices, including charge and discharge, or stewardship, accounting. For an interesting study of the importance of these practices in the eighteenth century, see Yannick Lemarchand, "Double Entry versus Charge and Discharge Accounting in Eighteenth-Century France," *Accounting, Business and Financial History* 4, no. 1 (January 1994): 119–145. A small slice of the massive literature on double-entry bookkeeping ranges from Basil S. Yamey, "Notes on the Origin of Double-Entry Bookkeeping," *Accounting Review* 22, no. 3 (1947): 263–272, to Jacob Soll, *The Reckoning: Financial Accountability and the Rise and Fall of Nations* (New York: Basic Books, 2014). For an overview of practices in the United States specifically, though not narrowly focused on the double-entry form, see Gary John Previts and Barbara Dubis Merino, *A History of Accountancy in the United States* (Columbus: Ohio State University Press, 1998).

26. "Jamaica Account, 1779, providing a list of slaves, stock, cattle and horses on various plantations," 1779, box 13, item 2.1, Wilberforce House Museum, AMD.

27. Ibid.

28. Ibid.

29. Ibid. For more on the importance of livestock and pen-keeping in Jamaica, see Shepherd, *Livestock, Sugar and Slavery*.

30. "Testimony of the Rev. John Thorpe on Colonial Slavery," *Negro Slavery Described by a Negro: Being the Narrative of Ashton Warner, a Native of St. Vincent's. With an Appendix Containing the Testimony of Four Christian Ministers, Recently Returned from the Colonies, on the System of Slavery as It Now Exists* (London: Samuel Maunder, 1831), 82–83.

31. James Logan, *Notes of a Journey through Canada, the United States of America, and the West Indies* (Edinburgh: Fraser, 1838), 228–229. Logan writes that these were

"allowed by law," reflecting legal requirements to retain a certain level of managerial oversight.

32. Peter Duncan, *A narrative of the Wesleyan mission to Jamaica, with occasional remarks on the state of society in that colony* (London: Partridge and Oakey, 1849), 367–368.

33. On the early development of management practice, see Russell R. Menard, *Sweet Negotiations: Sugar, Slavery, and Plantation Agriculture in Early Barbados* (Charlottesville: University of Virginia Press, 2006). On the early period in the Chesapeake, see Lorena Seebach Walsh, *Motives of Honor, Pleasure, and Profit: Plantation Management in the Colonial Chesapeake, 1607–1763* (Chapel Hill: University of North Carolina Press, 2010). Though this book focuses on the Anglophone Atlantic, some early examples of scale come from different geographies and imperial regimes, and further research in other regions might yield earlier examples. For an overview of the dating of the sugar revolution, the transfer of practices to and from other empires, and the importance of scale, see Stuart B. Schwartz, "Introduction," *Tropical Babylons: Sugar and the Making of the Atlantic World, 1450–1680*, ed. Stuart B. Schwartz (Chapel Hill: University of North Carolina Press, 2004). See also David Geggus, "Sugar and Coffee Cultivation in Saint Domingue and the Shaping of the Slave Labor Force," in *Cultivation and Culture: Labor and the Shaping of Slave Life in the Americas*, ed. Ira Berlin and Philip Morgan (Charlottesville: The University Press of Virginia, 1993), 73–98. For a broad perspective on New France, see Brett Rushforth, *Bonds of Alliance: Indigenous and Atlantic Slaveries in New France* (Chapel Hill: University of North Carolina Press, 2012).

34. Joshua Steele, *Mitigation of Slavery: In Two Parts* (London: R. and A. Taylor, 1814), 31.

35. Richard Ligon, *A True & Exact History of the Island of Barbadoes* (London: Peter Parker, 1673), 115–117. Interestingly, Ligon's accounts do not charge interest on capital invested in the enslaved but do posit that what might be included in interest or as depreciation would be made up for by increase. As he writes, "As also for the moderate decayes of our Negres, Horses, and Cattle, notwithstanding all our Recruits by breeding all those kinds."

36. Higman, *Plantation Jamaica*, 41.

37. Ibid., 56–64. The growing importance of attorneys was also reflected in new laws. For example, as early as the 1740s, regulations were designed to "prevent frauds and breaches of trust" by attorneys. These provisions set maximum commission rates and required that crop accounts be reported annually to an island secretary in Spanish Town. 41–42.

38. Ibid., 67.

39. Vere Langford Oliver, *Caribbeana: Being Miscellaneous Papers Relating to the History, Genealogy, Topography, and Antiquities of the British West Indies*, vol. 2 (London:

Mitchell Hughes and Clarke, 1919), 144; "John Shickle," Legacies of British Slave-Ownership, https://www.ucl.ac.uk/lbs/person/view/2146633558.

40. For the list, see "West Indies Inventories of Slaves etc.," 1754–1819, box 37 / 2, Barham Papers, CLAR. Barham II took over management in 1789 and maintained his father's system of record keeping. Dunn judges the choice not to purchase slaves from Africa to have been "a business mistake." On Barham II's decision, see Richard S. Dunn, *A Tale of Two Plantations: Slave Life and Labor in Jamaica and Virginia* (Cambridge, MA: Harvard University Press, 2014), 41, chap. 4.

41. For Falconer, see Parnassus Inventories in "Jamaica Account, 1779, providing a list of slaves, stock, cattle and horses on various plantations," 1779, box 13, item 2.1, Wilberforce House Museum, AMD.

42. Higman, *Plantation Jamaica*, 61. See also Lindsay, "Pennants and Jamaica," 62–62.

43. Muldrup was not the most senior manager at Parnassus. He is listed fourth on the schedule of staff, under Falconer and two clerks. For most of the other properties, the overseers are listed first. See Parnassus Inventories in "Jamaica Account, 1779, providing a list of slaves, stock, cattle and horses on various plantations," 1779, box 13, item 2.1, Wilberforce House Museum, AMD.

44. Newton Family Papers, Plantation Accounts, MS 523 / 119, SEN.

45. David W. Galenson, *Traders, Planters, and Slaves: Market Behavior in Early English America* (New York: Cambridge University Press, 1986), 139.

46. Duncan, *A narrative of the Wesleyan mission to Jamaica*, 367–368.

47. Parnassus Inventories in "Jamaica Account, 1779, providing a list of slaves, stock, cattle and horses on various plantations," 1779, box 13, item 2.1, Wilberforce House Museum, AMD.

48. "West Indies Inventories of Slaves etc.," 1819–1754, box 37, Barham Papers, CLAR. Some of the bookkeepers were called book posters, probably a slightly more sophisticated position.

49. Newton Family Papers, Plantation Accounts, MS 523 / 1–169, SEN. Among these, the vast majority are ledgers and journals. MS523 / 110, 111, and 123 are work logs. For a detailed analysis of work patterns on the Newton plantations, see Justin Roberts, *Slavery and the Enlightenment in the British Atlantic, 1750–1807* (New York: Cambridge University Press, 2013); Justin Roberts, "Working between the Lines: Labor and Agriculture on Two Barbadian Sugar Plantations, 1796–1797," *William and Mary Quarterly* 63, no. 3 (2006): 551–586.

50. Newton Family Papers, MS 523 / 110, SEN.

51. Newton Family Papers, MS 523 / 111, SEN.

52. Newton Family Papers, MS 523 / 117–118, SEN.

53. Though West Indian plantations devoted more time than American plantations to the production of cash crops, West Indian agriculture was less

monolithically devoted to sugar production than is sometimes assumed. Generally less than half of all days of slave labor were dedicated to sugar production. For an analysis comparing days spent in harvest of cash crops across plantations in different geographies, see Justin Roberts, "Sunup to Sundown: Plantation Management Strategies and Slave Work Routines in Barbadoes, Jamaica, and Virginia, 1776–1810" (PhD diss., Johns Hopkins University, 2008), 141.

54. William Weston, *The Complete Merchant's Clerk; or, British and American Compting House* (London, 1754), 22–23.

55. Ibid. Italics removed for clarity.

56. Roughley recommended awarding "a small quantity of rum or salt pork to each watchman, who may catch in the course of the week so many dozen of rats, keeping a daily book of account." But he warned the keeper to "be cautious, that the same rats are not brought twice by the watchmen." Thomas Roughley, *The Jamaica Planter's Guide* (London: Printed for Longman, Hurst, Rees, Orme, and Brown, 1823), 116.

57. Patrick Kein, *An Essay upon Pen-Keeping and Plantership* (Kingston, Jamaica: His Majesty's Printing-Office, 1796), 83.

58. Duncan, *A narrative of the Wesleyan mission to Jamaica*, 367–368.

59. "Ledger, Journal and Contingency Accounts: West Indies, 1777–1820," Barham Papers, CLAR. Jamaica seems to have had more complex systems of management than other islands, and bookkeepers may have been relatively higher up in the plantation hierarchy. In 1793, J. B. Moreton wrote that "in the wind-ward islands, book-keepers are not permitted to mess at overseer's tables, for which reason they are not so much respected as in Jamaica." J. B. Moreton, *West India Customs and Manners: Containing Strictures on the Soil, Cultivation, Produce, Trade, Officers, and Inhabitants; with the method of establishing and conducting a Sugar Plantation. To which is added, the practice of training new Slaves* (London: Printed for J. Parsons, Paternaster, Row, 1793), 93.

60. Parnassus Inventories in "Jamaica Account, 1779, providing a list of slaves, stock, cattle and horses on various plantations," 1779, box 13, item 2.1, Wilberforce House Museum, AMD. Based on the records consulted, the free white staff on these plantations (as well as their proprietors) appear to have been almost all men. However, new research on the American South suggests that though women were a minority of planters and slaveholders, they may have played a larger management role than previously understood. See Stephanie Elizabeth Jones-Rogers, "'Nobody Couldn't Sell 'Em but Her': Slaveowning Women, Mastery, and the Gendered Politics of the Antebellum Slave Market" (PhD diss., Rutgers University, New Brunswick, 2012).

61. Parnassus Inventories in "Jamaica Account, 1779, providing a list of slaves, stock, cattle and horses on various plantations."

62. Roughley, *Jamaica Planter's Guide*, 95–97. On enslaved healing and authority, see Sharla M. Fett, *Working Cures: Healing, Health, and Power on Southern Slave Plantations* (Chapel Hill: University of North Carolina Press, 2002); Londa L. Schiebinger, *Secret Cures of Slaves: People, Plants, and Medicine in the Eighteenth-Century Atlantic World* (Stanford, CA: Stanford University Press, 2017).

63. "Testimony of Hugh Hyndman, Return to an Address of the Honourable House of Commons, dated 6th March 1828; for The Minutes of Evidence taken before His Majesty's Privy Council, in the matter of the Berbice and Demerara Manumission Order in Council," 12, AMD.

64. Parnassus Inventories in "Jamaica Account, 1779, providing a list of slaves, stock, cattle and horses on various plantations," 1779, box 13, item 2.1, Wilberforce House Museum, AMD.

65. "Testimony of Colin Macrae, Return to an Address of the Honourable House of Commons, dated 6th March 1828; for The Minutes of Evidence taken before His Majesty's Privy Council, in the matter of the Berbice and Demerara Manumission Order in Council," 26–27, AMD.

66. Roughley, *Jamaica Planter's Guide*, 80–87.

67. Parnassus Inventories in "Jamaica Account, 1779, providing a list of slaves, stock, cattle and horses on various plantations."

68. Dunn, *Tale of Two Plantations*, 77, 84. On the work of raising workers, see Sasha Turner, *Contested Bodies: Pregnancy, Childrearing, and Slavery in Jamaica* (Philadelphia: University of Pennsylvania Press, 2017), chap. 7.

69. Roughley, *Jamaica Planter's Guide*, 106.

70. "List of Supplies wanted for 1795 on Prospect Estate," Accounts regarding Number of Slaves, Clothes for Slaves, Crops and Livestock, January 1784–March 1792, Records of the Jamaican Prospect Estate: Accounts for Prospect Plantation in Jamaica, Microfilm, ed. S. D. Smith, Barclays PLC.

71. Robert Plumsted to William Collier, July 31, 1753, Osborn fc 160, as quoted in Chris Evans, "The Plantation Hoe: The Rise and Fall of an Atlantic Commodity, 1650–1850," *William and Mary Quarterly* 69, no. 1 (2012): 71–100, 83. Evans describes the extraordinary range of hoes available to planters.

72. Roughley, *Jamaica Planter's Guide*, 105–109.

73. Kein, *Essay upon Pen-Keeping and Plantership*, 83.

74. Ibid.

75. Parnassus Inventories, "Jamaica Account, 1779, providing a list of slaves, stock, cattle and horses on various plantations."

76. Michael Craton, *Testing the Chains: Resistance to Slavery in the British West Indies* (Ithaca, NY: Cornell University Press, 1982), 17.

77. Parnassus Inventories, "Jamaica Account, 1779, providing a list of slaves, stock, cattle and horses on various plantations."

78. Roughley, *Jamaica Planter's Guide*, 88.

79. John J. McCusker and Russell R. Menard, *The Economy of British America, 1607–1789, with Supplementary Bibliography* (Chapel Hill: University of North Carolina Press, 1991), 154; Laurent Dubois, *Avengers the New World: The Story of the Haitian Revolution* (Cambridge, MA: The Belknap Press, 2004), 19.

80. Logan, *Notes of a Journey through Canada*, 228–229. Logan writes that these were "allowed by law," reflecting legal requirements to retain a certain level of managerial oversight.

81. Orlando Patterson, "Slavery and Slave Revolts: A Socio-Historical Analysis of the First Maroon War Jamaica, 1655–1740," *Social and Economic Studies* 19, no. 3 (1970): 289–325; Thomas W. Krise, "Cudjo (c. 1680–1744)," in *The Historical Encyclopedia of World Slavery*, ed. Junius P. Rodriguez (Santa Barbara, CA: ABC-CLIO, 1997), 203.

82. Diana Paton, "Tacky's Rebellion (1760–1761)," in *The Historical Encyclopedia of World Slavery*, ed. Junius P. Rodriguez (Santa Barbara: CA: ABC-CLIO, 1997), 625. See also Vincent Brown, "Slave Revolt in Jamaica, 1760–1761: A Cartographic Narrative," http://revolt.axismaps.com/.

83. Historians have used naming patterns as evidence of enslaved culture and family; however, it is difficult to know how much control enslaved people actually exercised over name choices. Indeed, some scholars have argued that enslaved names can tell us more about what free whites thought about slaves than about how they saw themselves. Trevor Burnard, "Slave Naming Patterns: Onomastics and the Taxonomy of Race in Eighteenth-Century Jamaica," *Journal of Interdisciplinary History* 31, no. 3 (2001): 325–346. Indeed, the evidence for this includes the fact that livestock were also named, and that some shared names with enslaved people. Philip D. Morgan, "Slaves and Livestock in Eighteenth-Century Jamaica: Vineyard Pen, 1750–1751," *William and Mary Quarterly* 52, no. 1 (1995): 47–76, 53. Still, on a very large plantation with an absentee owner such as Parnassus, it is possible that enslaved people exercised some influence. For work that uses naming patterns to unearth cultural practice, see Gutman, *The Black Family in Slavery and Freedom*; Jerome S. Handler and JoAnn Jacoby, "Slave Names and Naming in Barbados, 1650–1830," *William and Mary Quarterly* 53, no. 4 (1996): 685–728.

84. Parnassus Inventories in "Jamaica Account, 1779, providing a list of slaves, stock, cattle and horses on various plantations," 1779, box 13, item 2.1, Wilberforce House Museum, AMD.

85. For a synthesis, see Laurent Dubois, *Avengers of the New World: The Story of the Haitian Revolution* (Cambridge, MA: Belknap Press of Harvard University Press, 2004).

86. Clement Caines, *Letters on the Cultivation of the Otaheite Cane* (London: Printed for Messrs. Robinson, 1801), 245–247, 290. Slaves did sometimes gain access to arms; see the essays collected in Christopher Leslie Brown and Philip D. Morgan, eds., *Arming Slaves: From Classical Times to the Modern Age* (New Haven, CT: Yale University Press, 2006). Most of the examples cited were in circumstances of war, but in some cases, watchers and hunters were also armed. For more on the Haitian plantation guards, some of whom were armed prior to the revolution, see David Geggus, "The Arming of Slaves during the Haitian Revolution," in Brown and Morgan, *Arming Slaves*, 209–232.

87. On limiting access to religion, see Katherine Gerbner, "The Ultimate Sin: Christianising Slaves on Seventeenth Century Barbados," *Slavery and Abolition* 31, no. 1 (2010): 57–73; on religion and slave control, see Nicholas M. Beasley, *Christian Ritual and the Creation of British Slave Societies, 1650–1740* (Athens: University of Georgia Press, 2009).

88. Pickling is widely referenced in seventeenth-century sources and may have been used outside the slave regime as well. Other punishments referenced are included in Edward B. Rugemer, "The Development of Mastery and Race in the Comprehensive Slave Codes of the Greater Caribbean during the Seventeenth Century," *William and Mary Quarterly* 70, no. 3 (2013): 429–458. On mutilation and public punishment, see Trevor Burnard, *Mastery, Tyranny, and Desire: Thomas Thistlewood and His Slaves in the Anglo-Jamaican World* (Chapel Hill: University of North Carolina Press, 2004), 104, 150.

89. Vincent Brown, "Spiritual Terror and Sacred Authority in Jamaican Slave Society," *Slavery and Abolition* 24, no. 1 (2003): 24–53, 24, 27. See also Brown, *Reaper's Garden*, 157–200.

90. Burnard, *Planters, Merchants, Slaves*, 89, chap. 2.

91. Rugemer, "Development of Mastery," 429–458. See also David Barry Gaspar, "'Rigid and Inclement': Origins of the Jamaica Slave Laws of the Seventeenth Century," in *The Many Legalities of Early America*, ed. Christopher L. Tomlins and Bruce H. Mann (Chapel Hill: University of North Carolina Press, 2001), 78–96; David Barry Gaspar, "With a Rod of Iron: Barbados Slave Laws as a Model for Jamaica, South Carolina, and Antigua, 1661–1697," in *Crossing Boundaries: Comparative History of Black People in Diaspora*, ed. Darlene Clark Hine and Jacqueline McLeod (Bloomington: Indiana University Press, 1999), 343–366.

92. On ticketing, see Rugemer, "Development of Mastery," 440–441. Controlling slaves also required controlling planters, and information systems extended into the church. In seventeenth-century Barbados, Anglican ministers read the slave

NOTES TO PAGES 40-42

codes aloud in church biannually and posted notices of thefts and lost property at parish churches. See Katherine Gerbner, *Christian Slavery: Conversion and Race in the Protestant Atlantic World* (Philadelphia: University of Pennsylvania Press, 2018).

93. On Tacky's revolt, see Vincent Brown, "Slave Revolt in Jamaica, 1760–1761: A Cartographic Narrative," revolt.axismaps.com; Vincent Brown, *The Reaper's Garden: Death and Power in the World of Atlantic Slavery* (Cambridge, MA: Harvard University Press, 2008), chap. 4; Trevor Burnard and John Garrigus, *The Plantation Machine: Atlantic Capitalism in French Saint-Domingue and British Jamaica* (University of Pennsylvania Press, 2016), 126–128. For extensive literature on Maroon communities, see especially Richard Price, ed., *Maroon Societies: Rebel Slave Communities in the Americas*, 3rd ed. (Baltimore: Johns Hopkins University Press, 1996); Craton, *Testing the Chains*; Alvin O. Thompson, *Flight to Freedom: African Runaways and Maroons in the Americas* (Kingston, Jamaica: University of West Indies Press, 2006); Philip Wright, "War and Peace with the Maroons, 1730–1739," *Caribbean Quarterly* 16 (1970): 5–27; Mavis Campbell, *The Maroons of Jamaica, 1655–1796: A History of Resistance, Collaboration and Betrayal* (Granby, MA: Bergin & Garvey, 1988).

94. For a discussion of this alternation, see Vincent Brown, "Social Death and Political Life in the Study of Slavery," *American Historical Review* 114, no. 5 (2009): 1231–1249.

95. David Brion Davis, *Slavery and Human Progress* (New York: Oxford University Press, 1984).

96. Galenson, *Traders, Planters, and Slaves*, 137–142.

97. The proportion may have been as high as seven-eighths. Selwyn H. H. Carrington, "Management of Sugar Estates in the British West Indies at the End of the Eighteenth Century," *Journal of Caribbean History* 33 (1999): 28. Estimates vary somewhat based on definitions of plantations and estates. For further discussion, see B. W. Higman, *Plantation Jamaica*, 18–19. He writes that as of 1832, 81 percent of "dominant sugar estates" were owned by nonresident planters, though a larger proportion of smaller proprietors lived there.

98. Lowell J. Ragatz, *The Fall of the Planter Class in the British Caribbean, 1763–1833* (New York: Century, 1928), 44; Lowell Joseph Ragatz, "Absentee Landlordism in the British Caribbean, 1750–1833," *Agricultural History* 5, no. 1 (1931): 7–24. Ragatz also argued that absenteeism and decline laid the foundation for the abolition of the slave trade in 1807. The most famous account of the relationship between decline and abolition can be found in Eric Williams, *Capitalism and Slavery* (Chapel Hill: University of North Carolina Press, 1994). A persuasive recent reinvigoration of this view is David Ryden, *West Indian Slavery and British Abolition, 1783–1807* (Cambridge: Cambridge University Press, 2009). Seymour Drescher powerfully refuted this view, arguing instead that the British abolished slavery at

its zenith. Seymour Drescher, *Econocide: British Slavery in the Era of Abolition*, 2nd ed. (Chapel Hill: University of North Carolina Press, 2010).

99. I mean here the "separation of ownership and management" as generally discussed in business history, though that is sometimes confused with the overlapping and closely related "separation of ownership and control." Separation of ownership and control refers to a set of agency and incentive problems that have to be overcome in some cases of the separation of ownership and management, especially those with ownership by dispersed shareholders. Both literatures cite Adolf A. Berle and Gardiner Means, *The Modern Corporation and Private Property* (New York: Macmillan, 1933). For a business history perspective, see Brian Cheffins and Steven Bank, "Is Berle and Means Really a Myth?," *Business History Review* 83, no. 3 (2009): 443–474; Kenneth Lipartito and Yumiko Morii, "Rethinking the Separation of Ownership from Management in American History," *Seattle University Law Review* 33, no. 4 (2010): 1025; Eric Hilt, "When Did Ownership Separate from Control? Corporate Governance in the Early Nineteenth Century," *Journal of Economic History* 68, no. 3 (September 2008): 645–685.

100. B. W. Higman suggests a similar reframing of absentee proprietorship in *Plantation Jamaica*, 8–9. As Higman writes, "The basic organizing principles [of modern management] were founded on a separation of ownership and management, and the division of labour. . . . Most importantly, special roles were found for the 'manager' acting as agent or intermediary between the capitalist entrepreneur and the labour force of an enterprise. The Jamaican sugar economy of the eighteenth century saw the development of these principles in the separation of proprietor (ownership) and planter (management), and in the articulation of a refined managerial hierarchy." On managerial complexity and absenteeism generally, see Richard Sheridan, *Sugar and Slavery: An Economic History of the British West Indies, 1623–1775* (Kingston, Jamaica: Canoe Press, 1974), 360–388. Plantations were, of course, not the only colonial site where managers and owners negotiated the development of long-distance management practices. In Canada, the Hudson's Bay Company (HBC) dealt both with distance and with seasonal freezing, which intensified the need for detailed annual planning. On management and control at HBC during the seventeenth through nineteenth centuries, see Michael B. O'Leary, Wanda J. Orlikowski, and JoAnne Yates, "Distributed Work over the Centuries: Trust and Control in the Hudson's Bay Company, 1670–1826," in *Distributed Work*, ed. Pamela J. Hinds and Sara Kiesler (Cambridge, MA: MIT Press, 2001); Ann M. Carlos and Stephen Nicholas, "Agency Problems in Early Chartered Companies: The Case of the Hudson's Bay Company," *Journal of Economic History* 50, no. 4 (1990): 853–875. On management, HBC, and the fur trade more generally, see Ann M. Carlos, *Commerce by a Frozen*

Sea: Native Americans and the European Fur Trade (Philadelphia: University of Pennsylvania Press, 2010); Michael B. O'Leary, Wanda J. Orlikowski, and JoAnne Yates, "Managing by Canoeing Around: Lessons from the Hudson's Bay Company," *Knowledge Directions* 3, no. 1 (2001): 26–37.

101. Henry Drax and William Belgrove, *A treatise upon husbandry or planting* (Boston: D. Fowle, 1755); Peter Thompson, "Henry Drax's Instructions on the Management of a Seventeenth-Century Barbadian Sugar Plantation," *William and Mary Quarterly* 66, no. 3 (2009): 565–604.

102. Caines, *Letters on the Cultivation of the Otaheite Cane*, 246–247.

103. Ibid.

104. "Ledger, Journal and Contingency Accounts: West Indies, 1777–1820," Barham Papers, CLAR.

105. Roughley, *Jamaica Planter's Guide*, 28–29.

106. Ibid.

107. The earliest copies identified were for the mid-1720s. Newton Family Papers, box 523 / 2–3 and 523 / 4–5, SEN.

108. Newton Family Papers, box 523 / 32–45, SEN.

109. Higman, *Plantation Jamaica*, 97.

110. Drax's manuscript instructions are reproduced in their entirety in Thompson, "Henry Drax's Instructions," 600–603.

111. Thorstein Veblen, *Absentee Ownership: Business Enterprise in Recent Times: The Case of America* (New Brunswick, NJ: Transaction, 1923).

112. Though scholars have long debated the economic effects of abolition, the slaveholders themselves clearly opposed the loss of their property—or at least the loss of that property without substantial compensation. On planters and the politics of abolition, see, among many others, Ryden, *West Indian Slavery and British Abolition*. For an excellent overview of broader debates on the politics and economics of abolition, see Seymour Drescher, "Antislavery Debates: Tides of Historiography in Slavery and Antislavery," *European Review* 19, no. 1 (February 2011): 131–148. On compensation, see Nicholas Draper, *The Price of Emancipation: Slave-Ownership, Compensation and British Society at the End of Slavery* (New York: Cambridge University Press, 2010).

113. Sylvester Hovey, *Letters from the West Indies: Relating Especially to the Danish Island St. Croix, and to the British Islands Antigua, Barbadoes, and Jamaica* (New York: Gould and Newman, 1838), 131.

114. P. J. Laborie, *The Coffee Planter of Saint Domingo* (London: T. Cadell and W. Davies, 1798), 155.

115. Though plantations were not corporations, many were large partnerships, and some had multiple shareholders as the result of inheritance. Had slavery extended further into the period of general incorporation, it seems likely that

plantations might have become incorporated. For a list of commercial firms that had a stake in plantations when slavery ended in the British Empire (and thus applied for compensation), see the Legacies of British Slave-Ownership data, which as of July 29, 2017, included 532 "commercial firms" of various types. "Commercial Firms," Legacies of British Slave-Ownership, https://www.ucl.ac.uk/lbs/firms/.

116. Chandler, *Visible Hand*, 103; Alfred D. Chandler, *Henry Varnum Poor, Business Editor, Analyst, and Reformer* (Cambridge: Harvard University Press, 1956), 147–148; "Plan of Organization," New York and Erie Railroad, 1855, Geography and Map Division, Library of Congress. For a broader discussion of McCallum's chart, see Charles Wrege and Guidon Sorbo Jr., "A Bridge Builder Changes a Railroad: The Story of Daniel Craig McCallum," *Canal History and Technology Proceedings* 24 (2005): 183–218; and Caitlin Rosenthal, "Big Data in the Age of the Telegraph," *McKinsey Quarterly*, March 2013, http://www.mckinsey.com/business-functions/organization/our-insights/big data in the age-of-the-telegraph.

117. For Chandler's many hand-drawn charts, see the Alfred Dupont Chandler Papers, 1918–2007, Arch GA 12.50.1, box 24, Baker Library Historical Collections, Harvard Business School, Harvard University. Chandler explains that he never saw the Erie Railroad chart himself (at least as of 1988) in Alfred Chandler, "Origins of the Organization Chart," *Harvard Business Review* 66 (1988): 156–157.

2. Forms of Labor

1. Work Log for 1785, Records of the Jamaican Prospect Estate, ed. Simon D. Smith, Barclays PLC, Microform Imaging Ltd., 2003. Thanks also to Maria Sienkiewicz at Barclays Group Archives, Manchester, for providing additional photographs of these documents and offering details on their provenance. The books were left in the Pall Mall office of Ransom, Bouverie and Co., which later merged with Barclay, Bevan, Tritton and Co. Barclays did not own the plantation. On hurricanes in the region, see Stuart E. Schwartz, *Sea of Storms: A History of Hurricanes in the Greater Caribbean from Columbus to Katrina* (Princeton, NJ: Princeton University Press, 2015).

2. For biographical context on Attlay and his son, Oakeley Attlay Sr., see Simon D. Smith, "An Introduction to the Plantation Journals of the Prospect Sugar Estate," *Records of the Jamaican Prospect Estate*, Barclays PLC, Microform Imaging Ltd., 2003; Roberts, *Slavery and the Enlightenment in the British Atlantic*, 21–22.

3. The other industry where preprinted books were most common was shipping and the maritime trade. During voyages, captains could enter data into formatted journals designed to organize information on wind, speed, and cargo. See, for

example, *The Seaman's Journal: Being an Easy and Correct Method of Keeping the Daily Reckoning of a Ship, during the Course of Her Voyage* (New London, CT: James Springer, 1798), AAS. For other examples of preprinted journals outside of the plantation complex, see two copies of *The Workman's Account Book on an Easy and Economical Plan* (Boston, 1828), AAS, and *The Workman's Account Book on an Easy and Economical Plan* (Boston, 1849), LCP. See also David Young of Perth, *The Farmers Account-Book of Expenditure and Produce for Each Day, Month, and Year* (Edinburgh, 1788), LCP.

4. Work Log for 1785. Turnover is typically calculated as the number of separations (here the seven deaths) divided by the average size of the workforce: $7 / 159 = 4.4$ percent. Death totals omit at least one child who died within the week because he or she was left out of calculations of increase and decrease. New births were often not immediately recorded because infant mortality was so high. On levels of turnover in contemporary factories, see Jonathan Prude, *The Coming of Industrial Order: Town and Factory Life in Rural Massachusetts, 1810–1860* (New York: Cambridge University Press, 1983), 110. See also Dublin, *Women at Work,* 60. On labor turnover as a continuing problem into the twentieth century, see Laura Owen, "History of Labor Turnover in the U.S.," https://eh .net/encyclopedia/history-of-labor-turnover-in-the-u-s/.

5. See stationer's seal in Plantation journals for Prospect Estate, 1 January 1787–31 December 1793, Barclays Group Archives, Dallimore Road, Wythenshawe, Manchester. The shop also appears to have been used as a meeting place: merchants attempting to recruit clerks and accountants sometimes used the store to receive candidates. Classified ads, *Gazetteer and New Daily Advertiser* (London, England), August 19, 1779, *17th–18th Century Burney Collection Newspapers,* Gale. For the office as a site for recruiting clerks, see Classified ads, *World* (London, England), June 1, 1789, *17th–18th Century Burney Collection Newspapers,* Gale.

6. Plantation journals for Prospect Estate, 1 January 1787–31 December 1793, Barclays Group Archives, Dallimore Road, Wythenshawe, Manchester.

7. Ibid., 1787.

8. "Journal of Plantation Hope and Experiment, June 1812," Plantation Journals, 1812–1843, Wilberforce House Museum, box 9, item 1, AMD. The form for April is "Hope and Experiment plantations journal," South Carolina Historical Society, Addlestone Library at the College of Charleston, Charleston, South Carolina. I have been unable to find archival collections that contain both genres of account books, probably because reports were sent across the Atlantic while bound journals remained on the plantation. But the similar formats of surviving records suggest that one was copied into the other.

9. Ibid.

10. Ibid.

11. Ibid.

12. Ibid.

13. Ibid.

14. Ibid.

15. Andrew Thomson, *Review of Dr. H. Duncan's Letters on the West India Question* (Edinburgh: Printed for W. Whyte, 1831), 28–29, Slavery and Anti-Slavery: A Transnational Archive, Gale, http://www.gale.com/primary-sources/slavery-and-anti-slavery.

16. "Journal of Plantation Good Success, 1830–1831," Plantation Journals, 1812–1843, Wilberforce House Museum, box 9, items 8–9, AMD. "Monthly Report of Castle Wemyss," Records of Slaves, 1823–1828, Institute of Commonwealth Studies, 101/3/2/1–25, AMD. On the importance of the Netherlands in the earlier diffusion of accounting practices, especially double-entry bookkeeping, see Soll, *Reckoning*, chap. 5. On the Dutch Atlantic more broadly, see Gert Oostindie and J. Roitman, eds. *Dutch Atlantic Connections, 1680–1800: Linking Empires, Bridging Borders* (Boston: Brill, 2014).

17. "Journal of Friendship Plantation," Plantation Journals, 1812–1843, Wilberforce House Museum, box 9, items 7 and 28, AMD. Friendship appears to have belonged to William King. "William King, Profile & Legacies Summary," Legacies of British Slave-Ownership, https://www.ucl.ac.uk/lbs/person/view/28107. Friendship was a very popular plantation name, so it is difficult to confirm with absolute certainty whether this particular Friendship was in Jamaica, Barbados, or British Guiana. The one King owned appears most likely to be the one using these forms, because King's name appears on some of the other documents in the same collection at Hull. Regardless, King's many holdings suggest the breadth of what a proprietor might have been considering when he reviewed plantation returns.

18. Journal of Friendship Plantation, Plantation Journals, 1812–1843, Wilberforce House Museum, box 9, items 7 and 28, AMD.

19. Ibid.

20. Ibid.

21. For designs of desks with pigeonholes for sorting paper, see Thomas Chippendale, *The Gentleman and Cabinet-Maker's Director* (London, 1762).

22. For an example of bundled paper surviving, at least in part due to being wrapped, see the records of Drax Hall Plantation Records, Z9/3/1–3—Invoices and Receipts, 1818–1820, BNA.

23. Thomas Blount, *Glossographia Anglicana Nova* (London: Printed for Dan Brown, 1707). On a ship, a "pigeonhole" sometimes also referred to a window.

24. George Richardson Porter, *The Nature and Properties of the Sugar Cane* (London: Smith, Elder, 1830), 369.

25. Advertisement, *Barbados Mercury*, October 6, 1770, p. 4, Bridgetown, Barbados.

26. Advertisement, *Barbados Mercury*, October 13, 1770, p. 3, Bridgetown, Barbados.

27. Advertisement, *Gazette of Saint Jago de la Vega*, February 15, 1781, St. Jago de la Vega, Jamaica.

28. Advertisement, *Royal Gazette*, August 3, 1816, Kingston, Jamaica.

29. "Hamer Estate—Plantation Journals, 1821–1825," Plantation Journals, 1812–1843, Wilberforce House Museum, box 9, item 2, items 10–26, AMD. On William Attwick Hamer, see Legacies of British Slave-Ownership, http://www.ucl.ac.uk/lbs/person/view/45302.

30. One how blank books and forms both enable and encourage certain types of thinking, see Molly McCarthy, *The Accidental Diarist: A History of the Daily Planner in America* (Chicago: University of Chicago Press, 2013). On calculations as technologies that shape patterns of thought, see Seth Rockman, "Introduction: Paper Technologies of Capitalism," *Technology and Culture* 58, no. 2 (June 2017): 487–505; Caitlin Rosenthal, "Numbers for the Innumerate: Everyday Arithmetic and Atlantic Capitalism," *Technology and Culture* 58, no. 2 (June 2017): 529–544.

31. James Moore Swank, *History of the Manufacture of Iron in All Ages* (The American Iron and Steel Association, 1892), 144; Edward Harold Mott, *Between the Ocean and the Lakes: The Story of Erie* (Collins, 1899), 46–47; Advertisements, *National Advocate*, October 30, 1819; Advertisements, *National Advocate*, July 21, 1818.

32. Mott, *Between the Ocean and the Lakes*, 46–47.

33. Labor Ledger BD1, Isaac G. Pierson and Brothers, Records, 1795–1865, Mss. 501, HBS.

34. One occasional exception to this is "negro books," where planters paid incentives to enslaved people. See Justene G. Hill, "Felonious Transactions: Legal Culture and Business Practices of Slave Economies in South Carolina, 1787–1860" (PhD diss., Princeton University, 2015).

35. See memo tucked in Daybook AB1, 1796, Isaac G. Pierson and Brothers, Records, 1795–1865, Mss. 501, HBS. For other items exchanged, see Labor Ledger BD1.

36. Labor Ledgers BD2–BD3, Isaac G. Pierson and Brothers, Records, 1795–1865, Mss. 501, HBS. The labor ledger for the cotton mill (BD3) includes approximately 300 employees, a majority of whom were women; the general ledger (BD2), ostensibly covering nail manufacturing and the rolling mill, contains about 125–150 employees. Estimates are imprecise due to the difficulty of assessing full- and part-time workers and repeated entries as folios become full. A travel essay from 1906 claims that by 1816, the number of residents of Ramapo exceeded 700, suggesting that a majority of the local population labored for the firm. See *The Magazine of History, with Notes and Queries* (New York: W. Abbatt, 1906).

37. Labor Ledger BD2; Time Book LE1, Isaac G. Pierson and Brothers, Records, 1795–1865, Mss 501, HBS.

38. Time Books LE1-5, 1816–1828, Isaac G. Pierson and Brothers, Records, 1795–1865, Mss. 501, HBS.

39. Prude, *The Coming of Industrial Order*, 110; Dublin, *Women at Work*, 60; Owen, "History of Labor Turnover in the U.S."

40. Walter Licht, *Industrializing America: The Nineteenth Century* (Baltimore: Johns Hopkins University Press, 1995), 23.

41. Time book LE2.

42. Time book LE3.

43. Time book LE6, 1833, Isaac G. Pierson and Brothers, Records, 1795–1865, Mss. 501, HBS. Turnover seems to have plagued the firm from the start. Across an ad hoc sample taken from the first thirty folios of the earliest labor ledger, fewer than half of the workers were employed consistently during a six- to seven-month period. For the forty-three workers listed in these pages, only twenty show at least five months of work during the slightly more than half a year covered by the ledger; only thirty appear to have had "regular" employment for more than one or two months. See Labor Ledger BD1, 1795, 1–30.

44. Vol. 250, Hamilton Manufacturing Company, 1825–1917, Mss. 442, HBS.

45. John Bezís-Selfa, "A Tale of Two Ironworks: Slavery, Free Labor, Work, and Resistance in the Early Republic," *William and Mary Quarterly* 56, no. 4 (October 1999): 677–700, 688; John Bezís-Selfa, *Forging America: Ironworkers, Adventurers, and the Industrious Revolution* (Ithaca, NY: Cornell University Press, 2004), 28. Marx wrote about the importance of labor supply to maintaining capital: as long as business continued uninterrupted, capitalists did not take notice of "this gratuitous gift of labour," but any "interruption of the labour process by a crisis makes him sensitively aware" of his losses. Karl Marx, *Capital: A Critical Analysis of Capitalist Production* (London: Swan Sonnenschein, 1906), 189.

46. John Williams to George Bond, October 1, 1825, Letterbook I, Dover Manufacturing Co. Papers, New Hampshire Historical Society, Concord, NH, as cited in David J. Jeremey, "Innovation in American Textile Technology during the Early 19th Century," *Technology and Culture* 14, no. 1 (1973): 40–76, 47.

47. For samples of the abstracts prepared at Hamilton, see Vol. 258, Hamilton Manufacturing Company, 1825–1917, Mss. 442, HBS.

48. On the relative abundance of land relative to labor, the classic account is H. J. Habakkuk, *American and British Technology in the Nineteenth Century: The Search for Labour-Saving Inventions* (Cambridge: Cambridge University Press, 1962).

49. For an overview of labor turnover in the longer term, see Owen, "History of Labor Turnover in the U.S."

50. On eventual innovations along these lines, see JoAnne Yates, *Control through Communication: The Rise of System in American Management* (Baltimore: Johns

Hopkins University Press, 1989); Margaret Levenstein, *Accounting for Growth: Information Systems and the Creation of the Large Corporation* (Stanford, CA: Stanford University Press, 1998). Taking an even broader view, many of the managerial innovations of welfare capitalism and human relations can be seen as attempts to reduce or manage turnover, create worker loyalty, and thus enable continuity in production. See, for example, Gillespie, *Manufacturing Knowledge*; Sanford M. Jacoby, *Employing Bureaucracy: Managers, Unions, and the Transformation of Work in American Industry, 1900–1945* (New York: Columbia University Press, 1985); Sanford M. Jacoby, *Modern Manors* (Princeton, NJ: Princeton University Press, 1998); Laura J. Owen, "Worker Turnover in the 1920s: The Role of Changing Employment Policies," *Industrial and Corporate Change* 4 (1995): 499–530.

51. For another evocative use of the machine analogy, see Burnard and Garrigus, *Plantation Machine*.
52. Manuel Moreno Fraginals, *The Sugarmill: The Socioeconomic Complex of Sugar in Cuba, 1760–1860* (New York: Monthly Review Press, 1976), 41.
53. Ibid. 15. On packing of sugar by grade later in the nineteenth century, see 108–109.
54. William Young, *The West-India Common-Place Book; Compiled from Parliamentary and Official Documents . . .* (London: Printed for R. Phillips, 1807), 4.
55. Roberts, *Slavery and the Enlightenment in the British Atlantic*, 27.
56. While theories of interchangeable parts date to the late eighteenth century, they did not become a production reality until the mid-nineteenth. Even then, interchangeable parts in the service of mass production (without fitters) remained elusive, emerging only in the early twentieth century. David Hounshell, *From the American System to Mass Production, 1800–1932: The Development of Manufacturing Technology in the United States* (Baltimore: Johns Hopkins University Press, 1985).
57. "Price Current," *Columbian Herald*, Charlestown, South Carolina, June 13, 1785, Archive of Americana, *America's Historical Newspapers*.
58. On the interconnected business of slavery in New England, see Christy Clark-Pujara, *Dark Work: The Business of Slavery in Rhode Island* (New York: New York University Press, 2016); Seth Rockman, "Negro Cloth: Mastering the Market for Slave Clothing in Antebellum America," in *American Capitalism: New Histories*, ed. Sven Beckert and Christine Desan (New York: Columbia University Press, 2018), 170–194. Other individuals are directly linked to textile firms like those discussed here. For example, Patrick Tracy Jackson, a founder and treasurer of the Boston Manufacturing Company and an investor in several other Lowell mills, began his career as a supercargo on a voyage to Saint Thomas. He traveled there and to the East Indies extensively over the period between 1799 and 1808. Kenneth Wiggins Porter, *The Jacksons and the Lees: Two Generations of Mas-*

sachusetts Merchants, 1765–1844, vol. 1–2 (Cambridge, MA: Harvard University Press, 1937).

59. Weston, *Complete Merchant's Clerk.*
60. Advertisement, *London Chronicle,* January 16, 1762.
61. Weston, *Complete Merchant's Clerk,* unnumbered opening pages.
62. Weston, *Complete Merchant's Clerk,* front matter. Copy inscribed to Birly at JCB.
63. Thomas Langton and Joan Wilkinson, *The Letters of Thomas Langton, Flax Merchant of Kirkham, 1771–1788* (Carnegie Pub., 1994), 19, 32. On Birly, see Melinda Elder, *The Slave Trade and the Economic Development of Eighteenth-Century Lancaster* (Halifax, England: Ryburn, 1992), 76.
64. Meabry himself stayed only a few short weeks in Jamaica before illness forced him to return to London. Upon returning, he gave evidence against the slave trade. See Alexander Barclay, *A Practical View of the Present State of Slavery in the West Indies; or, An examination of Mr. Stephen's "Slavery of the British West India Colonies"* (London: Smith, Elder, 1826), 370.
65. Malachy Postlethwayt, *The Merchant's Public Counting-House; or, New Mercantile Institution* (London: John and Paul Knapton, 1750); Stanley C. Hollander, "Malachy Postlethwayt's British Mercantile College, 1755," *Accounting Review* 28, no. 3 (July 1953): 434–438.
66. Carrington, "Management of Sugar Estates," 27–53, 29.
67. "Wants Employment," *Boston-Gazette, and Country Journal,* October 29, 1764, supplement, 2.
68. See *World* (London), February 8, 1791, issue 1281; *World and Fashionable Advertiser* (London), February 19, 1787, issue 43.
69. "Wanted, An Experienced Book-keeper," *New-York Daily Advertiser,* January 3, 1820, issue 845, 3.
70. "Wanted to go to Jamaica," *City Gazette and Daily Advertiser* (Charleston, South Carolina), April 4, 1788, 3.
71. "To Merchants," *New-York Gazette and General Advertiser,* July 20, 1802, issue 5176, 2.
72. Richard S. Dunn, *Sugar and Slaves: The Rise of the Planter Class in the English West Indies, 1624–1713* (Chapel Hill: University of North Carolina Press, 1972); Alfred Chandler, "The Expansion of Barbados," *Journal of the Barbados Museum and Historical Society* 13, no. 3–4 (May–August 1946): 106–136; Russell R. Menard, *Sweet Negotiations: Sugar, Slavery, and Plantation Agriculture in Early Barbados* (Charlottesville: University of Virginia Press, 2006), chap. 6.
73. Trevor Burnard found that almost 10 percent of a sample of eighteenth-century indentured migrants to Jamaica were clerks and bookkeepers. Trevor Burnard, "European Migration to Jamaica, 1655–1780," *William and Mary Quarterly* 53, no. 4 (October 1996): 769–796, 789. Per Table 7, this was 9.4 percent of migrants between 1719 and 1759. A slightly different number is given in the text.

74. The movement of people and ideas also crossed imperial boundaries. Not only clerks, but also enslaved people and free people of color exploited the boundaries between imperial regimes to trade on their expertise. On these crossings, see Elena Schneider, *The Occupation of Havana: War, Trade, and Slavery in the Eighteenth-century Atlantic World* (Chapel Hill: Omohundro / UNC Press, forthcoming).

75. Farquhar Macrae, "On the Soils and Agricultural Advantages of Florida.—No. 1," *Farmers' Register*, July 1835, 179.

76. Ibid. See note 79 for Macrae's payout.

77. Nicholas Draper, *The Price of Emancipation: Slave-Ownership, Compensation and British Society at the End of Slavery* (Cambridge: Cambridge University Press, 2010).

78. "Jamaica Clarendon 1 (Parnassus Estate)," Legacies of British Slave-Ownership, http://www.ucl.ac.uk/lbs/claim/view/22211.

79. "Farquhar McRae," Legacies of British Slave-Ownership, http://www.ucl.ac.uk /lbs/person/view/16003. Macrae is also spelled "M'Rae" and "McRae" in the reports.

80. Farquhar Macrae, "Forms for an Overseer's Journal and Monthly Reports, Suited to a Southern Plantation," *Farmers' Register*, July 1835, 163–165.

81. Edward E. Baptist, *Creating an Old South: Middle Florida's Plantation Frontier before the Civil War* (Chapel Hill: University of North Carolina Press, 2002), 20–21.

82. Macrae, "Forms for an Overseer's Journal."

83. Ibid.

84. Albert Lowther Demaree, *The American Agricultural Press, 1819–1860* (New York: Columbia University Press, 1941), 362; "List of Subscribers," *Farmers' Register*, Supplement to Vol. 1, May 1834, 769–776.

85. Macrae's career as a booster for slave labor and Florida planting ended abruptly in 1838. When he died in the explosion of the steamship *Pulaski*, the *Farmers' Register* published an effusive note. En route from Charleston to Baltimore, the ship's boiler burst into flames. All told, more than half of the passengers and crew (likely including slaves accompanying their masters) died in the explosion and its aftermath. "To Correspondents and Contributors," *Farmers' Register*, December 31, 1838, 767. For an excellent account of southern steamboats, see Johnson, *River of Dark Dreams*, chaps. 1–3.

86. For reviews of the literature on the second slavery generally, see note 7 to the introduction. On technology transfer specifically, see Maria M. Portuondo, "Plantation Factories Science and Technology in Late-Eighteenth Century Cuba," *Technology and Culture* 44, nos. 231–257 (April 2003): 244–246, 256; Rood, *Reinvention of Atlantic Slavery*; Jos. Guadalupe Ortega, *The Cuban Sugar Complex in*

the Age of Revolution, 1789–1844 (PhD diss., University of California, Los Angeles, 2007), chap. 5. On a similar process with the law, see Gaspar, "'Rigid and Inclement,'" 78–97; Barry J. Nicholson, "Legal Borrowing and the Origins of Slave Law in the British Colonies," *American Journal of Legal History* 8 (1994): 38–54. Practices did not always transfer smoothly from merchants to planters. For one merchant's not very successful attempt to apply his skills on a slave plantation in Florida, see Hancock, *Citizens of the World*, chap. 5.

87. For thinking about laws enabling slavery as market regulation, see Holly Brewer, "Property in People and the Complexities of Capitalism," work in progress presented at the 2018 Business History Conference. On abolition as market regulation, see Caitlin Rosenthal, "Abolition as Market Regulation," *Boston Review Forum 1: Race, Capitalism, Justice* (2017).

88. *Extracts from a West India Plantation Journal, Kept by the Manager: Showing the Treatment of the Slaves and Its Fatal Consequences* (London: S. Bagster, 1831), 1–2.

89. Ibid. 3–5.

90. Ibid. 2. See also Teresa A. Goddu, "The Antislavery Almanac and the Discourse of Numeracy," *Book History* 12 (2009): 129–155.

91. Friendship Punishment Records, January–June 1829, 1829; Wilberforce House Museum, box 9 / 4, AMD.

92. For an example form and a discussion of regulations, see *State Papers: Relating to the Slave Population in the West Indies on the Continent of South America and at the Cape of Good Hope . . .* , vol. 2, 1827, https://books.google.com/books?id=QDdbAAAAQAAJ.

93. William Dickson, *Subscription Solicitation for "A Plan for the Mitigation of Slavery: Delineated, in a Series of Letters by the Late Honourable Joshua Steele, of Barbadoes"* (London: John Orphoot, Blackfriards Wynd, 1809), 2.

94. Stephanie E. Smallwood, *Saltwater Slavery: A Middle Passage from Africa to American Diaspora* (Cambridge, MA: Harvard University Press, 2007), 98.

95. Saidiya V. Hartman, *Lose Your Mother: A Journey along the Atlantic Slave Route* (New York: Farrar, Straus and Giroux, 2007), 17.

3. Slavery's Scientific Management

1. Picking of course varied from day to day, and the next day, when the cotton was "not so good" and the morning "quite cold," the hands brought in only 2,202 lb. Eli Capell, Plantation Diary for 1842, vol. 8, Capell Family Papers, LSU.

2. Though this chapter invokes the language of the laboratory, it's important to acknowledge that enslaved people were also subjected to more literal "experiments,"

both while alive and after death through the sale of cadavers. See Londa L. Schiebinger, *Secret Cures of Slaves: People, Plants, and Medicine in the Eighteenth-Century Atlantic World* (Stanford, CA: Stanford University Press, 2017); Daina Ramey Berry, *The Price for Their Pound of Flesh: The Value of the Enslaved from Womb to Grave in the Building of a Nation* (Boston: Beacon Press, 2017), chap. 6; Stephen C. Kenny, "Power, Opportunism, Racism: Human Experiments under American Slavery," *Endeavour* 39, no. 1 (March 2015): 10–20.

3. Eli Capell, Plantation Diaries, vols. 8–27, Capell Family Papers. See also Wendell Holmes Stephenson, "A Quarter-Century of a Mississippi Plantation: Eli J. Capell of 'Pleasant Hill,'" *Mississippi Valley Historical Review* 23, no. 3 (December 1936): 358.

4. Eli Capell, Plantation Diaries, 1843–1845, vols. 8–10, Capell Family Papers, LSU.

5. Eli Capell, Plantation Diaries, 1840–1862, vol. 15, Capell Family Papers. See also vols. 16–27 for additional Affleck books, by far the most common journals used by Capell during this period.

6. Thomas Affleck to James Henry Hammond, 3 January 1855, box 32, folder 10, pp. 262–266, Thomas Affleck Papers, LSU.

7. Ibid.

8. Farmer's Record and Account Book Advertisement, *Subscription Books* (Fairbanks, Palmer, 1850), 531.

9. Advertisement, *Affleck's Southern Rural Almanac, and Plantation and Garden Calendar* (Washington, MS, 1854), 2.

10. Eli Capell, Plantation Diary for 1857, vol. 23, Capell Family Papers, LSU.

11. Advertisement, *Affleck's Southern Rural Almanac,* 2.

12. Thomas Affleck, "Explanation of Records and Accounts," *Plantation Record and Account Book.* See, for example, G. R. Clark, Eustatia Plantation Account Book (1861), vol. 649, Ohio Historical Center Archives Library, http://dbs.ohiohistory.org/africanam/html/page2890.html?ID=13902&Current=F004. Ratios of picked to ginned cotton are inside the back cover.

13. Thomas Affleck, "Explanation of Records and Accounts."

14. Advertisement, *Affleck's Southern Rural Almanac and Plantation and Garden Calendar,* 1860, 1–6.

15. Affleck to Hammond, 3 January 1855, pp. 262–266, Thomas Affleck Papers, LSU. For the most comprehensive overview of the role of the overseer, see William Kauffman Scarborough, *The Overseer: Plantation Management in the Old South* (Athens: University of Georgia Press, 1984). See also Laura Sandy, "Supervisors of Small Worlds: The Role of Overseers on Colonial South Carolina Slave Plantations," *Journal of Early American History* 2, no. 2 (January 1, 2012): 178–210.

16. Thomas Affleck to B. M. Norman, January 6, 1851, box 32, folder 6, Thomas Affleck Papers, LSU.

17. On Affleck's troubled relationships with his printers, see various letters in box 32, folder 7, Thomas Affleck Papers, LSU.

18. For an example of Affleck's eighth edition, see example Thomas Affleck, *Cotton Plantation Record and Account Book*, No. 3, (New Orleans: Broomfield & Steel: 1859), identified as Turnbull and Bowman family diary, 1860, West Feliciana Parish, Louisiana, Southern life and African American history, PQHV (RASP, Series I: Part 4). For what appears to have been an overly optimistic estimate of 5,000, see note 16 above. In 1856, Affleck claimed a circulation of over 2000, Thomas Affleck, 25 March, 1856, box 19, folder 12, Thomas Affleck Papers, LSU. For estimate of 3,000, see Thomas Affleck, circular, box 31, folder 19, Thomas Affleck Papers, LSU. Other data for the calculations in this paragraph and the accompanying chart come from the Parker-Gallman Sample (see figure 3.2).

19. Though this book focuses on larger plantations and elite business practices, it is worth noting that more middling farmers also participated in broad debates about agricultural improvement. Plantation structures were echoed in miniature by small farmers. Yeomn built tiny hierarchies, sometimes including slaves, that made it easier for them to align their political values with elite planters. Stephanie McCurry, *Masters of Small Worlds: Yeoman Households, Gender Relations, and the Political Culture of the Antebellum South Carolina Low Country*, (New York: Oxford University Press, 1995). On the distinctive identity of middling southerners, see Jonathan Daniel Wells, *The Origins of the Southern Middle Class, 1800–1861* (Chapel Hill: The University of North Carolina Press, 2004).

20. Macrae, "Forms for an Overseer's Journal."

21. Andrew Flynn, Green Valley Plantation Book, no. 1057, Microfilm, Reel 1, SHC.

22. Some evidence suggests the author could have been Virginia planter and Confederate general Philip St. George Cocke. See a custom printed version "For the Use of the Manager on the Estate of Philip St. George Cocke," *Plantation and Farm Instruction, Regulation, Record, Inventory and Account Book*, 2nd ed. (Richmond, VA: J. W. Randolph, 1861), UVA. A biography of St. George Cocke from the 1890s lists him as author of a book on *"Plantation and Farm Instruction"* published in 1852 and also as president of the Virginia State Agricultural Society. Maj. Jed. Hotchkiss, "Brigadier-General Philip St. George Cocke," in *Confederate Military History, a Library of Confederate States History in Twelve Volumes*, vol. 3 (Atlanta: Confederate Publishing, 1899), 585; John Fiske and James Grant Wilson, eds., *Appletons' Cyclopædia of American Biography*, vol. 1 (New York: D. Appleton, 1887), 672. Further consultation of the Philip St. George Cocke papers held at UVA might confirm this possibility.

23. "Plantation Book," *The Southern Planter*, ed. Frank G. Ruffin, Esq. (Richmond, VA: P. D. Bernard, 1852), 188.

24. *Plantation and Farm Instruction, Regulation, Record, Inventory and Account Book*, 3–19.

25. Thomas Affleck to B. M. Norman, 14 February 1854, box 32, folder 9, Thomas Affleck Papers.

26. Affleck to Hammond, 3 January 1855, box 32, folder 10, Thomas Affleck Papers.

27. G. R. Clark, Eustatia Plantation Account Book, Ohio Historical Center Archives Library. On how Affleck's books were filled out, see work in progress by Ian Beamish, "A Complicated Humbug: Slavery, Capitalism, and Accounts in the Cotton South."

28. Work Records, Manuscript, vol. 1, folder 2, in the Francis Terry Leak Papers #1095, SHC. For another hand-lined book, though one not as consistent as Leak's, see Phanor Prudhomme, Cotton Book, 1836, folder 267, Prudhomme Family Papers #00613, SHC.

29. Charles Thompson, *Biography of a Slave* (Dayton, OH: United Brethren Publishing House, 1875), 37–41.

30. Henry Bibb, *Narrative of the Life and Adventures of Henry Bibb: An American Slave, Written by Himself* (New York: H. Bibb, 1849), 116–117.

31. Reproduced in James O. Breeden, *Advice among Masters: The Ideal in Slave Management in the Old South* (Westport, CT: Greenwood Press, 1980), 258–259.

32. Ibid., 257–258. This scheme resembled the fidelity funds that companies like Singer sewing machine would adopt to prevent embezzlement in the coming decades. On fidelity funds, see Robert Bruce Davies, *Peacefully Working to Conquer the World: Singer Sewing Machines in Foreign Markets, 1854–1920* (New York: Arno Press, 1976), 65.

33. Henry Watson, *Narrative of Henry Watson, a Fugitive Slave* (Boston: Bela Marsh, 1848), 19–20.

34. John Brown, *Slave Life in Georgia: A Narrative of the Life, Sufferings, and Escape of John Brown, a Fugitive Slave, Now in England*, ed. Louis Alexis Chamerovzow (London, 1855), 129.

35. Solomon Northup, *Twelve Years a Slave* (Auburn, NY: Miller, Orton & Mulligan, 1855), 167–168.

36. Brown, *Slave Life in Georgia*, 128–129. Baptist, *The Half Has Never Been Told*, 116–143, describes the structure of violence or what he calls the "pushing system" in more extensive detail. Some scholars in economics have objected to this description. See the next section, "King Cotton," for more discussion of this controversy and of the ways violence, accounting, and innovation worked together.

37. Cooke, "Denial of Slavery in Management Studies," 1905; Frederick Law Olmsted, *The Cotton Kingdom*, vol. 1 (New York: Mason Brothers, 1861), 128; Frederick Law Olmsted, *Walks and Talks of an American Farmer in England* (New York: G. P. Putnam, 1852), 38. As early as the 1940s, Bauer and Bauer described

the slowing of labor as a strategy of resistance. Raymond A. Bauer and Alice H. Bauer, "Day to Day Resistance to Slavery," *Journal of Negro History* 27, no. 4 (October 1942): 388–419. On the perils of overemphasizing resistance, see Walter Johnson, "On Agency," *Journal of Social History* 37, no. 1 (2003): 113–124. On these strategies beyond the slave context, see James C. Scott, *Weapons of the Weak: Everyday Forms of Peasant Resistance* (New Haven, CT: Yale University Press, 1985).

38. Thomas D. Morris, *Southern Slavery and the Law, 1619–1860* (Chapel Hill: University of North Carolina Press, 2004), 280.

39. Ibid., 281.

40. As quoted in Alfred L. Brophy, *University, Court, and Slave: Pro-Slavery Thought in Southern Colleges and Courts and the Coming of Civil War* (New York: Oxford University Press, 2016), chap. 7, 185–186.

41. Andrew Fede, "Legitimized Violent Slave Abuse in the American South, 1619–1865: A Case Study of Law and Social Change in Six Southern States," *American Journal of Legal History* 29, no. 2 (1985): 93–150, 119n54, 119n55. Eugene Genovese offered a contrasting portrait of the extent to which white masters were held accountable, arguing that "when whites did find themselves before the bard of justice, especially during the late antebellum period, they could expect greater severity than might be imagined." He cites a number of cases in which masters were punished. Eugene D. Genovese, *Roll, Jordan, Roll: The World the Slaves Made* (New York: Pantheon Books, 1974), 38.

42. Morris, *Southern Slavery and the Law,* 185–187. Slaves who attempted to defend themselves physically and did not lose their own lives in the process could be tried for murder. In these examples, most cases "did not pass beyond the county and a prompt execution." Morris found only one trial that ended in acquittal, resulting in an overall conviction rate near 100 percent: "No other crime, not even insurrection, came close to this conviction record."

43. On the ways enslaved people interacted with southern courtrooms, see Kimberly Welch, *Calling to Account: Black Litigants in the Antebellum American South* (University of North Carolina Press, forthcoming 2018); Dylan Penningroth, *The Claims of Kinfolk: African American Property and Community in the Nineteenth-Century South* (Chapel Hill: University of North Carolina Press, 2003); Ariela J. Gross, *Double Character: Slavery and Mastery in the Antebellum Southern Courtroom* (Princeton, NJ: Princeton University Press, 2000); Laura F. Edwards, "Status without Rights: African Americans and the Tangled History of Law and Governance in the Nineteenth-Century U.S. South," *American Historical Review* 112, no. 2 (April 2007): 365–393; Laura F. Edwards, *The People and Their Peace: Legal Culture and the Transformation of Inequality in the Post-Revolutionary South* (Chapel Hill: University of North Carolina Press, 2009).

44. Jonathan Bush, "Free to Enslave: The Foundations of Colonial American Slave Law," *Yale Journal of Law and Humanities* 5 (1993): 417–470, 426. Eugene Genovese describes this as "a kind of dual power: that which they collectively exercise as a class, even against their own individual impulses . . . and that which they reserved to themselves as individuals who commanded other human beings in bondage." Genovese saw this as an underlying contradiction that weakened the operation of the system, but masters' management practices suggest these "contradictions" placed relatively few practical limitations on their authority. Genovese, *Roll, Jordan, Roll,* 46–47. Some studies of slavery and the law suggest that deep contradictions in the law weakened its operation. (See, for example, Mark V. Tushnet, *The American Law of Slavery, 1810–1860: Considerations of Humanity and Interest* [Princeton, NJ: Princeton University Press, 1981]). However, an alternative reading might be to see the law as not contradictory but flexible, or as Thomas Morris has suggested, inconsistent but not cripplingly so (*Southern Slavery and the Law*). An even stronger reinterpretation suggests that inconsistencies reflect enslaved resistance. On how enslaved people contributed to legal "confusion," see, for example, Walter Johnson, "Inconsistency, Contradiction, and Complete Confusion: The Everyday Life of the Law of Slavery," *Law and Social Inquiry* 22, no. 2 (April 1997): 405–433.

45. Israel Campbell, *An Autobiography, Bond and Free . . .* (Philadelphia: C. E. P. Brinckloe, 1861), 33–35. For an example of planters estimating yield of lint per pound of cotton, see the account book completed by overseer George R. Clark of Eustatia Plantation. After tallying up weekly picking, Clark divided the running total by the total number of pounds he believed would produce a bale of lint. Over time he tried dividing by 1400 lbs, 1300 lbs, and 1350 lbs. G. R. Clark, Eustatia Plantation Account Book. A previous discussion of these calculations misidentified them as pounds per week per prime hand. Thanks to Alan Olmstead and Paul Rhode for their help in correcting this error. For the erroneous discussion, see Caitlin C. Rosenthal, "Slavery's Scientific Management: Masters and Managers," in *Slavery's Capitalism: A New History of American Economic Development,* ed. Sven Beckert and Seth Rockman (Philadelphia: University of Pennsylvania Press, 2016), 62–86.

46. Eli Capell, Plantation Diary for 1852–1853, vol. 18.

47. "The overseer used a slate on which to set down the weights of cotton, which was hanging in his cabin." Thompson, *Biography of a Slave,* 41. "He kept a slate with each hand's name on it, and would put each draft of cotton down as they brought it in." Campbell, *An Autobiography,* 33–35.

48. Cotton Record Book, 1859–1866, Robert H. Stewart Account Books, Mss. 404, 4732, LSU.

49. Ibid.

50. See Alan L. Olmstead and Paul W. Rhode, "Biological Innovation and Productivity Growth in the Antebellum Cotton Economy," *Journal of Economic History* 68, no. 4 (2008): 1123–1171. See also Olmstead and Rhode, *Creating Abundance,* chap. 4. For earlier estimates yielding similar magnitudes but not based on plantation records, see Stanley Lebergott, *The Americans: An Economic Record* (New York: Norton, 1984).

51. Olmstead and Rhode, "Biological Innovation," 1124.

52. Olmstead and Rhode attribute this gain to the arrival of new strains of Mexican cotton. Historian Edward Baptist's *The Half Has Never Been Told* places violence at the center of the picture, a useful corrective to accounts that emphasize technical innovation. And Walter Johnson's recent *River of Dark Dreams* emphasizes both seeds and violence. Olmstead and Rhode, "Biological Innovation," 1123–1171; Baptist, *The Half Has Never Been Told*, 126–130, 445n31. This most recent round of debate echoes an older literature. Economic historians have long agreed on the remarkable productivity of cotton production, but they have disagreed about its sources. One set of scholars, most prominently represented by Robert Fogel and Stanley Engerman, has argued that the productivity resulted from scale and the gang labor system—essentially a speedup in cotton growing and picking. By contrast, Gavin Wright has argued that crop mix was most important. Those who grew the most cotton earned the most profit, and scale worked only indirectly through crop mix. While plantation accounting practices do not show which of these had the greatest impact, they do show that the most managerially advanced planters attempted to use all of them: to increase the rate of picking, to adjust seasonal schedules to maximize the cotton crop, and to compare production of different varieties of cotton. Engerman and Fogel, *Time on the Cross*; Fogel, *Without Consent or Contract*; Gavin Wright, *The Political Economy of the Cotton South: Households, Markets, and Wealth in the Nineteenth Century* (New York: Norton, 1978). Notably, though the most recent set of debates has also been across disciplinary lines, the disagreement has not always broken down in the same way. For example, though Fogel and Engerman did not adequately emphasize violence, their explanation for high rates of productivity was essentially a "speed up" in the pace of labor, a mechanism more compatible with Baptist's "whipping machine" than Rhode and Olmsted's account.

53. For a discussion of the ease of picking new strains, see Olmstead and Rhode, *Creating Abundance*, chap. 4.

54. Rhode and Olmsted argue that only a relatively small number of slave narratives mention the lash-per-pound punishments described by Baptist and earlier in this chapter. Though they correctly identify a number of cases where Baptist should have been more careful with his sources, much of Baptist's larger

argument seems to be persuasive: innovation in technology was underpinned by innovation in violence. Counting mentions of whipping is not an adequate way to understand the prevalence of plantation violence, a situation in which it is particularly important for documents to be read against the grain. Baptist, *The Half Has Never Been Told*. For the critique, see Alan L. Olmstead and Paul W. Rhode. "Cotton, Slavery, and the New History of Capitalism," *Explorations in Economic History* 67 (January 1, 2018): 1–17. For a classic account of the perils of quantifying whipping, albeit from different sources, see Herbert G. Gutman, *Slavery and the Numbers Game: A Critique of Time on the Cross* (Urbana: University of Illinois Press, 1975), particularly chap. 2, "Enslaved Afro-Americans and the Protestant Work Ethic." Indeed, integrating both sides of the debate yields a fuller picture of a system that knit together biological innovation and violence. To take just one point of contention, Baptist argues that planters used "quotas," but Rhode and Olmstead suggest that no "quotas" were listed in account books and that, moreover, they would not have worked because picking rates declined toward the end of the season. But the absence of a flat quota over the course of a season does not preclude more nuanced attention to picking rates, particularly when slave narratives and scattered references in account books suggest paper records were only the top layer of record keeping in a system that also relied on verbal reports and on slates. Planters (at least the elite agriculturists described here) cared about picking the last pound of cotton, but they cared far more about the last bale. This outlook is also reflected in the fact that cotton-crazed planters did not become cotton monocroppers. On slates, see notes 46 and 47 above. On monocropping, see note 57 below.

55. Affleck to Hammond, 3 January 1855, box 32, folder 10, pp. 262–266, Thomas Affleck Papers. In Affleck's vision, such data could be shared in the lively southern agricultural press. See John F. Kvach, *DeBow's Review: The Antebellum Vision of a New South* (Lexington: University Press of Kentucky, 2013). On the longer history of agricultural innovation, and agricultural networks that made it possible, see Joyce E. Chaplin, *An Anxious Pursuit: Agricultural Innovation and Modernity in the Lower South, 1730–1815* (Chapel Hill: University of North Carolina Press, 1993); Lorena Seebach Walsh, *Motives of Honor, Pleasure, and Profit: Plantation Management in the Colonial Chesapeake, 1607–1763* (Chapel Hill: University of North Carolina Press, 2010).

56. Work Records, Manuscript, vol. 1, folder 2, in the Francis Terry Leak Papers #1095, SHC. For quote, see hand-numbered p. 20. Given these large numbers, Leak probably means 605,000 pounds baled, not 605,000 bales.

57. As Walter Johnson writes, "Throughout the antebellum period, the Lower Mississippi Valley . . . imported most of the wheat, corn, beef, and pork its residents required to live from the Midwest and the Ohio Valley. The entire economy was

devoted to agriculture, yet it could not feed itself . . . there were, scattered among the many plantation owners who planted nothing but cotton, a few planters who tried to diversify their crops." He continues a few pages later, "Allocation of either land or labor away from cotton and toward corn, cattle, or hogs represented an unaccountable loss in the minds of cotton-crazed planters." As I suggest later in this chapter, the fact that this misrepresentation lingers in the historical literature reflects slaveholders' real obsession with growing as much cotton as possible—an obsession that comes through in many archival sources. It is only the conclusion that this drove them to monoculture that is incorrect.

For the large literature on foodstuffs grown in the South, see, for example, Robert E. Gallman, "Self-Sufficiency in the Cotton Economy of the Antebellum South," *Agricultural History* 44, no. 1 (January 1970): 5–23; Diane Lindstrom, "Southern Dependence upon Interregional Grain Supplies: A Review of the Trade Flows, 1840–1860," *Agricultural History* 44, no. 1 (January 1970): 101–113; Albert Fishlow, "Antebellum Interregional Trade Reconsidered," *American Economic Review* 54, no. 3 (May 1964): 352–364.

58. Jacob Metzer, "Rational Management, Modern Business Practices, and Economies of Scale in the Ante-bellum Southern Plantations," *Explorations in Economic History* 12, no. 2 (1975): 123–150.

59. On incentives for smoothing in addition to Metzer, see Ralph V. Anderson and Robert E. Gallman, "Slaves as Fixed Capital: Slave Labor and Southern Economic Development," *Journal of American History* 64, no. 1 (June 1977): 24–46.

60. Diary of Francis Terry Leak, "Hints to Be Attended to Another Year," Tuesday, 15 April 1845, Manuscript, vol. 2, folder 8, p. 33, typed transcript, in the Francis Terry Leak Papers #1095, SHC; see also in the same collection, Manuscript, vol. 1, folder 2, 1841–1865, p. 142.

61. Work Records, Manuscript, vol. 1, folder 2, in the Francis Terry Leak Papers #1095, SHC. For quote, see hand-numbered p. 111.

62. George Washington, 15 July 1769, quoted in Lewis Cecil Gray, *History of Southern Agriculture in the United States* (Washington: P. Smith: 1958), 1:550. See also George Washington, *The Diaries of George Washington, 1748–1799*, ed. John Clement Fitzpatrick, vol. 1, *1748–1770* (New York: Houghton Mifflin, 1925), 338. Thomas Affleck cites Washington as a source (see, for example, Capell, Plantation Diary, 1858, vol. 24, Capell Family Papers, LSU), and the manual published by J. W. Randolph also quotes from Washington's instructions to his overseers. *Plantation and Farm Instruction, regulation, record, inventory and account book.*

63. Anderson and Gallman, "Slaves as Fixed Capital," 35; Gallman, "Self-Sufficiency in the Cotton Economy," 5–23.

64. As Gavin Wright has written about risk and slavery: "The landowner who committed acres to cotton was taking financial risk, and neither the planter

nor his creditors would have been willing to do so without some means of assurance that labor supply for the harvest would be available. Although there are other means of achieving such assurance, none was as effective or as certain as the legal property rights of a slaveowner." Wright, *Slavery and American Economic Development*, 88.

65. "Cotton Record Book, 1859–1866," Robert H. Stewart Account Books.

66. As Wright writes, "The capacity to take advantage of rare bumper crops highlights one of the crucial property-rights benefits of slavery: the power to mobilize harvest labor throughout the season, however protracted and however unanticipated. Many writers have portrayed the year-round character of slave labor as a kind of burden, an indivisibility that raised fixed costs and strained the manager's ability to keep slaves usefully employed. Under the right conditions, however, this fixed-cost investment in potential labor power could generate a great monetary return by allowing the owner to capture the full benefit of an abundant crop. Even in more normal years, knowing that the slave labor reserve was present made it feasible for planters to extend their acreage in commercial crops like cotton beyond the level that would otherwise be financially prudent." Wright, *Slavery and American Economic Development*, 93.

67. Diary of Francis Terry Leak, Manuscript, vol. 2, folder 8, typed transcript, in the Francis Terry Leak Papers #1095, SHC. On seed varieties, see April 1842, p. 7; on measuring stalks, see July 2, 1842, p. 9; on blight, see p. 11: "Scattered some cotton leaves affected with the rust on several stalks in the garden with the view of ascertaining whether rust can be propagated in that way." For experiments on manuring, see p. 228. (All page numbers refer to the typed transcription.)

68. The literature on double-entry bookkeeping is massive, from classic texts by Max Weber and Werner Sombart to Jacob Soll's recent *The Reckoning*. Max Weber, *General Economic History* (Glencoe, IL: Free Press, 1950); Werner Sombart, *The Quintessence of Capitalism: A Study of the History and Psychology of the Modern Business Man* (New York: H. Fertig, 1967); Soll, *The Reckoning*. For a discussion of the connection between double-entry bookkeeping and "rationality," see Bruce G. Carruthers and Wendy Nelson Espeland, "Accounting for Rationality: Double-Entry Bookkeeping and the Rhetoric of Economic Rationality," *American Journal of Sociology* 97, no. 1 (July 1991): 31–69. For a different analysis suggesting overemphasis on double-entry bookkeeping and on financial accounting generally, see Johnson and Kaplan, *Relevance Lost*.

69. The other chief source of profit was the appreciation of slaves, the subject of Chapter 4.

70. Richard Follett, *The Sugar Masters: Planters and Slaves in Louisiana's Cane World, 1820–1860* (Baton Rouge: Louisiana State University Press, 2007), 93.

71. Samuel Leigh, Observations of Weather and Crops, 1856–1857, A. Ledoux & Co. Plantation Journal, Pointe Coupee [Iberville?] Parish, Louisiana, Southern life and African American history, PQHV (RASP, Series I: Part 1, A. Ledoux & Co. Plantation Journal, LSU).

72. Account Book of overseer George W. Woodruff, Frogmoor Plantation of James Pirrie Bowman, 1857, Louisiana, Southern life and African American history, PQHV (RASP, Series I: Part 4, Turnbull-Bowman-Lyons Family Papers, LSU).

73. Ibid., Form D, 69–73.

74. Follett, *Sugar Masters*, 93.

75. As quoted in Follett, *Sugar Masters*, 45.

76. Claiborne T. Smith Jr., 1979, "Barrow, Robert Ruffin," in *Dictionary of North Carolina Biography*, ed. William S. Powell (Chapel Hill: University of North Carolina Press, 1979). Plantation Journal (original and typed transcription), vols. 1 and 2, 1857, in the Robert Ruffin Barrow Papers #2407-z, SHC.

77. Plantation Journal (original and typed transcription), vols. 1 and 2, 1857, Robert Ruffin Barrow Papers #2407-z, SHC.

78. Ibid.

79. On turnover as a barrier to production, see the discussion in Chapter 2; on continuing turnover rates of 100 percent or more into the twentieth century, see Sumner H. Slichter, *The Turnover of Factory Labor* (New York: D. Appleton, 1921), 17, http://catalog.hathitrust.org/Record/101712179.

80. Timothy Flint, *The History and Geography of the Mississippi Valley* (Cincinnati, OH: Flint and Lincoln, 1832), 1:244–245, quoted in Follett, *Sugar Masters*, 91.

81. Robert Russell, *North America, Its Agriculture and Climate* (Edinburgh: A. and C. Black, 1857), quoted in Follett, *Sugar Masters*, 90.

82. Plantation Journal (original and typed transcription), vols. 1 and 2, 1857, Robert Ruffin Barrow Papers #2407-z, SHC.

83. Sally Hadden, *Slave Patrols: Law and Violence in Virginia and the Carolinas* (Cambridge, MA: Harvard University Press, 2001), 129–132. See also Stanley Harrold, *Border War: Fighting over Slavery before the Civil War* (Chapel Hill: University of North Carolina Press, 2010), 46–47.

84. On the federal government's enforcement of the Fugitive Slave Law of 1850 and its efforts to rely on *posse comitatus* to do so, see Gautham Rao, "The Federal 'Posse Comitatus' Doctrine: Slavery, Compulsion, and Statecraft in Mid-Nineteenth-Century America," *Law and History Review* 26, no. 1 (2008): 1–56. On the ways informal knowledge networks helped escaped slaves avoid or delay capture, and the effect of their evasion on state building, see Ryan A. Quintana, "Planners, Planters, and Slaves: Producing the State in Early National South Carolina," *Journal of Southern History* 81, no. 1 (February 2015).

85. Morris, *Southern Slavery and the Law*, 83.

86. Ibid., 100.

87. "Management of Slaves," *Southern Cultivator,* March 1846, 44. See also Steven G. Collins, "System, Organization, and Agricultural Reform in the Antebellum South, 1840–1860," *Agricultural History* 75, no. 1 (January 2001): 1–27, 6.

88. Plantation Journal (original and typed transcription), vols. 1 and 2, 1857, Robert Ruffin Barrow Papers #2407-z, SHC. Nursing women were also put to a different kind of work: suckling the children of their masters. Stephanie Jones-Rogers, "'[S]he Could . . . Spare One Ample Breast for the Profit of Her Owner': White Mothers and Enslaved Wet Nurses' Invisible Labor in American Slave Markets," *Slavery & Abolition* 38, no. 2 (2017): 337–355.

89. On the labor of children, see Wilma King, *Stolen Childhood: Slave Youth in Nineteenth Century America* (Bloomington: Indiana University Press: 1995), chap. 3. On the ways enslaved children were "trained," in part, by the white children who were also being trained for mastery themselves, see Stephanie Jones-Rogers, "Mistresses in the Making: White Girls, Mastery and the Practice of Slaveownership in the Nineteenth-Century South," in *Women's America, Volume 8: Refocusing the Past,* ed. Linda Kerber, Jane Sherron De Hart, Cornelia Hughes Dayton, and Judy Wu (Oxford: Oxford University Press, 2015), 139–146.

90. Follett, *Sugar Masters,* 112–113.

91. Breeden, *Advice among Masters,* 197.

92. "Drinks for Harvest," in *The Merchants' & Planters' Almanac, for the Year of Our Lord and Saviour 1855* (New Orleans: Converse, 1854).

93. Follett, *Sugar Masters,* 5.

94. Frederick Law Olmsted, *Journeys and Explorations in the Cotton Kingdom of America* (London: S. Low, Son, 1861), 328.

95. Follett, *Sugar Masters,* 157.

96. Taylor, *Principles of Scientific Management,* 55.

97. Plowden C. J. Weston, *Rules for the Government and Management of Plantation, to be Observed by the Overseer* (Charleston: A. J. Burke, 18[??]), 8. Italics in original.

98. Pleasant Suit, *The Farmer's Accountant and, Instructions for Overseers* (Richmond, VA: J. MacFarlan, 1828), xiv. Suit recommended an array of strategies, including "calculation, trials, and inquiries of experienced persons."

99. Taylor, *Principles of Scientific Management,* 59.

100. Ibid., 55.

101. "A Day's Work," in *The Soil of the South,* vol. 6 (Columbus, GA: W. H. Chambers, 1848), 85–86.

102. "Reply to 'A Day's Work,'" in *The Soil of the South,* vol. 6 (Columbus, GA: W. H. Chambers, 1848), 103.

103. *Plantation and Farm Instruction, regulation, record, inventory and account book,* 15–16. The author's example explained that a man working with a good horse for

10 hours could walk 3 miles of 1,760 yards each hour. With acres of 70 yards × 70 yards and furrows of 9 inches wide (4 per yard), he estimated a task of 1 and 1 / 3 acres per day. The author included the equation as "(1760 × 3 × 10) / (70 × 70)) × (¼) = 1⅓ very nearly." The actual result is approximately twice this much.

104. Taylor, *Principles of Scientific Management*, 55–56.

105. For this influence on Taylor, see Spender and Kijne, *Scientific Management*, 50; Robertson Buchanan et al., *Practical Essays on Mill Work and Other Machinery* (London: J. Weale, 1841 [1814]), 89; Julius Weisbach, *Principles of the Mechanics of Machinery and Engineering*, ed. Walter R. Johnson, vol. 2, *Applied Mechanics* (Philadelphia: Lea and Blanchard, 1849). Buchanan may not be the original source. He footnotes "Dr. Young's Natural Philosophy, Vol. II, 165," which appears to be Thomas Young, *A Course of Lectures on Natural Philosophy and the Mechanical Arts* (London: Printed for J. Johnson, 1807), 165–167, http://archive.org/details/lecturescourseof02younrich.

106. See Chapter 2 for a broader discussion of how slaveholders' management advice crossed geographies.

4. Human Capital

1. James Green Carson, Record Books, 1856 and 1857, Canebrake Plantation Records, 1856–1858, DBC. The births were recorded in the book for 1856. They were listed for 1856 but not by value, the births of 1856 appear with values in the inventory to begin 1857.

2. Slaves often made up more of planters' wealth than land, a fact that shaped planters' behavior. This was true even for planters owning just a few slaves. As Gavin Wright notes, "If slave owners were capitalists, they were human capitalists." Gavin Wright, *Old South, New South* (Baton Rouge: Louisiana State University Press, 1996 [1986]), 20. On slaves as capital, see Anderson and Gallman, "Slaves as Fixed Capital," 24. This chapter focuses on owners' and traders' attempt to value slaves, but related practices also evolved in insurance. On slavery and insurance, see Jonathan Levy, *Freaks of Fortune: The Emerging World of Capitalism and Risk in America* (Cambridge, MA: Harvard University Press, 2012), chap. 4; Murphy, *Investing in Life*, chap. 7; Sharon Ann Murphy, "Securing Human Property: Slavery, Life Insurance, and Industrialization in the Upper South," *Journal of the Early Republic* 25, no. 4 (Winter 2005): 615–652; Ralph and Rankin, "Decoder: The Slave Insurance Market."

3. James Green Carson, "Form I," Record Book, 1857, Canebrake Plantation Records, 1856–1858, DBC.

4. In his pathbreaking comparison between Mesopotamia Plantation in Jamaica and Mount Airy in Virginia, historian Richard Dunn used more than a century

of inventories to track the evolution of plantation demography. For Mesopotamia alone, 87 surviving annual inventories cover the span of more than a
century. Dunn, *Tale of Two Plantations*, prologue, esp. 10–18. Inventories are also
the basis for the large data set built and analyzed by Trevor G. Burnard in *Planters,
Merchants, and Slaves*.

5. Several economic historians have explored the implications of thinking
about slaves as capital assets. These discussions generally pay more attention
to theoretical implications than to actual accounting practices. See, for example,
Roger L. Ransom, *Conflict and Compromise: The Political Economy of Slavery,
Emancipation, and the American Civil War* (New York: Cambridge University
Press, 1989), 42–44; Anderson and Gallman, "Slaves as Fixed Capital," 24–46.

6. Form I was Form M in Affleck's sugar books. Affleck, *Plantation Record and Account Book*; Randolph, *Plantation and Farm Instruction, Regulation, Record, Inventory
and Account Book*.

7. Affleck, "Explanation of Records and Accounts," *Plantation Record and Account
Book*.

8. James Green Carson, "Form I," Record Book, 1857, Canebrake Plantation Records, 1856–1858, DBC. By 1861, Carson had moved across the Mississippi River
to Airlie Plantation in Louisiana, taking most of his slaves with him. His inventory for 1861 lists 180 men, women, and children, with a total value of $75,075.
Of these, records from 1857 to 1861 account for all but six, who were likely new
purchases and thus are excluded from my calculations. The 174 owned in 1857
or born in the interim were worth $71,575 in 1861. With a starting value of
$59,450, this yields a rate of increase of nearly 4 percent over the period. A small
number of slaves appeared in the inventory of 1857 but not in the inventory for
1861. For purposes of calculation, I assume these slaves died instead of being
sold. If they were sold the actual rate of increase may have been significantly
higher. Green Carson, "Form I," Record Book, 1861, Airlie Plantation Records,
1846–1961, DBC, 121–122.

9. Green Carson, "Form I," Record Book, 1857, 116–117.

10. Ibid.

11. Green Carson, "Form I," Record Book, 1856, Canebrake Plantation Records,
1856–1858, DBC; Green Carson, "Form I," Record Book, 1861, 121–122.

12. Though an earlier generation of scholars dated the practice of depreciation to
the late nineteenth century, most now hold that sophisticated American accountants understood the concept by the early 1830s, when the Commonwealth of Massachusetts required corporations to provide estimates of the
value of real and personal corporate property. Upon issuing stock, they had to
revalue this property. Thus, those with large investments in machinery (primarily textile mills) occasionally estimated depreciation. However, these calcu-

lations were not performed annually, nor did they regularly appear in balance sheets when proprietors bothered to compile them. Similarly, accounting textbooks rarely mentioned depreciation before the late nineteenth century. For an overview of this literature, see Thomas Tyson and Richard Fleischman, "The History of Management Accounting in the U.S.," *Handbooks of Management Accounting Research* 2 (2006): 1071–1089; Previts and Merino, *History of Accountancy in the United States*, 98, 163, 218. On early examples of the use of depreciation outside the United States, see Lee Parker and Richard Fleischman, *What Is Past Is Prologue: Cost Accounting in the British Industrial Revolution, 1760–1850* (New York: Garland, 1997). Affleck's instructions and the ways a wide array of planters used them reflect a remarkably high level of standardization and sophistication for the period. The last decade has seen an explosion of research on slavery by accounting historians. Affleck's discussion of depreciation is noted in Richard K. Fleischman and Thomas N. Tyson, "Accounting in Service to Racism: Monetizing Slave Property in the Antebellum South," *Critical Perspectives on Accounting* 15, no. 3 (April 2004): 376–399. See also Richard K. Fleischman, David Oldroyd, and Thomas N. Tyson, "Monetising Human Life," *Accounting History* 9, no. 2 (July 2004): 35–62; Richard K. Fleischman, David Oldroyd, and Thomas N. Tyson, "Plantation Accounting and Management Practices in the US and the British West Indies at the End of Their Slavery Eras," *Economic History Review* 64, no. 3 (March 2011): 765–787; Cheryl S. McWatters and Yannick Lemarchand, "Accounting Representation and the Slave Trade," *Accounting Historians Journal* 33, no. 2 (December 2006): 1–37.

13. *Report of the Committee of Directors and Stockholders of the South-Carolina Canal and Rail-Road Company, at an adjourned meeting of the* . . . (Charleston, SC: 1833), 14, *Sabin Americana*, Gale, Cengage Learning, Gale Digital Collections; *Proceedings of the stockholders of the South-Carolina Rail-Road Company and of the South-Western Rail-Road Bank at their annual meeting* (Charleston, SC: 1849), 28, *Sabin Americana*, Gale, Cengage Learning, Gale Digital Collections; *Annual Reports of the President and Directors and the General Superintendent of the South Carolina Railroad Company for the year ending December, 1857* (Charleston, SC: Steam Power Press of Walker Evans, & Co., 1858), 18.

14. Several economic historians have explored the theoretical implications of thinking about slaves as capital assets, though these discussions generally pay less attention to actual accounting practices. See, for example, Ransom, *Conflict and Compromise*, 42–44; Anderson and Gallman, "Slaves as Fixed Capital," 24–46.

15. "The State of Georgia—Its Duties and Its Destiny," *Southern Quarterly Review* 8, no. 16 (October 1845): 458.

16. Henry Wiencek, *Master of the Mountain: Thomas Jefferson and His Slaves* (New York: Farrar, Straus and Giroux, 2012), 8–9, 90, 97.

17. Russell, *North America, Its Agriculture and Climate*, 137, 266. Russell is quoted in Frederick Law Olmsted, *The Cotton Kingdom: A Traveller's Observations on Cotton and Slavery in the American Slave States . . .* , vol. 2 (New York: Mason Brothers, 1861–1862), 256. He offered the further comparison: "Natural increase of slaves is no doubt a considerable item in the profits of the slave owner in Maryland and Virginia" and a "far larger item in the profits of the slave owners in the Southern States [where] the sum invested in slaves bears a much larger proportion to the gross amount of the capital," 256. For additional examples of rates of increase, see Marie Jenkins Schwartz, *Birthing a Slave: Motherhood and Medicine in the Antebellum South* (Cambridge, MA: Harvard University Press, 2006), 68. See also Breeden, *Advice among Masters*, 47.

18. These studies arose out of work on the internal slave trade that suggested that the older coastal states deliberately bred slaves for states added through westward territorial expansion, and direct evidence for this is indeed limited. See, for example, John Boles, *Black Southerners, 1619–1869* (Lexington: University Press of Kentucky, 1983); Richard G. Lowe and Randolph B. Campbell, "The Slave-Breeding Hypothesis: A Demographic Comment on the 'Buying' and 'Selling' States," *Journal of Southern History* 42, no. 3 (August 1976): 401–412. On the internal slave trade broadly, see Michael Tadman, *Speculators and Slaves: Masters, Traders, and Slaves in the Old South* (Madison: University of Wisconsin Press, 1989); Walter Johnson and Gilder Lehrman Center for the Study of Slavery, Resistance, and Abolition, eds., *The Chattel Principle: Internal Slave Trades in the Americas* (New Haven, CT: Yale University Press, 2004).

19. On reproduction and sexual violence, see Jennifer Morgan, *Laboring Women: Reproduction and Gender in New World Slavery* (Philadelphia: University of Pennsylvania Press, 2004); Daina Ramey Berry, "'We'm Fus' Rate Bargain': Value, Labor, and Price in a Georgia Slave Community," in *The Chattel Principle: Internal Slave Trades in the Americas*, ed. Walter Johnson (New Haven, CT: Yale University Press, 2004), 55–71; Amy Dru Stanley, "Slave Breeding and Free Love: An Antebellum Argument over Slavery, Capitalism, and Personhood," in *Capitalism Takes Command: The Social Transformation of Nineteenth-Century America*, ed. Michael Zakim and Gary J. Kornblith (Chicago: University of Chicago Press, 2012), 119–144; Adrienne Davis, "'Don't Let Nobody Bother Yo' Principle': The Sexual Economy of American Slavery," in *Sister Circle: Black Women and Work*, ed. Sharon Harley and the Black Women and Work Collective (New Brunswick, NJ: Rutgers University Press, 2002), 103–127; Edward Baptist, "'Cuffy,' 'Fancy Maids,' and 'One-Eyed Men': Rape, Commodification, and the Domestic Slave Trade in the United States," in *The Chattel Principle*, ed. Johnson, 165–202; Gregory D. Smithers, *Slave Breeding: Sex, Violence, and Memory in African American History* (Gainesville: University Press of Florida, 2012); Ned Sublette and Constance Sub-

lette, *The American Slave Coast: A History of the Slave-Breeding Industry* (Chicago: Lawrence Hill Books, 2016).

20. Follett, *Sugar Masters*, 71.

21. Ibid., 72.

22. Ibid., 71. Traders manipulated lactation by offering enslaved people for sale as wet nurses. See Jones-Rogers, "'[S]he Could Spare One Ample Breast . . .'"

23. Eli Capell, "Form I," Plantation Diary for 1850, vol. 14, Mss. 56, Capell Family Papers, LSU.

24. Capell, "Form I," Plantation Diary for 1851, vol. 16, Mss. 56, Capell Family Papers, LSU.

25. For an example of the critique that southerners did not calculate profitability, see Olmstead and Rhode, "Cotton, Slavery, and the New History of Capitalism," 1–17, 11.

26. See, for example, Mary Poovey, *A History of the Modern Fact: Problems of Knowledge in the Sciences of Wealth and Society* (Chicago: University of Chicago Press, 1998). With specific reference to slavery, see also Erik Dussere, *Balancing the Books: Faulkner, Morrison, and the Economies of Slavery*, Literary Criticism and Cultural Theory (New York: Routledge, 2003). These scholars have also drawn on the research of those working in "critical accounting studies" who have parallel points about aesthetics, power, and accounting practice. For a valuable overview of this approach, see Peter Miller, "Accounting as Social and Institutional Practice: An Introduction," in *Accounting as a Social and Institutional Practice*, ed. Anthony Hopwood and Peter Miller (New York: Cambridge University Press, 1994): 1–39.

27. Martin's sample focuses on Virginia, South Carolina, and Louisiana. Bonnie Martin, "Slavery's Invisible Engine: Mortgaging Human Property," *Journal of Southern History* 76, no. 4 (2010): 817–866, 821–822. See also her recent article, with an enlarged sample: Bonnie Martin, "Neighbor-to-Neighbor Capitalism," in *Slavery's Capitalism: A New History of American Economic Development*, ed. Sven Beckert and Seth Rockman (Philadelphia: University of Pennsylvania Press, 2016), 107–121.

28. Martin, "Slavery's Invisible Engine," 817–866, 822.

29. Ibid., 823.

30. See, for example, Richard Kilbourne's careful study of debt relations in East Feliciana Parish, Louisiana, between 1825 and 1885. Richard Holcombe Kilbourne, *Debt, Investment, Slaves: Credit Relations in East Feliciana Parish, Louisiana, 1825–1885* (Tuscaloosa: University of Alabama Press, 1995). As Gavin Wright sums up in the foreword, Kilbourne's work suggests that the unique liquidity of enslaved assets enabled them to serve "as the basis for a vast extension of collateralized credit" and that this "same store of wealth indirectly supported

another huge volume of uncollateralized credit." Several more local studies suggest that such mortgages may also have been important in the colonial period, both in North America and in the Caribbean. See S. D. Smith, *Slavery, Family, and Gentry Capitalism in the British Atlantic: The World of the Lascelles, 1648–1834* (New York: Cambridge University Press, 2006), chaps. 5–6; David Hancock, "'Capital and Credit with Approved Security': Financial Markets in Montserrat and South Carolina, 1748–1775," *Business and Economic History* 23 (Winter 1994): 61–84; Russell R. Menard, "Financing the Lowcountry Export Boom: Capital and Growth in Early South Carolina," *William and Mary Quarterly* 51, no. 4 (October 1994): 659–676. A work in progress by Sharon Murphy promises to expand this for both the colonial and antebellum periods.

31. Baptist, *The Half Has Never Been Told*, 246–248. See also Edward E. Baptist, "Toxic Debt, Liar Loans, Collateralized and Securitized Human Beings, and the Panic of 1837," in Zakim and Kornblith, *Capitalism Takes Command*, 69–92; Calvin Schermerhorn, *The Business of Slavery and the Rise of American Capitalism, 1815–1860* (New Haven, CT: Yale University Press, 2015), esp. chap. 4. On slavery and finance more broadly, see work in progress by Sharon Ann Murphy, "Banking on Slavery in the Antebellum South."

32. "Abram Childress, guardian of Angeline and John Turner, asks to sell two slaves allotted to his wards . . . ," 5 November 1855–6 March 1856, Franklin County, Virginia, folder 016453–010–0126, Slavery and the Law, PQHV.

33. "Thomas J. Couch, a resident of the Parish of Carroll, seeks $500 in damages from Matilda Bushey . . . ," 8 February 1854–21 February 1855, Orleans Parish, Louisiana, folder 101693–016–0649, Slavery and the Law, PQHV.

34. "Dr. Henry Daret seeks compensation from Captain A. G. Gray for harboring . . . ," 2 May 1854–25 May 1857, Orleans Parish, Louisiana, folder 101693–016–0985, Slavery and the Law, PQHV.

35. "Francois Barthelemy LeBeau claims that his two runaway slaves . . . ," 18 February 1840–30 November 1841, Orleans Parish, Louisiana, folder 101693–011–0329, Slavery and the Law, PQHV.

36. Northup, *Twelve Years a Slave*, 85.

37. Henry Bibb, *Narrative of the Life and Adventures of Henry Bibb, An American Slave, Written by Himself* (New York: The Author, 1849), from University of North Carolina at Chapel Hill, Documenting the American South, North American Slave Narratives, 203.

38. Daina Ramey Berry, *The Price for Their Pound of Flesh: The Value of the Enslaved from Womb to Grave in the Building of a Nation* (Boston: Beacon Press, 2017), 3.

39. Josephine Brown, *Biography of an American Bondman, by His Daughter* (Boston: R. F. Wallcut, 1856), 32.

40. J. D. Green, *Narrative of the Life of J. D. Green, a Runaway Slave, from Kentucky, Containing an Account of His Three Escapes, in 1839, 1846, and 1848* (Huddersfield, UK: Henry Fielding, Pack Horse Yard, 1864), 27.

41. Brown, *Biography of an American Bondman*, 32.

42. On the attempts of enslaved people, slave traders, and buyers to influence the shape of sales, see Walter Johnson, *Soul by Soul: Life inside the Antebellum Slave Market* (Cambridge, MA: Harvard University Press, 1999). On parallel attempts in courtroom settings particularly, see Ariela Julie Gross, *Double Character: Slavery and Mastery in the Antebellum Southern Courtroom* (Princeton, NJ: Princeton University Press, 2000).

43. Isaac D. Williams and William Ferguson Goldie (pseud. Tege), *Sunshine and Shadow of Slave Life: Reminiscences as told by Isaac D. Williams to "Tege"* (East Saginaw, MI: Evening News Printing and Binding House, 1885), 18.

44. For an example of slave traders attempting to turn their capital more quickly: "Some may say I would not sell my 90 or 60 days bills and lose the interest, but you do so, for 'why' says you, because the more Exchange we let the Banks have the more indulgence we can get and the more negroes we buy the more Exchange we can get . . ." Philip Thomas to Jack, Whitmell Pitta, VA, Oct. 6th, 1859, Folder 1, William A. J. Finney Papers, 1849–1876, RUB.

45. "Document detailing the prices of Betts & Gregory slave market, broken down by gender, age, and height," January 5, 1861, American Slavery Documents Collection (RL 11093), box 2, folder 3, RUB. For a reflection on another version of the Betts & Gregory price list and what it says about southern racism, see Charles B. Dew, *The Making of a Racist: A Southerner Reflects on Family, History, and the Slave Trade* (Charlottesville: University of Virginia Press, 2016).

46. William Cronon, *Nature's Metropolis: Chicago and the Great West* (New York: W. W. Norton, 1992), 109. The fact that slave traders used similar categories to those employed by the Chicago Board of Trade is less surprising when we compare the grading of wheat to the grading of cotton and sugar. While wheat has often served as a canonical example of the process of commodification, both sugar and cotton were graded in similar ways. Though the New Orleans Cotton Exchange was founded after emancipation, it built on existing grading practices which divided cotton into even more grades than wheat. David Pinzur, "Making the Grade: Infrastructural Semiotics and Derivative Market Outcomes on the Chicago Board of Trade and New Orleans Cotton Exchange, 1856–1909," *Economy and Society* 45, no. 3–4 (October 1, 2016): 431–453. On the grading of sugar, see Fraginals, *The Sugarmill*, 116–119.

47. Chicago Board of Trade, *Annual Statement of the Trade and Commerce of Chicago* (Chicago: S. P. Rounds, 1859). Grades for wheat were the most complex,

dividing by white and red, winter and spring, and finally quality. Practices also evolved over this first year, and "No. 2" wheat was also sometimes "Standard."

48. Walter Johnson, *Soul by Soul*, 58.

49. See various circulars in Folder 1, William A. J. Finney Papers, 1849–1876, RUB. One includes a handwritten list by height that precisely replicates the Betts & Gregory categories.

50. Tyre Glen to Thomas Glen, 9 January 1836, Tyre Glen Papers, RASP, series F: part 3, reel 15.

51. Brown, *Slave Life in Georgia*, 14–15. Biometric pricing can also be found in other contexts. For example, height was also used in pricing enslaved people in the extensive systems of indigenous forced labor described by Andrés Reséndez, *The Other Slavery: The Uncovered Story of Indian Enslavement in America* (Boston: Houghton Mifflin Harcourt, 2016), 51.

52. Brown, *Slave Life in Georgia*, 114.

53. Ibid., 115.

54. On manumission restrictions, see Sally E. Hadden, "The Fragmented Laws of Slavery in the Colonial and Revolutionary Eras," in *The Cambridge History of Law in America*, ed. Michael Grossberg and Christopher Tomlins (Cambridge: Cambridge University Press, 2008), 267, 270; Benjamin Joseph Klebaner, "American Manumission Laws and the Responsibility for Supporting Slaves," *Virginia Magazine of History and Biography* 63, no. 4 (October 1955): 444, 445, 450.

55. Duncan Clinch Slave List, 1859, RASP, series C: part 2, reel 1, 0134. On the breakup of families for court sales in order to increase revenues, see Thomas D. Russell, "Articles Sell Best Singly: The Disruption of Slave Families at Court Sales," *Utah Law Review* 4 (1996): 1161–1209. On sales in lots, which more frequently included children and the elderly, see Charles W. Calomiris and Jonathan B. Pritchett, "Preserving Slave Families for Profit: Traders' Incentives and Pricing in the New Orleans Slave Market," *The Journal of Economic History* 69, no. 4 (2009): 986–1011.

56. Sally E. Hadden, "The Fragmented Laws of Slavery," 267, 270; Benjamin Joseph Klebaner, "American Manumission Law," 444, 445, 450. On the treatment and sale of the elderly more broadly, see John Hope Franklin and Loren Schweninger, *Runaway Slaves: Rebels on the Plantation* (Oxford: Oxford University Press, 2000), 256–258; Stacey K. Close, *Elderly Slaves of the Plantation South* (Garland, 1997). For a study that suggests that legal restrictions had limited impact, see Calomiris and Pritchett, "Preserving Slave Families for Profit," 989.

57. Jenny Bourne Wahl, *The Bondsman's Burden: An Economic Analysis of the Common Law of Southern Slavery* (New York: Cambridge University Press, 1997), chap. 2, esp. 27–29.

58. Some judges reasoned that enslaved property was always unique, while others suggested that only certain slaves with ties to their owners or specific skills should be treated as such. For examples of specific performance, see Tushnet, *American Law of Slavery*, 166–170. Tushnet sees inconsistencies in the law as a reflection of underlying contradictions in the treatment of humans as property. But the fluidity of courts' treatment can also be seen as a reflection of the law's flexibility in meeting the unique needs of those trading in a distinctive class of property. Sometimes contracts provided specifically for substitution of one slave for another in case of death. For an example, see Martin, "Slavery's Invisible Engine," 822n9. On broader questions involving whether slaves should be treated as real versus personal property, see Morris, *Southern Slavery and the Law*, chap. 3. Morris's view aligns more closely with the one presented here: that the importance of consistency in the law should not be overestimated.

59. Morris, *Southern Slavery and the Law*, 80.

60. Wahl, *Bondsman's Burden*, 27.

61. Ibid., chaps. 3 and 4. On the law related to hiring, see chapter 3; on carrier law, see chapter 4. Recent research has shown that enslaved people made more use of the law than previously thought. But the cases in which they gained standing in court seem to be those that reflected a deference for private property—not for them as people. Slaves could gain standing before the law more readily as property and as owners of property than as people needing protection. On enslaved people's attempts to defend their property before the law, see Dylan C. Penningroth, *The Claims of Kinfolk: African American Property and Community in the Nineteenth-Century South*, John Hope Franklin Series in African American History and Culture (Chapel Hill: University of North Carolina Press, 2003); Welch, *Calling to Account*. This fits with a separate and emerging literature that shows how enslaved people traded on their own account, negotiating with masters and one another—sometimes even engaging in small-scale entrepreneurship—to gain access to cash and perhaps even accumulate capital. See Calvin Schermerhorn, *Money over Mastery, Family over Freedom: Slavery in the Antebellum Upper South* (Baltimore: Johns Hopkins University Press, 2011); Kathleen M. Hilliard, *Masters, Slaves, and Exchange: Power's Purchase in the Old South* (New York: Cambridge University Press, 2013); Justene G. Hill, "Felonious Transactions: Legal Culture and Business Practices of Slave Economies in South Carolina, 1787–1860" (PhD diss., Princeton University, 2015); David E. Patterson, "Slavery, Slaves, and Cash in a Georgia Village, 1825–1865," *Journal of Southern History* 75, no. 4 (2009): 879–930.

62. Chandler, *Visible Hand*, 119.

63. George Richardson Porter, *The Tropical Agriculturist: A Practical Treatise on the Cultivation and Management of Various Productions Suited to Tropical Climates*

(London: Smith, Elder, 1833), 40. Though slave owners in the British Atlantic do not appear to have used the system of hands before the early 1800s, slave traders in the Spanish and Portuguese Caribbean used a similar system as early as the sixteenth century. Slaves were rated as "piezas de esclavo" and later "piezas de Indias"—as pieces of slaves or of Indies. See David Wheat, *Atlantic Africa and the Spanish Caribbean, 1570–1640* (Chapel Hill: University of North Carolina Press, 2016), 102; Wim Klooster, "Piezas de Indias," *The Historical Encyclopedia of World Slavery*, ed. Junius P. Rodriguez (ABC-CLIO, 1997).

64. See "Account of an Agricultural Excursion Made into the South of Georgia in the Winter of 1832," *Southern Agriculturist and Register of Rural Affairs*, 1833. Hopeton's manuscript records include among them a cotton book, though it does not appear to contain an accounting by hands. "Volume 3: Account of Cotton Picked at Hopeton, 1818–1831," J. Hamilton Couper Plantation Records #185-z, SHC.

65. For the practice of combining multiple fractional hands to work a single plot, see Ulrich Bonnell Phillips, *American Negro Slavery: A Survey of the Supply, Employment and Control of Negro Labor as Determined by the Plantation Regime* (New York: D. Appleton, 1918), 247.

66. James Postell, Kelvin Grove Plantation Book #2771, SHC, pp. 5–9 of microfilmed transcription.

67. Ibid. Below "Plant 97 Acres" he subtracts 15 acres, settling on 82. The motivation for this final calculation is unclear.

68. For inventories to 1849, see John McPherson DeSaussure Plantation Book, 1 October 1842–1 October 1849, folder 002380–008–0817, Slavery and Southern Life, PQHV (RASP, series A: part 2). For 1850 hand list, see John McPherson DeSaussure Plantation Book, 1 January 1849–31 December 1861, folder 002380–008–0317, Slavery and Southern Life, PQHV (RASP, series A: part 2).

69. Olmsted, *Journeys and Explorations*, 177.

70. Frederick Law Olmsted, *A Journey in the Seaboard Slave States: With Remarks on Their Economy* (New York: Dix & Edwards, 1856), 420.

71. Ibid., 57.

72. "Practice of Agriculture," in *The Soil of the South*, vol. 4 (W. H. Chambers, 1846), 103.

73. "Sea Island Cotton Planting," *Southern Cultivator*, July 1848. Years covered are 1830–1847.

74. James D. B. DeBow, *DeBow's Review* 23 (New Orleans: J. D. B. DeBow, 1857), 126; Frederick Law Olmsted, *A Journey through Texas* (New York: Dix, Edwards, 1857), 208. On DeBow, see John F. Kvach, *"DeBow's Review": The Antebellum Vision of a New South* (Lexington: University Press of Kentucky, 2013).

75. Ibid. For another reprint of the calculations, see E. T. Freedley, *Opportunities for Industry and the Safe Investment of Capital; or, A Thousand Chances to Make Money* (Philadelphia: J. B. Lippincott, 1859).

76. On "eagle eye planters who could spot opportunity at a distance" and the work of the U.S. Land Office to bring lands to sale, see Adam Rothman, *Slave Country: American Expansion and the Origins of the Deep South* (Cambridge, MA: Harvard University Press, 2007), 44; Malcolm J. Rohrbough, *The Land Office Business: The Settlement and Administration of American Public Lands, 1789–1837* (New York: Oxford University Press, 1968); Johnson, *River of Dark Dreams*, 35–40; On the "movability" of slaves and its implications for southern economic development, see Wright, *Old South, New South*.

77. Lewis C. Gray, *History of Southern Agriculture in the United States*, vol. 1 (Washington: Carnegie Institute, 1933), 552–553. The "task acre" should not be confused with what Walter Johnson has evocatively but also misleadingly called a "trinomial algebra of bales per hand per acre" (and elsewhere bales per acre per hand). While Johnson gestures toward planters' general mind-set, I have never seen evidence of these specific calculations (though bales per hand and bales per acre were common). The "task acre" was a way of determining the optimal amount of land for one enslaved hand to farm, not a way of getting the most out of land production. On the "trinomial," see Johnson, *River of Dark Dreams*, 153, 197, 246.

78. Phillips, *American Negro Slavery*, 247–248. Phillips records the standard tasks for full hands in rice culture in 1843 as follows: "plowing with two oxen, with the animals changed at noon, one acre; breaking stiff land with the hoe and turning the stubble under, ten compasses; breaking such land with the stubble burnt off, or breaking lighter land, a quarter acre or slightly more; mashing the clods to level the field, from a quarter to half an acre; trenching the drills, if on well prepared land, three quarters of an acre; sowing rice, from three to four half-acres; covering the drills, three quarters."

79. For example, planters do not appear to have rated particularly productive slaves higher than a full hand. Further, if hands could be translated into profits in an easy and predictable fashion, a prime hand should cost twice as much as a half hand. In Olmsted's widely circulated plan for large-scale cotton growing, discussed earlier in this chapter, this was not the case, though a half hand was priced at twice the amount of a quarter hand. Olmsted, *A Journey through Texas*, 208.

80. Steven Deyle, *Carry Me Back: The Domestic Slave Trade in American Life* (New York: Oxford University Press, 2005), 241.

81. "Price Current," *Columbian Herald*, Charlestown South Carolina, June 13, 1785, from Archive of Americana, *America's Historical Newspapers*.

82. Though there appear to have been no futures contracts, some traders may have employed "standing orders," to be fulfilled by any slave of a particular description. For a reference to "standing orders," see "Lincoln's Election a Menace to Slavery," *Charleston Mercury*, Oct. 11, 1860, in *The Causes of the Civil War: Revised Edition*, ed. Kenneth Stampp (New York: Simon and Schuster, 1991), 151.

83. Johnson, *Soul by Soul*. For an account that brings the market into the home, see Stephanie Elizabeth Jones-Rogers, "'Nobody Couldn't Sell 'Em but Her.'"

84. Without legal protections to secure self-purchase at a fair price, slaves faced difficult and expensive negotiations. In Spanish-ruled territories, the system of *coartación* had long allowed slaves to sue for their freedom at a fair market price, and during the late eighteenth century, slaves living in the Louisiana territory could use this system. But the return of Louisiana to the French and then to the United States revoked this right. After the shift, not only did manumission become less common, but those who did manage to purchase their freedom often had to pay a substantial premium over market prices. Shawn Cole, "Capitalism and Freedom: Manumissions and the Slave Market in Louisiana, 1725–1820," *Journal of Economic History* 65, no. 4 (December 2005): 1008–1027.

85. For the story of Pamela Munro, see Stanley Engerman, "Pricing Freedom," in *Working Slavery, Pricing Freedom*, ed. Verene Shepherd, 1996, 281–282. The resulting debate highlighted the many possible approaches to the valuation of slaves. Was payment meant to compensate the owners for the market value of the asset, with the earnings they could expect from that asset, or with the cost of replacing the asset itself? The inherent and highly individual complexity of human chattel proved a knotty accounting problem.

86. The owner "refused to name any sum that he would take for you." Jermain Wesley Loguen, *The Rev. J. W. Loguen, as a Slave and as a Freeman: A Narrative of Real Life* (Syracuse: J. G. K. Truair, 1859), 255.

87. Northup, *Twelve Years a Slave*, 86–87. The narrative of Peter Still recounts his efforts to persuade his current owner to sell him to a Mr. Friedman. But his owner explains that he "didn't offer any price for you—only five hundred dollars." Kate E. R. Pickard, *The Kidnapped and the Ransomed: Being the Personal Recollections of Peter Still and His Wife "Vina," After Forty Years of Slavery*, 3rd ed. (Syracuse: William T. Hamilton, 1856), 221.

88. On the exploitation of difference as a management strategy more broadly, see David R. Roediger and Elizabeth D. Esch, *The Production of Difference: Race and the Management of Labor in U.S. History* (New York: Oxford University Press, 2012).

89. Abraham Lincoln, "Speech at Hartford, Connecticut," March 5, 1860, *Hartford Daily Courant*, March 6, 1860. Also appears in Abraham Lincoln, *Collected*

Works of Abraham Lincoln, vol. 4, 2001, http://name.umdl.umich.edu/lincoln4. On the role of slavery as property in sectional disagreement, see James L. Huston, *Calculating the Value of the Union: Slavery, Property Rights, and the Economic Origins of the Civil War* (Chapel Hill: University of North Carolina Press, 2003).

90. Jenny Bourne, "Slavery in the United States," *EH.Net Encyclopedia,* ed. Robert Whaples, March 26, 2008, http://eh.net/encyclopedia/slavery-in-the-united -states/.

91. "Confederate States of America—Georgia Secession," January 29, 1861, *The Avalon Project: Documents in Law, History and Diplomacy (Lillian Goldman Law Library, Yale Law School),* avalon.law.yale.edu/19th_century/csa_geosec.asp.

92. "A Declaration of the Immediate Causes which Induce and Justify the Secession of the State of Mississippi from the Federal Union," *The Avalon Project,* http://avalon.law.yale.edu/19th_century/csa_missec.asp.

93. Jefferson Davis, "The Indispensible Slaves," Message to the Confederate Congress, April 29, 1861, in *The Causes of the Civil War: Revised Edition,* ed. Kenneth Stampp (New York: Simon and Schuster, 1991), 154.

94. Edward B. Bryan, *The Rightful Remedy. Addressed to the Slaveholders of the South* (Charleston, SC: Walker and James, 1850), 58. Bryan borrowed a calculation of profitability published in 1848 by the *Southern Quarterly Review* and added to it his estimate of gains from capital increases. "The Growth and Consumption of Cotton," *Southern Quarterly Review* (Charleston: Burges and James, 1848), 122–123.

95. "Lincoln's Election a Menace to Slavery," 151.

96. For the additional examples of the circular beyond the one reproduced here, see "Price circular issued by Betts & Gregory, Richmond auctioneers . . ." August 2, 1860, Chapin Library, Williams College, Williamstown, MA; Betts and Gregory, "Circular . . ." March [?], 1861, Mss. 4, B4666 a 1, Virginia Historical Society, Richmond, VA.

97. By 1862, Carson had moved across the Mississippi River to Louisiana where he worked Airlie Plantation. James Green Carson, Record Books, 1862, Airlie Plantation Records, 1846–1951, DBC. The finding aid identifies the move as around 1846, though the records from the late 1850s are from Cane Brake. It is possible that an overseer rather than Carson completed these, but they are in a different hand than the daily records (and the same hand each year) suggesting Carson may have completed them.

98. Henry Clay, speech, February 7, 1839, as reproduced in Huston, *Calculating the Value of the Union,* 6.

99. George Washington, *Letters from His Excellency General Washington, to Arthur Young . . .* (London: W. J. and J. Richardson, 1801), 127–128. Young writes, "there is no man in the world who would not . . . change slaves to cows and sheep:

he cannot otherwise command labour, and therefore must keep them; but the profit in any other light than labourers, is inadmissible."

100. Henry Clay, speech, February 7, 1839. Planters' pursuit of capital is of course evident in efforts to oppose abolition, but it is also striking in planters' work to shape tax and trade policy. As Robin Einhorn has shown, much of the history of American tax resistance reflects southern efforts to protect and multiply their enslaved property. Robin L. Einhorn, *American Taxation, American Slavery* (Chicago: University of Chicago Press, 2006).

5. Managing Freedom

1. Publishing history of the original is recounted in I. D. Affleck, *Affleck's Farmer's and Planter's Record and Account Book*, 2nd ed. (New York: Fairbanks, Palmer, 1883), preface. (Collection of the author.) On Affleck's debt and schemes, see Fred C. Cole, "The Texas Career of Thomas Affleck" (PhD diss., Louisiana State University, 1942), chaps. 16–17.

2. I. D. Affleck, *Affleck's Farmer's and Planter's Record and Account Book*, preface. Collection of the author.

3. Ibid., C1–C6.

4. On the periodization of Reconstruction, see Eric Foner, *Reconstruction: America's Unfinished Revolution, 1863–1877* (New York: Harper & Row, 1988). For more recent discussions of Reconstruction as an analytical category and period, see Gregory P. Downs and Kate Masur's introduction to *The World the Civil War Made*, ed. Gregory P. Downs and Kate Masur (Chapel Hill: University of North Carolina Press, 2015), 1–21, as well as Luke E. Harlow's introduction to "Forum: The Future of Reconstruction Studies," *Journal of the Civil War Era*, https://journalofthecivilwarera.org/forum-the-future-of-reconstruction-studies/.

5. Capell's diary, as quoted in Wendell Holmes Stephenson, "A Quarter-Century of a Mississippi Plantation: Eli J. Capell of 'Pleasant Hill,'" *Mississippi Valley Historical Review* 23, no. 3 (December 1936): 355–374, 373. For legal restrictions, see *Laws of the State of Mississippi* (Jackson: J. J. Shannon, 1866), 82–93, 165–167.

6. Capell, as quoted in Wendell Holmes Stephenson, "A Quarter-Century of a Mississippi Plantation," 355–374, 373.

7. I have not seen any consistent records of picking per hand in my review of postbellum records. There may well be individual examples, but they are nowhere near as common as they were in the antebellum period. For one early mention of payment per pound in the 1880s, see W. Hilgard, *Report on Cotton Production in the United States; Also Embracing Agricultural and Physico-Geographical Descriptions*

of the Several Cotton States and of California, Part II (Washington, DC: Government Printing Office, 1884), 55.

8. Comparing the 1867 work logs with the contracts signed in January 1868 shows little continuity. Of the eight men and women who signed contracts with Capell in January 1868, only three appeared on the work logs from the prior year: Charles Hill, Israel Kinnison, and Stephen Allen. Israel and Steve are listed by first name only in 1867 and therefore difficult to confirm. "Agreement with Laborers," RSPE, series B, reel 3; Eli J. Capell Family Papers, vol. 3, Laborer's Record Book, LSU.

9. Tera W. Hunter, *To 'Joy My Freedom: Southern Black Women's Lives and Labors After the Civil War* (Cambridge, MA: Harvard University Press, 1997), 28. Quitting as a political strategy among the freedpeople deserves more scholarly attention. It emerged during the Civil War, when enslaved Americans withdrew their labor in support of the Union. W. E. B. Du Bois referred to this as a "General Strike." See W. E. B. DuBois, *Black Reconstruction in America* (New York: Russell & Russell, 1962), chap. 4. Studies of quitting have the potential to help us understand the varied ways in which different groups of freedpeople pursued different kinds of freedoms. On the need for intersectional studies of African Americans in this period, see Kidada E. Williams, "Maintaining a Radical Vision of African Americans in the Age of Freedom," *Journal of the Civil War Era*, https://journalofthecivilwarera.org/forum-the-future-of-reconstruction-studies/maintaining-a-radical-vision/.

10. Contract for 1866, DeSaussure Family Papers, 1716–1938, RSPE, series C, part 2.

11. Ibid.

12. Memo Book, 1866, DeSaussure Family Papers, 1716–1938, RSPE, series C, part 2.

13. Ibid.

14. Contract for 1867, DeSaussure Family Papers, 1716–1938, RSPE, series C, part 2.

15. Ibid.

16. Ronald L. F. Davis, *Good and Faithful Labor: From Slavery to Sharecropping in the Natchez District, 1860–1890* (Westport, CT: Greenwood Press, 1982), 3. For further description of contract negotiations, see Susan E. O'Donovan, *Becoming Free in the Cotton South* (Cambridge, MA: Harvard University Press, 2007), chap. 3.

17. Joseph D. Reid, "Sharecropping as an Understandable Market Response: The Post-Bellum South," *Journal of Economic History* 33, no. 1 (1973): 106–130, 107–108. Reid suggests that contracts were easily renegotiated to mutual advantage because planters and laborers shared similar incentives. Some of the harsh terms described by Reid raise questions about the extent to which shared incentives actually aligned interests. For a critique along these lines, see Harold D. Woodman, "Sequel to Slavery: The New History Views the Postbellum South," *Journal of Southern History* 43, no. 4 (1977): 523–554.

18. Reid, "Sharecropping as an Understandable Market Response," 109.

19. Cotton Book, folder 2, vol. 1: 1857–1874, Lewis Plantation Papers #2528, SHC, unnumbered pages, scans 70–71. For annual picking tallies, see two unnumbered pages at the end of the book. Intermittent pages are filled with scattered calculations from later years.

20. Ibid., unnumbered pages, scans 50–53. On the squad system as an intermediate step before sharecropping, see Gerald David Jaynes, *Branches without Roots: Genesis of the Black Working Class in the American South, 1862–1882* (New York: Oxford University Press, 1989), chap. 10.

21. Ibid., unnumbered page, scan 63. For a ledger of accounts with former slaves that contains tallies of debts for food and days lost, see folder 3, vol. 2: 1866, 1881, Lewis Plantation Papers #2528, SHC.

22. Louisa Jacobs, *The Freedmen's Record,* March 1866, 55–56, http://docsouth.unc.edu/fpn/jacobs/support14.html.

23. Tines Kendrick, FWP, vol. 2, Arkansas, part 4, Jackson-Lynch, 1936, 177–185. Spelling from this and other cited narratives has been slightly modernized for clarity. On the ways WPA interviewers transcribed interviews, sometimes imposing and exaggerating racialized dialects, see Lawrence W. Levine, *Black Culture and Black Consciousness: Afro-American Folk Thought from Slavery to Freedom* (New York: Oxford University Press, 1997). Scholars have used these narratives more in recent decades. Though the sources have biases, as all sources do, Dylan Penningroth asks, "Why assume that black-authored sources were more biased than things written by the men who owned them?" Dylan Penningroth, "Writing Slavery's History," *OAH Magazine of History* 23, no. 2 (2009): 13–20, 16. See also Catherine A. Stewart, *Long Past Slavery: Representing Race in the Federal Writers' Project* (Chapel Hill: The University of North Carolina Press, 2016).

24. Jennie Kendricks, FWP, vol. 4, Georgia, Part 3, Kendricks-Styles, 1936, 6.

25. Louis Thomas, FWP, vol. 20, Missouri, Abbot-Younger, 1936, 350–351.

26. Jake McLeod, FWP, vol. 14, South Carolina, part 3, Jackson-Quattlebaum, 1936, 163.

27. On the ascendance of contracts, narrowing of conceptions of freedom, and the rise of the market, see Amy Dru Stanley, *From Bondage to Contract: Wage Labor, Marriage, and the Market in the Age of Slave Emancipation* (Cambridge: Cambridge University Press, 1998).

28. Theodore Brantner Wilson, *Black Codes of the South* (Tuscaloosa: University of Alabama Press, 1965), 57. Despite his otherwise problematic interpretation of the black codes, Wilson incisively writes "the sum of army and Freedmen's Bureau policies was: protect the Negroes from violence and actual enslavement, but keep as many as possible on the plantations and *compel* them to work."

29. George R. Bentley, *A History of the Freedmen's Bureau* (Philadelphia: University of Pennsylvania, 1955). On contracting generally, see 148–152. On wages, see 80–81. For quotation and descriptions of ration-only revisions, see Joe M. Richardson, "The Freedmen's Bureau and Negro Labor in Florida," *Florida Historical Quarterly* 39, no. 2 (1960): 167–174, 171.

30. D. Davis, FWP, vol. 2, Arkansas, part 2, Cannon-Evans, 1936, 106.

31. Reid, "Sharecropping as an Understandable Market Response," 107–108.

32. Ibid., 108–109.

33. Folder 2, vol 1: 1857–1874, in the Lewis Plantation Papers #2528, SHC, unnumbered page, scan 28.

34. This number could be 167 or 168; the contract contains notations summing the signatures to both 167 and 168. Contract for 1866, DeSaussure Family Papers, 1716–1938, RSPE, series C, part 2.

35. Contract for 1870, DeSaussure Family Papers, 1716–1938, RSPE, series C, part 2.

36. For another example offered by Reid, consider the contracts signed in 1873 by E. Dromgoole, which blended a flat payment with a crop share. Tenants paid $225 and one-third of the balance of the crop. Dromgoole also specified that a ton of fertilizer selected by him be applied to the fields, with expenses shared in proportion to the shares. Further, the contract specified that the cost of tools be split fifty-fifty, that seed corn be advanced at 50 percent interest, and that spring oats be planted. Dromgoole also required that he be allowed to hire (at the expense of the freedmen) additional labor to work the farm. And he further mandated a bonus rent of 20 percent of the excess value of the crop (over $1,000). Reid, "Sharecropping as an Understandable Market Response," 119–120.

37. November 1867, as quoted in Reid, "Sharecropping as an Understandable Market Response," 110.

38. Miscellaneous accounts, 1866–1878, folder 166, Prudhomme Family Papers 1765–1997 #00613, SHC.

39. Ibid.

40. J. Alphonse Prudhomme I, 1867, folder 279, Prudhomme Family Papers 1765–1997 #00613, SHC. This ledger contains records for both 1865 and 1867: the former in pen, the latter in pencil. It is recorded in the 1859 edition of Affleck's record books, and it does contain some records of cotton weights. If these somewhat haphazard records are from 1867, they would be a rare example of cotton weighing after emancipation.

41. Contracts for 1866–1870, DeSaussure Family Papers 1716–1938, RSPE, series C, part 2; Roger L. Ransom and Richard Sutch, *One Kind of Freedom: The Economic Consequences of Emancipation* (New York: Cambridge University Press, 1977), 45, fig. 3.1. Ransom and Sutch base their assessments not on labor records but on census data and a set of estimates of reduced output. Account books could be

used to test their assumptions about relative decline in more detail, but at least at the aggregate level, DeSaussure's books suggest that fewer hands rated one-half or one-quarter were working under contract.

42. Though control over work patterns is not the focus, these activities seem connected to emerging political struggles like those described in Stephen Hahn, *A Nation under Our Feet: Black Political Struggles in the Rural South from Slavery to the Great Migration* (Cambridge, MA: Harvard University Press, 2003).

43. Thomas Chase to Thomas Affleck, August 19, 1865, box 31, folder 52, Thomas Affleck Papers, LSU. See also box 31, folders 52–63.

44. On Affleck's scheme, see also Barbara J. Rozek, *Come to Texas: Attracting Immigrants, 1865–1915* (College Station: Texas A&M University Press, 2003), 10–11; Fred C. Cole, "The Texas Career of Thomas Affleck" (PhD diss., Louisiana State University, 1942), chaps. 10–16.

45. "Art X. Department of Immigration and Labor," *DeBow's Review*, November 1867, 575–580.

46. Gavin Wright emphasizes that the nature of southern property rights in slaves, especially the movability of enslaved capital, was a key factor limiting southern investments in infrastructure. Wright, *Old South, New South*; Gavin Wright, *Slavery and American Economic Development* (Baton Rouge: LSU Press, 2006).

47. "Art X. Department of Immigration and Labor," 575–580.

48. Ibid.

49. *DeBow's Review*, July / August, 1867, 151–152. On indentured Asian migration to Louisiana, see Moon-Ho Jung, *Coolies and Cane: Race, Labor, and Sugar in the Age of Emancipation* (Baltimore: Johns Hopkins University Press, 2006). On race and management practices more broadly, see David R. Roediger and Elizabeth D. Esch, *The Production of Difference: Race and the Management of Labor in U.S. History* (New York: Oxford University Press, 2012), esp. chaps. 3–5 on the postbellum period.

50. Papers relating to the employment of Chinese labour in the West Indies, "Execution of the plan," 336 / 4, CLAR.

51. See "Prospectus," "Calculations," and "Execution of the plan," in Papers relating to the employment of Chinese labour in the West Indies, 336 / 4, CLAR.

52. On the revival of indenture in the nineteenth century, particularly related to emancipation, see David Northrup, *Indentured Labor in the Age of Imperialism, 1834–1922* (New York: Cambridge University Press, 1995). Not all indentured servants went to locations with a history of slavery, and some worked alongside slaves before abolition. For an overview in a broader context, see Walton Look Lai, "Asian Diasporas and Tropical Migration in the Age of Empire: A Comparative Overview," *Journal of Chinese Oversea* 5, no. 1 (2010): 28–54. See also *The Chinese in Latin America and the Caribbean*, ed. Walton Look Lai and Chee Beng Tan (Boston: Brill,

2010), 35–64, 40–42; Walton Look Lai, *Indentured Labor, Caribbean Sugar: Chinese and Indian Migrants to the British West Indies, 1838–1918* (Baltimore: Johns Hopkins University Press, 1993).

53. Cole, "The Texas Career of Thomas Affleck," 467–469.

54. Estimate by federal investigator A. J. Hoyt, cited in Pete Daniel, "The Metamorphosis of Slavery, 1865–1900," *Journal of American History* 66, no. 1 (June 1979): 88–99, 89. See also Pete Daniel, *The Shadow of Slavery: Peonage in the South, 1901–1969* (Urbana: University of Illinois Press, 1990).

55. On debt peonage see Jonathan M. Wiener, *Social Origins of the New South: Alabama, 1860–1885* (Baton Rouge: Louisiana State University Press, 1978); Jay R. Mandle, *The Roots of Black Poverty: The Southern Plantation Economy after the Civil War* (Durham, NC: Duke University Press, 1978); Pete Daniel, "The Metamorphosis of Slavery, 1865–1900," *Journal of American History* 66, no. 1 (June 1979): 88–99; Daniel A. Novak, *The Wheel of Servitude: Black Forced Labor after Slavery* (Lexington: University Press of Kentucky, 1978). Scholars have also pointed to debt as a potent form of control in other settings. In *One Kind of Freedom*, Roger Ransom and Richard Sutch describe the way southern storekeepers used debt relations to control the actions of former slaves. Their analysis may overstate the role of storekeepers, but it correctly points to debt as strategy in white southerners' extensive portfolio of tools to regain control. For a useful summary of critiques and influence, see Peter Coclanis, "In Retrospect: Ransom and Sutch's *One Kind of Freedom*," *Reviews in American History* 28, no. 3 (September 2000): 478–489.

56. Wright, *Old South, New South*, 64, 113.

57. Novak, *Wheel of Servitude*, 3–5, 40.

58. Daniel, *Shadow of Slavery*, x.

59. Richardson, "Freedmen's Bureau and Negro Labor in Florida," 174.

60. On southern convict labor, see Alexander C. Lichtenstein, *Twice the Work of Free Labor: The Political Economy of Convict Labor in the New South* (New York: Verso, 1996); Talitha Leflouria, *Chained in Silence: Black Women and Convict Labor in the New South* (Chapel Hill: University of North Carolina Press, 2015); Douglas Blackmon, *Slavery by Another Name: The Re-enslavement of Black Americans from the Civil War to World War II* (New York: Anchor Books, 2009); and Edward Ayers, *Vengeance and Justice: Crime and Punishment in the 19th Century American South* (New York: Oxford University Press, 1984). See also Matthew Mancini, *One Dies, Get Another: Convict Leasing in the American South, 1866–1928* (Columbia: University of South Carolina Press, 1996). Mancini is also careful to distinguish the key difference between slavery and the convict lease: the lack of ownership of human capital—hence his title, a quote from a businessperson describing the replaceability of convicts.

61. On the history of convict labor beyond the South, see Rebecca M. McLennan, *The Crisis of Imprisonment: Protest, Politics, and the Making of the American Penal State, 1776–1941* (New York: Cambridge University Press, 2008).

62. LeFlouria, *Chained in Silence*, 15–16, 86.

63. Ibid., 131, 134. Alex Lichtenstein describes the problems of using a task system in coal mining, where a host of conditions made it impractical to assign flat tasks, but the dispersed nature of the work made direct supervision impractical. Thus, many convicts were disciplined for failing to meet impossible tasks. Lichtenstein, *Twice the Work of Free Labor*, chap. 6.

64. Ibid., 155–158.

65. Ibid., 188.

66. Ibid., xvii.

67. Ibid., xvii–xviii.

68. For estimates of increases in labor turnover due to emancipation and their influence on the emergence of new institutional forms, see Martin Ruef, *Between Slavery and Capitalism: The Legacy of Emancipation in the American South* (Princeton, NJ: Princeton University Press, 2014), chap. 5 and tables on 122–123.

69. Wright, *Old South, New South*; Gavin Wright, "Postbellum Southern Labor Markets," in *Quantity & Quiddity: Essays in U.S. Economic History,* ed. Peter Kilby, Jeremy Atack, and Stanley Lebergott (Middletown, CT: Wesleyan University Press, 1987), 98–134.

70. On northern turnover rates in the early nineteenth century, see Chapter 2. These continued into the late nineteenth and early twentieth centuries. A study on the subject conducted in 1921 suggested that in a year of "normal prosperity," such as 1910–1913, turnover rates in industry were approximately 100 percent. Sumner H. Slicter, *The Turnover of Factory Labor* (New York: D. Appleton, 1921), 16.

71. Wright, "Postbellum Southern Labor Markets," 103.

72. Wright, *Old South, New South*, 9, 64–70; Wright, "Postbellum Southern Labor Markets," 98–134. On the reasons for persistence and eventual convergence, see Gavin Wright, "The Economic Revolution in the American South," *Journal of Economic Perspectives* 1, no. 1 (1987): 161–178. There are isolated earlier examples of immigration across state lines and even international boundaries. For a study of one case, see Karl Jacoby, *The Strange Career of William Ellis: The Texas Slave Who Became a Mexican Millionaire* (New York: W. W. Norton, 2016).

73. Oliver Martin Crosby, *Florida Facts, Both Bright and Blue: A Guidebook* (New York, 1877), 21, as cited in Richardson, "The Freedmen's Bureau and Negro Labor in Florida," 173.

74. For reviews of these debates, see Scott P. Marler, "Fables of the Reconstruction: Reconstruction of the Fables," *Journal of the Historical Society* 4, no. 1 (Jan-

uary 2004): 113–137; Alex Lichtenstein, "Was the Emancipated Slave a Prole-
tarian?" *Reviews in American History* 26, no. 1 (1998): 124–145; Adrienne Petty, "In
a Class by Itself: Slavery and the Emergence of Capitalist Social Relations during
Reconstruction," *Journal of the Civil War Era,* https://journalofthecivilwarera.org
/forum-the-future-of-reconstruction-studies/in-a-class-by-itself-slavery/.

75. In a way, this characterization of sharecropping resembles the comparison to
putting-out offered by Jaynes, *Branches without Roots,* 26–28.

76. The increasing importance of southern contracting has been described by
Amy Dru Stanley as part of a national shift in which freedom was increasingly
defined as the freedom to contract. Stanley, *From Bondage to Contract.* Though
this may have been the perspective of the Freedmen's Bureau, it remains unclear whether it applies to the outlook of the emancipated slaves or their
former masters. The freedpeople seem to have cared more intensely about re-
shaping labor conditions and control than about contracting.

77. On the ways freedpeople sought to reshape ideas that cast freedom as merely the
right to a wage, see Julie Saville, *The Work of Reconstruction: From Slave to Wage
Laborer in South Carolina, 1860–1870* (New York: Cambridge University Press,
1994). On labor law and the meaning of "free labor," see James D. Schmidt, *Free to
Work: Labor Law, Emancipation, and Reconstruction, 1815–1880,* Studies in the Legal
History of the South (Athens: University of Georgia Press, 1998); Mark A. Lause,
Free Labor: The Civil War and the Making of an American Working Class, Working
Class in American History (Urbana: University of Illinois Press, 2015).

78. The end of slavery not only transformed enslaved people's status as property
but also raised questions about how informal systems of property and cus-
tomary rights would intersect with formal market rights. The contested image
of property that emerged reflected "intense, far-reaching negotiation with
northern bureaucrats, white landlords, and other black folk about the ownership and meaning of property." On the ways the freedpeople sought to reshape
conceptions of property, based in part on their experience under slavery, see
Penningroth, *Claims of Kinfolk,* 131, chap. 5. For another useful perspective on
how "free labor" was seen by both the freedpeople and their former masters,
see Heather Cox Richardson, *The Death of Reconstruction: Race, Labor, and Politics in the Post-Civil War North, 1865–1901* (Cambridge, MA: Harvard University
Press, 2001).

79. For an overview of southern growth and the delay of wage convergence until
the mid-twentieth century, see Wright, "Economic Revolution in the American South," 161–178.

80. Marler, "Fables of the Reconstruction," 113–137, 128–129. This hybrid form
also varied considerably by region. For some contrasting regional studies, see,
for example, Barbara Fields, *Slavery and Freedom on the Middle Ground;* Joseph

Reidy, *From Slavery to Agrarian Capitalism in the Cotton South* (Chapel Hill: University of North Carolina Press, 1995).

81. I. D. Affleck, *Affleck's Farmer's and Planter's Record and Account Book*.

82. See, for example, Benj. Ashbrook to I. D. Affleck, September 11, 1883, Thomas Affleck Collection, A19–50, TAMU.

Conclusion: Histories of Business and Slavery

1. Moses Roper, *A Narrative of the Adventures and Escape of Moses Roper, from American Slavery* (Philadelphia: Merrihew & Gunn, 1838), 28–29; Masthead, *The American Cotton Planter*, 1853.

2. The multiplication of human capital in these multiple modes is described in detail in Chapter 4. On the intersections of violence and human capital, see especially the work of Jennifer Morgan, Marisa Fuentes, and Daina Ramey Berry: Morgan, *Laboring Women*; Marisa J. Fuentes, *Dispossessed Lives: Enslaved Women, Violence and the Archive* (Philadelphia: University of Pennsylvania Press, 2016); Berry, *Price for Their Pound of Flesh*. And on debt, collateral, and capital multiplication, see Bonnie Martin and Richard Kilbourne Jr.: Martin, "Slavery's Invisible Engine," 817–866; Richard Holcombe Kilbourne, *Debt, Investment, Slaves: Credit Relations in East Feliciana Parish, Louisiana, 1825–1885* (Tuscaloosa: University of Alabama Press, 1995).

3. Kilbourne, *Debt, Investment, Slaves*, 6. Another way of conceptualizing southern wealth can be found in *Time on the Cross*, in which Robert Fogel and Stanley Engerman point out that in 1860, the slaveholding South was the fourth wealthiest nation in the world, measured by per capita income (including slaves), and that the richest region of the South (the West South Central) was the wealthiest region of the United States by the same measure. Stanley L. Engerman and Robert William Fogel, *Time on the Cross: The Economics of American Negro Slavery* (New York: Norton, 1989 [197?]), 248.

4. On creative destruction, Schumpeter, *Capitalism, Socialism, and Democracy* ch 7. A formulation with more negative connotations can be found in what Jonathan Levy calls the "generative insecurity and radical uncertainty of capitalism." Levy, *Freaks of Fortune*, 18.

5. On patenting and education, see John Majewski, "Not All Inequality Is the Same," *Equitable Growth*, December 10, 2015, http://equitablegrowth.org/report/not-all-inequality-is-the-same/. And on institutions and paths of development, see Kenneth L. Sokoloff and Stanley L. Engerman, "History Lessons: Institutions, Factors Endowments, and Paths of Development in the New World,"

Journal of Economic Perspectives 14, no. 3 (2000): 217–232. See also Robert E. Wright, *The Poverty of Slavery: How Unfree Labor Pollutes the Economy* (Cham, Switzerland: Palgrave Macmillan, 2017).

6. Daron Acemoglu, Simon Johnson, and James A. Robinson, "Reversal of Fortune: Geography and Institutions in the Making of the Modern World Income Distribution," *Quarterly Journal of Economics* 117, no. 4 (2002): 1231–1294. Acemoglu, Johnson, and Robinson use this phrase to point out that nations that were wealthy in the early colonial period and featured geographical advantages and extractive institutions like slavery had grown poor by the twentieth century. The reverse is also true: neglected portions of the New World developed more equal institutions and became wealthier.

7. This literature is extensive; a small sampling of prominent examples might include John W. Blassingame, *The Slave Community: Plantation Life in the Antebellum South* (New York: Oxford University Press, 1979); Ira Berlin, *Many Thousands Gone: The First Two Centuries of Slavery in North America* (Cambridge, MA: Belknap Press of Harvard University Press, 1998); Philip D. Morgan, *Slave Counterpoint: Black Culture in the Eighteenth-Century Chesapeake and Lowcountry* (Chapel Hill: University of North Carolina Press, 1998).

8. For the concentration camp comparison and claims about the emergence of personality types, see Stanley M. Elkins, *Slavery: A Problem in American Institutional and Intellectual Life* (Chicago: University of Chicago Press, 1962).

9. A parallel example focusing on African American families and whether distinctive characteristics resulted from racial difference or from the system of slavery is E. Franklin Frazier, *The Negro Family in the United States,* rev. and abridged ed. (Chicago: University of Chicago Press, 1966).

10. Roots of this historiography date as early as the end of the Civil War. But for the most famous example and the comparison to schools, see Phillips, *American Negro Slavery*. Though this outlook, which valorized the Old South, would remain dominant in the mainstream historiography until the mid-twentieth century, there were major earlier countercurrents, most notably in the tradition of black radical scholars. For an overview of this earlier tradition and ongoing neglect of it, see Peter James Hudson, "The Racist Dawn of Capitalism," *Boston Review,* March 1, 2016, http://bostonreview.net/books-ideas/peter-james-hudson-slavery-capitalism. For a case study of the neglect of earlier African American scholarship in sociology, see Aldon D. Morris, *The Scholar Denied: W. E. B. Du Bois and the Birth of Modern Sociology* (Oakland: University of California Press, 2015).

11. For two examples of such critiques, see Walter Johnson, "On Agency," *Journal of Social History* 37, no. 1 (2003): 113–124; and Walter Johnson, "To Remake the

World: Slavery, Racial Capitalism, and Justice," *Boston Review Forum: Race, Capitalism, Justice* (2017). See also Peter A. Coclanis, "The Captivity of a Generation," *William and Mary Quarterly* 61, no. 3 (2004): 544–555. Coclanis writes, "More troubling is the heady, overexcited, overly upbeat, and ultimately (if unintentionally) condescending manner" of this work, 548–549.

12. On paths forward that bridge themes of domination and agency, see Vincent Brown, "Social Death and Political Life in the Study of Slavery," *American Historical Review* 114, no. 5 (2009): 1231–1249.

13. David Brion Davis, *The Problem of Slavery in the Age of Revolution, 1770–1823* (Ithaca, NY: Cornell University Press, 1975), 39.

14. Here, I want to suggest that a focus on rule and management (backed by violence) can explain far more than generally understood. This move follows Walter Johnson's critique of Eugene Genovese's explanation of the limits of enslaved resistance "in reference to the slaves' own culture rather than the balance of force in the society—by reference, that is, to 'hegemony' rather than simple 'rule.'" Walter Johnson, "A Nettlesome Classic Turns Twenty-Five," *Common-Place* 1, no. 4 (July 2001), http://www.common-place -archives.org/vol-01/no-04/reviews/johnson.shtml. In a similar vein, Stephanie M. H. Camp has written that "a focus on hegemony overestimates the extent of consent at the expense of the determining role of force." See "The Pleasures of Resistance: Enslaved Women and Body Politics in the Plantation South, 1830–1861," *New Studies in the History of American Slavery*, ed. Edward E. Baptist and Stephanie M. H. Camp (Athens: University of Georgia Press, 2006), 115.

15. Johnson, *River of Dark Dreams*, chap. 8. On the "carceral city," see Mike Davis, *City of Quartz: Excavating the Future in Los Angeles* (New York: Verso, 1990).

16. For a valuable take on paternalism that is sympathetic to Genovese but also attempts to clarify the stakes of each side, see Kathleen M. Hilliard, *Masters, Slaves, and Exchange: Power's Purchase in the Old South* (New York: Cambridge University Press, 2014), 2–5. As Hilliard points out, Genovese himself did not see paternalism and resistance as antithetical, writing in *Roll, Jordan, Roll* that "Accommodation itself breathed a critical spirit and disguised subversive actions and often embraced its apparent opposite—resistance." But she also recognizes that some of historians' criticisms result from the fact that though Genovese's work (and his collaborations with Elizabeth Fox-Genovese) was careful to say that paternalism was not kindness, it also evinced a certain admiration for slaveholders. Eugene D. Genovese, *Roll, Jordan, Roll* (New York: Pantheon Books, 1974), 597–598; Eugene D. Genovese and Elizabeth Fox-Genovese, *Fatal Self-Deception: Slaveholding Paternalism in the Old South* (New York: Cambridge University Press: 2011).

17. Stephen Meyer, *The Five Dollar Day: Labor Management and Social Control in the Ford Motor Company, 1908–1921* (Albany: State University of New York Press, 1981); Stuart D. Brandes, *American Welfare Capitalism, 1880–1940* (Chicago: University of Chicago Press, 1976); Sanford M. Jacoby, *Modern Manors: Welfare Capitalism since the New Deal* (Princeton, NJ: Princeton University Press, 1998). On different ways of specifying paternalism, some of which developed in early transitions to capitalism and others which reflect the maturation of welfare capitalism, see Philip Scranton, "Varieties of Paternalism: Industrial Structures and the Social Relations of Production in American Textiles," *American Quarterly* 36, no. 2 (1984): 235–257. Seen as a business strategy, paternalism can be interpreted as both modern and conservative—in some cases it draws on traditional economic relations and family businesses, but it can also be a strategy of large multidivisional corporations. As Andrea Tone has reflected, the apparent "paradox of capitalist paternalism"—the assumption that capitalism and paternalism are somehow opposites—rests on an unrealistic "projection of a perfect capitalist order in which paternalism and capitalism would indeed be diametrically opposed, a mythical market with an unlimited supply of labor, devoid of restraints curtailing employer's freedom . . ." *The Business of Benevolence: Industrial Paternalism in Progressive America* (Ithaca, NY: Cornell University Press, 1997), 55. Tone's analysis also describes paternalism as a political strategy intended to undercut unions and to cultivate support for pro-business policies.

18. Ira Berlin, *Many Thousands Gone: The First Two Centuries of Slavery in North America* (Cambridge, MA: Belknap Press of Harvard University Press, 1998). For a parallel set of critiques of Berlin and of the shortcomings of scholarship on agency as an explanatory force, see James Oakes, "Slaves without Contexts," review of *Many Thousands Gone: The First Two Centuries of Slavery in North America* by Ira Berlin, *Journal of the Early Republic* 19, no. 1 (1999): 103–109; Peter A. Coclanis, "The Captivity of a Generation," review of *Many Thousands Gone: The First Two Centuries of Slavery in North America* by Ira Berlin, *William and Mary Quarterly* 61, no. 3 (2004): 544–555. As Coclanis writes about scholarship focused on agency, "this generation of scholars, Berlin among them, seems more concerned with dwelling upon small triumphs of agency . . . than in confronting, much less explaining, the fact that masters' near monopoly of power and force allowed for the creation of a stable and economically vital regime . . . that was sufficiently flexible, portable, and recapitulative to have lasted in the South for at least a century and a half" (551).

19. In some ways, I am suggesting that scholars bring the questions we ask about enslaved people closer to the questions we ask about other groups. Business and labor historians rarely mistake employers' control for employees' consent.

Rather, coordination and control are seen as the outcome of negotiations in which one party enjoys disproportionate power. Just as soldiering among wage workers has been seen by labor historians as a sign of class consciousness that deprives managers and owners of knowledge of labor processes, soldiering (or sogering) on the part of slaves undermined the extent to which planters could know and control enslaved peoples' lives. Understanding plantation information systems can help to reveal the layers of meaning that James C. Scott has called "hidden transcripts." *Domination and the Arts of Resistance: Hidden Transcripts* (New Haven, CT: Yale University Press, 1990).

20. Describing what the slaves were "up against" in parallel to the abolitionists seems particularly valuable at a moment when scholars have shown that enslaved people were critical in bringing about the abolition of the system they suffered under. See, among others, *Freedom: A Documentary History of Emancipation, 1861–1867*, series 1, vol. 1, *The Destruction of Slavery*, ed. Ira Berlin, Barbara J. Fields, Thavolia Glymph, Joseph P. Reidy, and Leslie S. Rowland (Cambridge University Press, 1985), and Manisha Sinha, *The Slave's Cause: A History of Abolition* (New Haven, CT: Yale University Press, 2016).

21. See "Moral Reckoning," in Chapter 2.

22. On wrestling with the archives of slavery, see Saidiya Hartman, "Venus in Two Acts," *Small Axe* 12, no. 2 (July 17, 2008): 1–14; as well as the essays collected in a 2016 special issue of *History of the Present*, especially Brian Connolly and Marisa Fuentes, "Introduction: From Archives of Slavery to Liberated Futures?" *History of the Present* 6, no. 2 (2016): 105–116; Jennifer L. Morgan, "Accounting for 'The Most Excruciating Torment': Gender, Slavery, and Trans-Atlantic Passages," *History of the Present* 6, no. 2 (2016): 184–207; Stephanie E. Smallwood, "The Politics of the Archive and History's Accountability to the Enslaved," *History of the Present* 6, no. 2 (2016): 117–132.

23. In some ways, the argument that these technologies of distance helped people to see farther calls to mind Thomas Haskell's analysis of how the period from 1750 saw both the rise of capitalism and the extension of the humanitarian sensibility. However, I wish to suggest something narrower: it was not the market per se, but the technologies that evolved alongside the market—many of them quantitative—that connected people to distant causes. These tools have (and continue to have) many different kinds of politics. They can be tools for amelioration and for profit seeking, for remembering and for forgetting. Differently designed (and differently read), these systems can reveal and obscure dramatically different things. Thomas L. Haskell, "Capitalism and the Origins of the Humanitarian Sensibility, Part 2," *The American Historical Review* 90, no. 3 (June 1, 1985): 547–566.

Postscript: Forward to Scientific Management

1. Robert Kanigel, *The One Best Way: Frederick Winslow Taylor and the Enigma of Efficiency* (New York: Penguin Books, 1997), 459. See also Hugh G. J. Aitken, *Taylorism at Watertown Arsenal: Scientific Management in Action 1908–1915* (Cambridge, MA: Harvard University Press, 1960).

2. Hearings Before Special Committee of the House of Representatives to Investigate the Taylor and Other Systems of Shop Management, Oct. 4, 1911–Feb. 12, 1912, U.S. Government Printing Office, 1912, 1902.

3. Ibid., 1501.

4. Ibid., 1934, 1869–1870.

5. On clock time and plantation management, see Mark M. Smith, *Mastered by the Clock: Time, Slavery, and Freedom in the American South* (Chapel Hill: University of North Carolina Press, 1997).

6. Scudder Klyce to Kempton P. A. Taylor, 9 August 1915, Stephens Institute of Technology, online collections.

7. On the loss of control over labor processes under scientific management, see Harry Braverman, *Labor and Monopoly Capital: The Degradation of Work in the Twentieth Century* (New York: Monthly Review Press, 1975), chap. 4.

8. Taylor, *Principles of Scientific Management*, 39; H. L. Gantt, "Task and Bonus in Management," *Lecture Notes on Some of the Business Features of Engineering Practice*, by Alex C. Humphreys, rev. ed. (Hoboken, NJ: Stephens Institute of Technology, 1912), 485–497.

9. Taylor as quoted in M. McKillop and A. D. McKillop, *Efficiency Methods: An Introduction to Scientific Management* (London: G. Routledge, 1919), 104; Henry Laurence Gantt, *Wages and Incentives*, rev. ed. (Chicago, 1921), 54–55.

10. Henry Laurence Gantt, *Industrial Leadership* (New York: Association Press, 1921), 52; Henry Laurence Gantt, *Work, Wages, and Profits*, 2nd ed. (New York, 1913), 112.

11. As quoted in Carol Kennedy, *Guide to the Management Gurus: The Best Guide to Business Thinkers* (New York: Random House Business, 2007), 15. Kennedy does acknowledge that Gantt came from a slaveholding family. I have not been able to locate the original source or further documentation for this quotation.

12. James Mapes Dodge, "Scientific Management—Progressive and Irresistible," typed manuscript in the Papers of Frank and Lillian Gilbreth, Special Collections, Purdue University Libraries, West Lafayette, Indiana. N125 / NHL / 0816–172, 1.

13. Daniel Joseph Singal, "Ulrich B. Phillips: The Old South as the New," *Journal of American History* 63, no. 4 (1977): 876; Phillips, *American Negro Slavery*, 228, 398; and Phillips, *Life and Labor*, 132–133.

14. Hearings Before Special Committee of the House of Representatives to Investigate the Taylor and Other Systems of Shop Management, Oct. 4, 1911–Feb. 12, 1912 (U.S. Government Printing Office, 1912), 1403; see also similar text on 1402, 1413.

15. R. Keith Aufhauser, "Slavery and Scientific Management," *Journal of Economic History* 33, no. 4 (December 1973): 812.

16. Ibid., 823.

17. Mark M. Smith, "Time, Slavery and Plantation Capitalism in the Ante-Bellum American South," *Past and Present* 150 (February 1996): 142–168; Smith, *Mastered by the Clock.*

18. Cooke, "Denial of Slavery in Management Studies."

19. A much larger literature does not directly discuss parallels to scientific management but generally evaluates planters' sophisticated management practices. See, for example, Jacob Metzer, "Rational Management, Modern Business Practices, and Economies of Scale in the Ante-Bellum Southern Plantations," *Explorations in Economic History* 12, no. 2 (1975): 123–150; James Oakes, *The Ruling Race* (New York: Knopf, 1982); William Dusinberre, *Them Dark Days: Slavery in the American Rice Swamps* (New York: Oxford University Press, 1996); Fogel and Engerman, *Time on the Cross*; Follett, *Sugar Masters*; Chaplin, *Anxious Pursuit.*

20. See, for example, *Business: The Ultimate Resource* (Perseus Publishing, 2002), 986–987. The text's biographical sketch of Gantt repeats the elision that "the Civil War brought about changes to the family fortunes," from the Gantt's 1934 biography, quoted below.

21. Leon Pratt Alford, *Henry Laurence Gantt: Leader in Industry* (New York: American Society of Mechanical Engineers, 1934).

22. This broad point about the expansion of slavery and freedom going hand in hand has been made repeatedly by American historians. See, for example, Edmund S. Morgan, *American Slavery, American Freedom: The Ordeal of Colonial Virginia* (New York: Norton, 1975). Or, more recently, with reference to market freedoms, see Seth Rockman, *Scraping By: Wage Labor, Slavery, and Survival in Early Baltimore* (Baltimore: Johns Hopkins University Press, 2008).

23. Taylor, *Principles of Scientific Management*, 54.

ACKNOWLEDGMENTS

From its inception, this book has straddled the contentious divide between history and economics. It began as a paper on accounting in early New York and Massachusetts, and under the expert guidance of terrific co-advisors, Sven Beckert and Claudia Goldin, it evolved into a broader, comparative project on slavery and quantitative management. Sven encouraged me to consider politics and ideology, and to pay attention not just to what numbers revealed but also to what they concealed. Claudia made me define my terms, examine causal claims, and consider the ways accounting functioned as an information technology. Both kept me focused on big questions even as I considered the minute details of sometimes tedious ledgers.

Navigating the terrain between history and economics would not have been possible without support from scholars in economics departments. I thank Stan Engerman, who not only read my notes and hosted me in Rochester while I dug through boxes of records, but also offered a model for scholarship amid disagreement. Stan is always open-minded, always skeptical, always collegial, and always encouraging. Naomi Lamoreaux and Gavin Wright have both offered priceless input, and Eric Hilt has helped me maneuver disciplinary divides with humor and encouragement. All are truly committed to crossing the boundary between history and economics. Closer to the subject of slavery and capitalism, I am grateful to Paul Rhode and Alan Olmsted for their critiques and also their generosity with sources. Even if we have not always agreed, I have learned a tremendous amount from them, and my work is much better for it. A number of scholars and institutions have provided venues for cross-disciplinary conversations. In our interconnected era, many academic debates are happening in blog posts and online exchanges. These venues can obscure common ground, making it even more difficult to work across disciplinary boundaries. Peter Coclanis, Kenneth Janken, and Patrick Horn turned the 2017 Chandler Lecture at the University of North Carolina's Center for the Study of the American South into an immensely constructive conversation with Trevon Logan. Doug Irwin and the Nelson Rockefeller Center at Dartmouth University convened a lively "debate" on slavery and capitalism, and Dartmouth faculty and students joined for an even livelier discussion over dinner. Finally, I thank Ian Keay and the Economic History Association for inviting me to share my research at the Nevins Prize panel.

Even more important have been the many historians who have supported my writing, first at Harvard and later at Berkeley. Harvard's program on the History of American Civilization (now American Studies) offered a terrific community where my fellow students offered the first line of critique. I owe huge debts to Eli Cook, Katharine Gerbner, Noam Maggor, Stephen Vider, and Tom Wickman, who shaped the project with their insights and friendship. Beyond this core group, many members of the Harvard community supported the project: Arthur Patton-Hock, Caitlin Hopkins, Chambi Chachage, Christine Desan, Emma Rothschild, Glenda Goodman, Jeremy Zallen, Josh Specht, Joyce Chaplin, Kathryn Boodry, Robin Kelsey, Rudi Batzell, Shaun Nichols, Stefan Link, and others who were regular participants in the seminars and workshops that nurtured the project. These include the Economic History Tea, the Workshop on the Political Economy of Modern Capitalism, the Early America Workshop, and the Book History Workshop. I also owe a special thanks to the Business History Initiative across the river at Harvard Business School, and especially to Walter Friedman and Geoff Jones for their ongoing support and feedback. During my year as the Newcomen fellow I found a wonderful community, including Aldo Musacchio, Elisabeth Koll, Noel Maurer, and Tom Nicholas.

When I joined the faculty at Berkeley I found a new community that was both welcoming and challenging. Beginning with the first question in my job interview, the history faculty here has pushed me to make the book both broader and deeper. I am particularly grateful for feedback received at a 2016 conference on the book manuscript sponsored by the Institute for International Studies, which provided support to bring Gavin Wright, Adam Rothman, and Thomas LeBien to campus. There and in conversations before and after, I received amazing comments as well as extensive edits from colleagues: Brian Delay, Carolyn Zola, Daniel Robert, Daniel Sargent, David Henkin, Dylan Penningroth, Edward Evenson, Franklin Sammons, Jan De Vries, Robbie Nelson, Robin Einhorn, Rebecca McLennan, Margaret Chowning, Mark Brilliant, Mark Peterson, Sandra Eder, Stephanie Jones-Rogers, and

Waldo Martin. Carolyn and Franklin also offered spectacular research assistance. Many other colleagues have made the university a welcoming place to work and think: Abhishek Kaiker, Carlos Norena, Cathryn Carson, Emily Mackil, Ethan Shagan, Massimo Mazzotti, Maureen Miller, Paula Fass, Susanna Elm, and Tom Lacqueur. Beyond the history department, I am grateful to the Center for Science, Technology, Medicine, and Society and the members of the Economic History workshop, especially Barry Eichengreen, Brad DeLong, Christy Romer, and Marty Olney. I thank Marion Fourcade for inviting me to share my work in Sociology's Departmental Colloquium and the Peder Sather Center for funding a lively international conference on commodities that I organized with Espen Storli. The Townsend Center for the Humanities offered time off from teaching in my final year of writing, while the Abigail Reynolds Hogden fund supported images and indexing. Finally, teaching Berkeley's awesome undergrads has kept me motivated! Thanks especially to Marcus Tondre, Harry Rackmil, and Fabian Jacobo for enthusiastic research assistance.

The Business History Conference has been my academic home since my first meeting a decade ago in Athens, Georgia. Among many others who are part of that terrific community (and others already mentioned!), I thank Alexia Yates, Barbara Hahn, Calvin Schermerhorn, Colleen Dunlavy, Dan Bouk, David Carlton, Ellen Hartigan-O'Connor, JoAnne Yates, John Majewski, Josh Lauer, Justene Hill, Ken Lipartito, Laura Phillips Sawyer, Roger Horowitz, Richard John, Shane Hamilton, Stephen Mihm, and Susie Pak. Though I have presented at the BHC many times, I am especially thankful for the opportunities to share my research in the doctoral colloquium, then organized by Pam Laird, and the Krooss Prize Panel, chaired by Regina Blaszczyk.

Various chapters of the book have also been presented at the Organization of American Historians, the American Historical Association, the Economic History Association, the Omohundro Institute of Early American History & Culture, the Southern Historical Association, the Society for the History of the Early American Republic (SHEAR), and the Society for the Advancement of Socio-Economics. Just as important are the smaller workshops and thematic conferences where I have shared my research. Seth Rockman has supported my work at many stages, including inviting me to "Slavery's Capitalism" when the project was just getting started, putting together a lively workshop on "Paper Technologies," and inviting me to join the plenary at SHEAR. I thank Walter Licht and the Penn Economic History workshop Nelson Lichtenstein and the Political Economy Seminar at UC Santa Barbara; Rachel St. John and the Nineteenth Century Workshop at UC Davis (especially Justin LeRoy and Nickolas Perrone for comments); Bethany Johnson, Caleb McDaniel, John Boles, and Randal L. Hall for inviting me to join the Jefferson Davis Papers Conference at Rice University; Gerardo Okhuysen and Alex Borucki for a terrific seminar at UC Irvine; Gavin Wright and the Stanford Social Science Workshop;

Morgan Kausser and the faculty at Caltech; the Bay Area Seminar; William De-ringer for including me in "Calculating Capitalism" at Columbia; Carole Shammas at the USC / Huntington Early Modern Studies Institute; the Princeton Institute for International and Regional Studies and Deepak Mahlgan for including me in a work-shop on "Global Diffusion"; and Pierre Gervais and the participants at MARPROF. Thanks also to Ariel Ron for including me in a delightful year of writing and reading with Matt Karp and Dael Norwood. Beyond those already mentioned, I have bene-fited from comments and spontaneous conversations with Daina Ramey Berry, Dan Rood, Eric Rauchway, Greg Downs, Ian Beamish, Justin Roberts, Justin Si-mard, Michael Ralph, Richard Follett, Sarah Keyes, and Trevor Burnard, who also helped me to decode some very tricky handwriting!

Chapter 3 retraces aspects of the argument and also incorporates passages from "Slavery's Scientific Management: Masters and Managers," in *Slavery's Capitalism: A New History of American Economic Development*, ed. Sven Beckert and Seth Rockman (Philadelphia: University of Pennsylvania Press, 2016). Copyright © 2016 University of Pennsylvania Press. Chapter 2 is in some respects informed by examples previously discussed in "Seeking a Quantitative Middle Ground: Reflections on Methods and Opportunities in Economic History," in *Journal of the Early Republic* 36, no. 4 (Winter 2016): 659–680, also published by University of Pennsylvania Press.

Numerous libraries and archives have also shaped the manuscript. Among the many listed in the notes, I owe a special debt to Baker Library at Harvard Business School. Laura Linard pointed me to the very first set of account books I consulted, and the reference staff always made the reading room a great place to work. Thanks also to Paul Erickson and the American Antiquarian Society for supporting my re-search with a Botein Fellowship in Book History; to Cathy Matson and PEAES for inviting me to the Library Company of Philadelphia; and to the John Carter Brown Library, especially Kim Nusco (who knows more about business books than anyone) and Margot Nishimura. Finally, I thank Maria Sienkiewicz at Barclay's Group Ar-chives, for saving me a trip across the Atlantic.

At Harvard University Press, Brian Distelberg saw early promise in the project and Thomas LeBien saw it through. I am particularly grateful to Thomas for making the trip to Berkeley, where he expertly herded a big group of historians, keeping my manuscript workshop focused on the end goal of writing a good book. He also helped me to synthesize the immensely helpful feedback of two anonymous reviewers. Thanks to Kathleen Drummy and Mary Ribesky for keeping everything on track (and giving me a little extra time!) when I was editing with a newborn in arms. Be-yond HUP, I thank Liz Maples and Kate Epstein for edits and Molly Roy for helping me prepare the organizational charts in Chapter 1.

Among all of the historians who have shaped this book, I owe *by far* the greatest debts to Katharine Gerbner and Elena Schneider. They have read drafts that are in disorder and cheered me on when I needed encouragement. They are both amazing historians and absolutely spectacular friends. At Berkeley, I have also been supported by a writing group of fabulous women—the "quilters." Thank you to Andrea Sinn, Carolina Reid, Charisma Acey, Elena Conis, Elena Schneider, Karen Tani, Karen Trapenberg Frick, and Lisa Trever—for asking me again, and again, and again, what I am really trying to say.

Finally: my family. This book is dedicated to my amazing parents, Cindy and Jim Rosenthal. Without their love and support, this book could not have been written. The same is true of my wonderful husband, Matt, who helped me to finish a book while also starting a family. And though our children, Teddy and Eliza, have sometimes slowed my writing, their arrivals made the book different than it would have been. Every day they remind me what is at stake: that there are lives behind the numbers.

INDEX

after emancipation; Freed labor on
Southern plantations
Enslaved healers, 32–33
Enslaved managers, 31–40
Enslaved people: accounting used to
uncover resistance, 100; attempting to
influence own sale, 151–152, 156; balance
sheet of life and death, 9–13, 19; as both
labor and capital, 86; challenges faced
by, 194–195; communities of, 195;
depreciation of, 122, 127–137, 153–154, 155,
190; "head" positions, 32–37; health of,
60; informal networks among, 41;
intrusion of slaveholders into private
lives of, 130–131; managing resistance of,
40; market capitalization of, 153, 154–155;
naming patterns, 38, 224n83; price lists,
71, 77, 137–139, 149, 150–151, 152, 154, 155;
pricing of, 126–127, 136, 139–140;
resistance of, 4, 36, 37–39, 40, 41, 98, 100,
193–194, 196, 197; runaway, 38, 39, 114,
135–137; Shickle's abstract of, 19–20, 22;
slaveholders and reproduction among,
130–131, 137–139; threat of sale and
control of, 115; as unit of analysis, 69–70.
See also Human capital
"Essay upon Pen-Keeping and Plantership" (Kein), 31
Eustatia Plantation, 95
*Extracts from a West India Plantation
Journal, Kept by the Manager* (Stephens),
80–81

Factories, northern: account books, 50;
account books for labor management,
190; control over wageworkers, 4,
63–71; double-entry bookkeeping and,
64; labor turnover in, 63, 66–69,
192–193, 233n43; size of workforce in
textile mills, 14; use of accounting for
control in, 63–71
Factory accounting in the West Indies, 73
Fairbanks, Palmer & Company, 158

Falconer, Alexander, 27
Family groups, sale of enslaved, 141–142
Farmers' Register (magazine), 75, 76–78, 92
Farm Record and Account Book (Isaac
Dunbar Affleck), 157–158, 185
Fear: enslaved children and cultivation
of, 34–35; maintenance of control over
slaves using, 38–39, 97. *See also* Violence
Flint, Timothy, 114
Flynn, Andrew, 92
Follett, Richard, 111, 131
Ford, Henry, 8
Ford, Robert, 114
Ford Motor Company, 195
Forges, labor turnover and, 67–68
Forms. *See* Blank forms, Preprinted
forms, Paper
Fox, W. H., 101
Fractional hands, 144–148; after emancipation, 164, 165; imagining free
immigrants as, 177
Fraginals, Manuel Moreno, 69
Freed labor on Southern plantations:
contracts with, 159–170, 162–170, 171,
173; control of, 179–185; control over
shape of work, 175; efforts to control
private lives of former slaves, 168;
indebtedness and, 168–169, 179–180;
labor relations with women and
children, 174–175; laws to control,
179–180; "lost time" system, 170–172;
negotiations with ex-slaveholders,
114–115, 158–160; organization of,
173–175; peonage system and, 179–180,
183–185; turnover and, 160–162, 165,
182–183, 184; as wage laborers, 183–185.
See also Contracts with freed labor
on Southern plantations after
emancipation
Freedmen's Bureau: elimination of, 179;
labor contracts and, 168–169, 170
Freedom, relationship with depreciation,
136